IRELA

WHERE TO GO, WHAT TO DO

The upper lake of Killarney

CONTENTS

Editor: Donna Wood
Designer: Peter Davies
Advertising: Peter Whitworth
tel Basingstoke 20123
Maps: AA Cartographic Department

Produced and distributed by the Automobile Association, Fanum House, Basingstoke, Hampshire RG21 2EA
Irish Office: 23 Suffolk Street, Dublin 2
Distributed overseas by the British Tourist Authority, 64 St James Street, London SW1A 1NF

Phototypeset by Fakenham Press Limited, Fakenham, Norfolk and Petty & Sons Ltd, Leeds. Printed by Fakenham Press Limited.

Photographs are by courtesy of the Irish Tourist Board; Ulster-American Folk Park; Office of Public Works in Ireland. Engravings from the Mansell Collection.

Published by the Automobile Association.

Introduction

Think of a fresh, green land with 3,500 miles of beautiful coastline, splendid lakes, rivers and mountains and uncrowded, well-surfaced roads. This is Ireland – a motorist's paradise and a holidaymaker's joy. Although there are no sprawling motorways to eat away the miles, the pleasant, well-planned main roads and charming country lanes are tailor-made for relaxed and troublefree motoring.

The only problem, with such a wide canvas to explore, is in deciding on the type of accommodation that best suits the needs of your family. This book has all the answers. It is a comprehensive and detailed guide to the wealth of holiday opportunities Ireland can offer – presented in a format small enough to be slipped into the glove compartment or carried in a pocket.

In alphabetical order throughout, the easy-to-read gazetteer highlights graded hotels – ranging from the very grand to modest; country farmhouses, cosy guesthouses and well-appointed camping and caravanning sites – all with the AA seal of approval. The best restaurants, picnic sites, places of interest and most beautiful beaches are also listed, together with a full-colour, sixteen-page atlas.

With so much valuable information at your fingertips, you are now fully equipped to discover the real pleasures of Ireland for yourself. Go as you please – high into the mountains, or down to the sea – following the advice of our route planning experts as they map out a selection of seventeen one-day tours that cover not only the best drives in the Republic, but so much that is beautiful and unspoilt in Northern Ireland, too.

MOTORING IN IRELAND

Ross Castle, Killarney

The fame of Ireland as a touring ground is widespread; wherever you roam you will find spectacular scenery and well-surfaced roads. In this personal account a seasoned motorist and dedicated tourist leads you through the highways and byways of the beautiful south-west

Motoring In Ireland

Leisure motoring in Ireland can be a real joy, whether you're out for a short spin or a long hop. It's not important where you start from; Dublin, Cork, or for that matter anywhere else. The important thing is to decide where you're heading and how long it will take, making sure that you give yourself time enough to enjoy the pleasure of the countryside as you pass through on your journey.

For make no mistake, there is much to see all over Ireland. It is so easy once you're out of the city or town to work up speed and cover the miles, catching glimpses of old castles, fine houses, lovely rivers. But glimpses never make for memorable holidays. The secret of a motoring tour is to learn the joy of stopping . . . and looking.

You will never, ever, see all there is to see on a motoring trip in Ireland but if you learn to stop and get out of the car to look, you will return home from your holiday impressed by the variety of all that is Ireland – its scenery, its churches, its villages, its castles, its gentle countryside, its majestic mountains, deep valleys, lovely, empty beaches and sweeping, rolling hills.

For instance . . .

. . . drive out of Dublin and head south on the road to Carlow. If you're not careful you will pass through Moone without noticing it. But don't do that. There is a quaint stone Post Office on one side of the road and a church and a grocery on the other – and very little else. But if you turn right at the Post Office, passing through what appears to be old, derelict entrance gates, drive on for a mile or so. A sign post reads High Moone. Leave the car and follow a private avenue towards a farm house. You will come to the High Cross of Moone. Made of granite, it is seventeen and a half feet high and carved on all sides with the quaintest of saints and animals. The Twelve Apostles in three rows stand on each other's heads like a team of performing acrobats. Another panel has a fantastic tangle of lions and reptiles with horses' heads. This beautiful and graceful work is worth photographing and also is ideal for rubbing. So if you're interested in that sort of thing remember to take some

The richly-carved, 17½ foot-high Celtic cross at Moone, Co Kildare

wax and paper with you.

Or you could drive north from Dublin and head for Drogheda and the lovely valley of the River Boyne, to visit the ruins of Mellifont Abbey or the sleepy, pretty village of Slane, where you can picnic on its own noble stretch of the river . . .

Book your accommodation
As accommodation can be limited in the more remote areas, booking in advance is always to be recommended whether you are intending to stay at a luxury hotel or a more modest guest house. Many tourists use their hotel as a base from which to explore a region for a few days before moving on to a new hotel . . . a new base . . . a new region.

The tower of St Ann's church, Shandon which houses the famous eight bells

We booked in advance when we decided to tour the popular south-east region around Cork and Kerry, and received a wonderful welcome from the porters at Jury's Hotel in the heart of Cork, matched by a first-class evening meal served impeccably and most courteously by the head waiter himself. It was an impressive start to a lovely few days which we spent exploring the coast and countryside around the city.

Before embarking on our tour, we spent a happy day in Cork itself – a busy port and the second largest city in the republic. St Patrick's Street, in particular, has some fine shops and department stores which afford a nice morning break from touring. Like all of Ireland's major cities, Cork has a lot to offer the sight-seer. It has a long and often turbulent history. Everything seems to have started with the foundation of a monastery by St Finbarr in the 6th or early-7th

century and it is generally accepted that the present St Finbarr's Cathedral (CI), built in the 19th century, is on the site of that first monastery and is well worth seeing in its own right. Half a mile away is the University College, founded in 1845 and St Mary's Pro-Cathedral (RC) built in 1808 stands north of the River Lee. Other viewpoints worth noting are the Red Abbey Tower, south of George Street which was a vantage point used by John Churchill, later Duke of Marlborough, during the 1690 siege of Cork, and the National Monument at the end of Grand Parade which was erected to the memory of 18th- and 19th-century Irish patriots. On a more modern note, take time to visit the Marina down Victoria Road on the east side of the city. You can spend a pleasant half-hour or so there and you will get some nice views of the river too. Finally, if you have time, visit St Ann's (CI) church in Shandon, well known for its delightful and famous eight bells.

The following day we motored out to the

Motoring In Ireland

market town and fishing port of Youghal and spent a pleasant hour strolling around the old town, which lies at the foot of a long and steep hill. The town walls date back to the 15th century and the area, of course, was associated with Sir Walter Raleigh who was Warden in 1588–89.

From Youghal we went off on the road to Waterford, diverting through Lismore to picnic at The Gap in the Knockmealdown Mountains and enjoying the lovely vista in the warmth of the late morning before returning to Lismore and pushing on to Waterford. We were tempted to linger here to visit the famous Waterford Glass factory but we had set our hearts on visiting a new modern tourist attraction – the John F Kennedy Memorial Park near New Ross. It's off the main road and down a lovely meandering country lane and worth every moment's driving. We were lucky – it was a quiet, pleasant afternoon and we savoured the peaceful and beautiful setting – a 410-acre park in the heart of the Irish countryside with trees and shrubs from all parts of the world. Go there, if you can.

A breathtaking view of Lismore Castle

Winding out of Cork the other way is a memorable drive around the coast through Kinsale, Clonakilty and Skibbereen. In parts the road is twisting and narrow but if you're wise you will take it slowly – to enjoy the many magnificent views around almost every corner. Beyond Bantry we motored into the lovely little township of Glengarriff where we spent an hour having coffee and doing the usual tourist 'shopping' before setting off for a circuit of the Beara Peninsula. Beautiful views of Bantry Bay were followed by a right turn into the Slieve Miskish Mountains to Eyeries and on to Ardgroom and then to Lauragh for another right turn and up through the magnificent Healy Pass that is as breathtaking as anything you will find on the Continent. Allow yourself a little over two hours for this circuit to really enjoy it.

Breaking the journey in the heart of Kinsale

Rent a Car in Ireland

When you rent from Bolands you can be sure of a new 1980 car. At the beginning of March each year Bolands Car Hire Ltd., renew their entire fleet. With offices at all principal ports of arrival, whenever or wherever you arrive in Ireland our uniformed hostesses will be there to welcome you and start you on your best holiday ever.

Write for free illustrated brochure.

38 PEARSE STREET
DUBLIN 2
Telephone: Dublin 770704
Telex: 8662

Also at Wexford Road, Rosslare Harbour
Dublin Airport
Shannon Airport: Dun Laoire
Waterford Road, New Ross
and at 14 Bridge Street, Cork

Motoring In Ireland

The rushing waters of a mountain stream in Killarney, Ireland's famous beauty spot

Legendary Killarney is an ideal centre in which to stay a few days. This world-famous town is an attraction for all tourists no matter where they come from. Its beautiful setting on the serene lakeside is matched by its bustling life as a busy, typical Irish market town. If you happen to be there, as we were, on a Killarney Races day then get your parking space early! In and around the town there is a lot to see – the Franciscan Friary of Muckross, the magnificent Ross Castle, the view from the Hill of Aghadoe only two and a half miles out of town, Dunloe Castle and, of course, a visit to Killarney would not be complete without an excursion on the lakes themselves.

A most enjoyable long afternoon's driving will take you around the Ring of Kerry with its innumerable viewpoints from where you can have sight of sweeping seascapes and rugged mountains. Another afternoon you can go north out of Killarney on the road to Tralee, from where you can sweep into the Dingle Peninsula where Ryan's Daughter was filmed. Allow yourself plenty of time to turn right at Dingle itself to motor over the wild Connor Pass where you will get some memorable camera shots to take home.

Start each day with a full tank
Garages and filling stations are not available as frequently as they are in and around the major cities and towns. So remember to keep your tank filled at the start of your day's motoring.

Motoring In Ireland

The journey from Kerry to Clare takes time whichever way you head from Tralee. You can motor to historic Limerick by the main road – the N21 – via Castleisland, Abbeyfeale and Newcastle West – or you can be more adventurous and go through to Listowel from Tralee and then on to the ferry from Tarbert and cross the Shannon Estuary to Killimer in County Clare. We chose to go through Limerick – not because we were faint-hearted but simply because we wanted to visit one of the largest cities in Ireland – a city full of history and yet alive with modern life, because of its proximity to the world-famous Shannon Airport, gateway to Europe for thousands of American visitors.

The principal sights of Limerick are best seen from a short, circular walk which starts in O'Connell Street. Turn down Sarsfield Street, cross the river via Sarsfield Bridge then turn right along Clancy's Strand. At the west end of Thomond Bridge is the Treaty Stone dating back to the siege of the city in 1690 by the forces of William III. Between the Thomond and Sarsfield bridges are the Curragour Falls and King John's Castle stands on the far bank. On the other side of Thomond Bridge is the old High Town. Pass the castle at the top of Castle Street and turn right along the Parade, continue along Nicholas Street and you will come to St Mary's Cathedral (CI) whose fine tower stands 120ft high and gives excellent views of the area.

The landscape changes dramatically as you motor out past Shannon Airport and into the heart of Clare, especially after you pass through the small town of Ennis and head west to Ennistymon and on to the towering, dramatic Cliffs of Moher – a sight worth motoring miles to see. From there it is on inland to the incredible Burren country – ten square miles of moonscape. But don't be deceived – the bare limestone hills of the Burren are famous for the rarity and beauty of much of the flora to be found in the area. Take time also to follow the coast road to Black Head to view the remote but beautiful Aran Islands and thence inland to the spa of Lisdoonvarna and back on the road through Burren to Galway and Connaught.

The city of Galway stands at the mouth of the salmon-filled River Corrib and is the gateway to Connemara and Joyce's Country. It has a good shopping centre and is ideal as a base for two or three days' touring. We stayed at the three-star Ardilaun House Hotel which provided a comfortable room and excellent food. It is out of the city centre but convenient enough to take a half-hour's walk to sit on the Promenade and watch the sun go down on Galway Bay ... The city is a popular tourist centre with excellent local fishing, boating and sea bathing, not forgetting the famous Galway Races. It has a cathedral and a university and is a centre of Gaelic language and culture. In Eyre Square is the John F Kennedy Memorial Garden.

If you approach from the coastal road

Ennis – a busy market town in Co Clare

Slea Head, Co Kerry

Slow down on narrow roads
Although traffic is light in this area, many roads are narrow, occasionally rough and sometimes deceptively bumpy. Road surfaces can be excellent but high speeds cause discomfort because of the undulating nature of the road itself. So slow down, especially when you come to Maam Cross . . .

along Galway Bay, my advice is to go straight ahead and over the main road. If you come inland via Oughterard - which, incidentally, happens to be an important game fishing centre – then please turn right at Maam Cross and head your car for Joyce's Country. It is a changing landscape

of gaunt hills – watch for the Twelve Bens in view on the left – with deep dark lakes amid countless peat bogs. If you're lucky you will see the famous Connemara ponies – strong, beautiful animals and highly regarded the world over. You will motor through narrow vales under the shadow of lofty mountains until you come to the narrow inlet of Killary Harbour at Leenane. Turn left and motor gently along the inlet heading through well-wooded and hilly countryside for the small market town of Clifden.

At the small village of Moyard turn right and take the coastal road into Clifden and enjoy some truly wonderful views of the bay – it is some of the finest scenery in Ireland.

It is at Clifden in August or September every year that the famous Connemara Pony Show is held. Take time

Motoring In Ireland

Tranarossan Bay, Co Donegal

out to motor five miles or so to
Derrygimlagh Bog to see where Alcock and
Brown crash-landed in 1919 after their first
memorable West to East flight across the
Atlantic. Their feat is commemorated by a
cairn close to their landing spot at the edge
of the bog and there is a monument on high
ground about one and half miles away
which gives a good view of the landing spot.

We stayed overnight at the Abbeyglen
Hotel in Clifden, enjoying a pleasant meal
at their new restaurant before a cross-
Ireland journey the next day, back through
Galway following the N6 to Dublin – a
good motoring road, winding its way
mainly through open farming country.

Ireland is an ideal country for motor
touring. Waiting for us on another trip is
Westport and Ballina – that road overlooks
some splendid scenery. Sligo and Lough
Gill beckon with dramatic County Donegal
and the Inishowen peninsula, Ireland's
most northerly point, waiting beyond.

Some day we must go to see the great cliffs
of Slieve League near Glencolumbhille and
the lofty quartzite cone of Errigal
overlooking the Poisoned Glen near
Gweedore. We will enjoy, I am sure, the
famous Antrim Coast Road in Northern
Ireland and the Giant's Causeway with its
superb coastal scenery and view across the
North Channel to Scotland. Another time
. . . another tour.

However, Ireland is much more than a
long tour through unique scenery. Its
beauty lies as much in its country folk and
their friendly, relaxed way of life. Don't try
to cover too much ground. Meander rather
than tour. Enjoy the villages, the pubs, the
friendly farmhouses where you can often
find excellent and very reasonable
accommodation for a fiver a night. If you
fish, take your rod with you and sample
some of Europe's best fishing – much of it
free. And, of course, for the golfer and
those who enjoy walking, paradoxically, a
motoring holiday in Ireland can be a real
joy.

Mileage chart

This chart gives distances (to t[he] nearest mile) between 46 tow[ns]. The distances are given as a guide only, and are measured [to] the centre of each town along *AA recommended route* using classified roads. The towns ha[ve] been chosen solely for their geographical position.

Distances between places not included in this chart may be calculated by reference to the service map, on which point-to point mileages are shown.

The figures following the town names and shown in the marg[in] of the chart are cross-referenc[e]

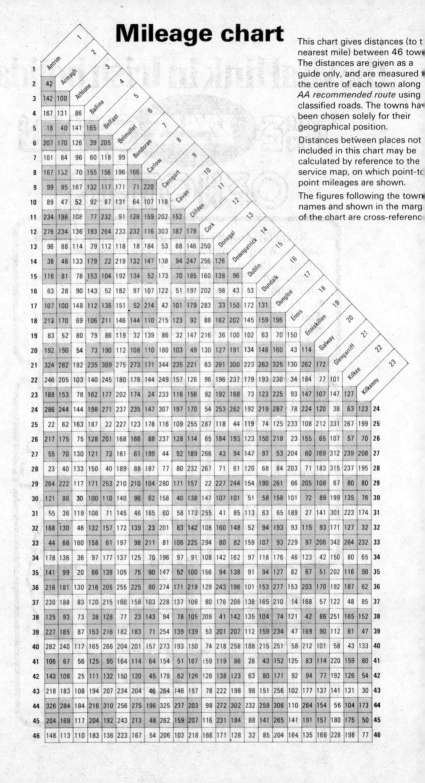

Diagonal town references:
1 Antrim, 2 Armagh, 3 Athlone, 4 Ballina, 5 Belfast, 6 Belmullet, 7 Bundoran, 8 Carlow, 9 Carrigart, 10 Cavan, 11 Clifden, 12 Cork, 13 Donegal, 14 Downpatrick, 15 Dublin, 16 Dundalk, 17 Dungloe, 18 Enniskillen, 19 Ennis, 20 Galway, 21 Glengarriff, 22 Kilkee, 23 Kilkenny

#	1	2	3	4	5	6	7	8	9	10	11	12	13	14	15	16	17	18	19	20	21	22	23
2	42																						
3	142	100																					
4	167	131	86																				
5	18	40	141	165																			
6	207	170	126	39	205																		
7	101	84	96	60	118	99																	
8	167	132	70	155	156	196	166																
9	99	95	167	132	117	171	71	220															
10	89	47	52	92	87	131	64	107	118														
11	234	198	108	77	232	91	128	159	202	152													
12	276	234	136	193	264	233	232	116	303	187	179												
13	96	88	114	79	112	118	18	184	53	68	146	250											
14	38	48	133	179	22	219	132	147	138	94	247	256	126										
15	116	81	78	153	104	192	134	52	173	70	185	160	138	96									
16	63	28	90	143	52	182	97	107	122	51	197	202	98	43	53								
17	107	100	148	112	136	151	52	214	42	101	179	283	33	150	172	131							
18	212	170	69	106	211	146	144	110	215	123	92	88	162	202	145	159	196						
19	83	52	80	79	86	119	32	139	86	32	147	216	36	100	102	63	70	150					
20	192	150	54	73	190	112	108	110	180	103	49	130	127	191	134	148	160	43	114				
21	324	282	182	235	309	275	273	171	344	235	221	63	291	300	223	263	325	130	262	172			
22	246	205	103	140	245	180	178	144	249	157	126	96	196	237	179	193	230	34	184	77	101		
23	188	153	78	162	177	202	174	24	233	116	156	92	192	168	73	123	225	93	147	107	147	127	
24	286	244	144	198	271	237	235	147	307	197	170	54	253	262	192	219	287	78	224	120	38	63	123
25	22	62	163	187	22	227	123	178	116	109	255	287	118	44	119	74	125	233	108	212	331	267	199
26	217	175	75	128	201	168	166	88	237	128	114	65	184	193	123	150	218	23	155	65	107	57	70
27	55	70	130	121	73	161	61	199	44	92	189	266	43	94	147	97	53	204	60	169	312	239	208
28	23	40	133	150	40	189	88	187	77	80	232	267	71	61	120	68	84	203	71	183	315	237	195
29	264	222	117	171	253	210	210	104	280	171	157	22	227	244	154	190	261	66	205	108	67	80	80
30	121	86	30	100	110	140	96	62	158	40	138	147	107	101	51	58	158	101	72	89	199	135	76
31	55	36	119	106	71	145	46	165	60	58	173	255	41	85	113	63	65	189	27	141	301	223	174
32	168	130	46	132	157	172	139	23	201	83	142	108	160	148	52	94	193	93	115	93	171	127	32
33	44	66	160	158	61	197	98	211	81	106	225	294	80	82	159	107	93	229	97	206	342	264	232
34	178	136	36	97	177	137	125	70	196	97	91	108	142	162	97	118	176	46	123	42	150	80	65
35	141	99	20	66	139	105	75	90	147	52	100	156	94	138	91	94	127	82	67	51	202	116	98
36	216	181	130	216	205	255	225	60	274	171	219	129	243	196	101	153	277	153	203	170	192	187	62
37	230	188	83	120	215	160	158	103	228	137	106	80	176	206	138	165	210	14	168	57	122	48	85
38	125	93	73	38	128	77	23	143	94	78	105	209	41	142	135	104	74	121	42	86	251	165	152
39	227	185	87	153	216	182	183	71	254	139	139	53	201	207	112	159	234	47	169	90	112	81	47
40	282	240	117	165	266	204	201	157	273	193	150	74	218	258	188	215	251	58	212	101	58	43	133
41	106	67	56	125	95	164	114	64	154	51	167	159	119	86	28	43	152	125	83	114	220	159	80
42	143	108	25	111	132	150	120	45	179	62	126	126	138	123	63	80	171	92	94	77	192	126	54
43	218	183	108	194	207	234	204	46	264	146	197	78	222	198	98	151	256	102	177	137	141	131	30
44	326	284	184	216	310	256	275	196	325	237	203	98	272	302	232	259	306	110	264	154	56	104	173
45	204	169	117	204	192	243	213	48	262	159	207	116	231	184	88	141	265	141	191	157	180	175	50
46	148	113	110	183	136	223	167	54	206	103	218	166	171	128	32	85	204	164	135	168	228	198	77

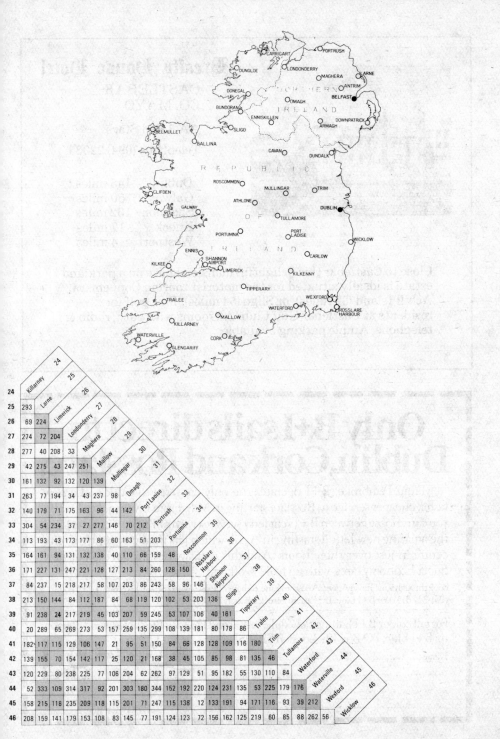

	Killarney																					
24																						
25	293	Larne																				
26	69	224	Limerick																			
27	274	72	204	Londonderry																		
28	277	40	208	33	Maghera																	
29	42	275	43	247	251	Mallow																
30	161	132	92	132	120	139	Mullingar															
31	263	77	194	34	43	237	98	Omagh														
32	140	179	71	175	163	96	44	142	Port Laoise													
33	304	54	234	37	27	277	146	70	212	Portrush												
34	113	193	43	173	177	86	60	163	51	203	Portumna											
35	164	161	94	131	132	138	40	110	66	159	48	Roscommon										
36	171	227	131	247	221	128	127	213	84	260	128	150	Rosslare Harbour									
37	84	237	15	218	217	58	107	203	86	243	58	96	146	Shannon Airport								
38	213	150	144	84	112	187	84	68	119	120	102	53	203	136	Sligo							
39	91	238	24	217	219	45	103	207	59	245	53	107	106	40	161	Tipperary						
40	20	289	65	269	273	53	157	259	135	299	108	139	181	80	178	86	Tralee					
41	182	117	115	129	106	147	21	95	51	150	84	66	128	128	109	116	180	Trim				
42	139	155	70	154	142	117	25	120	21	168	38	45	105	85	98	81	135	46	Tullamore			
43	120	229	80	238	225	77	106	204	62	262	97	129	51	95	182	55	130	110	84	Waterford		
44	52	333	109	314	317	92	201	303	180	344	152	192	220	124	231	135	53	225	179	176	Waterville	
45	158	215	118	235	209	118	115	201	71	247	115	138	12	133	191	94	171	116	93	39	212	Wexford
46	208	159	141	179	153	108	83	145	77	191	124	123	72	156	162	125	219	60	85	88	262	56	Wicklow

IN DUBLIN'S FAIR CITY

Dublin Castle

*Patrick O'Donovan, writer,
raconteur and committed
Dubliner (though more by
conviction than accident of birth)
writes warmly about the place
he calls 'the least lonely city
I know . . .'*

In Dublin's Fair City

The spire of Christ Church Cathedral seen across the famous River Liffey

Dublin is a Prince among cities Though greatly loved, it has the wrong reputation. It is misunderstood and under rated. It has an international reputation for a charm considered very rare in Northern Europe. It is said to be a rollicking sort of place where the girls are unsophisticated and pretty and the men given over to a Celtic machismo that is sustained on deep draughts of a dark and beery liquid that only they can make and which has various therapeutic properties. Like all the clichés about Ireland – and no other nation is so festooned with other peoples' fantasies and simplifications – there is just a little truth in this. Only a little. But that there is something special and rare about it, all people who have considered the city, even without setting foot in it, would agree. And they would be right.

Above all, it is a capital city. It was founded by Danes and grew around the heavy feet of foreigners and now has the purpose of all great capital cities, which is to provide a base for government, to make money and to ease this process by clustering together the counting houses that make the attendant farms and factories possible. To be a dormitory for the rich and

the half-way up and for the poor and, a long way behind, to be a centre for the Arts. It must also provide a reasonable ration of civilised pleasure.

Dublin is the capital of a country beginning to enjoy most of the worldly things that history denied it. And its citizens richly deserve their self-indulgence. But despite its conventional purposes, despite the curious and unsuitable romance in which it has been draped, there is still something very special about Dublin.

The English now love it. It appears to them unmistakably alien in a safe way. It confers no guilt upon them. Indeed it seems positively to liberate them. The Americans tend to treat it as a sacred subject. The French and the Germans tend to hurry through it on the way to a countryside of a legendary purity where there are still lobsters.

Basically this is a puritanical and respectable city which retains the elegance denied to many more pretentious cities and lifts the heart.

It has special qualities imposed upon it by its history. There is a haunting, pleasurable

by Patrick O'Donovan

sadness about it. You can see this in vast Georgian squares. They are of the utmost elegance, but have a curious two-dimensional quality about them, almost as if they were stage sets – and indeed they were the setting for a fascinating but artificial civilisation, that of the Anglo-Irish.

These people were fantastically gifted. True, some were bullies, exploiters, persecutors, drunks, horse maniacs. This brilliant minority also led the Irish struggle for independence and wrote most of the literature that the rest of the world thinks of as Irish. They were mixed up with the English Establishment that ran Ireland.

But the people who lived in these squares have gone. The army officers have decamped (there were once more British troops in Ireland than there were in India!)

The Bank of Ireland and Trinity College

the civil servants, the professional men had no work left to do and in leaving they left this vast pattern of magnificent town houses, each unit fit for a lordling when servants were cheap, and which are now a burden on an unsentimental Republic that is not greatly concerned with the preservation of that part of their past. The houses are tall, rose pink with fanlights over the door.

Those at the very centre are still superb. But others have become hellish slums with the front door gaping like a toothless mouth and some are uninhabitable and some have been pulled down and their sites ravaged.

In the same class is Dublin Castle from which the English once ruled. The Irish have sumptuously restored the state apartments buried in this elegant Kremlin. As expressions of confidence and power they are on a small scale but they are still used, occasionally, rather uneasily, to serve

In Dublin's Fair City

the Republic. Empty and open to the public, they elegantly mourn the departure of an alien rule.

Even stranger are Dublin's two Gothic cathedrals. Both are Church of Ireland (Protestant) and each separately is too big for the Protestant congregations that are left. But each is loaded with the history of Ireland which includes thickets of memorials to rulers and nobility that are not only dead but whose memory moulders. There is Christ Church, small and elaborate, and St Patrick's which is on an English scale. Both keep up the solemn choral services of their rich past.

To these, perhaps, should be added the library of Trinity College, a foundation of Elizabeth I. Within the restrained splendour of that long, mad room, there are shown the most holy of the most ancient books of Ireland, made before even the Normans came.

There can be no other city that has the GPO in working order at the centre of its capital city, as a national shrine. The Irish tricolour flies very high over its portico, because here the insurgents of the Easter Rising of 1916 proclaimed the Republic and made their last stand. A statue in the main hall commemorates this. Nothing else is necessary. (Dubliners still buy their stamps and postal orders here.) Or there is Kilmainham gaol where most of the leaders were shot. There is a memorial garden to them in Parnell Square. You can feel the proud anguish. Then there is Glasnevin cemetery which is the Irish equivalent of *Les Invalides* or Westminster Abbey, where many famous Irish men and women are buried.

But the Irish are practical. Dublin is no cenotaph and in fact I would put it as the most *cheerful* capital in Europe. It is not that they are content with themselves or rich beyond worry or uninhibited or dreadfully drunk. There is a quality of honest gaiety that changes me each time I am there.

They have a street of luxury shops, humble as Bond Street is humble, and a place where a rich man can get whatever a rich man dare ask for without shame. This

The 300ft-long, rectangular façade of Trinity College (1759) which was the first university to grant degrees to women and non-Christians

is Grafton Street. There is an alley off it which leads to a Carmelite church. It is not to my eyes even a stab at a work of art. But all day and every day it rustles and squeaks and patters to a stream of people, loaded with shopping, sensibly dressed, who come to kneel and 'pay a visit'. This matters as much as any monument.

It has in Phoenix Park the grandest park I know. Central Park is a dubious playground in comparison and Hyde Park a grand back garden. Phoenix Park was made for the Lords Lieutenants of Ireland to career across in their open carriages with a cavalry escort back to their villa where the President of Ireland now lives. It has the tumultuous walk along the Liffey Quais, tumultuous because there is so much to see. The river is dark and feels close to the sea. The sides are lined with houses and shops and churches and pubs painted by Victorian house painters who must have been creative artists slightly round the bend. It also has two great buildings that will stop you in your tracks, but like all the public buildings of Ireland, be they the Dail or the old Parliament, they seem made not to overawe, but to please. And that is the unservile character of Dublin.

Its museums are for pleasure and are man-sized. In the National Museum there is a collection of Irish metal work, of large, lowering chalices, of strange-shaped croziers for bishops, so beautiful and subtle that you wonder how anyone had the effrontery to try to conquer and subdue Ireland.

So why my delight in this sad and practical and elegant capital which was basically the creation of semi-foreigners, and which the Irish have characteristically made their own?

The place is endlessly entertaining. It is old-fashioned in a way that suggests luxury and good manners and friendliness – all, I would say, about fifty years out of date. This is to all the civilised world an advantage that confers envy.

It has countless pubs where you can sit and talk or read. The hotels are eccentric because they have not sold their souls. The theatres are unpredictable so that each visit

becomes an adventure which may end in greatness. The food is sound and, if you can pay, plainly as good as any in the world. No, better!

The place is civilised and sophisticated and makes no demands. You can relax there as you would on a farm. You can pursue the culture of the West in a highly specialised way. It is the least lonely city I know, but treat it gently and with respect, for it really is a Prince – a reigning Prince.

The O'Connell monument, which stands at the foot of O'Connell Street in the city

Entertainment in Dublin

Dublin's busy central area

Cabaret

Braemor Rooms, County Club,
Churchtown, Dublin 14 ☎ 988664.
Irish Cabaret (all year).

Burlington Hotel****, Upper Leeson
Street, Dublin 4 ☎ 785711 'Phil the
Fluter' Irish Cabaret (Apr–Oct).

Fitzpatrick's Killiney Castle Hotel****,
Killiney, Co Dublin ☎ 851533 (end
Apr–mid Oct) Irish Cabaret.

Jury's Hotel****, Pembroke Road,
Ballsbridge, Dublin 4 ☎ 767511 Irish
Cabaret (May–Oct).

Clontarf Castle, Castle Ave, Clontarf,
Dublin 3 ☎ 332271 (all year).

Jazz

Jazz in Dublin takes the form of regular
weekly sessions in city pubs (cover charge
approximately 40p and 60p) and hotels and
occasional concerts. At the time of going to
press, the following venues were offering
regular weekly sessions. Please check the
evening newspapers for changes.

Tue: Lawrence Hotel, Howth ☎ 322643.

Wed: South County Hotel, Stillorgan, Co
Dublin ☎ 881621.

Thu: Lawrence Hotel, Howth ☎ 322643.

Fri: South County Hotel, Stillorgan, Co
Dublin ☎ 881621.

Sat: Fitzpatrick's Killiney Castle
Hotel ****, Killiney, Co Dublin
☎ 851533.

Sun: Fitzpatrick's Killiney Castle
Hotel ****, Killiney, Co Dublin
☎ 851533 (lunchtime).

Court Hotel***, Killiney, Co Dublin
☎ 851622 (evening).

Lawrence Hotel, Howth ☎ 322643
(lunchtime).

South County Hotel, Stillorgan, Co
Dublin ☎ 881621 (lunchtime).

Traditional Irish Music Sessions (Comhaltas Ceoltóiri Éireann)

See also 'A Heritage of Song' page 76.

Pipers Club, CCE, An Culturlann, 32/33
Belgrave Square, Monkstown, Co Dublin.
Sat 10pm–12mdnt.

The Sean Treacy Branch, CCE, An
Culturlann, 32/33 Belgrave Square,
Monkstown, Co Dublin.
Fri 10pm–12mdnt.

Airport Branch, ALSAA Club, Dublin.
Airport. Fortnightly Mon 9–11.30pm.

Balbriggan Branch, CCE, Social Centre,
Hampton Street, Dublin.
Last Wed of the month. 10pm–12mdnt.

Churchtown Branch, CCE, The County
Club Churchtown, Dublin 14.
Sun 8.30–10pm.

Scoil Ard Ris, Griffith Avenue, Dublin 9
Thu 9.30–11pm.

Craobh U; Chearbhalláin, Room A

Entertainment in Dublin

An Culturlann, 32/33 Belgrave Square, Monkstown, Co Dublin. Sat 9–11.30pm.

Dúchas Branch, An Culturlann, 32/33 Belgrave Square, Monkstown, Co Dublin. Sun 9.30–11pm.

Ceili: First Thu of every month and weekly Jun–Sep. Comhaltas Ceoltóiri Éireann Headquarters, An Culturlann 32/33 Belgrave Square, Monkstown, Co Dublin. 9pm–12mdnt.

Concerts

Ballad and Popular Music Concerts are held throughout the year at the following venues:

Liberty Hall, Eden Quay, Dublin 1

New Stadium, South Circular Road, Dublin 8.

Focus Theatre, Pembroke Place, Pembroke Street, Dublin 2.

Project Arts Centre, 39 East Essex Street, Dublin 2.

Royal Dublin Society Concert Hall Ballsbridge, Dublin 4.

Trinity College Dublin, Dublin 2.

St Anthony's Hall, Merchant's Quay, Dublin 2.

University College Dublin, Belfield, Dublin 4.

Radio Telefis Éireann Symphony Orchestra Concerts take place regularly at St Francis Xavier Hall, Lower Sherrard Street, Dublin 1 during summer months and in the Gaiety Theatre, South King Street, Dublin 2 during winter months. Details of programmes and performances can be checked in the daily newspapers or by contacting Radio Telefis Éireann, Montrose, Donnybrook, Dublin 4. ☎ 693111.

Opera

The Dublin Grand Opera Society spring and winter seasons are held in the Gaiety Theatre, South King Street during Apr and Dec respectively.

Other Classical Music venues are –
Trinity College, and the Royal Dublin Society Concert Hall, Ballsbridge, Dublin 4.

Dancing

The following are the main ballrooms in the city for informal dancing:

Television Club, Harcourt Street, Dublin 2 ☎ 758891.

National Ballroom, Parnell Square North, Dublin 1 ☎ 746634.

Olympic Ballroom, Pleasants Street, Dublin 8 ☎ 754027.

Tara Ballroom, D'Olier Street, Dublin 2 ☎ 712019.

Theatres

The following are the main city centre theatres. Performances are generally from Mon to Sat inclusive and programmes normally commence at 8pm. Tickets may be reserved at the individual theatres or tourist information offices: 14 Upper O'Connell Street, Dublin 1, 51 Dawson Street, Dublin 2, Brown Thomas and Switzers, Grafton Street, Dublin 2. Amateur companies stage excellent 'basement' theatre and musical productions throughout the city.

Abbey and Peacock Theatres, Lr Abbey Street, Dublin 1 ☎ 744505

Gate Theatre, Cavendish Row, Parnell Square, Dublin 1 ☎ 744045

Gaiety Theatre, South King Street, Dublin 2 ☎ 771717

Eblana Theatre, Store Street, (Central Bus Station), Dublin 1 ☎ 746707

Project Arts Centre, 39 East Essex Street, Dublin 2 ☎ 713327

Olympia Theatre, Dame Street, Dublin 2 ☎ 778962

Focus Theatre, Pembroke Place, off Pembroke Street, Dublin 2 ☎ 763071

Player Wills Theatre, South Circular Road, Dublin 8 ☎ 758445/757901

Beaver Theatre, Ballinteer Ave, Dublin 14 ☎ 713609

The Puppet Theatre. For full information on programme contact: The Mews Theatre, Lambert Puppets, 5 Clifton Tce, Monkstown, Co Dublin ☎ 800974

Cinemas

Savoy 1, 2, 3, 4 & 5, Upper O'Connell Street, Dublin 1 ☎ 748487

Carlton 1, 2 & 3, Upper O'Connell Street, Dublin 1 ☎ 744098

Regent, Findlater's Place, Dublin 1 ☎ 748145

Adelphi 1, 2, 3 & 4, Middle Abbey Street, Dublin 1 ☎ 742667

Ambassador, O'Connell Street, Dublin 1 ☎ 787530

Film Centre, O'Connell Bridge House, Dublin 2 ☎ 778923

Plaza, Parnell Square, Dublin 1 ☎ 746416

Curzon, Middle Abbey Street, Dublin 1 ☎ 747469

Academy, Pearse Street, Dublin 2 ☎ 774994

Green 1 & 2, St Stephen's Green, Dublin 2 ☎ 751753

Odeon 1 & 2, Eden Quay, Dublin 1 ☎ 744611

Astor, Eden Quay, Dublin 1 ☎ 748641

Metropole, Hawkins Street, Dublin 2 ☎ 714988

Cameo, Abbey Street, Dublin 1 ☎ 742658

The Irish Film Theatre, St Stephen's Green House, Earlsfort Terrace, Dublin 2 ☎ 764207 and the Project Cinema Club, 39 East Essex Street, Dublin 2 ☎ 713327, are restricted to members only, but non-Irish visitors may avail of temporary membership for a nominal sum.

Dinner Dances
Informal dinner dances are held in the following hotels during the winter period (Sat nights – Oct–Apr). The charges for meal and dance average £6–£10 per person and advance reservations should be made. The Hunt Balls are arranged to coincide with Horse Show Week (beginning 5 Aug).

Fitzpatrick's Killiney Castle Hotel****, Killiney, Co Dublin ☎ 851533

Green Isle Hotel***, Naas Road, Clondalkin, Co Dublin ☎ 593406

Galleries
Bank of Ireland, Lr Baggot Street, Dublin 2 ☎ 785744. Mon–Fri 9.30am–5.30pm

David Hendricks, 119 Stephen's Green, Dublin 2 ☎ 756062. Mon–Fri 10am–6pm Sat 10am–1pm

Davis Gallery, 11 Capel Street, Dublin 2 ☎ 748169. Mon–Fri 11am–5.30pm Sat 10am–1pm

Douglas Hyde, Trinity College, Nassau Street, Dublin ☎ 772941. Mon–Sat 11am–5.30pm

Image Gallery, 22 Upr Leeson Street, Dublin 2 ☎ 765481. Tue–Sat 10.30am–5.30pm

Lad Lane Gallery, 34 Lad Lane, off Baggot Street, Dublin 2 ☎ 763143. Mon–Fri 11am–6pm Sat 11am–1pm

Municipal Gallery, Parnell Square, Dublin 1 ☎ 741903. Tue–Sat 10am–6pm Sun 11am–2pm

National Gallery, Merrion Square, Dublin 2 ☎ 767571. Mon–Sat 10am–6pm (9pm Thu) Sun 2pm–5pm

Neptune Gallery, 42 South William Street, Dublin 2 ☎ 715021. Mon–Fri 10am–5.30pm Sat 10am–1pm

Project Gallery, 39 East Essex Street, Dublin 2 ☎ 712321. Mon–Sat 11am–6.30pm

Robinson Gallery, 151 Leinster Road, Dublin 6 ☎ 960269. Mon–Fri 10.30am–5pm (8pm Thu) Sat 10.30am–1pm

Setanta, 37 Molesworth Street, Dublin 2 ☎ 765338. Mon–Fri 10am–6pm Sat 11am–2pm

Tom Caldwell Gallery, 32 Upr Fitzwilliam Street, Dublin 2 ☎ 688629. Mon–Fri 11am–5pm Sat 10.30am–1pm

Painting of the Month Dinner/Lecture
National Gallery of Ireland, Merrion Square, Dublin 2 ☎ 767571. On the first Thu of each month a special dinner is followed by a talk on a selected picture by the Director of the Gallery. Price £7 (approx) per head.

Outdoor Entertainment
Special Irish Concerts take place on weekdays at lunchtime during Jul & Aug in St Stephen's Green and band recitals take place regularly in some of the city parks. For details of these concerts contact Dublin Tourism, 14 Upper O'Connell Street, Dublin 1 or 51 Dawson Street, Dublin 2 ☎ 747733.

RELICS OF BYGONE DAYS

Druidical stone at Ballybrack, Co Wicklow

*Ireland is particularly rich in
buildings of the past, and the
traveller is immediately struck
by the number and variety of the
archaeological remains to be
seen in almost every part of the
country. The following pages
describe the most striking of
these monuments, and where to
find them*

Relics of Bygone Days

There are no certain traces of the Palaeolithic (Old Stone Age) inhabitation of Ireland, but man is known to have lived in the country in Middle Stone Age times – that is to say, roughly from about 6,000 BC. No structures can be assigned to these first settlers, but after the coming of Neolithic or New Stone Age peoples, some of the most spectacular of Irish field monuments were built.

Megalithic Tombs

These Neolithic colonisers first brought a knowledge of agriculture to Ireland between 3,000 and 2,000 BC and were responsible for the erection of the earliest stone-built, collective burial tombs known as megaliths – the Court Cairns. This type has produced Neolithic pottery and is, therefore, placed first in the series. Court cairns (so called because the tombs consist generally of a covered gallery for burial with one or more unroofed courts or fore-courts for ritual) are mainly to be found in the northern part of the country – north of a line between Clew Bay in the west and Dundalk Bay in the east. Elaborate examples are the full-court cairns at Creevykeel, Co Sligo, Ballyglass, Co Mayo (one of a group on the west shores of Killala Bay) and the cairn with double fore-court at Cohaw, near Cootehill, Co Cavan. Related to the court cairns is the most simple (but often very imposing) type of megalith – the dolmen or portal dolmen. This consists of a large, sometimes enormous, capstone and three or more supporting uprights. The distribution of the dolmen is more widespread but tends to be eastern; there are striking specimens in the neighbourhood of Dublin at Glendruid near Killiney and in Howth Demesne; one with a huge capstone at Mount Browne just outside Carlow town; and two fine monuments of tripod form at Proleek, Co Louth, and Legananny, Co Down. Another variety of megalith is the wedge-shaped gallery, of which the largest example is that at Labbacallee, near Fermoy, Co Cork. There are numbers of such tombs in the Burren area in Co Clare built from the

A simple type of megalith known as a dolmen, at Carrowmore, Co Sligo

characteristic limestone slabs. Most excavated wedges belong to the Early Bronze Age – 2,000 to 1,500 BC, a good example being at Ballyedmonduff, near Stepaside, Co Dublin.

The most spectacular of the great tombs are the passage-graves. The best known is Newgrange, one of a group on the River Boyne, west of Drogheda, Co Louth, which by its construction and by the carvings which occur on the stones ranks among the most imposing megalithic tombs in Europe. The decorative carving which covers many of the stones is abstract, composed of spirals, lozenges and other motifs, and is believed to have been of religious significance. Other very fine groups of passage-graves are those at Slieve-na-Calliagh (Loughcrew Hills), near Oldcastle, Co Meath, with an important collection of decorated stones, and the large cemeteries at Carrowkeel, near Castle Baldwin, and Carrowmore, both in Co Sligo, where, however, no carvings occur. Recent excavations of a passage-grave at Tara suggest a late Neolithic date for the type.

Early Irish Architecture

Before the Norman invasion most buildings in Ireland were of wood. Not one of these has survived. In the treeless country of the west, however, small stone buildings – beehive 'clocháns' of corbel construction, or tiny, dry-built oratories – were erected. Some, possibly as early as the 7th century, may still be seen. Clocháns are particularly common in Co Kerry: there are many in the Dingle Peninsula and some very perfectly preserved examples in the early monastic settlement on the Skellig Rock, off the Kerry coast. In Kerry also is the best-preserved example of an early boat-shaped oratory, that at Gallerus.

Most of the early mortared churches seem to derive from wooden prototypes. Like the boat-shaped oratories they were very small, but they embody several features which were to be characteristic of Irish buildings: antae (pilaster-like projections), steeply pitched roofs, inclined jambs to door- and window-opes, and a general tendency to make use of an inward batter in walls. An

West Cross at Clonmacnoise, Co Offaly

excellent example is the stone-roofed church on St MacDara's Island, Co Galway, which shows its timber ancestry clearly in the gable-finial of stone.

Many of these small churches must have been roofed with timber, shingled or thatched, but some were certainly roofed with stone. The problem of providing a pitched roof of stone over a rectangular structure was solved by inserting a relieving semi-circular arch below the roof. The small space over the arch forms a croft. Good examples may be seen at Ceanannus Mór (St Columba's House), Co Meath, and Glendalough (St Kevin's Church), Co Wicklow. Sometimes a small chancel, with a round chancel-arch in plain masonry, was added to or incorporated in the early churches. These buildings lack features by which they can be accurately dated; a conservative dating would be from the beginning of the 9th century onwards.

High Crosses

The carved stone cross, usually in the typical 'Celtic' ringed form, is found in considerable variety of detail in most parts of the country. Among the earliest Christian monuments in Ireland are simple crosses incised on standing stones. They are most common in the west and are numerous in the Dingle Peninsula, Co Kerry. Representations of the Crucifixion are first found on crude slabs, also in the west, as on the slab at Duvillaun, off the Co Mayo coast. These also are incised in some examples, but the development of low-relief carving can be traced in the 7th century, culminating in the tall cruciform slab at Carndonagh, Co Donegal, which is carved with representations of the Crucifixion, other figures and interlaced ornament.

The ringed high cross first appears at a somewhat later date; its carving is in the tradition of the slabs, but its form is probably derived from portable wooden crosses, such as are depicted in some early scenes. It is thought that the ring had a functional origin and derives from four stays used to brace the angles of a wooden cross.

The earliest group of the high crosses,

31

Relics of Bygone Days

dating from the 8th century, is in southern Kilkenny and Tipperary, and the finest examples are at Ahenny, Co Tipperary, and two miles away at Kilkieran, Co Kilkenny. In this group the cross-shafts and heads are magnificently carved with spirals and other decorative forms derived from metalwork, with figure-sculpture on the bases. Somewhat to the north, in the Barrow valley, is another group, slightly later in date and more crudely carved – in granite, unlike the Ossory (Kilkenny) group, which is carved in sandstone. The Barrow group has an interesting innovation: the faces of the shafts and heads are divided into panels, in each of which a scene, usually Biblical, is depicted. The finest of these crosses is at Moone, Co Kildare, but there are two very good examples at Castledermot in the same county.

At the beginning of the 10th century sandstone came into use again for the crosses, and from this period a splendid series of sculptural monuments survives at monastic sites scattered across the Central Plain. At Clonmacnoise, Co Offaly, there are two crosses, at Monasterboice, Co Louth, three, at Ceanannus Mór, Co Meath, four, and there are many single examples. The West Cross and Muiredach's Cross at Monasterboice are the best examples of the whole series. In each case the east and west faces are carved with scriptural scenes while the north and south faces have spirals, vine-scrolls, diapers or other ornament. The iconography of the figure-sculpture has not been fully interpreted, but some commonly occurring scenes are identifiable: the Crucifixion; the Last Judgment; Adam and Eve; Cain and Abel; and Arrest of Christ, etc. Later crosses in this tradition may be seen at Clones, Co Monaghan, Drumcliff, Co Sligo, and Arboe and Donaghmore, Co Tyrone.

Towards the end of the 11th century a new type of cross was carved. The ring was now often omitted, and the whole length of the shaft was taken up with a single figure – the crucified Christ in full relief; figures of ecclesiastics commonly occur on the opposite face and on the base. The ornament of the north and south faces usually consists of animal-interlacing of Scandinavian form. The type persisted, with minor variations of style, to the mid-12th century. Eleventh-century crosses may be seen at Roscrea, Co Tipperary, and Kilfenora, Co Clare. There is a good 12th-century cross at Taum, Co Galway, dated by an inscription, another of unusual form on the Rock of Cashel, Co Tipperary, and one at Glendalough, Co Wicklow.

Fine collections of Early Christian grave-slabs, with inscriptions in Irish, may be seen at Clonmacnoise, Co Offaly, and Iniscealtra, Lough Derg, Co Clare.

Castles

The Normans were already experienced castle-builders when they came to Ireland, but in the first years of the invasion they built fortifications of wood. The remains of these can be seen all over the eastern half of the country in the form of early earthen fortresses known as mottes-and-baileys.

Towards the end of the 12th century the construction of stone fortifications on a large scale began. The finest and one of the earliest castles of the period is at Trim, Co Meath, where there is a great square keep in a large bailey, defended by a high embattled wall, with turrets and barbicans. Other fine examples of the same type are at Carlingford, Co Louth, and Carrickfergus, Co Antrim. Late 13th-century ruins of great square keeps, with corner towers, may be seen at Carlow, Co Carlow and Ferns and Enniscorthy, both in Co Wexford. There are also many castles without keeps, like the well-preserved remains at Ballymoon, near Muine Bheag, Co Carlow.

One of the commonest antiquities of the Irish countryside is the ruined 15th- or 16th-century tower house. From about 1420 onwards, these buildings became common – fortified dwellings consisting of a tall, squarish tower which usually had a small walled bawn or courtyard. In most cases the bawn has disappeared, but good intact examples can be seen at Doe Castle (Creeslough), Co Donegal, Pallas, Co Galway, and Dungory, near Kinvarra, Co Galway.

DAY DRIVES

Roundstone Bay, Co Galway

The following seventeen one-day tours have been hand-picked to cover the most beautiful and interesting areas that Ireland has to offer—from Munster, Leinster, Ulster and Connaught. Places of scenic and historical interest are marked along each route

Day Drives

DAY DRIVE ABBREVIATIONS & MAP SYMBOLS

AA Viewpoint	☀	Mile(s)	m
Abbey	♖	Motorway	M1 ③
Airport	✈	National Boundary	
Avenue	Av	National Monument	(NM)
Battle Site	✕	National Trust	(NT)
Border Crossings		Other Roads	L62
Northern Ireland	⚑	Places off Main Route	Kenmare ○
Republic of Ireland	⚑	Places of Interest	■
Bridge	)(	Places on Route	*Ballin* ○
Castle	♜	Racecourse	○
Century(ies)	c	Railways	┼┼┼┼
Circa	c	Rivers and Lakes	*R Maine*
Crags	⛰	Road	Rd
Drive Route	T68	Signpost(s); Signposted	SP
Feet	ft	Street	St
Heights in Feet	2413 ▲	Tower	⚙
Houses Open to the Public	▥	TV or Radio Mast	⚡
Industrial Building	▥	Waterfall	
Lighthouse	⬈	Windmill	✹
		Yard(s)	yd(yds)

Peaks of Three Ranges
From Killarney
Drive 1   86 miles

Leave *Killarney* via the T29(N22) 'Cork' road, and in 2½m bear T30(N72) SP 'Mallow, Rathmore'. Proceed with the Mangerton Mountains on the right, and in 5½m pass through Barraduff. Drive to *Rathmore*, in ½m branch right on to the L41 SP 'Millstreet', and in 7m reach *Millstreet*. On meeting the memorial, turn right, and immediately bear right on to the L41 SP 'Cork, Macroom'. In 4m turn sharp right on to an unclassified road SP 'Ballyvourney'. Climb steadily through forestry plantations to the 1,340ft road summit, then descend through dense forest.

In 2m turn left SP 'Ballyvourney', and in 1½m meet a T-junction and turn left to the T29(N22). Pass through Ballyvourney, and in 1½m reach *Ballymakeery*. Turn right on to

DRIVE 1

mls SCALE 4
kms 0 2 4 6

1085

KILLARNEY

Rathmore

Millstreet

CLARAGH MOUNTAIN 1486

CAHERBARNAGH 2239

1574

1511

KNOCKNAGOWAN 1927
KNOCKNABRO ▲ 1903
1742
THE 2284 1958
PAPS 2273

MULLAGHANISH
2133 ▲1804
SUMMIT (1300)
1523

Barraduff

Race-course

Lough Leane

Inishfallen Abbey

Ross Castle

Muckross Abbey

Muckross House

Lough Guitane

CROHANE 2162

Muckross Lake
Torc Waterfall

STOOMPA 2281

TOMIES MOUNTAIN

PURPLE MOUNTAIN 2739

SHEHY MOUNTAIN 2503

TORC MOUNTAIN 1764

MANGERTON MOUNTAIN 2756

Upper Lake 1226

DROMDERALOUGH 2139

Black Valley

2020

1814 2005

1341

Morley's Bridge

1521

COOMAGEARLAHY 1671

1451

MWEELIN 1603

COOMATAGGART 1776

Ballymakeery

Ballyvourney

Renaniree

Coom Wood 1408

SUMMIT 1000

1126

SUMMIT 1200

1558

Looscatnagh Lough 1645

1280

1278

Kilgarvan

1633

1674

DERRY-GARRIFF 1617

PEAKEEN MOUNTAIN 1825

1675

1774

843

KNOCKBRACK 1452

CARRAN 1989

BEALICK 1764

1800 1828

DOUGHILL MOUNTAIN 1553

Lough Allua

GAP OF DUNLOE

2398

GWOUNAREEN

1254 GAP

2091

BOUGHILL 2065

1951

LETTER SOUTH 1186

Kenmare

1100

KNOCKANASKILL 1100 ▲ 1170

CULLABA HILL 1986

AKINKEEN 2099

KNOCKEIRKA 1407

KNOCKBOY 2321

CONIGAR 1886

DOUCE MOUNTAIN 1564

1797

2280

Lough Leane

---

an unclassified road SP 'Ballingeary, Renaniree', and shortly enter the Douglas River valley. In 2¾m turn left SP 'Renaniree', pass through rocky countryside, then in 1m meet a T-junction and turn right. In ¼m reach Renaniree and turn right. Ascend gradually for 3m to a 1,000ft summit and turn right SP 'Kilgarvan, Kenmare'. Follow the mountain side to a 1,147ft summit and make a long, winding descent. Climb to a 1,055ft pass and continue down into the Roughty Valley. Cross Inchee Bridge and drive alongside the river for 2½m to Morley's Bridge. Turn right across the bridge, then left on to the L62. Proceed to *Kilgarven*

and follow SP 'Kenmere' through the village.

Continue down the Roughty Valley to reach *Kenmare*. Follow SP 'Killarney' on the T65(N71) to drive along the Finnihy River valley and ascend between low hills. Climb to the summit of an 860ft pass known as Moll's Gap and bear right. Descend into the Owenreagh Valley; after 1½m pass the famous Gap of Dunloe – separating 2,739ft Purple and 2,503ft Shehy Mountains from the main part of the *Macgillycuddy* range – to the left. Beyond Looscaunagh Lough (on the right) pass Lady's View viewpoint, which lies to the left. Proceed through extensive woodland for several

miles to the shores of Upper Lake, then pass the conical 1,103ft Eagle's Nest Mountain before skirting the base of 1,764ft Torc Mountain with Muckross Lake on the left. Shortly pass the entrance to magnificent *Torc Waterfall* on the right. Continue through dense woodland, and after 1m (from the waterfall) pass the entrance to *Muckross* House and Gardens on the left. In another ¾m pass ruined Muckross Abbey (NM) on the left, and shortly catch sight of Lough Leane.

In 1¾m cross the Flesk, and after ¾m pass a left turn leading to ruined Ross Castle. Continue to Killarney town centre.

Day Drives

The Dingle Peninsula
From Tralee
Drive 2   104 miles

Leave The Mall in *Tralee* by turning left into Bridge St, then follow SP 'Dingle T68' along Princes Quay for ¼m before turning right. Drive between a ship canal on the right and the River Lee, and in 1¼m turn left over the river to enter Blennerville. The *Slieve Mish Mountains* are visible in the background.

Proceed along the T68 with Tralee Bay on the right and four mountains on the left. The latter are 2,160ft Glanbrack Mountain, 2,795ft Baurtregaum, 2,713ft Caherconree, and 2,423ft Gearhane. Continue for about 5m until the Stradbally Mountains can be seen ahead and *Fenit* Harbour can be made out across the bay. In 2¾m reach the edge of *Camp* village and turn right on to an unclassified road SP 'Stradbally, Connor Pass'. In 5m pass a road to the right which leads to *Castlegregory*, situated in the Magharee Peninsula between the bays of Tralee and Brandon. In 1¾m the drive affords distant views of *Lough Gill* to the right, with 2,627ft Stradbally Mountain and 2,713ft Beenoskee to the left. Proceed through *Stradbally* village, and continue with views ahead of 2,764ft Brandon Peak rising from the Brandon range. In a short distance the route offers right-hand views over Brandon Bay, Brandon Point, and the fine strand which extends along the W side of the Magharee Peninsula. After 2m (from Stradbally village) bear left SP 'Dingle, Connor Pass', and in 1½m cross the end of deep Glennahoo Valley below 2,017ft Coumbaun – which rises to the left. In 2m climb steeply away from the Owenmore River valley to the upper slopes of 2,026ft Slievanea. Brandon Peak and *Brandon Mountain* – at 3,127ft the fifth-highest peak in Ireland – are visible to the right; also to the right and beside the harbour is *Cloghane* village. Continue forward and shortly enjoy views ahead of numerous small loughs, then meet a sharp

bend where a small waterfall provides a high outlet for tiny Lough Doon.

After a further 1m reach the dramatic, almost knife-edged summit of the 1,500ft *Connor Pass*, with Slievanea rising to 2,026ft on the left. To the right are the impressive bulks of 1,579ft Beenduff and 1,961ft Beennabrack. Follow a long descent for panoramic views which extend across Dingle Bay to encompass 2,267ft Knocknadobar and *Valentia Island*, with *Dingle* town and Harbour in the foreground. On entering Dingle turn left and immediately right, then in ¼m turn right on to an unclassified road SP 'Ventry, Ballyferriter'. Drive out of the town and proceed alongside Dingle Harbour, then after ¾m reach *Milltown* and turn left SP 'Murreagh, Ballydavid' across the Milltown River. In ¼m keep straight ahead SP 'Slea Head', and in ½m keep forward again SP 'Slea Head' – with Dingle Harbour visible on the left. In 1¼m continue along a stretch of route which affords views on Mount Eagle, rising to 1,696ft beyond Ventry Harbour. After another 1¾m enter *Ventry*, in ½m turn left SP 'Slea Head, Dunquin', and in 1¼m turn right. In ¼m turn left again, then after 1¼m rejoin the coast. Continue for a short distance and pass through *Fahan* – the site of some 400 of the stone bee-hive huts known as clochans, plus numerous other ancient remains. Some of the huts are modern farm buildings, and opposite the village is the interesting Dunbeg promontory fort. Views S from here take in Bray Head on distant Valentia Island, with the remote *Skellig Islands* far beyond. After another 1m pass SP indicating 'Fahan prehistoric bee-hive huts' on the right. In a further 1½m drive round *Slea Head*, high above the shore and below the towering bulk of Mount Eagle. This section of the drive affords dramatic views of *Dunmore Head*, Blasket Sound, 961ft *Great Blasket Island*, and farther out to sea the smaller islands of Inishnabro and *Inishvickillane*.

Proceed for another 1m and pass through Coumeenoole. Pass behind Dunmore Head, before rejoining the coast, with views which extend beyond Beginish and Young's Island to distant *Inishtooskert*. Continue to *Dunquin* – claimed to be the farthest W place of habitation in Europe. Meet X-roads and turn left. In ½m pass Clogher Head on the left, with views ahead extending across a small bay to take in Sybil Point and a curious rock formation known as the Three Sisters. *Smerwick* Harbour and, to the N, 830ft Ballydavid Head can be seen to the right. Meet a T-junction and turn right SP 'Ballyferriter', then in 2m keep forward through *Ballyferriter* village. In 1m meet another T-junction and turn left SP 'Murreagh, Ballydavid', then in ½m turn right SP 'Dingle, Feohanagh'. Cross a bridge and keep forward. In 1¼m turn left SP 'Murreagh, Feohanagh, Gallarus Oratory', and proceed through barren, rocky countryside. In ½m meet a T-junction and turn left; the road to the right here leads to the ancient *Gallarus Oratory* – the only perfect example of its type in Ireland. After a further 1m enter Murreagh, turn right, and keep forward with SP 'Feohanagh'. Pass a radio transmitter on the left beyond the village, and after 1½m drive past Ardamore. In a further ¾m keep forward for views to the left of the Dooneen Cliffs. In ½m enter Feohanagh and turn sharp left SP 'Ballycurrane'. Pass Ballydavid Head on the left, with fine forward views of 2,509ft Masatiompan and 3,127ft Brandon Mountain, and proceed to Ballycurrane. Continue for ½m, meet X-roads, and turn right SP 'Dingle'. The road to the left here leads to Brandon Creek. Climb to a low pass, with views of the Brandon Mountains to the left, and continue to the summit for views which extend along the valley of the Milltown River to Dingle Harbour. Ballysitteragh rises 2,050ft on the left. In 4m reach Milltown and turn left, then in ¾m drive into Dingle via the main street. Proceed to the end of the street, cross a bridge, and immediately

36

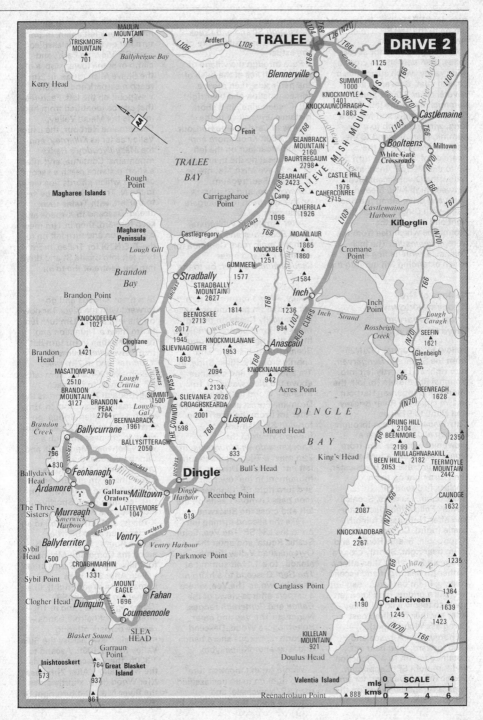

turn right SP 'Tralee'. In ¼m turn left on to the T68 SP 'Tralee, Anascaul'.

Ascend gradually for several miles, then descend to cross a wide valley which surrounds a coastal inlet. Slievanea and several other 2,000ft-plus summits rise to the left. After 5½m pass Lispole and follow a long, winding climb to a low summit, then descend to the edge of *Anascaul*. At the nearside of the village turn right on to the L103 SP 'Inch' and follow the Owenascaul River between high hills. Meet the coast and drive along the Red Cliffs, with Dingle Bay on the right and views of the mountains which rise from the *Iveragh Peninsula*. The Inch Peninsula, with its fine sandy beach extending 3m out into the estuary, can be seen ahead. *Rossbeigh* Strand and Creek occupy the opposite shore of the estuary.

Pass through the village of *Inch*, which lies at the base of the peninsula, then meet a forked junction and bear right SP 'Castlemaine'. In a short distance drive close to the shores of Castlemaine Harbour. Pass 1,860ft Knockmore and 1,860ft Moanlaur on the left before meeting the main group of the Slieve Mish Mountains – the peaks Baurtregaum, *Caherconree*, and Glanbrack – on the approach to Whitegate Crossroads.

After 1½m (from Whitegate) reach *Boolteens* and bear right with the main road. Continue for another 2¼m and enter *Castlemaine.* Turn left on to the T66(N70) SP 'Tralee', then immediately left again. In ¾m turn left on to an unclassified road SP 'Viewing Park', and climb over the lower slopes of the Slieve Mish range. In 2½m reach a carpark and 1,000ft viewpoint on the left. Features that can be identified from here include the Maine Valley, Castlemaine Harbour, the Laune Valley as far as *Killarney*, and the *Macgillycuddy's Reeks* mountains. Continue, and after a short distance reach a second carpark which affords fine views to the N. Tralee Bay can be seen to the left, with Tralee town ahead. Descend to X-roads and keep forward, then in 1½m meet a T-junction and turn left on to the T66(N70) for Tralee. In ¾m turn left into Castle St and drive into the centre of the town.

Valleys of the Knockmealdowns

From Dungarvan

Drive 3 96 miles

Follow SP 'Youghal T12(N25)' from the Square in *Dungarvan*, turn right and shortly left into Youghal Rd, then in ½m join the shores of Dungarvan Harbour. In 1¾m cross the River Brickey and climb to 919ft at Carronadavderg. Pass through the gap and continue to a viewpoint just over 12m from Dungarvan. After a further 4¼m turn left to cross the Blackwater, then turn right on to an unclassified road SP 'Cappoquin, Lismore, Scenic Route'. Follow the Blackwater, and after 1½m pass a ruined castle (right). Continue with SP 'Cappoquin, Scenic Route', and in ½m bear right. Shortly cross a bridge and turn left, then after a further ½m bear right and ascend steeply. In ¾m descend, keep left to cross a bridge, then keep left again to follow a small valley. After another 1m climb past Carnglass Wood (right).

Shortly meet X-roads and keep forward, then bear left. Continue for 1m to a T-junction and turn right SP 'Cappoquin, Scenic Route'. Descend for ½m to pass Strancally Wood on the left, and rejoin the Blackwater Valley. After a further ½m turn left, and in ¼m pass the entrance to Strancally Castle on the right. Meet a T-junction and turn right, In 1m turn right SP 'Cappoquin, Scenic Route, Lismore' and shortly cross the River Bride. In 1m enter a gap and continue above the Blackwater for 1m. Killahaly Wood (left) faces Dromana Forest across the river. After ¼m (from the river) keep forward SP 'Lismore' for forward views of the *Knockmealdown Mountains*. In 2¾m meet a T-junction and turn left into *Lismore*. Drive to the monument in the town centre and turn right SP 'Clogheen', then pass Lismore Castle on the left and cross the Blackwater.

Take the second turning left on to the L34 SP 'The Vee, Cahir, Scenic Route' and enter the Owennashad Valley. Climb steadily to a 1,114ft summit at *The Gap*. Descend to a hairpin bend known as The Vee, where a carpark affords views of the *Galtee* and *Comeragh* ranges. Negotiate The Vee and enter Bohernagore Wood. Descend through numerous sharp bends and later enter Killballyboy Wood.

Within ½m of *Clogheen* turn sharp right on to an unclassified road SP 'Newcastle' and continue along the Tar Valley. In 5½m meet X-roads and go forward with the River Tar now on the left, and in 1¼m turn left. In 1m meet a T-junction and turn right, then in ½m turn left into *Newcastle*. Follow SP '*Clonmel*' and in 2½m meet Ballymakee X-roads. Turn left SP 'Clonmel'. In ¾m reach Ballydonagh X-roads, cross the main road, and ascend. In 1¾m reach Kilmanahan Bridge, go forward on to the T27, and turn right. In 2m pass through a valley between Mountneill and Cannon Woods, then 1½m farther meet a T-junction and turn right. In ½m go forward on to the L27, and in a further ½m turn left then right. Shortly run alongside the river, meet X-roads, and turn right on to an unclassified road SP 'Nier Scenic Route'. Shortly climb along the Comeragh Mountain foothills, then turn S up a small valley. After 3½m pass Lyreanearca Wood (right). In a further ¾m turn right SP 'Comeragh Drive', and in 1m – after a pair of hairpin bends – reach a carpark offering mountain views across the Suir Valley from 1,100ft. Ascend to 1,300ft, then descend towards the Nier Valley. After 2½m pass Nier Wood (left), shortly cross the River Nier, and turn right SP 'Ballymacarbry'. Continue for

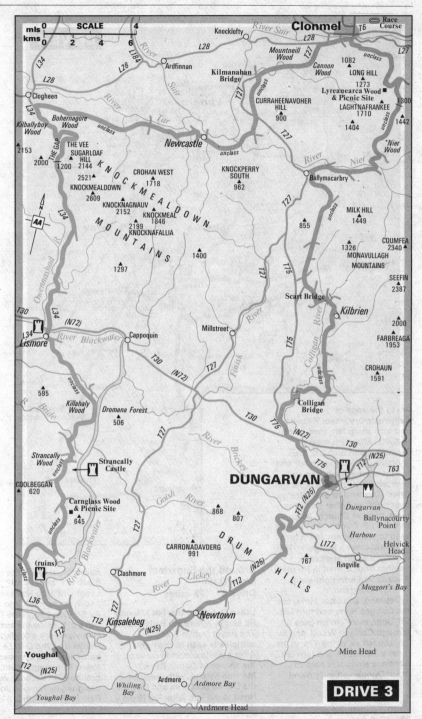

SCALE

mls 0 ——— 4
kms 0 —— 2 —— 4 —— 6

Clonmel

Knocklofty

Knockmealdown Mountains

Monavullagh Mountains

Drum Hills

Dungarvan

Lismore

Youghal

DRIVE 3

Day Drives

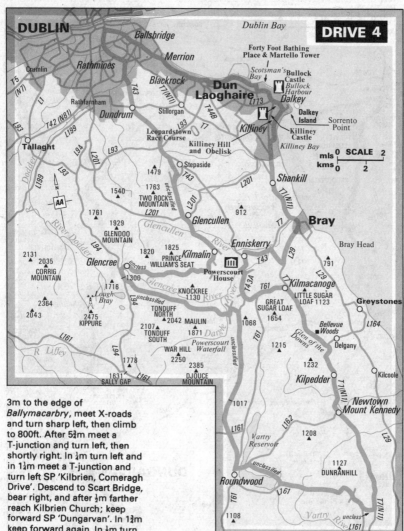

DUBLIN

Dublin Bay

Ballsbridge

Merrion

Rathmines

Crumlin

Blackrock

Dun Laoghaire

Forty Foot Bathing Place & Martello Tower

Scotsman's Bay

Bullock Castle

Bullock Harbour

Dalkey

Dalkey Island

Sorrento Point

Rathfarnham

Stillorgan

Killiney

Killiney Castle

Killiney Bay

Dundrum

Leopardstown Race Course

Killiney Hill and Obelisk

Tallaght

Stepaside

SCALE 2

mls 0

kms 0 2

1479

Shankill

1540

1763

TWO ROCKS MOUNTAIN

1761

912

Glencullen

Bray

1929

GLENDOO MOUNTAIN

Glencullen

Enniskerry

Bray Head

2131

2035

CORRIG MOUNTAIN

1820

1825

PRINCE WILLIAM'S SEAT

Kilmalin

791

Glencree

1300

Powerscourt House

Kilmacanoge

LITTLE SUGAR LOAF 1123

Greystones

1716

Lough Bray

KNOCKREE

1130

GREAT SUGAR LOAF 1654

2364

2043

TONDUFF NORTH

2042 MAULIN

1068

Bellevue Woods

Delgany

2475

KIPPURE

2107

TONDUFF SOUTH

1871

Powerscourt Waterfall

1215

Glen of the Downs

1778

WAR HILL

2250

2385

DJOUCE MOUNTAIN

1232

Kilpedder

Kilcoole

1631

SALLY GAP

1017

Newtown Mount Kennedy

1161

1208

L162

1127

DUNRANHILL

Vartry Reservoir

Roundwood

1108

Vartry River

3m to the edge of *Ballymacarbry*, meet X-roads and turn sharp left, then climb to 800ft. After 5½m meet a T-junction and turn left, then shortly right. In ½m turn left and in 1¼m meet a T-junction and turn left SP 'Kilbrien, Comeragh Drive'. Descend to Scart Bridge, bear right, and after ½m farther reach Kilbrien Church; keep forward SP 'Dungarvan'. In 1¾m keep forward again. In ½m turn right and cross a bridge. In 1¼m turn right again and cross another bridge, then in ¾m meet X-roads and turn right – still with SP 'Dungarvan'.

Descend, and after 1¾m cross the Colligan River and turn left SP 'Dungarvan'. In ¾m pass through Colligan Wood, and in ½m turn left on to the T75. In 1m meet a T-junction and turn left. Continue along this road to reach Dungarvan in 2½m and finish the drive.

Around the Sugarloaf
From Dublin
Drive 4   73 miles

Leave *Dublin* by the T44 Merrion Rd and in 2½m reach Ballsbridge. The Royal Dublin Society complex is seen to the right. After a while continue close to the shores of Dublin Bay at Merrion Strand, with views of the Dublin port area and Howrth Head to the left. After 3m (from Ballsbridge) reach the resort of *Blackrock*, bear left SP 'Dun Laoghaire' into Newtown Av, and in ½m turn left into Seapoint Av SP 'Dun Laoghaire Pier'. Drive alongside the seashore. Fine views are afforded across Dublin Bay and *Dun Laoghaire* harbour on the approach to the town. This magnificent, granite-built harbour was designed by famous John Rennie in the 19thC. It is the terminal for a ferry which crosses from Holyhead in Wales. Pass the car ferry on the left, meet traffic signals, and go forward SP 'Dalkey'. Continue along the shore, then in 1¼m meet a T-junction and turn right. The left turn here leads to the famous Forty Foot bathing place for men, plus a martello tower which houses a James Joyce museum and was once the poet's home. In 100yd meet X-roads and turn left on to the T44 SP 'Dalkey'. In ½m pass Bullock Castle on the approach to *Dalkey*. Meet a T-junction and turn left along Castle St. At the end of the street bear right SP 'Killiney' into Railway Rd, then bear left into Sorrento Rd. In ¾m turn right into Vico Rd. Ascend with views of Dalkey Head behind and *Killiney*, *Bray*, and Bray Head visible ahead. Pass wooded Killiney Hill, which is surmounted by an obelisk, and in ¼m turn left SP 'Coast Road, Bray'.

Descend steeply into Station Rd, Killiney, passing the station on the left. In ¼m meet staggered X-roads and go forward SP 'Bray, Wicklow'. After another ½m meet a T-junction and turn left on to the T44. In ¼m keep forward with the main road, then in ¾m go forward on to the T7(N11). Pass through *Shankill* and continue along a tree-lined road. In 1¾m keep forward on to the L29, then cross the River Bray to enter Bray. Keep forward through the main street to the town hall, then at the top of an ascent branch right SP 'Glendalough, Roundwood'. In 1¾m turn right on to the T7(N11) dual carriageway SP 'Dublin', and in ½m turn left on to the T43 SP 'Enniskerry'. Continue along the wooded Glencullen River valley to *Enniskerry*. Turn left SP 'Powerscourt', then on reaching a clock tower, bear left on to the T43A to ascend past the entrance of *Powerscourt* Demesne (right). The house was gutted by fire, but the magnificent gardens are open. Continue with SP 'Kilmacanoge', and in ¾m bear right; both the Great and Little *Sugarloaf* Mountains can be seen ahead. After 1m turn left on to the main T61 road and descend through fine rock scenery with the 1,654ft Great Sugarloaf on the right. Drive to *Kilmacanoge*, turn right on to the T7(N11) SP 'Wexford', and follow a main road between 1,123ft Little Sugarloaf and Great Sugarloaf. In 2m enter the *Glen of the Downs* and shortly pass the access to Bellevue Woods – with nature trails and a picnic site – on the left.

After 2m pass the edge of Kilpedder, from where the lower slopes of the Wicklow Mountains can be seen to the right. In 1½m pass through *Newtownmountkennedy*, and 5m farther turn right on to an unclassified road SP 'Roundwood'. In ½m meet a T-junction and turn right on to the L161. In ¾m meet X-roads and keep forward to pass through a gap between low hills. Continue to the edge of Varty Reservoir and bear right on to an unclassified road SP 'Sally Gap'. Follow the shores of the reservoir, with mountain views ahead. In 1½m meet a T-junction and turn left on to the L162. Cross the reservoir and in ½m reach the edge of *Roundwood*. Turn right on to the T61 SP 'Sally Gap, Bray', and in ¼m turn left on to an unclassified road SP 'Sally Gap, Enniskerry'. After a further 1½m go forward over X-roads SP 'Enniskerry'. Djouce Mountain rises to 2,385ft on the left, and Great Sugarloaf stands on the right. In 3¾m pass Djouce Wood on the left, and shortly enjoy a fine view over Bray Head and the coast (right). Some ¾m beyond this point, and 5½m from the X-roads, turn left SP 'Waterfall'. Descend steeply along a narrow road, then in ½m meet X-roads and turn left to continue the descent. In ½m pass the access to magnificent Powerscourt Waterfall (left) and bear right across the Dargle River SP 'Glencree'. Climb through forest, then after 5½m reach the 1,300ft head of Glencree Valley and turn right on to the L94 SP 'Rathfarnham'. A magnificent view to the right extends down the Glencree Valley to the distant Great Sugarloaf. In ½m branch right on to an unclassified road SP 'Glencree'. Descend to the area known as *Glencree* and shortly pass a World War Two German cemetery on the left.

Descend gradually below 1,825ft Prince William's Seat (left), with pleasant mountain and hill views across the valley. After 3¼m (from Glencree) drive past Curtlestown Church on the left. In 1¼m bear left SP 'Glencullen', pass the edge of Kilmalin on the right, and climb again to over 800ft. Descend steeply, cross the Glencullen River, and climb steeply. Meet Glencullen X-roads and keep forward SP 'Stepaside' to a 1,000ft summit below 1,763ft Two Rock Mountain. In ¾m descend, with views over Dublin Bay to the right, and after another 2m turn left on to the T43. Continue to *Dundrum* and go forward over X-roads. Follow SP City Centre' for the return to central Dublin.

Did you know . . .?

For 12 months after passing the driving test in Northern Ireland motorists must display 'R' plates (restricted driving) and limit their speed to 45mph.

Day Drives

The Historic Boyne Valley
From Drogheda
Drive 5 85 miles

Leave central *Drogheda* via West St and turn right into George's St T1(N1) SP 'Dundalk, Belfast'. In 4½m turn left on to an unclassified road SP 'Monasterboice Abbey, Round Tower', and in ½m turn left again. In ¾m pass ruined *Monasterboice* Abbey on the right. Continue with SP 'Mellifont Abbey' and in 1m turn right. After another 1m go forward on to the T25 SP 'Dublin, Drogheda'. In 1m turn right on to an unclassified road SP 'Mellifont Abbey', and in another 1m meet X-roads. Go forward for ¼m to ruined *Mellifont Abbey*, beside the Mattock River. Return to the X-roads and turn right. In 1¾m meet X-roads and go forward into King William's Glen, then in ¾m turn right on to the T26(N51) SP 'Slane'. In ¾m pass an unclassified left turn leading to the prehistoric tumuli at *Dowth*, *Newgrange*, and *Knowth*.

Follow the main road along the Mattock Valley and after 1¾m cross the River Mattock. After ¼m (from the bridge) pass another left turn leading to Knowth and Newgrange, then in a further 1½m pass a third, similarly signposted road. After another 2m enter *Slane*, meet X-roads, and keep forward on to the T26(N51) SP 'Navan'. In 1m with the Slane Castle estate on the left, turn right on to the L17 SP 'Kells'. In ½m turn left, and in 2½m meet a T-junction.

Turn right, then in ½m turn left SP 'Kells'. In 1¼m bear left, and in a further 1m reach *Kilberry*. Meet X-roads, go forward, and in 1m drive forward over a level crossing. In 4m meet X-roads and bear right then shortly left through Oristown. In a further 2½m cross the River Blackwater, and in 1½m bear right into the town of *Kells*. Pass the Headfort Hotel, branch left, then turn left on to the T9(N52) SP 'Athboy'. In ½m reach the edge of the town and branch left on to the L14. Bear right, and after another 6½m bear right SP 'Athboy'. The L21 left turn here leads to Rathmore Church (NM). In 1¼m, on entering *Athboy*, pass an unclassified left turn which leads to the Hill of Ward. Immediately beyond this road turn left on to the L3 SP 'Trim' and follow the line of the Athboy River. In 2½m bear right, and after a further 4½m enter the town of *Trim*.

Continue forward, and on meeting a T-junction turn right into the High St. Cross the River Boyne into the town square, and follow SP 'Dublin L3'. Pass castle ruins (left) and in ½m bear left to follow the River Boyne. After 1¾m turn left, cross a bridge, then turn left again on to an unclassified road SP 'Bective'. Continue along the Boyne Valley, then after 3m enter *Bective* and proceed to X-roads. Turn right SP 'Kilmessan'; the left turn here leads to a ruined fortress abbey. In 2¼m reach *Kilmessan* and turn left SP 'Tara' to cross a river bridge. Keep straight ahead, and in 1¼m turn right SP 'Tara'. Climb towards the ancient, royal hill of *Tara*, then in 1¾m meet a T-junction and turn right. In ½m turn left, and in 1¼m cross the T35(N3) SP 'Skreen Cross Church'.

In a further 1¼m pass the ruins of Skreen Castle on the right. Shortly pass Skreen Church and Cross (NM) on the left, meet X-roads and go forward, then in ½m meet the next X-roads. Drive forward and later descend. After 2¼m reach Edoxtown X-roads and turn left, then in ¾m meet more X-roads and drive forward, in ¼m bear left SP 'Duleek, Drogheda'.

Keep forward for ¾m, meet X-roads and turn left on to the T2(N2) SP 'Slane'. Keep forward for 6¾m along the T2 to McGruder's X-roads and turn right on to the L21 SP 'Drogheda'. In 1¾m pass an unclassified left turn SP 'Battle of the Boyne' – site of a crossing made by part of the Williamite force. Shortly bear left to reach the Boyne, then in 4m enter Donore and turn left SP 'Drogheda'. After another ½m pass another unclassified left turn SP 'Battle of the Boyne' – the site of the main battlefield. In 2¾m re-enter Drogheda.

Did you know . . . ?

You must slow down when driving into the Republic of Ireland. The maximum speed limit on main roads is only 55mph – 15mph less than on motorways and 5mph less than on main roads in the North.

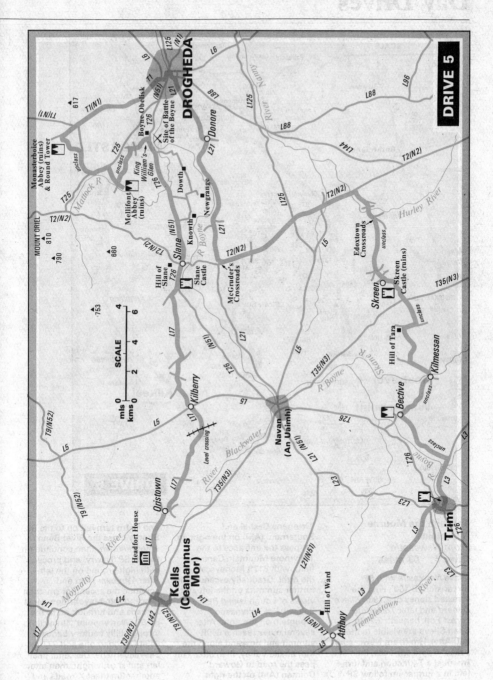

Day Drives

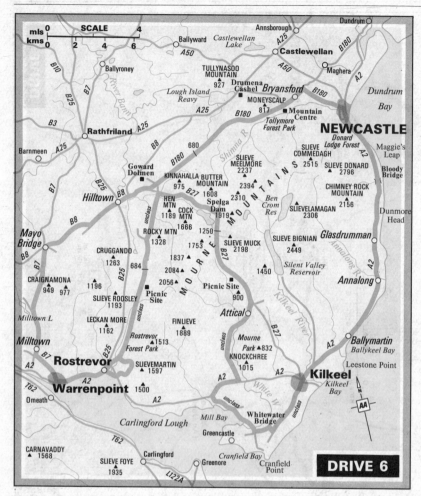

Through the Mourne Mountains area map. Scale: mls 0–4, kms 0–6.

DRIVE 6

Through the Mourne Mountains

From Newcastle

Drive 6   63 miles

Leave *Newcastle* with SP 'Bryansford B 180'. First the forested slopes of 2,796ft *Slieve Donard* and later *Tollymore Forest Park* beneath 2,203ft Shan Slieve are visible to the left. After 1½m (from Newcastle) pass the park entrance, then in ½m meet a T-junction and turn left. In a further ½m follow SP 'Hilltown' through *Bryansford* and pass Tollymore Forest Park below the *Mourne Mountains*. After ¾m pass a road to

'Drumena Cashel and Souterrain' (AM) on the right. In ½m pass the entrance to the Tollymore Mountain Centre (left), with 817ft Moneyscalp on the right. Gradually ascend with further summits on the left and views of Lough Island Reavy below 927ft Tullynasoo Mountain on the right. After several miles reach a 680ft summit and descend along the Kinnahalla Valley, then after 1½m pass the road to Goward Dolmen (AM) on the right. Views to the left extend across the upper Bann Valley to 1,189ft Hen and 1,666ft Cock. In ½m turn right on to the B27 SP 'Hilltown',

and in 1m turn left on to the B8. Shortly cross the River Bann to enter *Hilltown*, then continue on the B8 SP 'Newry' and proceed with high ground on the left. After 1½m bear right and continue the ascent for ¾m, then descend into Mayobridge. Meet X-roads and turn left on to the B7 SP 'Warrenpoint', then climb through hilly country beneath 949ft Craignamona and 977ft Slieveacarnane. Descend, bear left and shortly right, then after another 3m meet X-roads and turn left SP 'Warrenpoint'. After 1½m enter *Warrenpoint*. The Carlingford Mountains rise to over 1,500ft on the S side of

Carlingford Lough and include the isolated summit of 1,935ft Slieve Foye. Turn left on to the A2 and follow SP 'Rostrevor' through Warrenpoint. Proceed along the lough shores with mountain views to the right and Rostrevor Forest on the slopes of 1,597ft Slievemartin ahead. After 1m cross the Moygannon River, and in a further 1¼m cross the Ghann River into *Rostrevor*.

Here the main drive route keeps forward with SP 'Hilltown B25', and in ½m branches right on to an unclassified road before crossing the Kilbroney River in ½m. However, Rostrevor town centre offers an attractive alternative route through the Rostrevor Forest Park. To follow this turn right on to the A2 'Kilkeel' road SP 'Forest Scenic Drive', and in ½m turn left on to an unclassified road SP 'Rostrevor Forest'. Enter the forest and follow the signposted, one-way route. Climb steeply, with views of Carlingford Lough, and cross several mountain streams on the way through the forest. After 1¼m reach a picnic area and descend with fine views over Rostrevor, Carlingford Lough, and the Republic of Ireland. Warrenpoint can be seen in the distance. After 2m leave the forest and turn right on to an unclassified road SP 'Hilltown' to rejoin the main Drive. Climb the Kilbroney Valley, with part of Rostrevor Forest ahead and to the right; 1,162ft Leckan More rises to the left. After 1¾m cross a bridge and enter the forest. In ½m pass a picnic area SP on the right, then in another 1m leave the forest and reach a 684ft summit. Gradually descend along the valley of Shanky's River, with views of 1,328ft Rocky Mountain ahead, and after 1½m meet a fork and bear right SP 'Spelga Dam'. Pass Rocky Mountain on the right and in 1¼m cross the Rocky River. In ¾m cross the River Bann, meet X-roads, and turn right on to the B27 SP 'Spelga Dam, Kilkeel'. Follow the Bann River past Hen Mountain and the wooded lower slopes of 975ft Kinnahalla, then ascend steeply (1 in 10) into barren country between 1,500ft Spelga and Cock Mountain. This section of road is part of the *Spelga Pass* hillclimb route. Shortly reach the edge of the Spelga Dam reservoir, with some of the higher points in the Mourne range ahead. In ¾m meet a T-junction and turn right SP 'Kilkeel' to continue at over 1,250ft above sea level.

In ¾m cross the infant River Bann, then pass between Slieve Muck and 1,753ft Pigeon Rock Mountain to start the long descent towards 'Kileel'. After 1¾m skirt a small forest, with picnic areas SP on the right, and in another 1¾m branch right on to an unclassified road SP 'Newry'. Descend through agricultural country, and in ¾m pass the small village of Attical. After another ½m cross the White Water River, with 1,889ft Finlieve ahead and the wooded slopes of 1,015ft Knockchree on the left. Follow the White Water past Knockchree and the woods of the Mourne Park Estate, then continue the descent with some views of Carlingford Lough to the right. Meet a T-junction, turn right on to the A2 SP 'Newry', and in 1½m turn sharp left on to the unclassified 'Cranfield' road. Skirt Mill Bay with views of the Carlingford Mountains, and after 1m (from the A2) meet a fork and bear right. In a further 1½m cross the White Water bridge then meet X-roads and turn left for 'Kilkeel'. In ¾m meet a fork and bear right, then turn right SP 'Kilkeel'. In ½m meet a T-junction and turn left to proceed to *Kilkeel*. Enter this town and follow SP 'Newcastle' to join the A2. The road to the right leads to Kilkeel Harbour. Reach the end of the town, cross the Kilkeel River, and in ½m pass an unclassified road on the left leading to the *Silent Valley* reservoirs – situated deep in the Mourne range. The lower reservoir lies to the left of 2,449ft Slieve Bignian. In 1¾m pass through *Ballymartin*, descend almost to the shore, then after 2m (from Ballymartin) enter the straggling fishing village of *Annalong*. In ¾m pass the harbour (right).

Cross the Annalong River and continue along the A2 with views of Slieve Bignian to the left and 2,152ft Chimney Rock Mountain ahead. Follow the coastline, with views across Dundrum Bay to St John's Point, and after 5m (from Annalong) cross *Bloody Bridge*. *Slieve Donard*, the highest of the Mourne Mountains, rises to 2,796ft on the left. Rejoin the cliff edge, and in ¾m pass a ravine known as Maggie's Leap. Beyond this is the edge of extensive Donard Lodge Forest, and to the right are further views of Dundrum Bay. After 1m (from Maggie's Leap) pass Newcastle Harbour, and in ¾m re-enter the town.

Did you know...?

You must fasten your seat belts when driving across the border from Northern Ireland. The compulsory seat belt law came into force in the Republic in April 1979.

Day Drives

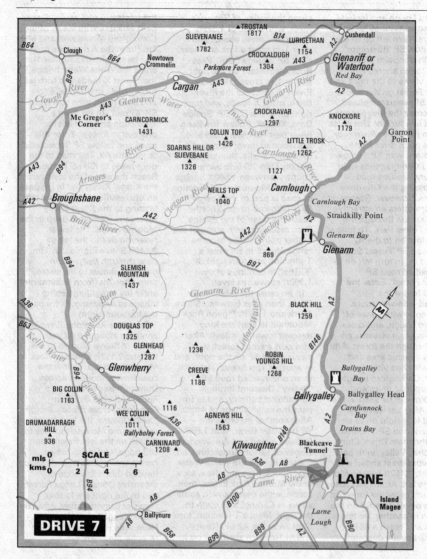

A Spectacular Sea Drive
From Larne
Drive 7   58 miles

This route follows part of the
Antrim Coast Road – rightly
considered to be one of the
finest marine drives in the
whole of Europe – through
some of the spectacular scenery
around the famous nine *Glens
of Antrim*. Most of these glens
are accessible from the road and

comprise a series of deep,
wooded rifts which cut across a
range of coastal hills. The most
distinctive is *Glenariff*, which
extends 5m inland from *Red Bay*
and includes attractive
waterfalls.
  From *Larne* follow SP
'Glenarm' to leave by the A2
along the Antrim Coast Road. In
2m pass through Black Cave
Tunnel to drive along the bays
of Drains and Carnfunnock, then

round 300ft Ballygalley Head
and continue to *Ballygalley*. The
fine fortified manor house in
this village is now used as a
hotel. Continue along the coast
for 6½m to enjoy lovely hill and
sea views before reaching
Glenarm, a village on the
Glenarm River at the head of
one of the Nine Glens of Antrim.
The village's chief attraction is
the beautiful park and glen
which adjoins its imposing

castle, built by the Earl of Antrim in 1636 but subsequently altered. Leave the village by following SP 'Carnlough' and cross the Glenarm River, then continue along the coast to *Carnlough*. The latter is beautifully situated at the foot of Glencloy – famous for its waterfalls – and features one of the mesolithic raised beaches for which this coast is famous. On leaving Glencloy pass beneath a stone arch, with the harbour to the right, then follow SP 'Cushendall, Waterfoot'. In 4m pass Garron Point Post Office, where *Garron Point* itself towers above the road and offers views which extend to the Scottish coast.

Veer W with road to follow shoreline of Red Bay. After 4m reach *Waterfoot*. Drive to the end of the village, cross the Glenariff River, and on meeting a T-junction turn left on to the A43 SP 'Glenariff, Ballymena'. Begin the ascent of Glenariff,

often considered the most beautiful of the nine Glens. A particularly attractive feature of this place is the contrast between the green of cultivated land and the black of basalt cliffs. Keep the Glenariff River on the left and wind along the cultivated, tree-shrouded slopes of 1,154ft Lurigethan Mountain, which rises to the right. This road affords fine views across the glen to the left, and to imposing cliffs with several waterfalls on the right. After 3m bear right and continue the ascent, then in 1¼m pass the entrance to Glenariff Glen on the left. *Parkmore Forest* is later seen to the right, and N of this is 1,817ft Trostan Mountain – the highest of the Antrim Hills. Proceed through rugged hill country with views of Cargan Water to the right, then descend through pastoral scenery to reach the village of Cargan. In 2¾m cross the Clough River, and after another 1¾m meet X-roads

and turn left on to the B94 SP 'Broughshane'. Continue through undulating countryside for 4m, then cross the Braid River and join the A42 to enter Broughshane.

Leave the latter by following SP 'Ballyclare' along the B94. Drive through pleasant, hilly country along a stretch of road which affords views of 1,437ft *Slemish Mountains* to the left, then after 6m meet X-roads and turn left on to the A36 SP 'Larne'. Follow the valley of the Glenwhirry River to *Glenwhirry*, then after this village bear right and in 2m cross the Glenwhirry river. Ascend through hilly countryside with fine views of the river now on the left, and in another 1½m reach Ballyboley Forest. Beyond the forest climb for a short distance and attain a 1,025ft summit, then descend over bleak moorland. Later pass the Kilwaughter House Hotel, and in 1m turn left on to the A8 for the return to Larne.

The Lower Erne Shoreline
From Enniskillen
Drive 8   64 miles

Enniskillen is an island town strategically sited in the River Erne between Upper and Lower Lough Erne. Its position has made it of great military importance for hundreds of years; as such it has been the centre of numerous battles and the site of several castles.

From Enniskillen follow SP 'Omagh' to leave the town on the A32. In 3½m branch left on to the B82 SP 'Kesh' and pass the road to *Devenish Island*. This is situated in beautiful Lough *Erne* and boasts one of the most complete monastic settlements in Ireland. St Molaise first founded a monastery here in the 6thC, and the small, rectangular oratory which carries his name is typical of many such structures built by the early-Irish church. Other interesting remains to be seen on the island, which can be reached by passenger ferry, include the Great Church and an 85ft round tower of 12th-C date.

After another 1½m pass

Ballycassidy Post Office and cross the Ballymallard River via a hump-backed bridge. Beyond this the road affords a fine view over the island-studded waters of Lower Lough Erne. Continue through the small angling resort of *Killadeas* and follow the wooded shores of attractive Rossclare Bay, then after a further 1m pass the road to Rossigh Bay Picnic Area on the left. Continue through the village of Lisnarrick and in 1m turn left on to an unclassified road SP 'Kesh Scenic Route', passing the entrance to *Castle Archdale* on the way. This castle now serves as a Ministry of Agriculture Grassland Experimental Centre. Ascend through part of the Castle Archdale Forest and reach a stretch of road which offers further excellent views of Lough Erne.

Drive through more open, undulating countryside, still with views of the lough, and in 3m meet a T-junction. Turn left here SP 'Kesh' and proceed to the sailing and angling centre of *Kesh* village, then turn left on to the A47 and cross the Kesh

River. In a further 1m turn left SP 'Boa Island, Belleek' to pass through pleasant scenery alongside the N shore of Lower Lough Erne. In 2½m cross a bridge on to narrow *Boa Island*, the largest of the many islands in the lough, and in another 4½m cross over to the mainland.

Meet a T-junction and turn left SP 'Belleek, Castle Caldwell', and in 3½m pass the entrance to *Castle Caldwell* Forest Wildlife Park (left). Beside the park gate is the 18th-C Fiddle Stone, which carries a curious inscription. The castle which gave its name to this park was one of the numerous 'Plantation' structures which dot the shores of Lough Erne. Continue to *Belleek*, which is noted for its pottery, then leave this small town on the A46 – passing the Hotel Carlton on the right. Follow SP 'British Customs, Enniskillen'. After a further ½m follow SP 'Garrison, Scenic Forest Drive' on to the B52.

Ascend, and in 1½m turn on to an unclassified road SP Derrygonnelly Forest Drive. Continue through barren, hilly

Day Drives

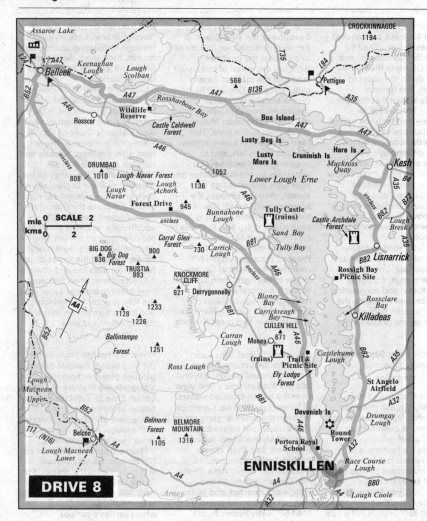

DRIVE 8

countryside with distant views of Lough Navar Forest and Corral Glen Forest ahead, plus Big Dog Forest to the right. After 6¾m proceed along a pleasantly tree-lined road, first passing the Lough Navar Forestry Office and then the entrance to the circular Lough Navar Forest Drive. The latter offers an interesting diversion from the main drive and visits a viewpoint situated at about 900ft on Magho Cliffs.

The magnificent panorama which spreads from here includes Lough Erne, the distant Donegal Hills, and far-off

Donegal Bay on the W coast. The signposted return follows a descent past Lough Achork and rejoins the main road, where a left turn is made to complete the circuit and once again pass the forestry office. A road opposite the entrance to the Forest Drive leads into wooded Glen Corral.

Continue along the unclassified road which forms part of the main route, and in ¾m pass picturesque little Carrick Lough. Follow SP 'Lough Erne', then in 2¼m meet X-roads and keep forward. After another 1½m turn right on to the A46 SP

'Enniskillen'. In 1m pass the road to Camagh Bay on the left, then after another 1½m pass the road to Carrickreagh Viewpoint on the right. Skirt the shore of Lower Lough Erne and pass the entrance to Ely Lodge Forest Loughshire Trail and Picnic Area on the left, then drive through part of the Ely Lodge Forest. Later pass a road leading right to *Monea* Castle ruins, and continue along the A46 for the return to Enniskillen. Portora Royal School can be seen on the hill before the route enters the town.

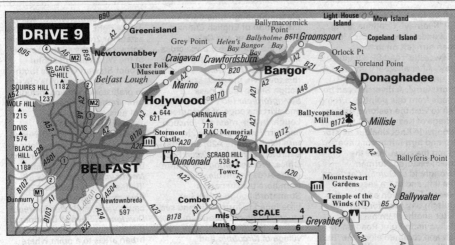

Peninsula Villages
From Belfast
Drive 9   81 miles

Leave *Belfast* by following SP 'Bangor A2' and join the Sydenham Bypass. In 3½m enter the Tillysburn Roundabout and take the first exit, then continue along a stretch of road which affords views over the coastal Belfast Lough to the left. Skirt *Holywood* and stay on the 'Bangor' road to pass through Marino village. After another ¾m pass Cultra Manor on the left. The manor and its grounds form the *Ulster Folk Museum*, which was originally created to illustrate traditional Ulster life. Re-erected buildings in the 136-acre park include a thatched barn, a farm, and a spade foundry.

Paintings by William Conor can be seen inside the house, and other interesting exhibits include a fine collection of transport vehicles. Adjacent to the museum is the proposed site of the projected Transport Museum. Proceed through Craigavad and in 2m turn left on to the B20 SP 'Crawfordsburn', then follow a pleasantly tree-lined road to the attractive village of this name. At the Crawfordsburn Inn bear left and drive to the outskirts of *Bangor*. This town is Northern Ireland's largest seaside resort and boasts all the usual amenities,

including good sandy beaches and the annual regatta of the Royal Ulster Yacht Club.

Drive into the town, cross a railway bridge into Bryansburn Rd, and at the ensuing roundabout keep forward. On meeting a T-junction turn right along the sea front. Views from here extend over Bangor Bay. In a further 1m pass Ballyholme Yacht Club on the left, then at the end turn left on to Ballyholme Esplanade to run alongside *Ballyholme Bay*. In almost ½m turn right into Sheridan Drive, then left into Groomsport Rd. In ¾m enter a roundabout and take the first exit SP 'Groomsport' on to the B511 to reach the small resort of *Groomsport*. Leave the latter with SP 'Donaghadee' and turn left on to the A2. Fine seascape views which now open up to the left include the off-shore *Copeland Islands*.

Enter the resort of *Donaghadee*, leave by following SP 'Millisle' to stay on the A2, then continue along the E coastline of the fertile *Ards Peninsula* to *Millisle*. To the W of this small resort is the restored Ballycopeland Windmill of 1784, which stands on the B172. Remain on the A2 and continue, with fine sea views, for 5m to pass through *Ballywalter* – a little resort noted for its extensive sands. Proceed to *Ballyhalbert*; on entering this village the drive affords views of

the off-shore Burial Island, which marks the extreme E limit of Irish soil. Leave Ballyhalbert and keep forward on to the unclassified Portavogie Coast Road, then in 1m bear right and continue into the small fishing village of *Portavogie*. On entering the village turn right then left and drive to the harbour.

After ½m turn left to rejoin the A2 SP 'Cloughey'. Follow a stretch of road which offers views of *Kirkistown Castle* to the right, and reach the little resort of Cloughey – situated near Cloughey Bay. Drive through the village, then at the church turn

49

left on to an unclassified road SP 'Kearney'. Continue along this undulating road for 1¾m, then turn left on to the 'Newcastle' road SP 'Quintin Bay'. After another 1½m meet a T-junction and turn right SP 'Portaferry'. A diversion can be made from this point by turning left to visit the restored fishing village of Kearney (NT). Drive alongside Knockinelder Bay for ½m and turn left to continue along the coast. Pass the much-restored Norman stronghold of *Quintin Castle* on the left, and in ¾m keep left. Meet a T-junction and take the Quintin Bay road for Barr Hall. After another 1½m pass the Ballyquintin Point Road on the left and continue along the 'Barr Hall' road.

On reaching the shores of Barr Hall Bay turn right on to the 'Portaferry' road and proceed N along the narrow straights of *Strangford Lough*. In some places the lough is as deep as the section of English Channel between Dover and Calais. Continue, with fine views across the water, and drive into the small port of *Portaferry*. Leave this town via the unclassified Lough Shore Road, pass *Strangford* car ferry on the left, and skirt the edge of Strangford Lough. In 3¼m meet a T-junction and turn left. In another 2¼m turn left on to the A20, and after a further ¾m reach *Ardkeen* Post Office. Proceed along the W arm of the Ards Peninsula. Views from here take in part of Strangford Lough which has broadened to form an inland sea studded with numerous small islands. In 4m pass through the village of *Kircubbin* and continue to *Greyabbey*, which features one of the most complete Cistercian abbeys in Ireland. Drive to the Police Station and turn left SP 'Newtownards', then after 1¼m pass the *Mountstewart* Estate on the right. Skirt the wall of the estate for 2m before passing the entrances to the 18th-C Temple of the Winds and beautiful Mount Stewart Gardens (both NT). The estate grounds are rich in prehistoric remains including three raths and a perfect dolmen.

Continue along the 'Newtownards' road with views which extend across the lough to the Londonderry Monument on distant *Scrabo Hill*. Enter *Newtownards* and follow SP 'Belfast' to leave by the A20. Pass through undulating countryside, and after 5m reach *Dundonald*. Beyond Dundonald drive through increasingly urban areas to a point where views to the right take in Stormont – the parliament buildings of Northern Ireland which are built in the English Palladian style. Proceed to Belfast city centre.

Over the Derryveagh Range

From Dunfanaghy

Drive 10 77 miles

Leave *Dunfanaghy* via the T72(N56) with SP 'Portnablagh and Carrigart', then in 1¾m reach *Portnablagh*. In ¼m reach a garage and turn left uphill on an unclassified road SP 'Marble Hill Strand'. After 1¾m join *Marble Hill* Strand (left) and shortly pass a well-wooded hillside (right) as the route turns away from the beach. In 1½m turn left to rejoin the T72(N56), and in ½m pass through *Ballymore*. After a further 1m pass the Ards Forest Park entrance (left). In 2m – close to a new church at the edge of *Creeslough* – branch right on to an unclassified road and ascend. Later pass beneath 2,197ft Muckish (right), and in 4¾m meet a T-junction. Turn left; the right turn here leads to 800ft Muckish Gap. In ¾m cross the Calabber River and immediately turn left on to the L82. Skirt 1,068ft Kingarrow on the right, cross the Owencarrow River at the end of Lough Veagh, and in ½m pass the *Glenveagh* Castle Estate entrance. Continue for 1½m, reach a T-junction, and turn right. In ½m bear right SP 'Gartan', then in 1¾m reach the bottom of a small valley and turn sharp right uphill.

Continue above the W shore of Lough Akibbon, later enjoying views of Gartan Lough, then descend past another Glenveagh Estate entrance (right). Bear left, pass between the two loughs, then in ½m drive forward on to the L82. Cross a river, bear right, and in ½m turn right on to an unclassified road to follow the shores of Gartan Lough. Brown Mountain stands at 746ft on the left, and 1,461ft Leahanmore rises to the right. After 1¼m reach the entrance to Church Hill Wood.

Drive forward past the end of Gartan Lough and enter the Bullaba Valley. Later climb to an 800ft pass, with Leahanmore and 1,388ft Farscollop to the right and the *Glendowan* range left. Ahead the peaks of 2,147ft Dooish and 2,240ft Slieve Snaght rise from the Derryveagh Mountains, and views right extend towards Lough Veagh. Follow the road left and descend into the Barra Valley between Moylenanav and Slieve Snaght, then continue past Lough Barra with high ground to the right. In 5½m reach the nearside of *Doochary*. Turn sharp right on to the L75, then ascend steep Corkscrew Hill.

Isolated Croaghleconnell rises to 882ft on the left. Proceed, with small lakes on both sides of the road, and after 5½m turn right on to the T72 (N56) 'Dungloe' road. In 2¼m reach a garage on the nearside of *Dungloe* and turn right on to the L130 (N56) SP 'Gweedore'. Follow a broad road, and after 5m pass Loughanure village and lough. In 2½m turn right to rejoin the T72, then continue and shortly pass through Crolly. In 1m keep forward on to the L130 and gradually ascend. After 1¼m cross the end of Lough Nacung Lower, then in ½m reach *Gweedore* and meet a T-junction. Turn right here on to the L82 SP 'Gortahork', follow the shores of Lough Nacung Lower, and pass the peat-fired Gweedore Power Station. In ½m keep forward on the L130 and ascend; the L82 right turn here leads to *Dunlewy* and the famous *Poisoned Glen*. Magnificent views right extend over Lough Nacung Upper and

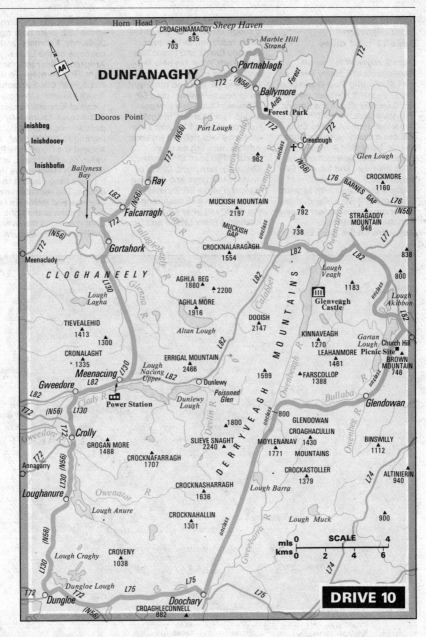

Horn Head
CROAGHNAMADDY
835
703
Sheep Haven
Marble Hill Strand
Portnablagh
Ballymore
Forest Park
DUNFANAGHY
T72 (N56)
T72
Ards Forest
T72
T72
Dooros Point
Port Lough
Creeslough
Glen Lough
962
CROCKMORE 1160
Inishbeg
Inishdooey
Inishbofin
Ballyness Bay
Ray
Falcarragh
Gortahork
Meenaclady
L83
L82
BARNES GAP
L76
L76
(N56)
792
STRAGADDY MOUNTAIN 946
738
MUCKISH MOUNTAIN 2197
MUCKISH GAP
CROCKNALARAGAGH 1554
L77
L82
838
800
C L O G H A N E E L Y
AGHLA BEG 1860
2200
AGHLA MORE 1916
Lough Lagha
Altan Lough
DOOISH 2147
Lough Veagh
1183
Lough Akibbon
Glenveagh Castle
L82
TIEVEALEHID 1413
1300
CRONALAGHT 1335
Meenacung
Gweedore
Crolly
ERRIGAL MOUNTAIN 2466
Dunlewy
Lough Nacung Upper
Power Station
Dunlewy Lough
Poisoned Glen
1599
KINNAVEAGH 1270
LEAHANMORE 1461
FARSCOLLOP 1388
Gartan Lough
Picnic Site
Church Hill
BROWN MOUNTAIN 746
1800
SLIEVE SNAGHT 2240
GROGAN MORE 1488
CROCKNAFARRAGH 1707
Annagarry
Loughanure
800
GLENDOWAN
CROAGHACULLIN
MOYLENANAV 1771
1430
MOUNTAINS
Glendowan
BINSWILLY 1112
CROCKASTOLLER 1379
CROCKNASHARRAGH 1636
Lough Barra
ALTINIERIN 940
L74
CROCKNAHALLIN 1301
Lough Muck
900
Lough Craghy
CROVENY 1038
Dungloe Lough
Dungloe
Doochary
CROAGHLECONNELL 882
L75
L75
L75
L74

mls   SCALE   4
kms 0 2   4   6

DRIVE 10

---

take in the highest mountain in
Co Donegal – conical, 2,466ft
Errigal.
    Continue to a low summit,
with Tievealehid and 1,300ft
Carntreena on the left, then

gradually descend and turn right
on to the T72 (N56). Views from
this section extend down the
Glenna River valley towards
Gortahork and the coast. In 1m
pass through Gortahork, then in

2¼m proceed through *Falcarragh*
and re-enter Dunfanaghy in a
further 8m.

*Places marked in italic type are
of special interest.*

Day Drives

Around Bear Haven
From Glengarriff
Drive 11   84 miles

From *Glengarriff* follow SP 'Castletownbere, Healy Pass' on the L61, skirting Poul Gorm pool and Glengarriff Harbour on the left. Continue above the Bantry Bay coast with the 1,887ft Sugarloaf, highest of the Caha Mountain foothills, to the right. Descend and skirt Adrigole Harbour. Continue to *Adrigole*, cross the river, and turn left SP 'Coast Road'.

After 2½m ascend with forward views of 800ft Bere Island, then follow the shores of *Bear Haven* with the Slieve Miskish Mountains on the right. Enter *Castletownbere*, keep forward through the town on the L61 coast road, and in 1½m pass Dunboy Castle and Picnic Site on the left. After 1m bear left and ascend to a 500ft summit. Descend for 1½m and turn right on to an unclassified road SP 'Allihies'. Climb to a low pass and in 1½m bear left. In 1m turn right on to the L61A, and after ½m turn sharp right. In ½m enter *Allihies*, turn left on to an unclassified road SP 'Eyeries', and in ¾m turn right. Climb to another low pass and descend steeply. Follow SP 'Eyeries', with the Slieve Miskish range on the right, and after 6m reach Kealincha River bridge and bear left.

Meet X-roads and turn left on to the L62. In ¼m bear right SP 'Killarney, Kenmare' and continue on the L62 to Ardgroom. Bear left, then turn right SP 'Kenmare'. To the right rise 1,969ft Coomacloghane and Tooth Mountain. Shortly enjoy views of *Kilmakilloge* Harbour; in 3m reach Lauragh Bridge and pass an unclassified right-turn leading to 1,000ft *Healy Pass*. Ascend the Glantrasna River valley to a 600ft pass, with mountain views to the right, and follow a long descent to Ardea Bridge. The mountain-ringed Cloonee and Inchiquin Loughs can be seen to the right. Continue along the river for another 8m to *Kenmare*

52

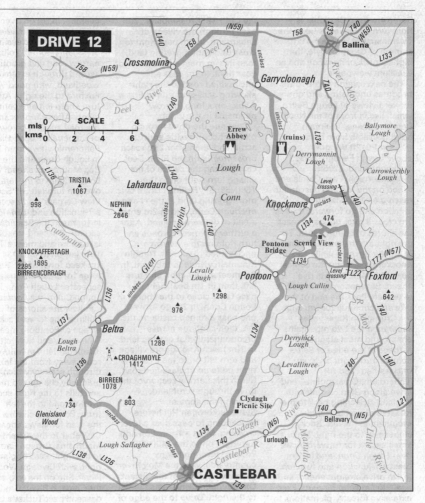

DRIVE 12

Suspension Bridge, then turn right on to the T65(N71) SP 'Glengarriff'. Drive along Sheen Valley and after 7½m cross the Baurearagh River.

Climb through several short tunnels to reach a long tunnel which marks the summit of a 1,000ft ridge. Descend with the Caha Mountains to the right, into the densely-wooded valley bottom and pass the entrance to Barley Wood Picnic Site on the right before re-entering Glengarriff.

Places marked in italic type are of special interest.

To the Shores of Lough Conn
From Castlebar
Drive 12   60 miles

Historic *Castlebar* is the county town of Mayo and has many interesting associations with Ireland's past. It was here, at the Imperial Hotel, that Michael Davitt founded the Land League during the time when the notorious Lord Lucan was forcing eviction on his tenants. Lucan was a member of the hated Bingham family.

Leave the town centre via the L136 Shamble St and cross a river bridge. Turn right SP

'Foxford, Ballina' into Chapel St and pass a church on the right, then meet X-roads and turn left into an unclassified road. Keep straight on to enter hilly, rather infertile country, then in 2m look left for distant views of 2,510ft *Croagh Patrick* and the *Connemara* mountains. Croagh Patrick is one of the most famous mountains in Ireland, and is traditionally the place where St Patrick withdrew to fast for the Lent period. After a further ½m pass through extensive forestry plantations, and shortly ascend to the top of a low rise. This affords views of Lough Sallagher to the left.

Day Drives

Some 4m from Castlebar is a right turn which leads up to the TV transmitter on the 1,412ft summit of Croaghmoyle, the highest peak of its range and an excellent viewpoint.

The next section of the route becomes undulating and offers forward views of Lough Beltra, which lies in front of the Nephin Beg Mountains. The main heights visible from here include 1,912ft Bengorm above Lough Feeagh, 1,935ft Buckoogh, and 2,295ft Birreencorragh. Pass Glenisland Wood on the left and descend to reach the L136. Meet this junction and go forward, then in 1m cross a river bridge to reach the shores of Lough Beltra. To the right are the wooded slopes of 1,078ft Birreen, while 1,695ft Knockaffertagh and the conical peak of 2,646ft Nephin rise ahead. Birreencorragh is visible to the left. Pass the end of the lake and continue for ¾m, with the Crumpaun River valley separating the two mountains ahead, and meet staggered X-roads at the edge of *Beltra* hamlet. Turn right on to an unclassified road SP 'Lahardaun, Crossmolina', and drive along Glen Nephin with bogland stretching back to the forested slopes of Nephin Mountain to the left. Rocky slopes rise to the right. Make a small ascent for forward views over *Lough Conn*, and in 1½m meet a T-junction and turn left. In 1m drive straight ahead, and again in 1m keep forward. Pass extensive forestry plantations to the right, and beyond these enjoy good views over Lough Conn. Shortly go forward on to

the L140 SP 'Crossmolina', and pass through the village of Lahardaun. In 2m bear right to cross undulating grazing land, then in 1½m meet a junction and bear right. In ¼m pass an unclassified road to the right allowing access to ruined Errew Abbey on a long, narrow peninsula in the lough.

Continue the drive through pleasant countryside and scrubland, then after 2¾m reach *Crossmolina* on the River Deel. On reaching the centre of the village turn right on to the T58(N59) SP 'Ballina'. Drive over more grazing land at the N end of Lough Conn, and in 2m enter a belt of dense woodland. After a further 2m meet X-roads and turn right on to a narrow unclassified road, with Nephin Mountain visible to the right. In 2m meet a T-junction and turn left, then in 1m bear right to pass fairly close to the shores of Lough Conn. In 2m go forward and pass a ruined castle on the left, then continue across predominantly flat grazing land. In 3½m reach Knockmore village and turn left on to the L134, then right on to an unclassified road. Climb this narrow section of the drive through scrubland, crossing the edge of Stoneparkbrogan Hill before descending to pass over a level crossing. Meet a T-junction and turn right on to the T40(N58). Proceed through boggy countryside, with the Moy River to the left in front of the distant Ox Mountains, and dense forest to the right. Drive to the edge of *Foxford* and before reaching the river bridge turn sharp right on to the L22 SP 'Pontoon', then

bear left. In ¾m go over a level crossing, then immediately turn right on to an unclassified road SP 'Scenic Route'. Follow this narrow road and gradually ascend through extensive woodland, with good views over Foxford to the right. After 1½m turn sharp left and continue to climb. After a further ¾m reach the road summit below the top of Stoneparkbrogan Hill. Panoramic views from here take in Lough Conn and the Nephin Beg Mountains ahead, with Lough Cullin to the left. In just over ½m turn left SP 'Scenic View Carpark' and ascend. Meet a T-junction and turn right, then in ½m reach the Scenic View carpark. Descend steeply to the lake shore and meet a T-junction. Turn left on to the L134, and in 1m keep forward SP 'Pontoon'. After 1m cross the stream which separates Lough Conn from Lough Cullin, via *Pontoon Bridge*.

Follow the shores of Lough Cullin to the forest-backed village of Pontoon, meet a T-junction, and turn left SP 'Castlebar'. In 1m follow the route away from the lake, through scenery which gradually changes to moorland and hills to the right and poor grazing land to the left. After 5m (from Pontoon) climb a rise in the road for views ahead over Castlebar to the distant Partry Mountains. Croagh Patrick rises to the right. Pass bogland to the right, with Clydagh Wood and Picnic Site on the left, and cross the Clydagh River. Gradually descend past Tucker's Lough. After a while go forward on to the T40(N5) to re-enter Castlebar.

Now with the coming in of the spring the days will stretch a bit,
And after the feast of Brigid I shall hoist my flag and go,
For since the thought got into my head I can neither stand nor sit
Until I find myself in the middle of the County of Mayo.
James Stephens (from the Irish of Raftery)

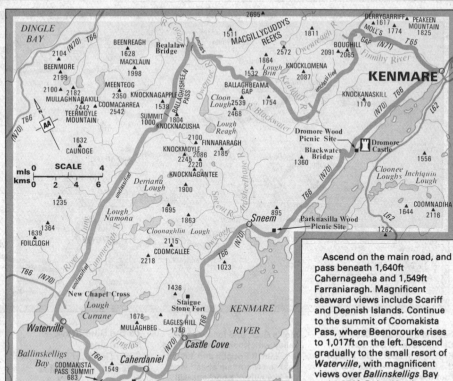

Map labels (Drive 13):

DINGLE BAY · R Caragh · 2695 · MACGILLYCUDDYS REEKS · 1511 · 1811 · DERRYGARRIFF 1617 · PEAKEEN MOUNTAIN 1825 · MOLL'S 1774 · BEENREAGH 1628 · Bealalaw Bridge · MACKLAUN 1998 · 2572 · KNOCKLOMENA 2091 · 2065 · BOUGHILL · GAP (N71) · T65 · Finnihy River · BEENMORE 2199 · 2104 (N70) T66 · Lough Brin 1532 · 1864 · 2087 · KENMARE · 2100 · 2182 · MEENTEOG 2350 · KNOCKNAGAPPLE 1538 · BALLAGHBEAMA GAP · 2539 · 1754 · KNOCKANASKILL 1170 (N70) T66 · MULLAGHNARAKILL 2442 · COOMACARREA 2542 · SUMMIT 1000 · 1804 · Cloon Lough · 2468 · Dromore Wood Picnic Site · Dromore Castle · AA · KNOCKNACUSHA · Lough Reagh · Blackwater Bridge 1360 · 1556 · 1632 CAUNOGE · 2100 · FINNARARAGH · KNOCKMOYLE 2245 · 2086 2185 · 2220 · Cloonee Loughs · Inchiquin Lough · SCALE · KNOCKNAGANTEE · Derriana Lough · 1900 · T66 (N70) · COOMNADIHA 1644 · 2116 · 1235 · Lough Namona · 1695 · 1863 · 895 · Sneem · Parknasilla Wood Picnic Site · 1262 · 1364 1639 FOILCLOGH · Cloonaghlin Lough · 2115 · 2218 · COOMCALLEE · T66 · 1023 · River Inny · Cummeragh River · New Chapel Cross · Lough Currane · 1436 · Staigue Stone Fort · KENMARE RIVER · Waterville · 1678 · MULLAGHBEG · EAGLES HILL 1786 · Castle Cove · Ballinskelligs Bay · T66 · Caherdaniel · COOMAKISTA PASS SUMMIT 683 · 1549 · 1017 · Derrynane House · Hogs Head · Abbey Island · Lambs Head · **DRIVE 13**

Through the High Passes
From Kenmare
Drive 13   80 miles

Take the T65(N71) and follow SP 'Killarney, Ring of Kerry' to leave *Kenmare*. In ½m bear left on to the T66(N70), then follow the N shore of Kenmare River with views of the Caha Mountains to the left. To the right the 1,186ft hills of Letter South and 1,170ft Knockanaskill rise above the waters of the bay. After 5m (from Kenmare) pass the entrance to Dromore Castle on the left, and 1¾m farther pass Dromore Wood Picnic Site on the left. In another 1m cross *Blackwater Bridge* and continue along the bay.

After 7m pass another picnic site at *Parknasilla* Wood. Continue from here to *Sneem* along a tree-lined road, with

glimpses of Kenmare River to the left. Approach Sneem with views of mountains which ring the town. This group is dominated by 2,155ft Coomcallee, which rises to the W. Cross the Sneem River by a narrow bridge and turn inland. Ascend along an afforested valley to the summit of a low pass, with Coomcallee on the right. Descend through wild, rocky scenery to rejoin Kenmare River. Views afforded by this stretch extend across the bay to the Slieve Miskish Mountains, which rise from the *Beare Peninsula*. Continue to Castle Cove, situated beneath 1,786ft Eagles Hill; an unclassified road here leads to *Staigue Fort* (NM). Follow the coast below the mountain to reach *Caherdaniel*. Restored, 17th-C Derrynane House (NM) can be visited here.

Ascend on the main road, and pass beneath 1,640ft Cahernageeha and 1,549ft Farraniaragh. Magnificent seaward views include Scariff and Deenish Islands. Continue to the summit of Coomakista Pass, where Beenorourke rises to 1,017ft on the left. Descend gradually to the small resort of *Waterville*, with magnificent views over *Ballinskelligs* Bay and 1,350ft Bolus Head. Approach the town and pass Lough Currane on the right. Proceed to the N end of the town and bear left, then right. In 1¾m reach New Chapel Cross and go forward on to an unclassified road SP 'Ballaghisheen, Glencar'. Follow the broad valley of the River Inny along a narrow but level road, with 1,639ft Foilclough in the distance to the left. Approach the head of the valley, with 1,632ft Caunoge to the left, and shortly reach a vantage point for views of 2,541ft Coomacarrea, 2,350ft Meenteog, and 2,258ft Colly. The foothills of 2,250ft Knocknagantee and 2,245ft Knockmoyle rise to the right. Ascend past extensive woodland to the 1,000ft summit of *Ballaghisheen Pass*, between 1,538ft Knocknagapple and 1,804ft Knocknacusha. Descend steeply through desolate bogland, along a narrow road with several difficult bends, to the valley floor. Continue for 4m

Day Drives

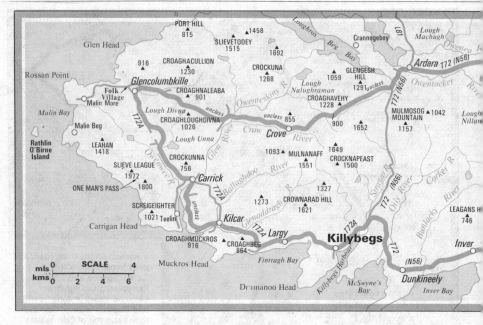

beyond the pass, cross the Caragh River at Bealalaw Bridge, and bear right. Follow the Caragh Valley with the foothills of *Macgillycuddy's Reeks* on the left. After 1½m turn right SP 'Ballaghbeama, Parknasilla', and recross the Caragh River.

Ascend between towering rock faces, with 2,539ft Mullaghanattin on the right, to reach the 1,000ft summit of *Ballaghbeama* Gap. The 1,532ft summit on the left is part of Knockaunanattin. Pass the road summit and descend along the valley of the River Kealduff, with 2,097ft Knocklomena ahead and Lough Brin to the left. On reaching the valley floor, continue through forestry plantations and cross the river. After 1m turn left SP 'Killarney,

Moll's Gap', and follow a wide valley with Knocklomena on the left, 2,091ft Boughil and 1,825ft Peakeen Mountain ahead, and the low hills of Knockanaskill and Letter South on the right. Climb to over 700ft and join the top end of the Finnihy Valley, with Boughil towering on the left. Shortly pass little Lough Barfinnihy on the left, then skirt an unnamed, 1,254ft hill for views of the Owenreagh Valley to the N. Meet the main road and turn right on to the T65(N71). Pass through Moll's Gap, situated between the unnamed hill and 1,617ft Derrygarriff at a height of over 900ft. Complete the drive by returning to Kenmare via a long, winding descent, which affords excellent views of Kenmare Bay and the surrounding mountains.

To the Blue Stack Mountains
From Donegal
Drive 14   100 miles

Leave *Donegal* from The Diamond and follow SP 'Killybegs, Mountcharles' on the T72(N56). Drive alongside Donegal Bay, passing *Mountcharles* after 3¼m, and ascend inland for several miles. Rejoin the coast at Inver Bay. After 7m (from Mountcharles) pass through *Dunkineely*, which lies at the base of a narrow peninsula separating Inver and McSwyne's Bays. This peninsula can be explored by an unclassified road. In 4½m turn left on to the T72A and drive alongside *Killybegs* harbour before entering the town. In ½m bear right and ascend, then in 1m descend to the edge of sandy *Fintragh Bay*. After 4m bear right SP 'Kilcar', and climb a low pass between 864ft Croaghbeg and 1,621ft Crownarad Hill. Descend along Glenaddragh Valley into *Kilcar*. Meet X-roads and keep forward SP 'Coast Road' on to an unclassified road. In ½m ascend steeply, with distant views of

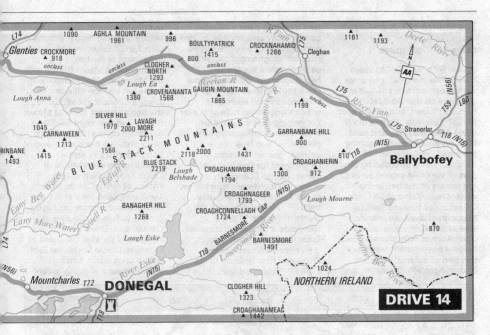

the Co Mayo mountains to the left. Summit views extend across Teelin Bay to the famous 1,972ft *Slieve League*.

Rejoin the T72A at the edge of *Carrick*, a village which provides access to *Teelin* and Slieve League. Pass through Carrick, shortly enter the Owenwee Valley, then climb to 600ft before descending towards *Glencolumbkille*. At the edge of the village keep forward on an unclassified road SP 'Ardara'. A left turn here allows a detour to the Folk Village. In ½m bear left over a river. Meet a T-junction and turn right SP 'Glengesh', then in 1m cross a river and bear right. Climb to a 700ft pass between 901ft Croaghnaleaba and 1,026ft Croaghloughdivna, then descend to the Glen River valley. Bear left SP 'Ardara' then drive forward to cross the river and enter the Crow River valley.

Follow an easy ascent past Crow village, with mountains ahead and to the right, and climb to 900ft below 1,228ft Croaghavehy at the head of Glen Gesh. Descend, with maximum gradients of 1 in 4 and hairpin bends. Meet a

T-junction and turn left on to the T72(N56) for *Ardara*. Enter the town and bear left SP 'Glenties', then ascend and bear right. Continue for 6½m to reach *Glenties*. Pass the school and church on the right, and immediately turn right on to an unclassified road, keeping the town to the left. Follow the Owenea Valley. After 4m the road affords views of 1,961ft Aghla Mountain on the left plus 1,713ft Carnaween and 1,979ft Silver Hill. Lough Ea lies to the right after several more miles. In 3m reach an 800ft summit, then make an easy descent into the Reelan Valley. Ahead is 1,865ft Gaugin Mountain, and views to

the right include the Blue Stack Mountains. Continue for 4m and bear right across a river, then in 1m join the valley of the River Finn. Follow the river for 3½m and drive forward on to the L75, then proceed to *Ballybofey*. Turn right here on to the T18(N15) SP 'Donegal', and skirt Lough Mourne after 5½m. The mountains beyond this include 1,793ft Croaghnageer on the right, plus 1,724ft Croaghconnellagh and 1,491ft Barnesmore ahead. Drive between the latter two mountains via *Barnesmore Gap*. Once clear of the range pass Lough Eske (right), and later re-enter Donegal.

Did you know...?

Red reflective rear number plates are legal in the South, while in Northern Ireland the British style yellow rear plates are used.

57

Day Drives

The Shores of Lough Corrib
From Galway
Drive 15   92 miles

Follow SP's 'Salt Hill' to leave *Galway* via the L100, and drive to the seaside resort of *Salt Hill*. Continue on the 'Spiddal' ('Spiddle') road, and in 1½m keep left SP 'Carraroe'. Follow the N coast of Galway Bay and pass through Barna before reaching the small angling resort of *Spiddal*. Views afforded by this part of the drive extend across the waters of the bay to the distant mountains of Co Clare.

Seascapes beyond Spiddal encompass the *Aran Islands*, while landward views take in a patchwork of little stone-walled fields – a prominent feature of this part of Ireland. After 9m branch right SP 'Costelloe', and turn inland to pass through barren rocky countryside. In 2¾m turn right on to an unclassified road SP 'Oughterard'. After a short distance the scenery becomes mountainous and the drive route affords views of numerous small lakes as it winds through the hills of the Iar Connaught district. After 8m enter a newly-afforested pine plantation, and later make a gradual descent towards *Oughterard* for fine views of distant *Lough Corrib*. On reaching Oughterard turn left on to the T71, then immediately right SP 'Westport'. Cross the Owenriff River and drive alongside it for a short distance. Enter the *Connemara* district, then after 10m reach *Maam Cross* and turn right on to the L100 SP 'Maam Bridge'. Drive over barren, open countryside before crossing higher ground with 2,012ft Leckavrea Mountain prominent to the left.

Continue to Maam Bridge with the Maumturk Mountains rising to the left and the hills of *Joyce's Country* ahead. Cross the Bealanabrack River at Maam Bridge and turn right SP 'Cong' to remain on the L101. After a short distance there are views of Lough Corrib's W arm – including the island-ruins of *Castle Kirke*, which is also known as *Hen's Castle*. After 1½m turn inland for a short distance and cross more high ground before continuing to *Cornamona*. Drive beyond this village and parallel the shore of attractive Lough Corrib for 2½m before once again turning inland. Make a winding ascent

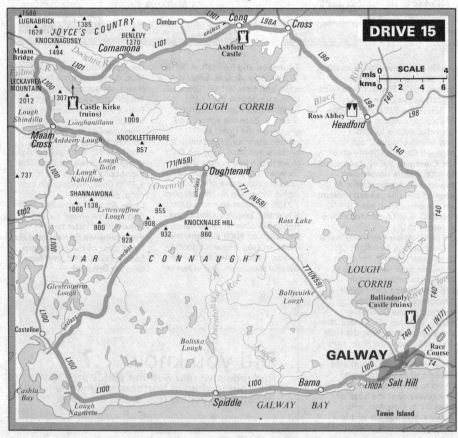

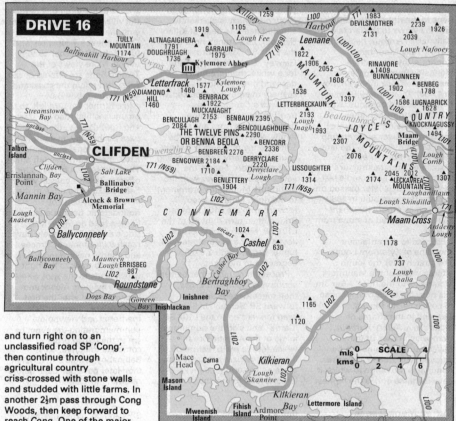

and turn right on to an unclassified road SP 'Cong', then continue through agricultural country criss-crossed with stone walls and studded with little farms. In another 2½m pass through Cong Woods, then keep forward to reach *Cong*. One of the major features offered by this interesting village is its largely-rebuilt Augustinian friary, a royal foundation dating from the 13thC. Drive to the old Market Cross in Cong and keep left SP 'Galway'. Leave the village, and after ½m pass the impressive gates of 19th-C *Ashford Castle*, which now serves as a hotel but was originally built for Arthur E Guinness. Keep forward with the L98 'Headford' road, and in 2½m turn right for the village of Cross. Continue along the L98 through undulating livestock-grazing country, and after 1½m keep left. After another 4¾m pass the ruins of Ross Abbey on the right and proceed into the small country town of *Headford*.

Join the T40 SP 'Galway', and continue the drive through flat,

rather uninteresting countryside for almost 11m before crossing the River Clare. This river flows into Lough Corrib, which lies only 1m to the right but is not clearly visible from the road. In 2¾m pass the remains of Ballindooly Castle, then complete the drive by continuing along the T40 to Galway.

To help motorists, places of special interest have been marked in italic type in the text and tourists are recommended to stop at them.

Into Joyce's Country
From Clifden
Drive 16   92 miles

Take the unclassified Sky Rd to leave *Clifden*, and follow the coast of a peninsula which is bounded to the S by Clifden Bay. Climb above the bay to cliff tops, which afford superb island views and Atlantic seascapes. In 4m keep right in order to return along the N side of the peninsula, and later follow the shore of Streamstown Bay. This part of the drive affords distant views of the *Twelve Bens*, or Pins; the highest of these mountains rises to 2,395ft. After 3¾m turn left on to the T71 SP 'Letterfrack, Leenane', and continue through barren countryside. In 1¾m bear right to cross open moorland, with

Day Drives

further views of the Twelve Bens to the right. After another 1¾m the views to the left take in Ballynakill Harbour, backed by 1,174ft Tully Mountain. Continue, and later drive alongside Barnaderg Bay to reach *Letterfrack* in the shadow of 1,460ft Diamond Hill. Leave Letterfrack and continue, with 1,736ft Doughruagh ahead, before following the valley of the Dawros River and entering the Pass of Kylemore. The late 19th-C *Kylemore Abbey*, a castellated granite structure which was one of Ireland's last castle houses, is later passed on the left. This was built in 1860 for a rich Liverpool merchant and is constructed of stone from Dalkey.

Proceed to the attractive shoreline of Kylemore Lough. The stretch after the lough affords views of the Maumturk Mountains to the right. After 3m it is possible to catch a glimpse of Lough Fee to the left. Descend to the shores of picturesque *Killary Harbour*, from which views of the Mweelrea Mountains can be enjoyed. The 2,688ft Mweelrea dominates the range to which it gave its name and is the highest

peak in Connacht. Continue to *Leenane*, which is pleasantly situated near the head of Killary Harbour, and branch right on to the L101 SP 'Maam Cross and Galway'. Cross higher ground for a while, then gradually descend through moorland scenery to enter the area known as *Joyce's Country*. This unofficially-named region derives its title from a Welsh family who moved here in the 13thC. Many of the local people count these early settlers among their ancestors. Follow the valley of Joyce's River with the Maumturk Mountains prominent to the right. Later on keep forward with the L100 to Maam Bridge, then turn right on to the L101 SP 'Maam Cross'. Cross Joyce's River and continue over higher ground with 2,012ft Leckavrea to the right.

Proceed through rather barren countryside to *Maam Cross*, then meet X-roads and go forward SP 'Screeb'. In 5½m keep forward on to the L102 SP 'Carna', and skirt the numerous inlets of the Atlantic Ocean which form a main feature of the S *Connemara* coast. In 4¾m cross a river bridge, then keep left and later follow the W

shores of Kilkieran Bay to reach the village of *Kilkieran*. Continue with the L102 to the outskirts of *Carna*, meet a T-junction, and turn right SP 'Cashel' to turn inland. More views of the Twelve Bens are offered ahead. After 3½m rejoin the coast and skirt Bertraghboy Bay.

In a further 4m turn left on to an unclassified road SP 'Cashel and Roundstone', then after 1m pass Cashel Bay. In 4m turn left SP 'Roundstone' and rejoin the L102, then in 1m turn left again. The next section of the route offers extensive coastal views before taking the drive to the little fishing village of Roundstone. Continue along the Clifden road and later skirt Dog's and Ballyconneely Bays to reach *Ballyconneely*. Proceed N and shortly pass Mannin Bay. In 3¼m pass a track to the right which leads to the spot where famous aviators Alcock and Brown landed after the first trans-Atlantic flight in 1919. A memorial and viewpoint commemorating the event lie ½m to the left. In order to complete the drive, cross Ballinaboy Bridge and turn left, then later pass Salt Lake before returning to Clifden.

Burren Moonscapes
From Ballyvaughan
Drive 17   79 miles

Depart from the monument in *Ballyvaughan* with SP 'Black Head' on the L54 and drive along the shores of Ballyvaughan Bay. Pass beneath 1,024ft Cappanawalla and 1,045ft Gleninagh Mountain, then after 6m round *Black Head* for views of the *Aran Islands*. After 4½m pass Craggagh Post Office on the right, with 1,134ft Slieve Elva to the left.

Continue, passing 976ft Knockauns on the left, then after 4m (from Craggagh) turn inland and ascend with 15th-C Ballynalackan Castle visible ahead. *Galway* Bay and the Aran Islands can be seen behind during the climb. After 1¾m reach the castle gates and turn right on to an unclassified road SP 'Cliffs of Moher'. Pass

through farmland with distant forward views of the famous, 600ft *Cliffs of Moher*. Descend to Roadford, cross the River Aille, and in ¼m turn left SP 'Cliffs of Moher'. The road ahead leads 1m to Doolin Strand. In 1¼m meet X-roads and turn right on to the L54. Ascend with fine views right and 678ft Knocknalarabana on the left, then after 4½m pass a right turn leading to the Cliffs of Moher carpark. Steps from here lead up to cliff-top O'Brien's Tower, which affords magnificent views of the 3m cliff range. After another 2m along the L54 pass St Bridget's Well and a monument on the right. In ¾m meet a T-junction and turn left SP 'Liscannor, Lahinch', then in 1½m enter *Liscannor* on the shores of Liscannor Bay. Continue along the shore with the L54 and in 1m pass a fine (but dangerous) beach. Follow

SP 'Lahinch', cross the Inagh River by *O'Brien's Bridge* with castle ruins on the left, then skirt Lahinch Championship Golf Course among the sand dunes on the right. Meet a T-junction, turn right on to the T69, then immediately left into the main street of *Lahinch*. Drive to the church, turn right, then immediately left SP 'Kilkee, Milltown Malbay'. Ascend, with views back and to the right over Liscannor Bay, and in 1m turn right SP 'Kilkee' to continue along the coast road. Views right extend across Liscannor Bay to the Cliffs of Moher. Proceed through farmland with hilly country to the left, and in 4m enjoy views of *Mutton Island* ahead.

After a further 2½m turn right into *Milltown Malbay*, continue to the end of the town, and turn left on to the L52 SP 'Inagh, Ennis'. In 1½m turn left on to the

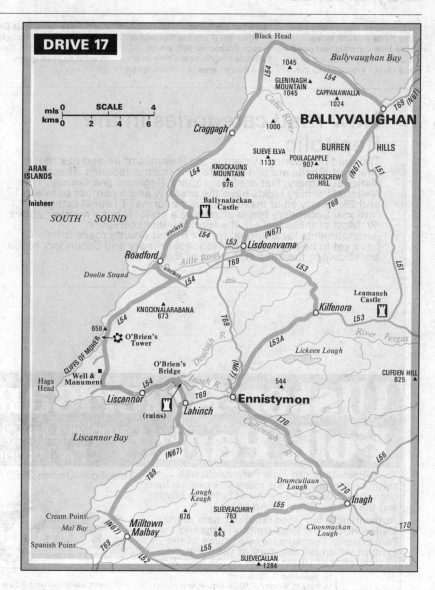

DRIVE 17

SCALE
mls 0   4
kms 0 2 4 6

Black Head

Ballyvaughan Bay

1045
GLENINAGH ▲ MOUNTAIN
1045
CAPPANAWALLA
1024

T69 (N67)

BALLYVAUGHAN

Caher River

1000

Craggagh

BURREN   HILLS

SLIEVE ELVA
1133   POULACAPPLE
907 ▲

ARAN
ISLANDS

CORKSCREW
HILL

KNOCKAUNS
MOUNTAIN
976

T69

Inisheer

SOUTH   SOUND

Ballynalackan
Castle

unclass

L54

L53

Lisdoonvarna

Roadford

Aille River

T69

L53

Doolin Strand

unclass

L54

KNOCKNALARABANA
673

Leamaneh
Castle

Kilfenora

L53

River   Fergus

658 ▲

O'Brien's
Tower

L53A

Lickeen Lough

CLIFDEN HILL
625 ▲

CLIFFS OF MOHER

O'Brien's
Bridge

Dealagh R.

Inagh R.

(N67)

544

Hags
Head

Well &
Monument

L54

Ennistymon

Liscannor

T69

(ruins)

Lahinch

T70

Liscannor Bay

Cullenagh R.

(N67)

T69

Drumcullaun
Lough

T70

Inagh

Lough
Keagh

L55

Cream Point

676

SLIEVEACURRY
763

Mal Bay

Milltown
Malbay

843

Cloonmackan
Lough

T70

Spanish Point

(N67)

T69

L55

L52

SLIEVECALLAN
▲ 1284

L55 SP 'Inagh' and follow a
winding road between 843ft
Slieveacurry (left) and 1,284ft
Slieve Callan. After another 4m
pass between several loughs as
the drive approaches Inagh.
Enter the village and turn left on
to the T70 SP 'Ennistymon' to
follow the valley of the Inagh or
Cullenagh River. Drumcullaun
Lough is glimpsed to the left.

Reach *Ennistymon*, go forward
through the town and climb on
the T69 SP 'Lisdoonvarna', and
in 1m branch right on to the
L53A SP 'Kilfenora' to enter low,
hilly country. In 4½m enter
Kilfenora, drive to the end of the
village, and turn left on to the
L53 SP 'Lisdoonvarna'. Climb
steadily with views ahead and
right of the *Burren* – a vast

moonscape of bare limestone.
After about 2m pass bogland.
Continue, and in another 1m
turn right on to the T69(N67)
across the Aille River. Enter the
well-known spa town of
Lisdoonvarna, follow SP
'Galway, Ballyvaughan', and in
½m bear left. In another ½m meet
a T-junction and turn right SP
'Galway' to follow a narrow

Day Drives

road between stone walls with rocky fields on both sides. Slieve Elva – the highest point in the area – rises to the left as the route climbs steadily into the heart of the Burren.

After 6m (from Lisdoonvarna) reach Corkscrew Hill, which affords magnificent views over the Burren area to Ballyvaughan and Galway Bays, plus *Lough Corrib*. Descend steeply through hairpin bends, and in 3½m re-enter Ballyvaughan.

New road categories in the Republic

The road numbering system in the Republic of Ireland has been changed. Roads are divided into four main categories. These are National Primary, National Secondary, Regional and County. The National Primary roads have the prefix N and a number between 1 and 25. Nearly all of these were in the former T (trunk) category. National Secondary roads also have a prefix N but a number above 50. Most of these were in the former L (link) category. Arrangements for Regional (prefix R) and County roads (prefix C) have yet to be finalised. The National Primary and Secondary roads are shown in the atlas at the end of this book.

A LAND OF COLOUR

Cahir Castle, Co Clare

A sightseeing holiday such as cruising on the Shannon reveals Ireland at its best. Add to that the strains of an impromptu folk music session from a darkened bar, and the mementoes of the strong ancestral links forged with America, and you are near to finding the essence of Ireland, as captured in the following pages

I think it's another car!

DRIVING LIKE IT USED TO BE

Ireland has just about the lowest traffic-density in the whole of Europe. That's why the roads are as clear and as empty as you could wish for. It's like the good old days your father told you about!

Not that you'll go short on facilities. There are plenty of places along your way to eat, to shop, to stay or just look at. And plenty of services for your car, of course, whether you bring your own or hire one.

Get all the information you need from any of the four Irish Tourist Board offices in Britain. Road maps, lists of hotels, scenic guides, things to do and see: they're all there for you.

TOURIST
i
INFORMATION

And when you get over there just look for the green-and-white sign with the big **i** on it. There are visitors' information offices dotted all over Ireland, and the people there are always happy to help you with regional or national information, routes, itineraries, etc. – they'll even book accommodation for you. See list of year-round Tourist Information Offices on the inside front cover.

Get in touch with us before you go, and we'll do all we can to make your trip an even happier one.

Ireland

Just ask anyone who's been there.

Sightsee by the Shannon
by DONNA WOOD

It was the last week in August and by some strange freak of nature the weather had turned unexpectedly warm and sunny. I stretched out fully on the seat of the cabin-cruiser, watching the lovely scenery drift by and enjoying the sensation of sun on my skin. At that moment I could have been almost anywhere in the world, from St Tropez to the most exotic South Sea island. . . .

And then I awoke – shaken out of my reverie by the collective gaze of a herd of complacent-looking cows which had come down for a paddle at the water's edge. There were even some sheep with a shamrock stamped on their backs. After that there could be no doubt about it at all.

This was Ireland, a land where the visitor is constantly reminded – and often surprised – by the uniqueness of his surroundings.

Twilight on the Shannon

Persistent rain and subnormal temperatures had ruined crops and dashed spirits throughout the Irish summer of '79, so it was with mixed feelings that my parents and I, with my young brother Jonathan, aged ten, prepared to embark upon our first visit to Ireland and first-time boating holiday.

Not being all that used to 'roughing it', nor able to claim to be the most organised of families, we wondered how, as novice sailors (and not even very good swimmers!) we would fare on the idyllic-sounding Shannon-cruise holiday – making a gentle, floating progress through the heart of Ireland, stopping only to explore the

Sightsee by the Shannon

fascinating waterside towns and villages along the way. We booked a four-berth craft with Cormacruisers, one of the ten or so hire companies which operate on the Shannon, and prepared to find out.

Our first glimpse of the Emerald Isle reinforced everything we had ever heard in praise of it – lush, green fields stretched as far as the eye could see, often stitched haphazardly together with white stone walls, and dotted with 'doll's house' cottages. Best of all, a watery sun was struggling to shine overhead, making our journey to Killaloe, in County Clare (the southern-most point for cruiser hire) all the more enjoyable.

Our first stop was Cormacruisers' modern reception room at the Marina, where we watched a film (available in several languages) giving valuable instruction on the basics of handling a cabin cruiser; safety precautions, use of the dinghy, and emergency procedure. Then we were shown to our boat the 'Lady Eva' by twinkling-eyed Irishman Jim Nevin, who showed us where everything was kept, explained a few complexities about the engine and took us for a short 'spin' to

Making sure the boat is securely moored at Mountshannon harbour

demonstrate steering and control.

Left alone to explore what was to be our home for the next week, we were immediately impressed by the cosiness and 'compactness' of the boat – a Freeman Super 8 metre, with two single berths in the forward section and, in the main part of the cabin, a dinette area that, when converted into a bedroom, had space for a double bed.

Single-lever control meant that the craft (powered by a Ford diesel engine) was extremely easy to manage and cruised at eight knots, with fuel consumption about five litres per hour. The only drawback was the absence of a fuel gauge.

As promised in the brochure, almost everything was provided, including kitchen utensils, towels (two per person), bed linen, dishcloths and toilet paper. The only items we found lacking were a pair of kitchen scissors, a tin or airtight box in which to keep bread, cake or biscuits fresh and – most important of all – a torch. There was a refrigerator, oven, flush toilet (albeit rather primitive and no room to swing even the smallest of cats), hot and cold running water, shaving point and an excellent radio.

Although the fuel tank was filled to its fifteen gallon capacity and it was still light enough for us to make our way to the next harbour that evening (one of the few rules is that craft must not be navigated after sunset), we decided to stay at Killaloe for the first night.

The next morning we made an early start and headed northwards up the river towards our first destination – Mountshannon. It was rather misty and overcast when we started our journey and the mountains were swaddled in cloud. Not the gentlest introduction to Lough Derg – the great inland sea of the Shannon, as on even the finest of days this wide stretch can be daunting, particularly to the novice sailor. But once we got used to the choppiness of the waves and accustomed ourselves to the boat's motion, we found plenty of scope for en route sightseeing. Mooring was the most difficult task to get

The waters teem with marvellous perch, pike, bream and trout

the hang of. It necessitated the person who was doing the 'driving' getting near enough to the side for someone to clamber on the front of the still-in-motion boat and either jump off, pull the vessel in and tie it up or

throw the rope to a friendly native. This seemingly simple act can become a nightmare if you do not 'pack' the rope properly before throwing. It will get taken by the wind and fall lamely into the water.

Once the boat was safely moored, we could begin to explore our surroundings and perhaps get to know our multi-national boating 'neighbours'. We found that a great feeling of camaraderie existed between boating people; hearty shouts of good wishes and much energetic waving accompanied each boat out of harbour.

Our mid-afternoon arrival in Mountshannon coincided with that of the large and buttery sun. We walked up to the sleepy, flower-decked village, where the locals stopped to chat about the welcome change in the weather (and anything else besides) and we noticed, with pleasure, how neat and well-kept everything looked, from window-boxes to waste-paper bins. This is the sort of place in which you are told by the locals that at 9.45am you are 'too early for Mountshannon'. At one little shop, known as 'McNamara's', we completely threw the system by asking for a receipt. The girl was willing, but obviously perplexed. 'How do you spell "McNamara"?' she asked, and throwing down her pen, ran outside to look above the door.

That evening, we had dinner of frothy, home-made mushroom soup, 'T' bone steak, a sweet and coffee for roughly £5 per head (half-price for Jonathan) in a local restaurant, where we could hear as many Dutch and German voices as Irish. A brisk walk in the now-chilly night air brought us back to the harbour in time to see the last of the sunset suspended, pink and golden, over the calm and shimmering water.

Our next destination was the bridge at Portumna and the large harbour beyond. However, we found Portumna itself rather a disappointment. The closely-packed, regimental lines in which the boats were moored produced a rather depressing effect (we all favoured the more haphazard, eccentric layout of the smaller harbours) and, Monday being early closing day, the majority of the shops were shut.

Sightsee by the Shannon

A fleet of cruisers at Lock Victoria

Before leaving we thought it would be wise to fill up with diesel, as the absence of a fuel gauge meant relying on guess-work. We were surprised to find we had used only four gallons of our fifteen-gallon tank.

Next stop was at Lock Victoria, Meelick, where we found a small fleet of cruisers already moored and waiting to pass through. We recognised many people we had seen along the river, or at the harbours, so the time spent waiting for the lock to open quickly passed in friendly conversation. Once inside the lock, we were unable to hide our inexperience as sailors. The idea is to manoeuvre the craft alongside a wall and for two people, one at the front, the other at the back, to grab the lengths of chain that hang from the wall without pulling the boat near enough to hit it.

Once you have got this far (we only just managed it, thanks to the broken English instructions shouted to us by our French, German and Dutch fellow sailors) you merely hang on for grim death. Suddenly, a deputation of Irishmen appear on the ground which is, by now, several feet above your head, and throw you a rope which has to be linked into a steel ring on the wall. This holds you fast while the water goes down.

From the lock our next port of call, Banagher, in County Offaly was only half an hour away. This charming little town, with its large, safe harbour (complete with floating dock) and its meandering street of delightful shops, was my favourite. A leisurely walk down the main street revealed a host of tiny, intriguing emporia which yielded interiors like Aladdin's cave – Irish-style. Fishing tackle, curios, crockery, underwear, groceries, Arran jumpers and of course, dark, creamy Guinness were obtainable everywhere and the shopkeepers were always friendly.

The Crannog pottery works, opposite the marina was another delightful surprise and not to be missed. The wrought-iron gate and picturesque, flower-decked courtyard (complete with Romany gipsy caravan) made a pleasant enough entrance, but the interior was a positive fairy grotto. A beautiful room hung with vines and furnished with uneven, stone tables and a turf fire held home-made produce and cosmetics, while pottery, handycrafts, tweeds, Connemara marble and woodwork were on sale in the cavernous showrooms.

That evening, there was live entertainment in the harbour as we watched a group of water-skiers skim the surface of the still river. Jonathan was overjoyed at being taken for a ride in the speed boat and whisked along the river at an exhilarating twenty-five miles per hour.

On returning to the boat we realised that the remaining half of our week would have to be spent on the return journey. One week on the Shannon is not long enough in which to penetrate the waterside towns and villages in any depth and keep on the move. – we found ourselves wishing for a few extra days in which to travel further and reach Athlone, Glassan, Lecarrow and all the other enticing places further up-river.

We headed homeward on Wednesday afternoon, to a chorus of squawking seagulls and a sky full of racing sunlight. Careful consultation of the maps and guides had revealed to us the tiny harbour of Terryglass in County Tipperary, a place we did not see on our outward journey.

Although recent extension to the harbour had just taken place, only three mooring spaces existed and these were occupied on our arrival. We were preparing to go on to the next harbour, when four Dutchmen, who we had seen earlier at Portumna bridge, invited us to tie up to their larger boat for the night. No sooner was this done, than a French couple, whom we had met at Banagher arrived, singing 'There's a place for us' at the top of their voices and secured their craft to ours.

On Thursday morning the four Dutchmen, Fred, Chiel, Paul and Joep, invited us to their boat for some good, strong Dutch coffee, before we all went to visit Terryglass's 13th-century, quadrilateral ruin, Old Court Castle, but that afternoon, we had no choice but to move on from Terryglass in order to reach Killaloe at the appointed time. But not before we exchanged addresses with our Dutch friends and promised to keep in touch. The last lap of our journey took us to the large, safe harbour of Dromineer, dominated by its castle ruins.

From there, we travelled onwards to Garrykennedy, on a day when the sharp tang in the air was cut by intermittent rain showers. Garrykennedy boasts an ancient and natural-looking harbour built with strong Irish stone, and the predictable castle ruins. We sheltered from the rain in a tiny, dark pub with oildrum seats and enjoyed the lively jokes and stories of the

Peace and quiet isn't hard to find

local fishermen. Beautiful winding footpaths shaded by sturdy trees led to the drowsy village, where the locals call out 'Welcome to Ireland'.

Our very last journey in the boat was quite an experience. By late Thursday night the weather had begun to change for the worse and when we came to cross Lough Derg on Friday afternoon, the 'great inland sea' was whipping up some wild-looking waves. Once we had started across the lake there was no going back, so we tried to grit our teeth and ignore the sound of the waves thudding against the hull. Although our journey was, for a time, rather nerve-racking, we reached Killaloe without casualty.

We all agreed that it had been a holiday to remember, and one to suit all tastes. The feeling of freedom is unlimited – you can stay all week at a little town you particularly like, or see three different ones in a day. You can get up when you want to, eat when you're hungry, relax or be extremely active whenever the fancy takes you. In short, a boating holiday is the best possible answer for those who like to please themselves and Ireland's shimmering River Shannon, the most beautiful inland waterway in Europe, is in itself enough to please anyone!

All things considered, is it so remarkable that Ireland also runs a rather enjoyable airline?

Aer Lingus

From Ulster to the USA *by RENÉE McRANDAL*

The Ulster-American Folk Park is seventy miles from Belfast, five miles north-west of Omagh on the road to Strabane in Northern Ireland's County Tyrone. An imaginative National Trust venture, it exists to tell part of the story of Irish emigration to America in the early eighteenth and nineteenth centuries, and the fact that 55,000 or more people visit the Folk Park every year is measure of its success and popularity.

Tour operators such as CIE include the Folk Park on their itinerary for twice-weekly visits, and coach parties are well-received, whether they be of local schoolchildren or American holidaymakers seeking their roots. Special meals should be ordered in advance, but good, basic fare is always available in the café.

The Folk Park is open daily throughout the year (except Christmas Day, Boxing Day and New Year's Day), when demonstrations of traditional Ulster cooking, thatching, flailing, winnowing, spinning, weaving and natural dyeing take place. Admission is 30p for adults, 15p for children.

Conestoga wagon – it carried the migrants

Although it was built as a monument to the Scotch-Irish (descendants of lowland Scots settled in Ulster) in general, the Ulster-American Folk Park tells the story of one man in particular, Thomas Mellon, who at the age of five emigrated with his parents in 1818.

His family were by no means typical emigrants, for they realised the then equivalent of one thousand dollars on the sale of their farm before leaving. This precious nest-egg was sewn into a special belt which Thomas's mother wore around her waist on the journey. They settled on a farm in Pennsylvania and the little boy became Judge Thomas Mellon, who

From Ulster to the USA

founded the Mellon Banking Company of Pittsburgh. It became one of the most important investment banks in the United States.

One of his sons became a financier and was appointed by President Harding as Secretary of the Treasury in 1921. Under his guidance the United States government reduced its World War One debt by nine billion dollars, and Congress was enabled to cut income tax rates substantially. The National Gallery of Art in Washington DC – part of the Smithsonian Institute – was his gift to the nation to house the twenty-five million dollar art collection he had already given.

The story of the Folk Park, believed to be the only one of its kind in the Western Hemisphere, began in the 1960s when the ancestral homes of notable Americans were being restored in Northern Ireland. The Mellon family provided funds for the

restoration of their family's old homestead, and when restoration was complete in 1968, it was decided to open it to the public. Out of this small beginning came the idea to create an entire complex, and The Ulster-American Folk Park was officially opened in 1976, the year of America's Bi-centennial celebrations.

The buildings in the Park can be divided into two categories. First, the thatched, whitewashed buildings showing life as it was in the North of Ireland when the emigrants left it; the second giving a

Striking fire from the anvil

The rustic exterior of the thatched-roofed Blacksmith's Forge

The Presbyterian meeting house, place of worship for the Ulster people

glimpse of the log cabins and dwellings they built for themselves in their new country.

The area of the Park covers twenty-six acres, and there is a guide to accompany you for the estimated one and a half hours it takes to tour the site. Modern exhibition techniques, audio-visual shows and lectures take place in the small auditorium within the Matthew T Mellon building.

From the entrance take the pine walk through the part of the Park devoted to the 'Old World'. The first building is the Blacksmith's Forge, where the brawny smith can be seen hammering the red-hot metal into shoes for an unseen horse. Alongside him are shoes for ponies, donkeys and the solid workhorses that used to plough the fields of Ulster, and which were once an essential part of the rural economy.

Indeed, the visit to the Blacksmith's Forge with its roaring fire will bring back childhood memories for many people – particularly those brought up in Belfast, for whom the local blacksmith tending the feet of the horses which pulled the carts of the bakers and milkmen in the city was a familiar sight, often accompanied by that strange, acrid smell that clung to the nostrils as he struck fire from his anvil.

Next along the pine walk is the Weaver's Cottage. In the old days there was a room set aside in almost every house in which the mother could make some extra money for the family by producing beautiful, handwoven products. In the holiday season a local woman gives demonstrations of spinning and weaving here. There is a turf fire glowing brightly and you can sample traditional Irish bread, baked on a griddle over the open fire, just as it was baked centuries ago.

Near to the Weaver's Cottage is the Meeting House, as Presbyterians called their place of worship. This is a replica of the Meeting House at Castletown where the Mellon family prayed every Sunday. It

73

From Ulster to the USA

contains the very high-backed pews that must have dwarfed young Thomas.

Next is the actual Mellon homestead where Thomas was born on 3 February 1813. It was built by his father and his uncle 'chiefly by the labour of their own hands' and is still a tribute to their workmanship almost 170 years later. Thomas was only five when he left Ulster, but the memory of his home environment remained clearly with him all his life.

The Old Schoolhouse – a single room, thirty-four feet by twenty feet, built of stone and lime mortar – is also original. It was taken from its site at Castletown, on the banks of the River Strule and re-erected in the Folk Park. The records show that the average daily attendance was seventy, and that Patrick Mulligan and his daughter Mary taught the children. He worked in one half of the room with the older children, she in the other half with the infants. The children brought sods of turf each morning for the two open fires, one at each end of the room, to make sure they

Thomas Mellon's actual birthplace in 1813

would be warm throughout the day.

The New World section begins with the picturesque Log Cabin, a reminder that the Ulster settlers were also frontiersmen. They had to prepare the land for their dwellings by cutting through the scrubland, felling the trees and then splitting them down the centre, so getting them ready to serve as walls for their homes. In such a setting one might expect to come face to face with Davy Crockett at any minute, and, strangely enough, his name is among other notable Americans whose families have their roots in Ireland.

There is also a replica of the larger house the Mellons moved to some time later, giving us a glimpse of their enhanced standard of living. Thomas Mellon relates: 'in less than a year we had as fine a six-roomed dwelling as the best of our neighbours, and that fall and winter as good a square log double barn as was to be seen thereabouts'.

An interesting wooden structure stands at the back of the house. It consists of four walls made from split logs, enclosing a spring well. The cool atmosphere generated by the well in the middle of the floor enabled the family to store their provisions, confident that they would retain their freshness. The forerunner of today's freezer?

Nearby is the Smokehouse, where the family supply of bacon and fish would have been hung over a fire made from twigs to give it that sought-after smokey tang.

Development of the Folk Park is by no means complete, and among additions planned is the cottage home of the first Archbishop of the Roman Catholic Church in New York, Archbishop John Hughes.

A Pennsylvania log farmhouse

This humble dwelling contrasts sharply with the magnificent neo-gothic St Patrick's Cathedral on Fifth Avenue, which we owe to Archbishop Hughes.

There are very strong links between Ireland and America, and every year about 26,000 Americans visit the North of Ireland, some in search of their roots. Their journey by plane to Belfast can take anything from five to ten hours. From Belfast to the Ulster-American Folk Park takes perhaps another two hours.

Consider that and remember that the Mellon family left Ireland from Derry and did not arrive at their destination, Greensburg in Westmoreland county until eighteen weeks later. The last lap of their journey, over the mountainous trail by Conestoga wagon – one of the features of the Park – lasted three weeks. Travellers then were made of sterner stuff!

A Heritage of Song

Michéal O'hEidhin is official Music Inspector for Irish schools and for nearly thirty years has been a key figure in the revival of folk music in Ireland. He arranged and conducted the instrumental music for the papal visit to Knock in September 1979.

Spontaneous entertainment in a Co Sligo pub

There are basically four styles of singing that could qualify as Irish folk song. Firstly, the traditional song in Gaelic, fully adorned and ornamented called 'Sean-Nós' (Old style), and unaccompanied. Secondly, there is the simple ballad in Gaelic, rarely adorned, or ornamented and generally of a rhythmic character. This is more often used in group singing, normally accompanied or arranged.

The third and fourth styles are identical to the first two, but rendered in the English language. There is the traditional song, fully adorned and ornamented and, of course, unaccompanied, and the familiar English ballad as sung by most groups in Ireland today.

'Sean-Nós' singing, the fore-runner of all other styles, is indeed the purest form of Irish folk song. It is also a technically difficult art-form to reproduce or execute accurately when it has to pass on from generation to generation. While it develops, some loss in traditional content is inevitable.

The ballads, on the other hand, live on because they have a commercial value. Indeed many can be heard almost any night in most parts of Ireland, whether it is at a festival or in the 'local'. The instrumental side of the music is in good hands – thanks to artists like Seán O Riada and his 'Ceoltóirí Cualann' who paved the way for a fresh look at this side of our traditional music. They gave groups who followed later the courage to develop it further. Until then music only for jigs, reels, hornpipes and set dances was being played. Now, one can hear beautiful slow airs, marches and O Carolans music being executed expertly on a wide range of instruments.

What stage has 'Sean-Nós' singing then reached? Some years ago, this particular style was on the wane.

by Mícheál O'hEidhin

A platform to perform is required to keep any music-form alive. Apart from a few festivals such as 'AntOireachtas' (a yearly festival, generally in November, alternating between Dublin and one of the Gaelic-speaking districts) and 'Fleadh Ceoil na hÉireann' (all-Ireland music festival, generally in August) no other opportunities have existed for it to be heard.

Then along came 'Radio na Gaeltachta' (Radio for Gaelic speaking districts), sponsored by the state, and its great revival began. As one of the first to produce a weekly programme of music and song for the station, I had to search the highways and byways for established 'Sean-Nós' singers, most of whom were getting on in years by that time. A new generation needed to be encouraged and trained. After four years one could pick and choose more readily from a younger age group who in turn recruited a new generation. Nowadays, teenagers who have pretty well mastered the art of 'Sean-Nós' singing are abundant in the Gaelic speaking areas.

So the wheel has turned full circle, making this ancient form of singing popular and fashionable again. The best attended competitions at 'AntOireachtas' are for

Paddy Tunney is one of the best known traditional singers in Ireland today, and has helped to keep the 'Sean Nós' idiom alive

'Sean-Nós' singing. And so great is the enthusiasm that 'Sean-Nós' is being examined, tabulated, nurtured and developed in many areas of Ireland at the moment. Recently, there was even a televised seminar on traditional 'Sean-Nós' singing, in my Co Galway village.

Radio and TV have played a significant part in the revival of Irish folk music. The main station of 'Radio na Gaeltachta' is at Cashla, in the Connemara Gaeltacht of Co Galway. On its two sub-stations, all broadcasts are in Gaelic, and some very fine 'Sean-Nós' singers can be heard, as well as excellent instrumentalists. These are the same musicians who can be heard at sessions most of the year around in the Gaelic speaking areas, nearly all of which are on the Western Seaboard, Donegal, Mayo, Galway, Kerry, Cork and Waterford. There is also one in Rath Cairn, Co Meath, where they have recently opened a community centre which is doing a lot to keep the music, dance and customs of the area alive.

The fine style of traditional singing in English, when performed properly, is practically a direct imitation in words and music of the 'Sean-Nós' idiom. One of the best exponents of this style is Paddy Tunney, whose book 'The Stone Fiddle' (My way to traditional singing) is in its way a work of art. Among the younger people, Seamus Mac Mathuna, who works with a Government backed body formed to preserve the music and dance of Ireland, is a fine flautist and traditional singer.

This Government initiative goes back to 1951 when 'Comhaltas Ceoltóirí Éireann; as it is called, was formed to preserve the musical heritage of Ireland, its culture and language. Since then it has spread to 400 branches at home, with others in Britain, the United States, Canada and Australia. It publishes a bi-monthly magazine 'Treoir', has hundreds of weekly classes to teach instrumental music, and stages annual concert tours abroad. At home it arranges music sessions in forty-seven areas, with displays of song, music and dance. A yearly festival of music is held at different venues and smaller musical events take place

A Heritage of Song

Traditional entertainment is popular at banquets

throughout the country during the year. 'Comhaltas Ceoltóirí Éireann' also runs a cultural institute and meeting place called 'An Culturlann' in Dublin, where one can have a drink, and enjoy 'Fonntraí', a twice-weekly show. There is also an educational–recreational musical weekend, held yearly, at the Franciscan College, Gormanston, Co Meath.

Another sign of the growing interest in the folk music scene is the important role being played by a Catholic priest from Moyvan, Co Kerry. Father Pat Ahern is Artistic Director of 'Siamsa Tíre', the National Folk Theatre of Ireland.

In our student days we used to play a lot of music together, while studying for our Bachelor of Music at Cork University. Father Ahern worked for some time in television, directed an annual folk festival and eventually settled in his native county, where with some Government sponsorship two Folk Centres were built in 1974–75 in the form of old Irish thatched cottages with open fireplaces and flagged floors.

One is in Finuge near Listowel, in North Kerry, and the other at Carraig near Ballyferriter in the western tip of the Dingle peninsula, Co Kerry. Each of these folk cottages are known as 'Teach Siamsa', a house of musical entertainment.

Marvellously rich in the traditions of the area they keep alive the culture of music, dance, folklore, storytelling, and are the centres for nightly classes. Each 'Teach Siamsa' is like the spoke of a cartwheel, with the hub being the Folk Theatre established in Tralee, Co Kerry in 1975 as an outlet to stage shows from the folk cottages.

As a result of all this activity, a group of players, now internationally recognised for recreating the traditional music, mime and dance of life in the Gaelic-speaking rural Ireland many years ago, stage a fascinating show at the Folk Theatre in Tralee during the summer. It is, of course, directed by Father Ahern.

There is also a Celtic Festival week in Killarney every May called 'Pan Celtic Festival' where six Celtic nations, Ireland, The Isle of Man, Wales, Cornwall (England), Scotland and Brittany (France) hold competitions for the 'Sean-Nós' singing, traditional fiddle playing and the traditional dancing of each country. It is refreshing to watch these Celtic musicians, songsters and dancers exchange ideas, styles and folklore.

But don't let us forget the week at

Performers in the Pan Celtic festival, which takes place every May in Killarney (above)

A scene from the Siamsa Tíre (below)

Limerick in March, where among four competitions, is one for harp playing, and another for traditional Instrumental groups.

There are, of course, many other festivals, which help encourage the impression that the musical heritage of Ireland is on solid foundations, and is developing more rapidly than any other European folk music.

For further information contact:
Comhaltas Ceoltóirí Éireann
An Culturlann
32 Belgrave Square
Monkstown
Co Dublin
☎ Dublin 800296

Siamsa Tíre
c/o Father Pat Ahern
Director
Finuge
Co Kerry

Pan Celtic Festival
Pan Celtic Office
Killarney
Co Kerry

Limerick Civic Week
c/o Fergus Quinlivan
Co-ordinator
Civic Week Office
Royal George Hotel
O'Connell Street
Limerick

An tOireachtas
6 Harcourt Street
Dublin 2
☎ Dublin 757401

The cream is real, the whiskey is real – only the taste is magic

R. & A. Bailey & Co. Ltd., Naas Road, Dublin 12, Ireland. Telephone Dublin 503313.

GAZETTEER

Delgany, Co Wicklow

Turn these pages for detailed information on beaches, forest parks, sports, AA-inspected accommodation, restaurants and camping and caravanning sites

The Cliffs of Moher, Co Clare

Beautiful Beaches

Ireland boasts a wealth of unspoilt beaches, some noted for a stark and haunting beauty, others for their safe and sheltered location. For the first time, the AA has devised this comprehensive guide to nearly one hundred of the best, with details of the kind of facilities each has to offer.

Co Antrim

BALLINTOY Map 15D04 A picturesque village with a charming bay of clean sand, situated close to Whitepark Bay. Carrick-a-Rede rope bridge is nearby.

BALLYCASTLE Map 15D14 Situated on the Glenshesk River, this resort has a fine stretch of sandy beach. Excellent facilities for fishing, golf and tennis. South is Ballycastle Forest Park on Knocklayd Mountain, and to the east are the ruins of Bonamargy Friary (AM). At the end of August the famous 'Ould Lammas Fair' takes place here.

Off the coast is Rathlin Island. Toilets are available.

BROWNS BAY Map 15D40 A small resort on Islandmagee, a tiny peninsula seven miles long by two miles wide, joined to the mainland at Blackhead. Small, sandy beach. To the south-west is Ballylumford Dolmen (AM) and there is a golf course close at hand.

CARNLOUGH Map 15D21 Situated on the Antrim Coast road at the foot of Glencloy, this resort has a fine beach and a pretty limestone harbour, with boating and fishing facilities. There is an old coaching inn here and toilets are available.

CARRICKFERGUS Map 15J48 This resort has Ulster's newest and widest promenade, with bathing beach on one side and Marine Gardens on the other. Close by is a leisure centre with two swimming pools. Carrickfergus Castle, the finest and biggest Norman castle in Ireland, and now housing a fascinating military museum, overlooks the harbour. The landing place of King William III on his way to the Battle of the Boyne is marked by a plaque at the end of Carrickfergus jetty. Toilets are available.

CUSHENDALL Map 15D22 This resort has a small, sandy beach and a golf course, and lies astride the winding Dall River. Toilets are nearby.

PORTBALLINTRAE Map 14C94 This small port has a sandy beach. At the Causeway a team of Belgian divers brought up the greatest Spanish Armada treasure ever recovered from a wrecked galleon. It is exhibited at the Ulster Museum in Belfast. Good fishing can be had from the rocks.

PORTRUSH Map 14C84 This is a major resort with two long beaches. It has excellent bathing, boating and charming walks. The famous Giants Causeway is seven miles east of the town and the beautiful caves of the Whiterocks are close at hand. Portrush also has a very fine golf course. Lifeguards are on duty, toilets nearby.

WHITEHEAD Map 15J49 Situated between Larne and Carrickfergus and sheltered by the cliffs at Whitehead and Blackhead. The beach is shingly and the resort has two golf courses, an outdoor swimming pool, squash and tennis courts. It also contains Ireland's main railway museum. Toilets are available along the seafront.

WHITEPARK BAY Map 15D04 This is one of Ireland's most beautiful beaches, surrounded by sand dunes and cliffs. To the east is the small village of Ballintoy, with the well-known Carrick-a-Rede rope bridge. Whitepark Bay is also of much archaeological interest.

Co Clare

BISHOPSQUARTER Map 7M20 Set one and a half miles south-west of the picturesque fishing port of Ballyvaughan is this fine beach on the southern shore of Galway Bay. Lifeguards are on duty at weekends. Nearby are the notable ruins of Drumcreechy Church, set amid a rewarding variety of coastal and mountain scenery.

DOOLIN Map 6R09 There are shopping and toilet facilities at this attractive resort and fishing village. This small, sandy bay is the nearest point to Inisheer, the most southerly of the Aran Islands. Lifeguard on duty.

FANORE Map 6M10 This charming beach lies on the lonely coast to the south of Black Head. Lifeguard on duty. Toilet facilities. Sandhills.

KILKEE Map 6Q85 This is a pleasant resort with a fine strand, sheltered from the full force of the Atlantic by the Duggerna rocks. Magnificent cliff scenery. Lifeguard on duty. Shopping and toilet facilities.

LAHINCH Map 6R08 A popular resort on Liscannor Bay, with excellent sandy beaches, safe for bathing. A fine golf course is nearby. The famous Cliffs of Moher rise four and a half miles north-west. Cars can be taken close to beach. Good shopping facilities are offered in town. Unspoilt scenery. Sandhills. Toilets close to beach.

SPANISH POINT Map 6R07 Two miles west of the small market town of Milltown Malbay is this

attractive resort with a good bathing beach. A popular spot for sea fishing and golf. The resort takes its name from the Armada Spaniards shipwrecked thereabouts in September 1588. Toilets and shopping facilities. Lifeguard on duty.

Co Cork

BARLEY COVE Map 2V72 Near Crookhaven is this extremely sheltered, beautiful sandy beach. There is parking quite close to the cove.

CROSSHAVEN Map 4W75 Popular yachting and seaside resort with bathing at Church, Myrtleville and Graball Bays. About one mile north-east, one of the finest views of Cork harbour may be obtained. Toilet facilities are available.

GARRETTSTOWN Map 3W54 The beach is sheltered by the Old Head of Kinsale and has interesting cliff scenery. Lifeguard on duty. Toilet facilities.

GARRYVOE Map 4X06 The remains of a church and 'pocket castle' can be seen here, near the pleasant beach.

INCHYDONEY Map 3W43 Overlooks Clonakilty Bay. There are fine sands and excellent bathing facilities, with lifeguards on duty. Shops and toilets nearby.

OWENAHINCHA Map 3W33 A favoured bathing place near Rosscarbery, patrolled by lifeguards. Toilets and shops nearby.

ROSSCARBERY Map 3W33 There is a lighthouse on Galley Head, east side of the bay. Sandy beach with good bathing. Toilet facilities. Interesting castles, high crosses and monuments in the vicinity.

YOUGHAL Map 4X17 Fine, sheltered harbour with five miles of sandy bathing beach. The town itself has many historic connections, and shopping and toilet facilities may be found there.

Co Donegal

BUNDORAN Map 16G85 A popular resort on the shores of Donegal Bay, Bundoran offers good bathing and recreational facilities – golf, tennis, and fishing one and a half miles west on the River Drowes. There is a short strand and deep rockpool with a diving board. Lifeguards are on duty. The force of the Atlantic has worn the rocks into many peculiar shapes; a fine example is the Natural Arch, known as the Fairy Bridge (24ft span). Shops and toilet facilities are nearby.

MARBLE STRAND Map 16C03 Small resort and bathing strand on an inlet of Sheep Haven.

PORT-NA-BLAGH Map 16C03 Excellent sandy beach. The name, roughly translated, means Harbour of Buttermilk.

PORTNOO Map 16G69 Extensive sands, rocks and beautiful scenery which takes in mountains and various coastal features, make this village an ideal place for a holiday.

PORTSALON Map 16C23 This picturesque harbour and two-mile long sandy beach are superbly situated at the north end of Ballymastocker Bay.

RATHMULLAN Map 14C22 This attractive resort with sandhills and a sandy beach is situated on the west shore of beautiful Lough Swilly.

ROSAPENNA Map 16C13 Rosapenna boasts a fine strand and a notable golf links.

ROSBEG Map 16G69 There is a good sandy beach at this Dawros Bay resort, and magnificent sand

Why Sealink's a better way to drive to Ireland.

Cheaper for you

No matter what car you have, nor how many passengers you take, you'll find that Sealink is cheaper to Ireland on four out of five Irish Sea crossings. And not just a pound or two. A Sealink return fare for a family can save you *£20 or more* on most of these crossings. Check with any travel agent.

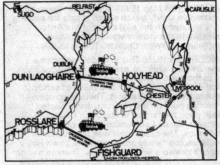

Better off-peak bargains for you

"Aim if you can for an off-peak time, you'll get our cheapest fare" our TV advertisement says. Certainly when things aren't so busy, you'll find our bargain ideas very tempting. We cut fares to the bone to let you 'sample' the delights of Ireland so you'll want to come again.

More convenient for you

Enjoy our big, comfortable ships. Enjoy too, a choice of 1st or 2nd Class on the superb St Columba to the 'gateway' to Ireland, Dun Laoghaire. From here, Dublin is just down the road, but you can also zoom off west or south and avoid Dublin, if you wish. Alternatively, Fishguard to Rosslare is the ideal crossing from the Southern Counties of England and Wales to the Southern Counties of Ireland. And don't forget, you can take your dog on holiday to Ireland with Sealink, without fuss, without quarantine. But it must stay in the car while on board ship.

Shorter and faster for you

Sealink has the two shortest routes to Ireland, from Holyhead to Dun Laoghaire and from Fishguard to Rosslare. Both are around 3½ hours, the fastest car ferry crossings on the Irish Sea.

More holiday choice for you

An inclusive holiday? You can choose from eleven types with Sealink. There's something for everyone here, from caravans to farmhouses to hotels. Ask your Sealink Travel Agent for the 'Holidays to Ireland|brochure.

So easy to plan for you

One price for all cars and only three seasonal tariffs. Couldn't be simpler. Your Sealink Travel Agent, principal rail station or motoring organisation will be happy to oblige.

Sealink's for *you.*

You and your car and
Sealink
It's a better way to get away

dunes at Tramore Beach. Opportunities for bathing and surfing are good.

ROSSNOWLAGH Map 16G86 One of the finest strands in Ireland can be enjoyed at this resort, which is well sited on the coast north of Ballyshannon. The three-mile beach stretches along Donegal Bay (patrolled by lifeguards) and is backed by fine dunes. Shops and toilet facilities nearby.

Co Down

BALLYHALBERT Map 15J66 This small village has a short, sandy beach. Offshore lies Burial Island, which marks the extreme eastern limit of Irish soil.

BALLYHORNAN Map 15J54 This small village has a fine stretch of sandy beach. It is situated in the Lecale Peninsula and the tiny Guns Island lies offshore. Good fishing can be had from the rocks.

BALLYWALTER Map 15J66 This small village has an extensive sandy beach which is safe for bathing and is situated on the east coast of the Ards Peninsula. In the vicinity stands the ruined Templefinn or 'White Church'. Toilets locally.

BANGOR Map 15J58 This seaside resort has a four-mile long seafront stretching from Smelt Mill Bay to the west, Bangor Bay and Ballyholme Bay to the east. Approximately two miles of sandy beaches are safe for bathing. There is an open-air swimming pool on the seafront, and a heated indoor pool, the largest in Northern Ireland, is situated in Castle Park, which is rich in rare trees and shrubs. The castle itself was the residence of the Clanmorris family and is now the Town Hall. Bangor has also a fine golf course. There is a wide promenade and coastal walks through the Marine Gardens along six miles of coastline. Toilets are available.

CLOUGHEY Map 15J54 This small resort has a fine, sandy beach. It has a golf course, car-park and toilets. Nearby is 17th-century Kirkistown Castle, with a massive keep and bawn with circular southern wall towers. Motor-cycling and car racing take place on the disused Kirkistown Airfield which is nearby.

CRANFIELD BAY Map 13J21 This is a long, south-facing beach, ideal for bathing. There is a caravan site here and Cranfield Point, Ulster's southern most promontory. Close by is the strategically-situated fortress of Greencastle, which guards the entrance to Strangford Lough. To the north-east is Kilkeel which has the coast's main fishing fleet.

CRAWFORDSBURN Map 15J48 One of the most charming villages near Belfast. It is situated midway between Helens Bay, a delightful cove to the north, and Clandeboye to the south, the seat of the Marquis of Dufferin and Ava. At the southern end of the demesne stands Helens Tower, erected by the fifth Earl in memory of his mother. Nearby is Crawfordsburn Country Park, a delightful place where the woods grow to the edge of a sandy beach. There is a golf course in the vicinity. Toilets are available.

DONAGHADEE Map 15J58 Situated on the east coast of the Ards Peninsula, Donaghadee's beach is of two textures. There is a large, sandy expanse suitable for bathing, while at intervals the surface is rocky and studded with pools. To the south of the town is a sixteen-acre park, The Commons, which incorporates lawns, playing fields, pavilion and car park. The harbour has a lighthouse and boats can be hired if desired. The Copeland Islands lie off the coast and the waters are

excellent for fishing. Donaghadee Moat was built in 1818 for storing gunpowder during the building of the harbour. Donaghadee has an excellent golf course. Toilets are available on the seafront.

KEARNEY Map 15J65 This village, which is a National Trust property, has been restored to its 19th-century character. It is situated three miles east of Portaferry, the berthing point for the Strangford Ferry across Strangford Lough. The coastline is rocky but there are small, sandy bays in the vicinity. Toilets nearby.

KILKEEL Map 13J31 At one time the centre of the Kingdom of Mourne, this town has a fine strand, good fishing and a busy harbour. A 14th-century ruined church stands in a rath at the town centre and there is a golf course a little inland. To the east lies the Silent Valley Reservoir. Toilets available.

MILLISLE Map 15J57 This small resort lies two miles south of Donaghadee and has a fine, sandy beach safe for bathing. To the west stands the restored Ballycopeland Windmill (AM) which may date from 1784. Toilets available in the vicinity.

NEWCASTLE Map 13J33 At the foot of the Mournes is this charming resort. There is five miles of sandy beach stretching through to Dundrum Bay. Close by is the famous Royal County Down golf course, and in the vicinity the magnificent Tollymore and Castlewhellan Forest Parks. South is the National Trust's coastal path from Bloody Bridge picnic site at the end of the Brandy Pad right through the mountains. Also south of the resort on the coast is Donard Cave and the cliff ravine known as Maggie's Leap. Toilets and shops nearby.

ROSTREVOR Map 13J11 This resort is on the north shore of Carlingford Lough. Protected by high hills and open only to the south, it is the most sheltered place in Northern Ireland, with mediterranean plants growing by the seashore in the lee of the Mournes. The beach is of two textures, stony in places, with a section of sand south of the harbour. Rostrevor Forest Park on Slieve Martin has a fine viewpoint, Cloghmore. There is also a forestry caravan park. Toilets in public park only.

WARRENPOINT Map 13J11 This resort stands on the northern shore of Carlingford Lough, an inlet of the sea which separates Co Down from Co Louth in the Republic of Ireland. The beach is shingly but suitable for bathing. There is an outdoor swimming pool and toilets are available at the nearby boating pool and park with facilities for handicapped people. The town has been called the Gateway to the Mournes and their foothills. Two miles to the east is the first rounded peak of the Mourne Mountains. To the west is Narrow Water Castle. There is a golf course and a caravan park in the vicinity. A Sunday market is held in the square. Warrenpoint has a new yachting marina and excursion boats travel to Omeath in the Republic.

Co Dublin

BALBRIGGAN Map 13O26 A quiet resort with a fine pier and dock and sandy beaches. Lifeguards are on duty. Shops and toilets nearby. Golf in the vicinity.

DONABATE Map 13O24 There is a lifeguard on duty at this sandy resort, easily reached by rail, and a nearby golf course, shops and toilet facilities.

MALAHIDE Map 13O24 A quiet, small, town resort

with good sands. There is a promenade with access to the shore. Lifeguards are on duty. Shops, toilets and golf nearby.

PORTMARNOCK Map 13O24 A small seaside resort with a splendid expanse of sandy beach known as 'Velvet Strand'. Championship golf course located here. Lifeguards, toilets, shops.

RUSH Map 13O25 One of the finest bathing strands on the east coast, with lifeguards, shops and toilets.

SKERRIES Map 13O26 A popular resort which derives its name from the rock islands off its coast. It is a sea fishing centre and has shops, toilets and lifeguards.

Co Galway

BALLYCONNEELY Map 10L64 The bay to the north, Mannin, contains a coral strand. There are sandhills and many small coves.

CARNA/KILKIERAN Map 6L73 Long, sandy beaches at Callowfeanish, Mweenish and Moyrus.

CARRAROE Map 6L92 Four sandy beaches nearby.

CLIFDEN Map 10L65 Amidst scenery of wild grandeur, the town has some trade in fish and lobsters, and there is bathing from a number of strands and sandy coves. There is ample scope for walks and excursions in the neighbourhood.

RENVYLE Map 10L65 A beautiful, sandy stretch of coastline, with shooting and fishing in the neighbourhood. Fine panoramic views are available from Renvyle Hill.

ROUNDSTONE Map 10L73 A busy fishing village on the western side of Bertraghboy Bay. There is a roomy, well-sheltered harbour which is almost landlocked and sandhills on the beach.

SPIDDAL Map 6M12 A small resort with a sandy beach, on the edge of the Irish-speaking part of the Iar Connacht district. Shops and toilets nearby. Lifeguards on duty.

Co Kerry

BALLYBUNION Map 6Q84 A popular little Atlantic coast resort with a fine beach, at the mouth of the Shannon. There are many caves in the sea cliffs. Excellent surfing and bathing are offered from the fine strand. Lifeguards are on duty here. Toilet facilities are available nearby.

BALLYHEIGUE Map 2Q72 Lifeguards patrol this quiet resort with its excellent sandy beaches and sand dunes. Toilet facilities and shops.

BARNA Map 6M22 Miles of safe, sandy beach patrolled by lifeguards. Toilets and shops nearby.

CASTLEGREGORY Map 2Q61 This small village and quiet seaside resort enjoys a beautiful situation at the head of the sandy Rough Point Peninsula. The beach is patrolled by lifeguards.

INCH Map 2Q60 This beautifully situated four-mile long beach is backed by sand dunes and set amid a magnificent sheltered seaside resort. There is a lifeguard on duty and shopping facilities are available.

ROSSBEIGH Map 2V69 Lifeguards are on duty at this resort with its splendid expanse of sandy bathing beach, backed by sandhills and the slopes of Curra Hill. Shopping and toilet facilities nearby.

WATERVILLE Map 2V56 Situated on a narrow neck of land between Ballinskelligs Bay and the beautiful Lough Currane. Toilet facilities and shops nearby.

Co Londonderry

CASTLEROCK Map 14C73 This small resort near the mouth of the River Bann has a fine beach and golf course. It also has an open-air heated swimming pool. Situated nearby are the ruins of the Downhill Palace and cliff top demesne of the 18th-century Earl-Bishop of Bristol and Derry, who filled it with works of art from Europe. On the cliffs by the castle gate stands the curious circular building known as Mussenden Temple (NT) which is open to the public. Toilets.

MAGILLIGAN Map 14C63 This splendid, six-mile long strand is one of the finest in Ireland and stretches from Downhill to the narrows of Lough Foyle facing Greencastle in Co Donegal. There are neolithic and other prehistoric habitation sites in the sandhills of the district. Binevenagh Mountain soars above the beach and record-size bass are caught from the shore. Lifeguards on duty.

PORTSTEWART Map 14C83 This small resort has a fine, sandy beach of some two miles in length. It also has a number of golf courses in the close vicinity. To the south-west is a fine stretch of strand with sandhills. Lifeguards are on duty.

Co Mayo

KEEL Map 10F60 The spectacular bay has a sandy strand two miles long, bounded by cliffs. Lifeguards are on duty. Shops and toilets nearby. Golf.

MULRANY Map 10L89 A picturesque resort with good bathing. Kitchen middens in the sand dunes yield many prehistoric finds. Lifeguards on duty, toilets, shops. Renowned for mild climate which encourages the growth of fuchsias and rhododendrons.

Co Meath

BETTYSTOWN Map 13O17 This small resort offers a six-mile long sandy beach (patrolled by lifeguards at the weekend), shops and toilet facilities, and is well known as the place in which one of the country's most valuable archaeological treasures, the 'Tara Brooch', was found.

LAYTOWN Map 13O17 A long stretch of fine, sandy beach connects Laytown with its twin resort Bettystown. Amenities as Bettystown.

MORNINGTON Map 13O17 The splendid six-mile stretch of fine bathing beach for which Mornington is noted extends along the south side of the Boyne estuary.

Co Sligo

ENNISCRONE Map 11G22 A small Killala Bay resort with good sands for surf bathing. To the north-east is the ruined Castle Firbis. Golf nearby.

MULLAGHMORE Map 16G75 Here are found many sheltered little resorts with superb bathing. Lifeguards on duty. Toilets and shops nearby.

ROSSES POINT Map 11G64 Well-known golfing resort with excellent boating. Splendid views across Drumcliff Bay, with toilets and shops nearby.

STRANDHILL Map 11G63 A well-known Sligo Bay resort with good, sandy beaches, shops, toilets and lifeguards. The ancient church of Killaspugbrone stands to the north of the village.

Co Waterford

ARDMORE Map 4X17 Ardmore Bay, on which this pleasant resort is sited, is edged by a fine sandy beach and rugged cliffs. Interesting sea caves can

be explored in Ardmore Head.

BUNMAHON Map 4X49 Natural amenities offered by this pleasant coastal resort include a sandy, sheltered beach backed by impressive 200ft cliffs. Shopping and toilet facilities nearby.

CLONEA Map 4X39 Small resort with fine bathing sands and sandhills situated on Clonea Bay. Toilet facilities and shops available.

DUNMORE EAST Map 5S60 A small angling and seaside resort at the mouth of Waterford Harbour, Dunmore East faces the long peninsula of Hook Head and derives its name from the great dunn which partially survives here. Black Knob Cliff with its promontory fort known as the Shanooan can be seen on the south side of the village, and access to Merlin's Cave beneath the Black Knob is by footpath. Lifeguard on duty here. Toilet facilities nearby.

STRADBALLY Map 4X39 Lifeguards patrol this pleasant resort and toilet facilities are available.

TRAMORE Map 5S50 The three-mile long strand boasted by this popular resort is washed on the south side by open sea and on the north side by a large lagoon.

Co Wexford

BALLYMONEY Map 9T26 Small seaside resort with a sandy beach, toilets and shops.

COURTOWN Map 9T25 A seaside village with a fine, one and a half-mile stretch of sandy beach with lifeguards on duty. There are toilets and shops nearby and several other more secluded strands in the vicinity. Golf in the area.

CURRACLOE Map 5T12 This beach is situated about six miles north-east of Wexford town, near Wexford Bay. Lifeguards are on duty at weekends and bank holidays.

KILMORE QUAY Map 5S90 The village, which is full of thatched and whitewashed cottages, has been described as the most attractive in Ireland. Toilet facilities are available near the beach.

KILMUCKRIDGE Map 5T14 Situated inland from a low stretch of coast, with fine sands to the north-east. Toilet facilities are available. Lifeguards on duty at weekends and bank holidays.

ROSSLARE Map 5T11 A well-known seaside and golfing resort boasting a beautiful, six-mile long silvery strand. Excellent boating and bathing. Shops and toilets nearby. Lifeguards on duty at weekends and on bank holidays.

Co Wicklow

ARKLOW Map 9T27 A bustling seaside resort which overlooks the sea from the mouth of the Avoca River at the foot of the Wicklow Mountains. Its fine sands extend north and south of the river, providing access for safe sea bathing. The town, once a shipping port, offers shops and toilet facilities.

BRAY Map 9O21 Once one of the best known holiday resorts in Ireland, Bray boasts a one-mile esplanade which extends from the harbour in the north to the approaches of 791ft Bray Head. Lifeguards are on duty here. Shopping and toilet facilities nearby. Bray is a convenient base for exploring some of the more celebrated beauty spots of Co Wicklow.

BRITTAS BAY Map 9T38 The lovely two and a quarter-mile beach is backed by sand dunes and patrolled by lifeguards. Toilet facilities available.

Forest Parks

Due to the large number of forest parks listed in this guide, the map location references can be found on the larger scale Ordnance Survey Maps of Ireland ($\frac{1}{2}$ inch series), and not in the atlas starting after page 192.

Season tickets (price £1.50) are obtainable from any of the parks and entitle you to unlimited free car parking facilities throughout the year. For further information contact: Forest and Wildlife Service, 22 Upper Merrion Street, Dublin 2 *tel* Dublin 789211.

Co Antrim

GLENARIFF FOREST PARK Map D2220 This park, situated in the world-famous Glens of Antrim, has walks, a teahouse, touring-caravan site & car parks. There is an admission charge for cars & pedestrians. Guided walks & illustrated talks can be arranged for schools & organised groups. Contact: Head Forester, Glenariff Forest Park, Parkmore, Ballymena ☎ Martinstown 232. For touring caravan site: Forest service, Room 23A Dundonald House, Belfast.

Co Armagh

GOSFORD FOREST PARK Map H9541 Not as mountainous as the others in Ulster, this park includes some fine panoramic views over South Armagh. There are planned walks, parking for 200 cars, picnic tables, toilets & caravan & campsites (not AA-classified).

Co Carlow

BAHANA ARROW BRIDGE GRAIGUENAMANAGH Map S7239 Forest walks via canal bank.

BALLINTEMPLE Map S8965 3m NW of Clonegal village. Car park, picnic place, forest walk.

CLASHGANNY Map S7345 3m S of Borris on L18A. Car park, picnic place, forest walk, River Barrow & canal.

DRUMMIN Map S7239 1½m S of St Mullins near Drummin House. Views of River Barrow from forest walks.

KILBRANISH NORTH Map S8557 Adjoins Bunclody/Mt Leinster rd. Car park, picnic place, forest walks in scenic setting.

RAHEENKYLE Map S8355 6m from Bunclody on Mt Leinster rd. Lay-by, parking, picnic place, walks.

Co Cavan

CASTLEHAMILTON Map H3207 ½m N of Killeshandra on T52. Forest walks.

CASTLE LAKE Map N6698 ½m N of Bailieborough on T24. Car park, picnic place, forest walks, fishing.

CASTLESAUNDERSON Map H4219 8m N of Cavan town off T52 near junction with T10. Car park, picnic place, forest walks.

CORRONAGH Map N6086 On S shore of L Ramor. Turn N off T35 (3m S of Virginia) or E off L49 (3m SW of Virginia). Car park, lakeside picnic place, walks.

DUN A' RI FOREST PARK Map N7997 1m N of Kingscourt on L35 to Carrickmacross. Car park (30p), picnic place, planned walks, wishing well, nature trail etc. (Booklet available on site.)

HEADFORD/DEERPARK Map N5887 1m W of Virginia off L49. Walks through broadleaf/conifer woodland, fishing.

KILLYKEEN FOREST PARK Map H3505 8m W of Cavan town. Turn NW off L15. Car park (30p), picnic place, boating, swimming, forest walks, fishing, shop/restaurant/toilets, nature trails, marina. (Booklet available on site.)

MULRICK Map N2990 1½m SW of Lough Gowna village. Forest walk & views of Lough Gowna.

Co Clare

CAHERMURPHY Map R5495 Near Flagmount village on shores of Lough Graney. Car park on lake shore. Forest walks.

CRATLOE AND WOODCOCKHILL Map R5261 At Cratloe village. 7m from Limerick on T11. Car park, picnic place, walks in mixed woodland.

CULLAUN Map R4674 1½m from Kilkishen off L11. (Enquire at village.) Car park, lakeside picnic place, forest walks, ruins of Cullaun House.

DOON Map R5674 3m from Broadford on Tulla rd. Lay-by, lakeside picnic place, walks.

DRIMMEEN/VIOLET HILL Map R5773 1m N of Broadford on Mountshannon rd. Walks in mixed woodland.

DROMORE Map R3588 Off T11 (Ennis-Gort) near Crusheen village. Car park, picnic place, walks, wooded lakeland area.

DROMOLAND Map R4070 1½m from Newmarket-on-Fergus off T11 to Ennis. Car park, picnic place, forest walks, access to Mooghaun fort.

GALLOWS HILL Map R5063 1½m above Cratloe off T11. Car park, picnic place, viewing point.

GRAGANS WOOD Map M1902 5m N of Lisdoonvarna on T69. Forest walks.

KILRUSH Map R0154 ½m from Kilrush on Killimer rd. Car park, picnic place, walks in mixed woodland.

Co Cork

ARDAROU Map W7188 Adjacent to Glenville on R Bride. Car park, picnic place, forest walks.

AULTAGH Map W2458 4m N of Dunmanway on L58. Car park, picnic place, forest walks.

BALLYNOE Map W9389 8m S of Tallow on L34. Car park, picnic place, forest walks.

BALLINABOOLA Map R5718 Turn E off T11 at Ballyhea Church, 4m S of Rathluirc & travel 1m along secondary rd. Car park, picnic place, forest walks, scenic views over Golden Vale.

BALLINTLEA/GLENANAAR Map R6413 10m NE of Mallow on T38. Car park, picnic place, forest walks (Canon Sheehan country).

BALLYGIBLIN Map R4613 6m E of Kanturk. Forest walks.

BARNEGEEHY Map V9942 3m from Bantry on L42. Lay-by, picnic place, viewing point.

CASTLEFREKE Map W3335 Off L42 on sea coast 6m from Clonakilty. Car park, picnic place, walks.

CASTLEMARTYR Map W9572 1m W of Castlemartyr on T12. Car park, picnic place, lakeside walks through mixed woodland.

CLASHNACRONA Map W2049 On T65 3m W of Dunmanway. Lay-by, picnic place, forest walks.

CLOGHVOLIA Map W6798 2½m SE of Killavullen on S rd from Fermoy. Forest walks, scenic views.

CORRIN HILL Map W8196 1m S of Fermoy on T6. Turn r to golf course. Car park, picnic place, forest walks, access to Carntiarna (Iron Age fort).

CURRABINNY Map W7962 Entrance 4m from Carrigaline. Turn l off Cork/Carrigaline rd at Carrigaline RC Church. Car park, picnic place, nature trail (leaflet available on site), scenic view of Cork Harbour, Bronze Age cairn.

CURRAGH Map W8677 3m N of Midleton on L35. Car park, picnic place, forest walks, ring fort.

DROMILIHY Map W2538 4m from Rosscarbery on L42 (to Skibbereen). Car park, picnic place, forest walks.

DUKES WOOD (SCARTNAMUCK) Map W4861 3m N of Bandon on L41. Lay-by, picnic place, riverside & forest walks.

DUNBOY Map V6644 2m W of Castletownbere on L61. Forest & seashore walks.

FARRAN Map W4871 3m SE of Coachford on Coachford/Farran rd. Car park, picnic place, scenic views, forest & lakeside walks, wildlife displays.

GARRETSTOWN Map W5945 On unclassified rd to Kilbrittain. Car park, picnic place, woodland walks.

GLENAGEAR Map W6799 1m S of Killavullen on Cork/Killavullen rd. Lay-by, picnic place, walks.

GLENBOE Map W7998 1m W of Fermoy on S Fermoy/Killavullen rd. Forest walks.

GLENBOWER Map W9978 Entrance at Killeagh village on T12 (Cork/Youghal). Car park, picnic place, forest & lakeside walks, nature trail (leaflet available on site).

GLENDAY Map W2481 2m W of Carriganimmy on L41. Turn l off Macroom/Millstreet rd & travel 2m W on unclassified rd. (Enquire at Carriganimmy.) Extensive area of forest providing fine scenery & walks.

GLENGARRIFF Map V9157 Adjacent to town on T65 to Kenmare. Car park, picnic place, forest walks, nature trail (leaflet available on site).

GLENNAHAREE EAST Map W4588 2m W of Bweeng off L40 from Mallow. Forest walks.

GLENSHESKIN Map R8403 1m NE of Kilworth. Forest walks.

GORTNACARRIGA Map W2165 2½m SW of Inchigeelagh. (Enquire at village.) Forest walks, scenic views.

GORTNATUBBRID Map W1976 Adjacent to Ballyvourney. Car park, picnic place, forest walk, view of R Sullane, access to St Gobnet's Shrine.

GORTROCHE Map W7296 2m S of Ballyhooley on Carrignavar rd. Car park, picnic place, forest & mountain walks.

GUAGANE BARRA FOREST PARK Map W0866 2m off T64 at Pass of Keimaneigh. Car parks (30p), picnic place, scenic walks, nature trail & car trail. (Booklet available on site.)

KILLIMER-TARBERT CAR FERRY

m.v. "Shannon Willow" — 44 Cars

Summer Sailing Schedule — April/September

Sailings from Killimer, Co Clare
Every hour on the hour

First Sailing . . . . 7.00 am
Last Sailing . . . . 9.00 pm

Sailings from Tarbert, Co Kerry
Every hour on the half hour

First Sailing . . . . 7.30 am
Last Sailing . . . . 9.30 pm

Sailings:
The Ferry Service operates every day of the year except Christmas Day. In peak periods two ferry boats operate to give a half-hourly service from each side. During October/March period last sailings are 2 hours earlier than above.

Distance:
Killimer/Tarbert. By road — 85 miles. By Ferry — 2¼ miles.   Average crossing time 20 mins.

SHANNON FERRY LTD, Kilrush.

91

GURTEEN Map W7598 1m S of Ballyhooley on S Fermoy/Killavullen rd. Forest walks.

INCHIGEELAGH Map W1965 On South Lake Drive 3m SW of Inchigeelagh. Car park, picnic place, forest walk to Memorial Cross, extensive views over Lee valley.

INNISHANNON Map W5456 Off Cork/Bandon rd (T65) on L41 to Ballinadee. Lay-by, picnic place, scenic views, walks.

ISLAND WOOD Map R3207 1m S of Newmarket on by-rd. (Enquire at town.) Car park, picnic place, forest & riverside walks, viewing point.

KILBRITTAIN Map W5246 On L65 from Bandon. 1m beyond Kilbrittain. Lay-by, picnic place, walks.

KNOCKAWODDRA/BWEENG MTN Map W4988 Beside Bweeng village off L40 from Mallow. Forest walks.

LOUGH HYNE Map W0829 Turn S beyond golf course on Skibbereen/Baltimore rd (L59). Lay-by, picnic place, viewing points, scenic walks.

LYRADANE Map W5686 8m S of Mallow off T11. Forest walks.

MARLOGE Map W8567 Off Cobh/East Ferry rd. Turn r just before East Ferry. Car park, picnic place, forest walks, viewing points over Cork Harbour.

MODELIGO Map W9297 5m W of Tallow Bridge on L36. Forest walks.

MT HILLARY Map W4296 2m SE of Banteer off L9. Forest walks.

MOANBAWN Map W8082 1m from Watergrasshill on Midleton rd. Forest walks.

MUSHERAMORE Map W3285 9½m N of Macroom. (Enquire at Ballinagree.) Car park, picnic place, holy well, forest & mountain walks.

QUITRENT Map R6814 12m from Mallow. Turn l off T38. Forest walks.

RATHGASKIG Map W1669 On Ballingeary/Kilgarvan rd. Approx 2m from Ballingeary. Lay-by, picnic place, forest walks.

RINNEEN Map W1833 On coast rd from Glandore to Castletownshend. Lay-by, picnic place, forest walks.

ROSTELLAN Map W8766 Turn W off Midleton/Whitegate rd at Farsid. Car park, picnic place, forest walks, access to 'Mrs Siddons Tower' at seashore.

ROWLS Map R2916 8m W of Dromcolliher on by-rd off L71. Forest walks.

SHIPPOOL Map W5755 2m from Innishannon on L41 (to Kinsale). Lay-by, picnic place, forest walks to riverside viewing points.

STREAMHILL Map R6112 3m N of Doneraile. Forest walks.

UMMERA Map W3772 3m E of Macroom on T29 to Cork. Car park, picnic place, forest walks.

WALSHTOWN Map W8781 7m N of Midleton on Castlelyons rd. Forest walks.

WARRENSCOURT Map W3565 Turn S off T29 (Cork/Macroom) to Poulanairgid (also access from Kilmurray village). Car park, picnic place, forest and lakeside walks.

Co Donegal

ARDS FOREST PARK Map C0735 On Sheephaven Bay 2m N of Creeslough on T72. Car park (30p), picnic place, toilets, forest walks, scenic views, swimming.

CHURCHILL Map C0515 Overlooking Gartan Lough near Glendowan RC Church, 2m from Churchill on Churchill/Doochary rd, 11m from Letterkenny. Car park, picnic place, paths to viewing points and to lake, access to St Columcille's well, forest walks.

CLONASILLAGH Map G6576 Turn N 6m W of Killybegs on T72. Forest walks.

CLOONEY Map G7499 5m W of Glenties on Portnoo rd. Car park, picnic place, forest & lakeside walks.

CROCKNACUNNY Map H1075 6m N of Pettigo on L6. Lay-by, picnic place, riverside walk, access to Lough Derg, scenic views.

DERRYLOUGHAN Map G8300 5m N of Glenties on Doochary rd. Forest walks adjacent to Gweebarra Bay.

DERRYVEAGH Map C0516 3m N of Churchill on cul-de-sac off L82. Car park, picnic place, forest walk, view of Claggan Lough.

DRUMBOE Map H1495 200yds from Stranorlar on T18. Car park, picnic place, riverside walk.

DRUMMONAGHAN Map C2221 ½m E of Ramelton on L77. Forest walks.

GLENGESH PASS Map G7088 On Ardara/Glencolumbkille rd. Car park, picnic place, forest walk, scenic views.

KNADER Map G9061 2m E of Ballyshannon on back rd to Belleek. Car park, picnic place, forest walks, scenic views.

LACKCROM Map G9061 4m N of Donegal. Car park, forest walks, scenic views.

LOUGH DERG Map H0772 6m N of Pettigo. Car park 1m from Pier for Station Island. Picnic place, lakeshore drive, forest walks & viewing points. Access to St Brigid's well.

LOUGH ESKE Map G9583 5m N of Donegal town on ring rd around Lough Eske. Car park, picnic place, forest walks & view of lake.

MEENGLASS Map H0891 Off T18 (Ballybofey/Donegal). Turn S 1½m from Ballybofey. Entrance at Meenglass Church. Forest walks.

MEENIRROY Map C0108 12m W of Letterkenny on L74. Forest walks.

MONELLAN Map H1992 4m E of Ballybofey near Crossroads village. Forest walks.

MONGORRY Map C2305 First turn r NW of Raphoe on Raphoe/Letterkenny rd. Forest walks, scenic views.

MULLAGHAGARRY Map H1798 2m NE of Stranorlar-Ballybofey. Turn l off T18 or r off L80. Car park, picnic place, forest walks & views over twin towns of Stranorlar & Ballybofey.

MURVAGH/MULLINASOLE STRAND Map G9073 5m W off Leahy T18, 9m from Donegal & 15m from Ballyshannon. Car park, picnic place, forest walk, beach access.

RATHMULLAN WOOD Map C2827 1m SW of Rathmullan on L77. Car park, picnic place, forest walks overlooking Lough Swilly.

WOODQUARTER Map C1828 2m NW of Milford on T72. Car park, picnic place, forest walks overlooking Mulroy Bay. Scenic views.

Co Down

CASTLEWHELLAN FOREST PARK Map J3336 This park has one of the finest arboreta in the British Isles and includes a lake and mountain viewpoints. Facilities include planned walks, parking for 800 cars, picnic & toilets. Admission fee per car. Campsite: see Gazetteer under Castlewhellan.

TOLLYMORE FOREST PARK Map J3433 In the Mourne Mountains. Facilities include planned walks & parking for 500 cars, picnic tables and toilets. Admission fee per car.

Co Dublin

BALLINASCORNEY LOWER Map O0721 8m from Rathfarnham on L199. Keep r at first junction beyond Ballinascorney Gap. Lay-by, picnic place, forest walks.

BALLINASCORNEY UPPER Map O0720 8m from Rathfarnham on L199. Keep l at first junction beyond Ballinascorney Gap. Lay-by, picnic place, forest walks, access to summit of Seechon Mountain.

BARNASLINGAN Map O2220 On Barnaslingan lane – E off T43 near Kilternan. Car park, picnic place, forest walks, scenic view overlooking the Scalp.

CARRICKGOLLOGAN Map O2321 2m W of Shankill near Ballycorus lead mines, or E off Barnaslingan Lane (off T43 near Kilternan). Forest walks.

CRUAGH Map O1222 5m S of Rathfarnham E off L94 or W off L201. Car park, picnic place, forest walks, nature trail (leaflet available on site). Wilderness trek via Featherbed Mountain to Military Road car park (below).

HELL FIRE CLUB Map O1223 4m S of Rathfarnham on L201. Car park, picnic place, forest walks on both sides of rd, access to Hell Fire Club & panoramic view.

KILMASHOGUE Map O1523 On cul-de-sac S off L93 (Rockbrook/Sandyford), 1m E of Rockbrook. Car park, picnic place, forest walk to Three Rock Mountain (below). Bronze Age tomb.

MILITARY ROAD Map O1220 On L94 (Rathfarnham/Glencree). 7m S of Rathfarnham. Lay-by, parking to facilitate users of wilderness trek via Featherbed Mountain to Cruagh car park (above).

SEECHON Map O0721 9m from Rathfarnham via L199. Keep l at first junction beyond Ballinascorney Gap. Car park, picnic place, panoramic views, access to summit of Seechon Mountain.

THREE ROCK MOUNTAIN Map O1623 5m S of Rathfarnham. Turn S on signposted cul-de-sac off L93. Car park, picnic place, forest walks, panoramic views, access to summits of Three Rock & Two Rock Mountains & to Kilmashogue car park (above).

TIBRADDEN Map O1322 5m S of Rathfarnham on L201. Car park, picnic place, forest walks, nature trail (leaflet available on site). Paths to Cruagh Wood & Military Road (above).

Co Galway

AGHRANE Map M7854 Adjoins Ballygar village on T15 from Mountbellew to Roscommon. Lay-by, parking, picnic places, forest walks.

ARDNAGEEHA Map M1354 1m W of Cong Sawmill on L101. Car park, picnic place, forest walks, view of Lough Corrib.

CLONBUR Map M0956 N of Clonbur village on the shores of Lough Mask. Forest walks.

CONG WOOD Map M1454 Entrance from Cong village through Abbey grounds & across river. Forest walks, viewing tower.

COOLE DEMESNE Map M4304 1½m N of Gort on T11. Car park, picnic place, site of Lady Gregory's home garden 'autograph tree', forest walks, nature trail (leaflet available on site).

DERREEN Map L9156 4m SE of Leenane on L100. Forest walks.

GLANN Map M0448 6m NW of Oughterard on shore of Lough Corrib. Car park, picnic place, forest walks.

KELLY'S CAVE WOOD Map M1554 ½m E of Cong on L101. Forest walks, Kelly's Cave, Captain Webb's Hole.

KILCORNAN Map M4220 ½m S of Clarinbridge on T11. Forest walks.

KYLEBRACK Map M6810 5m SE of Loughrea on L99. Forest walks.

LOUGH INAGH Map L8453 6m from Recess on Kylemore rd. Car park, picnic place, forest walk.

MONIVEA Map M5336 Adjoining Monivea on L54. Forest walk.

MOUNTBELLEW DEMESNE Map M6646 Adjoining Mount Bellew. Car park, picnic place, forest walks.

PIGEON HOLE WOOD Map M1355 ½m N of Cong Sawmill on L101. Car park, picnic place, forest walks, cave, underground river.

PORTUMNA FOREST PARK Map M8303 Adjoining Portumna. Car park (30p), picnic place, toilet/shelter/information building, forest walks, deer herds, stands for viewing wildlife, wildfowl, ponds, nature trail (leaflet available on site).

ROSTURRA Map M7500 6m SW of Portumna on T41. Forest walks.

TOBBERROE Map M4526 3m W of Athenry on T4. Forest walks.

TOORLEITRA Map R6998 3m W of Woodford. Forest walks.

Co Kerry

BALLAGHISHEEN/DERREENAGEEHA Map V6578 W of Ballaghisheen Pass on Waterville/Glencar rd 13m from Waterville. Car park, picnic place, walks.

BALLYGAMBOON Map Q8506 On Tralee/Castlemaine rd T66, 2m from Castlemaine. Lay-by, picnic place, forest walks.

DERRYCUNNIHY (LADIES VIEW) Map V9282 11m from Killarney on T65 to Kenmare. Lay-by, parking, picnic place. Famed view of Killarney lakes.

DOONEEN Map R0012 2m N of Castleisland on T28 to Limerick. Car park, picnic place, forest walks.

DROMORE Map V8168 On Kenmare/Sneem rd T66 6m W of Kenmare. Car park, picnic place, forest walks, viewing point over Kenmare Bay. Also lay-by/picnic place with seashore walk.

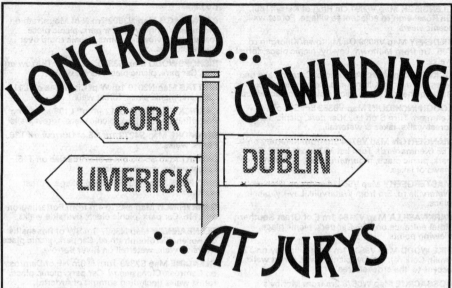

GLEENSK Map V5888 On Ring of Kerry (T66) 8m W of Glenbeigh. Lay-by, picnic place, forest walk to seashore.

GLENBEIGH Map V6691 On Ring of Kerry (T66). On Rossbeigh rd adjacent to village. Forest walk, scenic views.

KILDERRY Map V8099 On Milltown/Killorglin rd T66, 1m from Milltown. Lay-by, picnic place, forest walks.

LICKEEN Map V6988 At S end of Caragh Lake on lakeside rd from Killorglin to Ballaghbeama & Ballaghisheen. Lay-by, picnic place, scenic walks.

LOUGH INCHIQUIN Map V8363 8m SW of Kenmare. Turn S off L62. Car park, picnic place, forest walks, lakes & waterfall.

MANGERTON Map V9784 5m from Killarney on T65 (Kenmare rd). Turn l at Muckross hotel. Car park, picnic place, mountain walks, panoramic views of lakes.

MASTERGEEHY Map V5571 Lay-by on Glencar/ Waterville rd, 5m from Waterville. Lay-by, picnic place.

PARKNASILLA Map V7164 1m E of Great Southern Hotel entrance on T66. Car park, picnic place, viewing points.

PIKE WOOD Map V9891 1m from Killarney on T29 (main Cork rd). Lay-by, picnic place, forest walks, access to 'the crooked tree'.

ROSSACRUE Map W0678 2m from Morley's Bridge on L62 linking Kilgarvan with main Cork/Killarney rd. Lay-by, picnic place, walks.

Co Kildare

BLACKWOOD Map S6998 4m N of Athy on Athy/Kildare rd. Forest walks.

DONADEA DEMESNE Map N8333 5m SW of Kilcock on L181. Car park, picnic place, castle ruins, lake and & forest walks.

KILKEA CASTLE/MULLAGHREELAN Map S7488 2½m N of Castledermot on Castledermot/Athy rd. Car park, picnic place, forest walk to Wishing Well ring fort.

MOORE ABBEY Map N6409 ½m S of Monasterevin on L18. Car park, picnic place, forest walks.

RAHAN Map N6237 On the River Boyne on by-rd off L18, 3m S of Kinnegad. Forest walks, picnic place, lay-by, parking.

Co Kilkenny

BRANDON HILL Map S6740 Turn E off Graiguenamanagh/Inistioge rd 2m S of Graiguenamanagh. Forest walks, scenic views of Barrow valley.

CASTLEMORRIS Map S4835 3m W of Knocktopher on L32. Lay-by, picnic place, forest walk.

GRAIGUENAMANAGH Map S7042 Adjacent to village. Car park, picnic place, riverside walk.

JENKINSTOWN Map S4864 6m N of Kilkenny on T6. Car park, picnic place, riverside walks.

TREMCHMORE Map S4040 2m S of Callan on T6. Lay-by, picnic place, forest walk.

WOODLANDS Map S4652 3m W of Kilkenny on T6. Turn r at Tennypark. Lay-by, picnic place, forest walk.

WOODSTOCK PARK Map S6435 1m S of Inistioge

(turn r off T20 in Inistioge travelling from Kilkenny). Car park, picnic place, arboretum, walks.

Co Laois

BAUNREAGH Map N3002 7m N of Mountrath on Mountrath/Kinnitty rd. Car park, picnic place, forest walks, viewing points, scenic route over Slieve Blooms.

BISHOPSWOOD Map S3875 2m SW of Durrow on T36. Car park, picnic place, forest walks.

BRITTAS Map N3010 1m W of Clonaslee on L116. Car park, picnic place, forest walk.

CARRICK HILL Map N5412 ½m off L108 adjoining Portarlington. Car park, picnic place, forest walk.

DUNMORE Map S4279 1m NE of Durrow off T36. Forest walks.

DYSART Map S5296 5m E of Portlaoise on T16. Forest walks, viewing points.

EMO PARK Map N5305 In Emo village. Forest walks.

GARRYHINCH Map N4910 4m from Portarlington on L116. Car park, picnic place, riverside walks.

GLENBARROW Map N3607 3m SW of Rosenallis off Rosenallis/Mountrath rd. Car park, picnic place, riverside walk, waterfall on River Barrow.

GLENDINE Map S2399 Turn N 3m NE of Camross on Camross/Clonaslee rd. Car park, picnic place, forest walks (including summit of Arderin).

GLENDINEOREGAN Map N3006 4m S of Clonaslee on L116. Car park, picnic place, forest walks, viewing points, scenic route over Slieve Blooms.

MONICKNEW Map N3002 7m N of Mountrath on Mountrath/Clonaslee rd. Car park, picnic place, forest walks, viewing points, scenic route over Slieve Blooms Nature Trail (leaflet available on site).

OUGHAVAL Map S5895 1m SE of Stradbally on T16. Car park, picnic place, forest walks.

RATHDAIRE Map N5705 1m S of Ballybrittas on T5. Forest walks.

SHEFFIELD Map S4995 3m SE of Portlaoise on L26. Forest walks.

THE CUT Map N9904 5m S of Clonaslee on Clonaslee/Mountrath rd. Car park, picnic place, forest walks, viewing point, scenic route over Slieve Blooms, access to Wolftrap Mountain.

TOGHER Map S4696 2m S of Portlaoise on by-rd off T14.

Co Leitrim

CARTRON Map G9836 Off L16 (Sligo/Dromhaire). Turn N just E of Parks Castle. Car park, picnic place, forest walks.

DERRYCARNE Map N0291 Turn W off T3 N of Dromod. Car park, picnic place, access to Shannon.

GLENCAR Map G7443 By-rd along N shore of Glencar Lough. Co Council car park, forest walks, scenic views, Glencar Waterfall.

GLENFARNE Map H0138 E side of Glenfarne/Kiltyclogher rd at Glenfarne. Car parks & picnic places at L Macnean, forest walks.

KINLOUGH Map G8155 N of Kinlough village on T54. Car park, picnic place, forest walks.

KNOCKATEEN Map H0236 1½m W of Tarmon Church. Car park, picnic place, forest walk, scenic view.

LAVAGH Map G9025 1m N of Drumkeeran on T54. Car park, picnic place, forest walks.

MILLTOWN Map G8640 1m W of Manorhamilton on by-rd to Lurganboy. Forest walks.

Co Limerick

BALLINRUANE/CORRONAHER Map R4131 12m E of Newcastle West, 3m E of Kilmeedy village. Forest walks.

COOLFREE/GLENANAAR Map R6614 10m NE of Mallow off T38. Forest walks, hill climbs (Canon Sheehan country).

COMBAUN Map R8218 2m SE of Anglesboro. Lay-by parking, picnic place, forest walks.

CURRAHCHASE Map R4048 On Limerick/Askeaton rd T68. Car park, picnic place, gardens, arboretum, ruin of Curranchase House formerly home of Aubrey de Vere (area in course of development as Forest Park).

FANNINGSTOWN/GREENWOOD Map R6418 3m W of Kilfinnane or 6m S of Kilmallock off Kilmallock/Kildorrerry rd L36. Car park, picnic place, forest walks, hill climb (Canon Sheehan country).

FOYNES Map R2451 Near Foynes village on T68 to Tarbert. Lay-by, picnic place, views over Shannon, forest walks.

GALTEE CASTLE Map R8819 5m NE of Mitchelstown on T6 to Cahir. Car park, picnic place, forest walk.

MOORESTOWN Map R6924 2m NE of Kilfinnane. Forest walks.

THOMASTOWN Map R6821 Near Kilfinnane on L28. Forest walks.

Co Longford

DERRYCASSAN Map N3186 4m N of Granard turn W off Granard/Gowna rd. Forest walks, fishing.

NEWCASTLE DEMESNE Map N1856 1m E of Ballymahon. Forest walks.

Co Louth

BELLURGAN Map J1009 5m from Dundalk. Turn N at Ballymackellett off Ravensdale/Carlingford rd. Car park, picnic place, scenic views overlooking Dundalk Bay, walks.

RAVENSDALE Map J0913 4m N of Dundalk. Turn E off T1. Car park, picnic place, forest walks, nature trail (leaflet available on site).

SLIEVE FOYE Map J1613 2m from Carlingford on T62 towards Omeath. Scenic drive to car park overlooking Carlingford Lough, picnic place.

TOWNLEY HALL Map O0376 4m W of Drogheda on Boyne Valley rd at side of Battle of the Boyne. Car park, picnic place, forest walks, nature trail (leaflet available on site).

Co Mayo

BELLEEK Map G2421 ½m N of Ballina on W bank of Moy estuary. Car park, picnic place, forest walks.

BRACKLOON Map L9780 5m from Westport on T71. Forest walks.

BREAFFY Map M1889 3m from Castlebar on T39. Forest walks.

CASTLEMAGARRETT Map M3473 1½m from Claremorris on L27. Forest walks.

CLYDAGH Map G1794 3m from Castlebar on Pontoon rd L134. Car park, picnic place, fishing, waterfall, forest walks.

CORYOSLA/CORYOSLA BRIDGE Map G1904 1m from Pontoon towards Crossmolina on L140. Car park, picnic place, forest walks.

DRUMMIN/LOUGH CULLIN Map G2404 2m S from Foxford on Pontoon rd. Lakeside car & bus parking, picnic place, panoramic view, fishing, forest walks.

KNOCKRANNY/COLONEL'S WOOD Map M0083 Adjoining Westport off T39. Forest walks.

LAPALLAGH Map M0792 5m from Castlebar off L138. Forest walks, viewing point.

LAUGHIL Map G2003 On shores of Lough Conn (from Pontoon Bridge to Coryosla Bridge). Forest walks.

MOOREHALL Map M1974 E off T40 Castlebar/Ballinrobe via Ballintober Abbey to Carnacon. Turn S at Carnacon. Car park, picnic place, ruin of Moore Hall, access to lake, fishing, forest walks, scenic views.

OLD HEAD Map L8282 2m E of Louisburg off T139. Car park, picnic place, scenic views, forest walks.

SHEEFREY Map L8967 14m SW of Westport on Liscarney/Doolough rd. Car park, picnic place, viewing point.

SRAHMORE Map F9704 On L136 by Keenagh cross or T71 by Furnace. Forest walks, viewing points, riverside drive.

TOURMAKEADY DEMESNE Map M1067 At

Tourmakeady village on W shore of Lough Mask.
Car park, picnic place, forest walks including walk
to waterfall. Nature trail (leaflet available on site).

Co Meath

LOUGH BRACKEN Map N8787 1m SW of
Drumcondrath off L24. Car park, picnic place,
fishing, forest walks.

ROSS Map N4682 On S shore of Lough Sheelin,
turn I 4½m from Finea on Mountnugent rd. Forest
walks.

SUMMERHILL Map N8448 Near Summerhill
village S of Trim. Car park, picnic place, walks.

Co Monaghan

ANNAGHMAKERRIG Map H5821 On side rd off
L40 5m NW of Cootehill. Car park, picnic place,
forest walks.

BELLAMONT AND DARTRY Map H6045 1m N of
Cootehill towards Monaghan town. Car park,
picnic place, forest walks.

BLACK ISLAND Map H8320 Eastern outskirts of
Castleblayney. Lakeside walks, fishing.

CASTLESHANE Map H7331 5m E of Monaghan on
T2. Forest walks, Castleshane Waterfall.

CONCRA Map H8417 2m SE of Castleblaney on
T22. Forest walks, fishing.

ROSSMORE FOREST PARK Map H6531 1m S of
Monaghan on L44. Car park (30p), picnic place,
forest & lakeshore walks, fishing. Park booklet
including nature trail notes in course of
preparation.

Co Offaly

GLENREGAN Map N2001 Turn S off L116 of
Kinnitty village & travel 2m. Forest walk.

GLOSTER Map S0894 5m from Roscrea off T32
(Roscrea/Birr). Forest walks along lakeshore.

GLENLETTER/FINGER BOARD Map N2504 5m SE
of Kinnitty on Kinnitty/Mountrath rd. Car park,
picnic place, viewing point, forest walks.

GOLDENGROVE Map S1191 2m from Roscrea on
T32 (Roscrea/Birr). Forest walks.

LIME KILN GROVE Map N2101 Turn S off L116 E of
Kinnitty village & travel 2½m. Lay-by, car park,
picnic place, forest walks.

Co Roscommon

CORREEN Map M9226 5m SE of Ballinasloe on
L27. Forest walks.

DERRYDONNELL/MOTE PARK Map M8961 1½m S
of Roscommon town. Forest walks.

DOUGHILL/SLIEVE BAN Map M9575 5m S of
Strokestown. Forest walks, viewing points.

KILRONAN Map M8812 Turn I 1m from Keadue on
rd to Ballyfarnon. Forest walk.

LOUGH KEY FOREST PARK Map G8302 2m E of
Boyle 7m NW of Carrick-on-Shannon on T3. Car
park (30p), picnic place, caravan park, camping
area, service buildings, shop, restaurant, viewing
tower, boating, cruising, fishing, swimming, deer
compound, forest walks, bog garden, nature trail.
(Booklet available on site.) Caravan/camping
enquiries: ☎ Boyle 224 Restaurant/Shop ☎ Boyle
214 Cruises: ☎ Cootehill 7 Boats: enquire at Shop.

MOTE PARK Map M9161 Entrance off rd opposite
Ballymurry PO. Forest walks.

Co Sligo

CARNS Map G7134 1½m from Sligo on Holywell rd.
Car park, picnic place, forest walks, access to Cairn
(NM).

CARROWNASKEAGH Map G5525 Off T40 4m W of
Coolaney on Coolaney/Screen by-rd (route to
Ladies Brae). Lay-by, car park, picnic place, walks.

CASTLEDARGAN Map G7027 From L3 at
Ballygawley on L117. Forest walks.

CORREAGH Map G7231 5m from Sligo on L117.
Forest walks.

DEERPARK Map G7436 5m from Sligo on old rd to
Manorhamilton. Car park, picnic place, forest
walks & national monuments (Giants' Graves).

DOONEY/DOONEY ROCK Map G7131 4m from
Sligo on L117. Car park, picnic place, viewing
points, forest walks, nature trail (leaflet available
on site).

GLEN WOOD Map G6226 3m W of Ballisodare and
1m S from T40. Forest walks, scenic views.

GLENIFF Map G7347 S off T18 at Cliffoney (on
Gleniff Horseshore). Car park, picnic place, walks.

HAZELWOOD Map G7335 ½m off L16
(Sligo/Dromahaire). Turn r 3m from Sligo. Car
park, picnic place, scenic views, forest walks.

LISADELL Map G6244 W off T18 at Drumcliff,
travel 3m through Carney. Car park, picnic place,
forest walks. Important mainland refuge for
Barnacle Geese.

MASSHILL Map G4417 Turn N at Bellanagraugh
bridge on Cloonaghcool/Aclare rd. Forest walk.

RATHCARRICK/KNOCKNAREA Map G6334 1½m S
from L132 between Sligo & Strandhill. Car park,
picnic place, forest walks, scenic views of Sligo Bay.

SESSUE GILROY Map G4318 S end of rd from
Dromore West by Lough Easkey. Forest walks.

SLISHWOOD Map G7431 5m from Sligo on L117.
Car park, picnic place, forest & lakeside walks,
paddling pool.

UNION WOOD/BALLYGAWKEY LOUGH Map
G6929 5m S of Sligo on L3. Car park overlooking
lake, picnic place, forest walks.

Co Tipperary

BALLINACOURTY Map R8629 On
Tipperary/Lisvernane scenic route 1m from Statue
of Christ the King & 4m from Tipperary. Car park,
picnic place, forest walks, walks.

BALLYDAVID Map R9728 On by-rd leading to
Youth Hostel from T13. Car park, picnic place,
forest walks.

BISHOPSWOOD Map R9746 1½m from Dundrum
on L119 to Thurles. Entrance near Bishopswood
school. Lay-by, picnic place, forest walks.

BOHERNAGORE Map S0312 At Vee hairpin bend
on L34 (Clogheen/Tallow). Viewing point on
Knockmealdown Mountains, forest walks, picnic
place.

CAHIR PARK Map S0523 1½m S of Cahir on L184 to
Ardfinnan. Car park, picnic place, forest & riverside
walks, scenic views.

COOPERS WOOD Map R8820 Turn N off T6 at
Skeheenarinky School on Cahir/Mitchelstown rd.
Car park, picnic place, riverside/forest walk.

CORDANGAN AND BANSHA WEST Map R9432 1m from Bansha, 5m from Tipperary town on T13. Car park, picnic place, forest walks, viewing points.

GLENGARRA Map R9220 8m SW of Cahir on T6. (Dublin/Cork rd). Car park, picnic place, forest & riverside walks, unusual tree & shrub species, nature trail (leaflet available on site).

GORTAVOHER Map R8621 On Tipperary/Lisvernane rd at Statue of Christ the King 4m from Tipperary. Car park, picnic place giving extensive views of Glen of Aherlow, forest walks.

KILLURNEY Map S3228 Beside Kilcash village, also off by-rd adjacent to Killurney school. Viewing points, forest walks.

KILCASH Map S3227 Off T6 beside Kilcash Castle, 8m from Clonmel. Forest walks, Kilcash Castle (ruins) close by.

KNOCKBALLINERY Map S0812 Approx mid-way on the Clogheen/Newcastle rd linking with L28 S of Clogheen. Car park, picnic place, riverside walks & woodland drive to viewing point.

KNOCKNACREE Map R9889 1½m from Cloughjordan on Shinrone rd. Forest walks.

MARL BOG Map R9645 On Dundrum/Tipperary rd approx 1m from Dundrum. Car park, picnic place, forest walks giving access to game sanctuary.

MARLFIELD Map S1722 Close to Clonmel ½m E of Knocklofty Bridge. Riverside walk.

SCARAGH Map S0225 On mountain rd off T13 NW of Cahir. Forest walks, viewing point.

TOUREEN Map S0127 4m N of Cahir off T13. Forest walks.

Co Tyrone

DAVAGH FOREST PARK Map H6986 On the N slope of Beleevnamore Mountain on E edge of Sperrin Mountains 12m W of Cookstown. Walks, scenic drive, viewpoints, picnic sites & visitor centre which houses an exhibit. Toilets. Admission fee per car.

DRUM MANOR FOREST PARK Map H7677 Small forest park with facilities which include planned walks, parking for 200 cars, picnic tables & toilets. Admission fee per car.

GORTIN GLEN FOREST PARK Map H4988 Around the rugged Sperrin Mountains. Facilities include planned walks, a scenic drive, parking for 200 cars, picnic tables, toilets & a campsite (not AA-classified). Admission fee per car.

Co Waterford

BALLYLEMON/COLLIGAN WOOD Map X2196 5m N of Dungarvan on T75. Car park, picnic place, riverside & forest walks.

BALLYSCANLON Map S5403 Adjacent to Tramore. Car park, picnic place, forest walks adjacent to lake.

BOHADOON/MAW MAW ROAD Map S2502 On Comeragh Drive near Kilrossanty village. Lay-by, picnic place, forest walks, viewing points.

CARNGLASS Map X0987 8m S of Cappoquin on Hill Route to Youghal. Lay-by, picnic place, walks.

COOLATOOR Map X1990 6m W of Dungarvan (The Drum Hills). Forest walks, viewing points.

COOLFIN/GLENHOUSE Map S4712 ½m beyond RC church in Portlaw. Forest walks, rhododendron paths.

COOLNAMUCK EAST AND WEST/CHURCHTOWN Map S3521 Carrick-on-Suir/Tramore rd or back rd Carrick-on-Suir/Clonmel. Forest walks, viewing points.

COOLEYDOODY Map W9796 On Tallow/Fermoy rd L36 2m W of Tallowbridge. Lay-by, picnic place, walks.

CREHANAGH NORTH Map S4220 1m E of Carrick-on-Suir. Forest walks.

DRUM HILLS/MONAMEEN Map S3207 7m W of Dungarvan on T12. Entrance lay-bys, picnic place, walks.

GLENAREY/RUSSELSTOWN Map S1812 2m S of Clonmel off T27. Car park, picnic place, castle ruins, forest & riverside walks.

GLENDALLIGAN SOUTH Map S2997 2m from Dungarvan on T12 (Waterford rd). Lay-by picnic place, viewing point, forest walks.

GLENDALLIGAN NORTH Map S2901 1m off T12 8m from Dungarvan (on scenic Comeragh Drive). Forest walks, viewing point.

GLENSHELLANE Map S1202 2m N of Cappoquin. Turn r at Grotto off Mount Melleray rd. Car park, picnic place, forest & riverside walks. Also viewing lay-by on Cappoquin/Mt Melleray rd.

GURTEEN Map S2723 2m from Kilsheelan on L27. Lay-by, picnic place on river bank. Walks.

KILCLOONEY Map S3409 On Dungarvan/Carrick-on-Suir rd T56. Car park, picnic place, forest walks, access to Crotty's Rock & lakes.

KILLAHALEY Map X0995 On Blackwater opposite Dromana on Cappoquin/Youghal rd. Entrance lay-by, picnic place, walks, scenic views of Blackwater River.

KILNAMACK Map S1620 1m N of Clonmel. Entrance lay-by, forest walks leading to viewing point from Tower.

KILSHEELAN WOODS – TICKINCOR DERRINLAUR GURTEEN BOOLA Map S2422 1m S of Kilsheelan on T13 also bordering old Clonmel/Kilsheelan rd W of River Suir. Forest & riverside walks, scenic views.

KNOCKATOURNEY/CROGHAUN HILL Map S3710 Turn E off Dungarvan/Waterford rd 12m from Dungarvan & travel 2m. Forest walks, viewing points.

KNOCKNASHEEGA Map S1005 7m N of Cappoquin. 3m N of Mount Melleray Abbey. Viewing points, forest walks.

KNOCKAUN Map X0287 4m S of Tallow on Tallow/Youghal rd T36. Entrance lay-by, picnic place, forest walks.

LACKEN Map X2796 2m NE of Dungarvan on T12. Forest walks, viewing points.

LISMORE Map S0306 8m NW of Cappoquin beside Vee rd (to Clogheen).

MACALLOP GLEN Map R9400 ½m N of Ballyduff/Fermoy rd, 2m W of Ballyduff village. County Council lay-by, rhododendron paths.

MONEYGOOUR Map S1205 5m N of Cappoquin. Forest walks.

NIER VALLEY Map S2013 On scenic route from Clonmel, 4m from Ballymacarbery. Car park, picnic place, walks.

ROCKET'S CASTLE/CURRAGHMORE Map S4416

2m N of Portlaw on L26 to Carrick-on-Suir. Car park, picnic place, forest walks.

STRANCALLY Map W8690 On Blackwater rd, 10m W of Tallow beside Blackwater river. Viewing points, forest walks.

TOWER HILL Map S4417 1½m from Portlaw. (Enquire at village.) Forest walks, viewing points.

Co Westmeath

CARRICK Map N4144 On shores of Lough Ennell 6m S of Mullingar off Mullingar/Kilbeggan rd. Forest walks.

LYNN/KILPATRICK Map N4349 Off T9 1m from Mullingar at Butlers Bridge & further W. Forest walks.

MULLAGHMEEN Map N4679 5m E of Finea on Finea/Oldcastle rd. Forest walks.

Co Wexford

BALLYNASTRAGH Map T1564 Turn W off Arklow/Gorey rd at Tinnock Bridge for ½m. Car park, picnic place, forest walks.

BIG WOOD Map S7434 On New Ross/Borris rd 7m from New Ross. Forest walks.

BREE HILL Map S9433 1½m from Dunanore on Bree rd. Forest walks.

CAMOLIN PARK Map T0555 On Gorey/Enniscorthy rd 8m from Gorey, 10m from Enniscorthy on T7. Car park, picnic place, forest walks.

CARRICKBYRNE HILL Map S8224 9m from New Ross on main Wexford/New Ross rd. Co Council car park, picnic place, forest walks.

COURTOWN Map T1957 ½m W of Courtown on L31 (Gorey/Churchtown rd). Car park, picnic place, forest walks into Courtown.

DUNANORE Map S9636 At Dunanore Bridge 3m from Enniscorthy. Car park, picnic place, viewing points, riverside & forest walks.

GURTEEN LOWER/BALLYFAD Map T1768 1m from Coolgreany off Killinierin rd. Forest walks.

JOHN F KENNEDY PARK Map S7220 8m from New Ross on L159. Car park (30p), picnic place, arboretum & forest garden, shop/restaurant, viewing point, planned walks. (Brochure available on site.) Shop/restaurant – ☎ (051) 88195

OAKLANDS Map S7125 1m S of New Ross on Campile road. Co Council lay-by, picnic place, forest walks.

SHELMALIER COMMONS/FORTH MOUNTAIN Map S9718 4m from Wexford town on Wexford/Duncannon rd. Lay-by, parking, viewing points, forest walks.

TARA HILL Map T2062 N of Courtown 4m from Arklow, 5m from Gorey on T7. Forest walks, viewing points.

WILTON/PARK WOOD Map S9534 1½m from Dunanore on Bree rd. Forest walks.

Co Wicklow

AUGHAVANNAGH Map T0686 Entrance beside Aughavannagh Bridge (near Youth Hostel) on Rathdangan/Glenmalure rd. Forest walk to foot of Lugnaquilla Mountain.

AVOCA Map T2080 1m S of Avoca on T7. Car park, picnic place, forest walks.

Royal Marine Hotel

DUN LAOGHAIRE, CO. DUBLIN

Fifteen minutes from the city, thirty minutes from the Airport and just a few minutes from the Holyhead/Dun Laoghaire Car Ferry, the Royal Marine stands in a beautiful garden of flowers overlooking Dublin Bay. With over 100 bedrooms (many with private bathroom) — elevator — central heating — television lounge — luxury restaurant and bars — "Gay Nineties" Grill — sauna bath suite — Beauty salons — and fashion boutique — the hotel offers every modern comfort and amenity.

Tel: 801911 Cables: "Comfort" Dun Laoghaire

AVONDALE FOREST PARK Map T1886 1m S of Rathdrum. Car park (30p), picnic place, planned walks, nature trails. Avondale House (home of Charles Stewart Parnell) open to public 2pm–6pm Fri–Mon May–Sep. (Booklet available on site.)

BALLARD Map T1495 1m S of Laragh (T61). Keep l off T61 near Bookey's Bridge. Car park, picnic place, forest walks.

BALLINAGEE Map O0402 Annalecky Bridge 1m W of Wicklow Gap on Hollywood/Laragh rd. Car park, picnic place, forest walk, scenic views.

BALLINAMONA Map T1877 1m NW of Woodenbridge on Woodenbridge/Aughrim rd. Car park, picnic place, forest walks.

BALLINASTOE Map O1908 On Old Long Hill rd (Enniskerry/Roundwood). 2m S of Djouce Woods (see below). Car park, picnic place, forest walks linking to Lough Tay.

BALLYBOY Map T1091 Near Drumgoff Cross on Glenmalure/Glendalough rd. Forest walks, viewing points.

BALLYCULLEN Map T2296 2m W of Ashford via Nun's Cross. Forest walks.

BALLYGANNON Map T1888 ½m N Rathdrum on T61. Car park, picnic place, forest walks.

BALLYMANUS Map T2592 Turn off T7 200 yards N of Glenealy. Forest walks, viewing points.

BALLYMOYLE HILL Map T2679 On L29 2m S of Jack White's Cross, turn r at Scratenagh Crossroads then 1½m NW to entrance. Car park, picnic place, forest walks, scenic views.

BALLYREACH Map O1715 Take rd on S side of Glencree off L94 (Military Rd) for 2m. Forest walks.

101

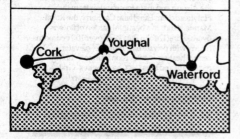
BARRAVORE Map T0694 Entrance from Co Council car park. 3m NW of Glenmalure Hotel. Forest walks, viewing points.

BELLEVUE Map O2612 5m S of Bray on T7. Car park, picnic place, forest walks, nature trail (leaflet available on site).

CALLOWHILL Map O2503 On by-rd off T7 turn W 2m S of Newtown Mountkennedy. Forest walks.

CARRIGEENDUFF Map O1107 On L94 (Military Rd) 3m S of Sally Gap. Lay-by, parking, picnic place, forest walk.

CLARAMORE Map T1793 On Laragh/Glenealy rd 2½m SE of Laragh. Forest walks.

CLONKEEN Map T0893 2m NW of Glenmalure Hotel, Glenmalure/Barravore rd. Forest walks, viewing points, access to river.

CLOON Map O1717 4m from Enniskerry on Glencree N rd. Car park, picnic place, forest walks.

COOLGARROW Map T1183 3½m NW of Aughrim village on Aughrim/Aughavannagh rd. Forest walks, access to river.

CRONE Map O1914 Take rd on S side of Glencree off L94 (Military Rd) for 2m. Car park, picnic place, forest walks, wilderness trek to Djouce Woods.

CRONEYBYRNE AND BALLINASTRAW Map T1893 2m N of Rathdrum on Rathdrum/Moneystown rd. Forest walks, fishing, access to river.

CULLENTRA Map T1089 On Military Rd (Glenmalure/Aughavannagh) S of Drumgoff Cross. 3 lay-by car parks & picnic places.

CURTLESTOWN Map O2117 On Enniskerry/Glencree N rd, 2m from Enniskerry. Forest walks.

DEVIL'S GLEN Map T2399 2½m W of Ashford on rd to Glendalough via Nun's Cross. Car park, picnic place, forest walks, waterfall, nature trail (leaflet available on site).

DERRYBAWN Map T1495 1½m S of Laragh on T61. Car park, picnic place, forest walk, access to river.

DJOUCE WOODS Map O2112 On Old Long Hill rd from Enniskerry to Roundwood. 3 car parks on Old Long Hill rd, each with picnic place, interconnecting forest paths, scenic views of lake waterfall & mountain wilderness trek (from Paddock Lake) to Glencree. (Crone car park.)

GLASAMULLEN Map O1807 On Old Long Hill rd (Enniskerry/Roundwood) 2m S of Djouce Woods (see above). Car park, picnic place, forest walk.

GLENART Map T2174 ½m from Woodenbridge on Woodenbridge/Arklow rd. Car park, picnic place, forest walks, rhododendron area.

GLENDALOUGH Map T1396 1m W of Laragh on L107. Co Council car park, picnic place, forest walks, nature trail (leaflet available on site), boat trips to St Kevin's Bed. (Boating enquiries ☎ (0404)5156.)

GLEN DING Map N9615 On L181 (Blessington/Naas), 1m from Blessington. Lay-by, picnic place, forest walks.

KILLAVENY Map T0774 2½m NE of Tinahely on L19. Lay-by, parking, picnic place, forest walks.

KILMURRAY Map O2506 2m W of Newtown Mountkennedy on L162. Forest walks.

KILNAMANAGH/DEPUTY'S PASS Map T2390 Turn off T7 about 2m SW of Glenealy on the Brittas Bay rd. Car park, picnic place, forest walks, viewing points.

KINDLESTOWN Map O2712 5m S of Bray near Delgany turning l at Glen of the Downs off T7. Car park, picnic place, forest walks, viewing point overlooking Greystones & sea.

KIPPURE Map O0814 On L161 (Kilbride/Sally Gap), 3m from Kilbride. Car park, picnic place, forest walks.

KNICKEEN, KNOCKAMUNNION, STRANAHELY AND LEITRIM Map S9995 Glen of Imaal forests – 5 entrances on rds from Seskin Bridge & Ballinclea to Knickeen Ford. Forest walks.

KNOCKSINK Map O2117 1m on Dublin side of Enniskerry village. Car park, picnic place, forest walks.

LACKEN Map O1917 On by-rd S off Enniskerry/Glencree N rd 2m from Enniskerry. Forest walks.

LUGNAGROAGH Map N9507 S of Pollaphuca Bridge on Valleymont rd. Car park, picnic place, forest walk, viewing point.

MUCKLAGH Map T0883 5m NW of Aughrim on Aughrim/Aughvannagh rd. Take the by-rd to river. Car park, picnic place, forest walks, viewing points.

REDCROSS Map T2580 ½m N of Barranisky on Barranisky/Redcross rd. Car park, picnic place, forest walk, scenic view.

TROOPERSTOWN Map T1696 1m NE of Laragh on T61. Car park, picnic place, forest walks.

WOODENBOLEY Map N9301 Through Hollywood Glens on Hollywood/Donard rd. Car park, picnic place, forest walk.

Racecourses

Please refer to the Ordnance Survey Maps (½" series) for racecourse locations.

Co Cork
Mallow
Map W5698

Co Down
Downpatrick
Map J4742
Down Royal
Map J2061

Co Dublin
Leopardstown
Map O2125
Phoenix Park
Map O1037

Co Galway
Galway
Map M2925

Co Kerry
Killarney

Map V9589
Listowel
Map Q9833
Tralee
Map Q8414

Co Kildare
Curragh
Map N7713
Naas
Map N8919
Punchestown
Map N9215

Co Kilkenny
Gowran Park
Map S6252

Co Limerick
Limerick
Map R5655

Limerick Junction
Map R8639

Co Louth
Dundalk
Map J0507

Co Mayo
Ballinrobe
Map M1765

Co Meath
Bellewstown
Map O0967
Fairyhouse
Map N0248
Navan
Map N8767

Co Roscommon
Roscommon
Map M8565

Co Sligo
Sligo
Map G7035

Co Tipperary
Clonmel
Map S2022
Thurles
Map S1258

Co Waterford
Tramore
Map S5801

Co Westmeath
Kilbeggan
Map N3337

Co Wexford
Wexford
Map T0322

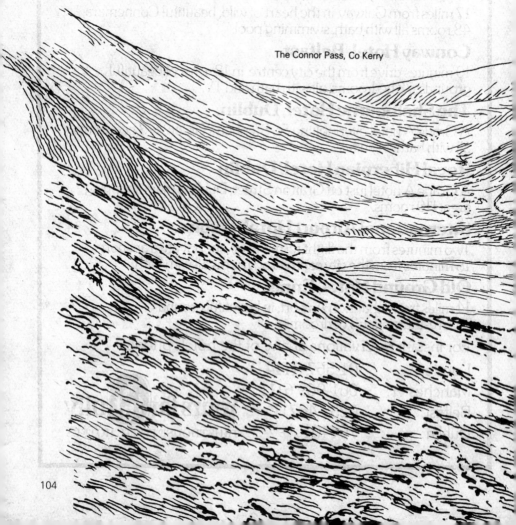

The Connor Pass, Co Kerry

Greyhound Tracks

Belfast
Map 15J37
Celtic Park
Dunmore Stadium

Co Cork
Cork
Map 3W67
Youghal
Map 4X17

Co Donegal
Lifford
Map 14H39

Co Dublin
Dublin
Map 9O13

Harolds Cross
Shelbourne Park

Co Galway
Galway
Map 7M22

Co Kerry
Tralee
Map 2Q81

Co Kildare
Newbridge
Map 9N81

Co Kilkenny
Kilkenny
Map 8S55

Co Limerick
Limerick
Map 7R55

Co Longford
Longford
Map 12N17

Co Louth
Dundalk
Map 13J00

Co Meath
Navan
Map 13N86

Co Tipperary
Thurles

Map 8S15

Co Tyrone
Dungannon
Map 14H76

Co Waterford
Waterford
Map 5S61

Co Westmeath
Mullingar
Map 12N45

Co Wexford
Enniscorthy
Map 5S93

Football Grounds

Co Antrim
Ballymena — Showgrounds
Map 15D10
Larne — Inver Park
Map 15D30

Co Armagh
Lurgan — Mournview Park
Map 15J05
Portadown — Shamrock Park
Map 15J05

Belfast — Seaview
Map 15J37 — Solitude
The Oval
Windsor Park

Co Cork
Cork — Flower Lodge
Map 3W67

Co Donegal
Ballybofey — Finn Park
Map 16H19

Co Down
Ballyskeagh — Distillery
Map 15J58
Bangor — Clandeboye Park
Map 15J47
Newtownards — Castlereagh Park
Map 15J47

Co Dublin
Dublin — Belfield Park
Map 9O13 — Dalymount Park
Glenmalure Park
Richmond Park
Tolka Park

Co Galway
Galway — Terryland Park
Map 7M22

Co Limerick
Limerick — Markets Field
Map 7R55

Co Londonderry
Coleraine — Showgrounds
Map 14C83

Co Louth
Drogheda — Lourdes Stadium
Map 13O07
Dundalk — Oriel Park
Map 13J00

Co Sligo
Sligo — Showgrounds
Map 11G63

Co Tipperary
Thurles — Thurles Park
Map 8S15

Co Waterford
Waterford — Kilcohan Park
Map 5S61

Co Westmeath
Athlone — St Mel's Park
Map 12N04

Rugby Grounds

Co Armagh
Portadown — Chambers Park
Map 15J05

Co Antrim
Ballymena — Eton Park
Map 15D10 — Academy Sports
Mallusk — Ground
Map 15D28 — Hydepark

Belfast — CIYMS
Map 15J37 — Collegians
Gibson Park
North of Ireland
Rugby FC
Queens
Ravenhill Park
Shanes Park

Co Cork
Cork — Musgrave Park
Map 3W67

Co Down
Bangor — Uprichard Park
Map 15J58
Newtownards — Ards
Map 15J47

Co Dublin
Dublin — Lansdowne Park
Map 9O13

Co Limerick
Limerick — Thomond Park
Map 7R55

Co Tyrone
Dungannon — Stevenson Park
Map 14H76

Ladies' View, Co Kerry

Castles, Houses and Gardens

The Municipal Museum, Cork

All entries have a grid reference and can be located on the atlas (from page 192), the *Touring Map of Ireland* or in the *Irish Members' Handbook*. The abbreviation NM indicates a National Monument, NT preserved by the National Trust and HM denotes an Historic Monument. *NOTE* You are advised to verify the opening times and admission fees before undertaking a journey as these may be revised without notice.

Co Antrim

ANTRIM Map D1080 North of the town in grounds of District Council Offices in Steeple townland. Site of important early monastery, marked by complete round tower 93ft high. (HM)

BALLYCASTLE, *Bonamargy Friary* Map D1040 East of the town at golf course. Extensive remains of Franciscan friary, founded about 1500 with gatehouse, church and remains of cloister. (HM)

BALLYLUMFORD DOLMEN Map D4000 on B90 on NW tip of Island Magee, situated in front garden of a house. Remains of a Neolithic burial monument 4000 to 5000 years old. (HM)

CAUSEWAY COAST LION PARK (6m E of Coleraine near Ballymoney) Map C9030 Open Mar and then weekends until Jun, daily Jun–Sep.

CRANFIELD CHURCH (At Churchtown Point, 3½m SW of Randalstown) Map J0080 Ruins of medieval parish church. (HM)

CULLYBACKEY, *Arthur House* (4m NW of Ballymena) Map D0505 Farmhouse. Open Apr–Sep, daily (except Tue) 2–6pm. Admission 25p, children 10p. (NT)

DALWAY'S BAWN Map J4090 On B90. 17th–C fortified enclosure. (HM)

DUNLUCE CASTLE (3m E of Portrush) Map C9040 Open Apr–Sep, weekdays 10am–6pm, Sun 2–6pm; Oct–Mar, Tue–Sat 10am–4pm, Sun 2–4pm. Admission: adults and unaccompanied children 30p, accompanied children 10p. (HM)

KINBANE CASTLE (3m WNW of Ballycastle) Map D0040 Ruins of 16th–C castle on chalk cliffs. (HM)

LARNE, *Olderfleet Castle* Map D4000 On Curran Point. Ruin of 16th–C tower. (HM)

SHANE'S CASTLE (3m NW of Antrim) Map J1080 Area includes Nature Reserve and railway. Open Apr, May & Sep, Sun & Bank Hols 12–6pm, Jun, Sat, Sun & Bank Hols 12–6pm, Jul & Aug, Wed, Sat, Sun & Bank Hols 12–6pm. Reserve open by arrangement in winter. Accessible by Lodge on A6, ½m out of Antrim.

TEMPLEPATRICK, *Templetown Mausoleum* Map J2080. In graveyard of Castle Upton. Open daily during daylight hours. Admission free. (NT)

Co Armagh

ARDRESS HOUSE (7m W of Portadown) Map H9090 17th–C house. Open Apr–Sep, daily (except Fri, but open Good Fri) 2–6pm. Admission 40p, children 20p. (NT)

ARMAGH COUNTY MUSEUM Map H8040 Open Mon–Sat 10am–5pm. Closed Sun & certain Bank Hols. Admission free.

ARMAGH PLANETARIUM ASTRONOMY CENTRE Map H8040 Open Mon–Sat 2–4.45pm, with star shows in the Planetarium each Sat throughout the year 3–4pm & every afternoon in Jul–Aug. For further details ☎ Armagh 523689.

ARMAGH FRIARY Map H8040 on SE edge of town. Ruined church of Franciscan Friary founded 1263–64. ((HM) Guide card available.

DERRYMORE HOUSE (1½m NW of Newry) Map J0020 18th–C Manor House. Open by appointment only ☎ Saintfield 510721. (NT)

NAVAN FORT Map H8040 (2m W of Armagh city) This huge earthwork enclosure (18 acres) marks the site of *Emhain Mhacha*, seat of the Kings of Ulster, prominent in heroic literature and legend. Extensively excavated in recent years. (HM)

KILLEVY CHURCHES Map J0020 3m S of Camlough on the lower East slopes of Slieve Gullion. Remains of two churches stand in a graveyard on the site of one of Ireland's most important early nunneries. (HM)

KILNASAGGART INSCRIBED STONE Map J0010 (1m S of Jonesborough) 7th–C tall granite pillar. (HM)

MOYRY CASTLE Map J0010 (7m S of Newry) Tall, square tower on rocky height. (HM)

Belfast

BELFAST, *Ulster Museum* Map J3070 One of the major museums and art galleries in Europe. Situated in the Botanic Gardens. Lectures, concerts and films in winter. Open weekdays 10am–4.50pm, Sun 2.30–5.20pm. Admission free.

BELFAST ZOOLOGICAL GARDENS (6m NW of Belfast) Map J3080 Open Mar–Oct 10am–5pm, Nov–Feb 10am–3.30pm only. Admission 60p, children 35p.

CARRICKFERGUS CASTLE (10m NE of Belfast on N shore of Belfast Lough) Map J4080 Open Apr–Sep weekdays 10am–6pm, Sun 2–6pm; Oct–Mar closes at 4pm. Admission: adults and unaccompanied children 35p, accompanied children 5–16 years 10p. (HM) Guide book and card available.

Co Carlow

BALLYMOON CASTLE (2m E of Muine Bheag) Map S7060 Accessible at reasonable times. Admission free. (NM)

Co Clare

BUNRATTY CASTLE Map R4060 Medieval banquet twice nightly. Admission £11.90. Bunratty Folk Park lies in the grounds behind the castle. Open daily 9.30am–5.30pm. Admission (incl. Castle and Folk Park) £1, children 50p.

QUIN, *Knappogue Castle* (5m SE of Ennis) Map R4070 Medieval banquet twice nightly. Admission £11.90, May–Oct. Open daily 9.30am–5.30pm. Admission 80p, children 40p.

Co Cork

BANTRY HOUSE Map V9040 Georgian mansion. Open 15 Feb–15 Dec. House and gardens weekdays 10am–6pm. Admission to house and grounds £1, children under 12 years half price; grounds only 20p.

BLARNEY CASTLE (6m NW of Cork) Map W6070 Open May Mon–Sat 9am–7pm; Jun–Jul 9am–8.30pm; Aug 9am–7.30pm; Sep 9am–6.30pm; Oct–Apr 9am–sunset. Sun 9am–5.30pm all year. Admission 60p, children 20p, includes admission to curious and picturesque Rock Close.

CORK MUSEUM, *Fitzgerald's Park* Map W6070 Open Jun–Aug weekdays 11am–1pm & 2.15–6pm (Wed 8pm); Sep–May weekdays 11am–1pm & 2.15–5pm; Sat all year 11.30am–1pm.

GARNISH ISLAND (*Ilnacullin*) (2m S of Glengarriff by boat) Map V9050. The Island is open Mar–Oct weekdays 10am–5.30pm; Sun & Church Holy Days 1–6pm; Bank Hols 10am–6pm. Admission 60p, children 25p. Boat charge about £1 per head.

GLANMIRE, *Riverstown House* (4m NE of Cork) Map W7070 Open May–20 Sep, Thu–Sun 2–6pm; Admission 50p. Tours any time by appointment. ☎ (021) 821205.

YOUGHAL, *Clock Gate* (museum) Map X1070 Open 31 May–Sep, Mon–Sat 11am–1pm & 2–7pm. Admission 10p.

Co Donegal

CASHEL, *Doe Castle* (10m NW of Kilmacrenan) Map C0030 Open at all reasonable times. Admission free. (NM)

DONEGAL CASTLE Map G9070 Open at all reasonable times. Admission free. (NM)

GLENCOLUMBKILLE FOLK MUSEUM Map G5080 1m W of the village. Accessible from May–1 Oct. Guided admission 20p. Grianan of Aileach (10m NW of Londonderry) Map C3010 Cashel (stone fort). Accessible at all reasonable times. Admission free. (NM)

Co Down

ARDGLASS, *Jordan's Castle* Map J5030 15th–C tower house. Open weekdays (except Mon) 10am–6pm, Sun 2–6pm, from Oct–Mar, Sat 10am–4pm, Sun 2–4pm. Admission: adults and unaccompanied children 15p, accompanied children 5p. (HM)

AUDLEY'S CASTLE (1½m W of Portaferry by S shore of Strangford Lough) Map J5050. (HM)

CLOUGH Map J4040 Norman earthwork castle with motte (mound) and bailey (enclosure) and remains of stone tower. (NT & HM)

DRUMENA (2m SW of Castlewellan) Map J3030 Good example of circular stone 'cashel', farmstead enclosure, of early Christian times with accessible souterrain (underground stonebuilt passage) probably used for taking refuge. (HM)

DUNDRUM CASTLE (4m N of Newcastle) Map J4030 12th–C stronghold. Open Apr–Sep weekdays (except Mon) 10am–6pm, Sun 2–6pm; Oct–Mar closes at 4pm. Admission free. Car Park. Guide card available. (HM)

GREEN CASTLE (5m SW of Kilkeel) Map J2010 13th–C Royal Castle. Open Apr–Sep, Tue–Sat 10am–6pm, Sun 2–6pm; Oct–Mar, Sat 10am–4pm, Sun 2–4pm. Admission free. (HM)

GREY ABBEY (½m W of Ballywalter) Map J5060 Cistercian Abbey founded in 1193. Extensive remains of church and cloister. Open Apr–Sep weekdays 10am–6pm, Sun 2–6pm; Oct–Mar weekdays 10am–4pm, Sun 2–4pm; closed Mon. Admission: adults and unaccompanied children 15p, accompanied children 5p. Guide card available. (HM)

HILLSBROROUGH FORT Map J2050 Artillery fort built in the mid–17th C. Open all year Mon–Sat 10am–6pm, Sun 2–6pm summer, Mon–Sat 10am–4pm, Sun 2–4pm winter closed Tue. Admission free. Guide card available. (HM)

HOLYWOOD, *Ulster Folk and Transport Museum* (7m NE of Belfast, S of Belfast Lough) Map J4080 Cultra Manor. The Transport Museum is in a 40-acre estate adjacent to the Folk Museum. Open May–Sep, Mon–Sat 11am–7pm, Sun 2–7pm; May–Jun, Tue & Wed 11am–9pm; Oct–Apr, Mon–Sat 11am–5pm, Sun 2–5pm. Admission 30p, children and pensioners 10p. Yearly family ticket £2.

INCH ABBEY Map J4040 On the River Quoile, North of Downpatrick. Beautifully situated remains of Cistercian Abbey, founded in 1187–88 with ruined church and cloister in large earthwork enclosure. (HM)

KILCLIEF CASTLE (On A2 3m S of Stagford) Map J5040 15-C tower house built by John Cely, Bishop of Down as a manorial residence. Open Jul & Aug, Tue–Sat 10am–6pm, Sun 2–6pm; Apr, May, Jun & Sep, Sat 10am–6pm, Sun & Wed 2–6pm. Admission: 15p, accompanied children and pensioners 5p. (HM)

LOUGHINISLAND CHURCHES (4m W of Downpatrick) Map J4040 This island graveyard is reached by a causeway. The ruins of three churches cluster on the hill overlooking the lake. (HM)

MAGHERA CHURCH (3m N of Newcastle) Map J3030 The stump of a round tower survives from the early monastery with a ruined 13th-C church nearby. (HM)

MILLISLE, *Ballycopeland Windmill* (3m S of Donaghadee) Map J5070 The only complete windmill in Co Down. Build in late 18th C and used until 1915. Open Apr–Oct, Tue–Sat 10am–6pm, Sun 2–6pm; Nov–Mar, Sat 10am–4pm, Sun 2–4pm. Admission: adults and unaccompanied children 15p, accompanied children 5–16 years old 5p. Guide book and card available. (HM)

MOUNT STEWART HOUSE, *Gardens and Temple of the Winds* (5m SE of Newtownards on N side of A20) Map J5060 Open Apr–Sep daily (except Fri, but open Good Fri) 2–6pm, Gardens open to end of Oct 12–6pm. Admission: House, Gardens & Temple 90p, Gardens & Temple 60p. (NT)

NARROW WATER CASTLE (1m NW of Warrenpoint) Map J1010 Open Apr–Oct, Tue–Sat 10am–6pm. Admission: adults and unaccompanied children 15p, accompanied children 5p. (HM)

ROWALLANE (11m SE of Belfast on A7) Map J4050 50-acre garden. Open all the year, Mon–Fri 9am–6pm, Sat & Sun 2–6pm. On fine evenings in May & Jun open 7–9pm. Admission: Apr, May & Jun 60p, children 30p; Jul & Mar 25p, children 10p. (NT)

STRANGFORD, *Castle Ward* (7m NE of Downpatrick) Map J5040 Open Apr–Sep daily (except Fri) 2–6pm. Admission: 75p, children 35p. Car park 50p. Grounds and wildfowl collection open all year from dawn to dusk. Admission free. (NT)

STRANGFORD, *Strangford Castle* Map J5040 A much-altered, fortified 16th-C town house with a small tower. Open Jul–Aug, Tue–Sat 10am–6pm, Sun 2–6pm; Apr, May, Jun & Sep 10am–6pm, Sun 2–6pm. Admission 15p, accompanied children and pensioners 5p. Guide card available. (HM)

STRUELL WELLS (1m W of Downpatrick) Map J4040 A ruined chapel with drinking and eye wells and men's and women's bath-houses nearby. (HM)

Co Dublin

DUBLIN CASTLE Map 01030 State apartments open Mon–Fri 10am–12.15pm & 2–5pm, Sat & Sun 2–5pm, Admission 30p (children and students 15p). Guided tour of Heraldic Museum Open Mon–Fri 9.45am–1pm & 2.15–4.45pm. Admission free. The chapel is open Mon–Fri 8.30–12pm & 2.30–5.45pm; Sat 2–5pm. Opening times subject to alteration (especially the State Apartments).

DUBLIN, *Civic Museum* Map 01030 Open Tue–Sat 10am–6pm; Sun 11am–2pm.

DUBLIN, *Guinness Museum* Map 01030 For free

admission contact the Curator ☎ 756071 ext 114.

DUBLIN, *Kilmainham Jail* (Museum) Map 01030 Open Sun only 3–5pm. Admission 40p, children 20p.

Marsh's Library, Dublin

DUBLIN, *Marsh's Library* Map 01030 Open Mon 2–4pm, Wed, Thu & Fri 10.30am–12.30pm & 2–4pm; Sat 10.30am–12.30pm. Admission free.

DUBLIN, *National Botanic Gardens, Glasnevin* Map 01030 Open all the year weekdays 9am–6pm; Sun 11am–6pm; in summer; 10am–4.30pm; Sun 11am–4.30pm; in winter. Greenhouses not open before 2pm Sun. Admission free. Closed 25 Dec.

DUBLIN TRINITY COLLEGE, *Old Library* Map 01030 Open Mon–Fri 10am–1pm. Closed Bank Hols.

DUBLIN, *Zoological Gardens, Phoenix Park* Map 01030 Open weekdays 9.30am–6pm, Sun 12–6pm. Closes at sunset in winter.

DUN LAOGHAIRE, *James Joyce Tower, Sandycove* Map 02020 Open May–Sep, Mon–Sat 10am–1pm & 2–5.15pm, Sun 2.30–6pm. Admission 20p, students 15p, children 10p. Special winter openings may be arranged by phone ☎ (01)808571.

FINGLAS, *Dunsoghly* (4m NW of Dublin) Map 01030 Accessible at reasonable times. Apply to caretaker at nearby cottage. Admission free. (NM)

HOWTH CASTLE DEMESNE (10m NE of Dublin) Map 02030 Open daily throughout the year 8am–sunset (except Christmas Day). Admission Apr–Jun 25p, children 10p. Season ticket 50p. Jul–Mar admission free.

MALAHIDE, *Malahide Castle* (9m N of Dublin) Map 02040 Home of the Talbot family from the 12th-C until 1973, the castle now houses a National Portrait Gallery and a collection of Irish period furniture. Open all year Mon–Sun 10am–4pm. Admission 80p, children 35p. Reduction for parties.

Co Fermanagh

BELLEEK POTTERY Map G9050 Open Mon–Fri 10.15am–4.15pm. Tours at half-hourly intervals. Admission free.

CASTLECOOLE (1½m SE of Enniskillen) Map H2040 Open Apr–Sep daily (except Fri, but open Good Fri) 2–6pm. Admission 70p, children 35p. (NT)

DEVENISH ISLAND (2m N of Enniskillen) Map

H2040 In the S of Lower Lough Erne. Churches, Abbey and round tower. Access to the island by signalling the Island Custodian from mainland boathouse, which is signposted on E shores of Lower Lough Erne, he will ferry passengers. Boats can also be hired. Open Apr–Sep, Tue–Sat 10am–6pm, Sun 2–6pm; Oct–Mar, Tue–Sat 10am–6pm, Sun 2–4pm. Ferry charges: adults 10p, children 5p. Guide card available. (HM)

ENNISKILLEN CASTLE Map H2040 Houses the County and Regimental Museums. The tower dates from the 16thC and was remodelled as a military barracks in the 18thC. Guide card available. (HM)

FLORENCE COURT (7m SW of Enniskillen) Map H1030 18th-C mansion. Open from Apr–Sep daily (except Fri, but open Good Fri) 2–6pm. Admission 55p, children 25p. (NT)

LISNASKEA, *Castle Balfour* (11m SE of Enniskillen) Map H3030 Dates from 1618. T-plan house with vaulted rooms. Open at all times. Admission free. (HM)

MONEA CASTLE (6m NW of Enniskillen) Map H1040 Plantation castle dating from 1618. Guide card available. (HM)

TULLY CASTLE Map H1050 On W shore of Lower Lough Erne, 3m N of Derrygonnelly. Substantial remains of T-shaped stronghouse and enclosing bawn, built by Sir John Hume 1618–19. (HM)

WHITE ISLAND CHURCH Map H1060 In Castle Archdale Bay. No regular ferry service but a boat is often available from Castle Archdale Forest Park. Small ruined church of about 1200AD on early monastic site, with famous carved stone figures. (HM)

Co Galway

THOOR BALLYLEE (11m SE of Kinvarra) Map M4000 De Burge tower house, which was a source of inspiration to the poet, Yeats. Open 14 Mar–Oct 10am–6pm, Jul–Aug 9am–9pm. Adults 30p, students and large groups 25p, children 10p & 5p. Enquiries Miss F MacNally, ☎ Peterswell 8. Sound guide. Tea rooms.

Co Kerry

CAHERDANIEL, *Derrynane House* Map V5050 Open May–Sep 10am–1pm & 2–7.30pm; Oct–Apr 2–5pm. Admission 30p, children 10p. (NM)

KILLARNEY NATIONAL PARK Map V9090 Admission free. Opening hours for private cars, May–Aug 9am–9pm. Closing at 8pm in Apr, Sep, Oct & 5pm Nov–Mar. Pedestrians and cyclists have 24-hour access to the Park. The National Park comprising 20,254 acres in all is centered on the Bourne Vincent Memorial Park (or the Muckross Estate) some 3m S of Killarney. Entrance via Muckross Abbey and the main gate. Cars admitted to the car park at Muckross House (½ mile away). In recent years extensive areas have been acquired near Killarney with entrances at Kings Bridge, (near Cathedral) and Ross Castle.

MUCKROSS HOUSE (3m S of Killarney) Map V9090 Open Etr–Jun, Sep–Oct 10am–7pm; Jul–Aug 9am–9pm daily; Nov–Etr 11am–5pm daily except Mon. Houses Museum of Kerry Folklife, also traditional craftworkers. Craft shop. Beautiful demesne and gardens free. Special car entrance to car park at rear of house. Admission to house: adults 70p, children (accompanied by adult) 30p. Reductions for groups of 20.

STAIGUE FORT (5m SW of Caherdaniel) Map V6060 Cashel (stone fort). (NM)

Co Kildare

CELBRIDGE, *Castletown House* (14m W of Dublin) Map N9030 Open Apr–Sep daily except Tue 11am–6pm. Rest of year Sun 2–5pm. Admission 70p (children and students 30p)

KILDARE, *Japanese Gardens, Horse Museum* (1m SE of Kildare) Map N7010 Open Etr–Oct weekdays 10.30am–5.30pm (closed 1–2pm) Sun 2–5.30pm. Admission 50p, children 20p.

MAYNOOTH CASTLE (15m W of Dublin) Map N9030 Access by obtaining keys from caretaker who lives opposite castle. (NM)

ROBERTSTOWN, *Falconry of Ireland* Map N7020 Open all year from 11am. Admission 80p, children 30p.

Co Kilkenny

KILKENNY DESIGN WORKSHOPS Map S5050 Exhibition shop. Open Mon–Fri 9am–6pm, Sat 10am–6pm, Sun 10am–6pm. Also at Nassau St, Dublin, open Mon–Sat 9am–6pm. Admission free.

KILKENNY CASTLE Map S5050 Open Jun–Sep weekdays 10.30am–6.30pm, Sun 2–7pm. Off season Tue–Sat 11am–1pm, 2–4pm, Sun 2–4pm. Admission 30p, children 10p (includes guided tour).

KILKENNY, *Rothe House Museum* Map S5050 Open Mon–Sat 10.30am–12.30pm & 3–5pm, (Sun 3–5pm) Apr–end of Oct; Nov–Mar: Mon, Fri, Sat & Sun 3–5pm. Admission 30p, students 20p, children 10p.

Co Laois

ABBEYLEIX HOUSE GARDENS (9m S of Port Laoise) Map S4080 The gardens open daily from Etr–Sep. Admission 45p, children 25p. Free car park. Shop & cafe.

STRADBALLY, *Traction Engine Museum* Map S5090 Open by appointment only. ☏ (0502) 25136. Admission 30p, children 10p. Special rates for groups.

Co Limerick

ADARE MANOR Map R4040 Open May–end of Sep, Mon–Fri 10am–5.30pm, Sun 2–5.30pm, closed Sat. Also open Apr–Oct 10.30am–4pm, Sun 2–4.30pm, closed Sat. Admission to manor and grounds 60p, children 6–12 30p. Grounds only 30p, children 10p. Children under 6 years not admitted.

LIMERICK ART GALLERY Map R5050 Open Mon–Fri 10am–1am & 2.30–7pm, Sat 10am–1pm. Admission free.

Co Londonderry

BANAGHER (2m SSW of Dungiven) Map C6000 Impressive ruin of church built about 1100 AD and altered a century later, with saint's tomb, cross and base of tower (the vicar's house) nearby. (HM)

BELLAGHY BAWN (7m SE of Maghera) Map H9090 Farm house. Open by previous appointment only ☏ Bellaghy 217. Admission free. No parking.

BISHOP'S VIEW *AA Viewpoint* Map C7030 Situated 800ft above sea level 8 miles W of Coleraine.

DOWNHILL, *Mussenden Temple Bishop's Gate and Black Glen* (9m NW of Coleraine) Map C7030 Open from Apr–end Sep daily (except Fri, but open Good Fri) 2–6pm. Admission free. Black Glen open all the year, from dawn to dusk. Admission free. Entrance by Bishop's Gate of Downhill Castle. (NT)

DUNGIVEN Map C6000 Priory, SE of town overlooking River Roe, an early monastery was followed by a priory of Augustinian canons. Extensive remains of church of many periods with fine late 15th-C tomb in chancel. Church open at all times, chancel only when caretaker in attendance. (HN) Guide card available.

HEZLETT HOUSE Map C7635 (4m W Coleraine on Coleraine/Downhill coast road). Open Apr–end Sep daily (except Fri, but open Good Fri) 2–6pm. Admission 40p, children 20p.

LIMAVADY, *Rough Fort* (1m W of Limavady) Map 6020 Celtic Rath. Open at all times. Admission free. (NT)

LONDONDERRY, *City Walls* Map C4010 Finest surviving city walls in Ireland. Accessible free of charge from various points. (HM)

MAGHERA Map C8000 Church at E approach to the town. Important early monastery, later cathedral and finally parish church. The much-altered church has a magnificent decorated door under the west tower. Cross-carved stone marks founder's grave west of the church. Key to graveyard from nearby house. (HM)

MOUNT SANDEL Map C8030 Mound on east bank of River Bann south of Coleraine possibly a fort of early Christian date, remodelled at a later period. (HM)

SPRINGHILL (5m NE of Cookstown on B18) Map H8080 17th-C manor house. Open from Apr–Sep daily (except Fri, but open Good Fri) 2–6pm. Admission 50p, children 25p. (NT)

Co Louth

CARLINGFORD, *King John's Castle* Map J1010 Accessible at all reasonable times. Caretaker: Mr B Fretwell, Castlehill. (NM)

The Great Cross of Drumcliff, Co Sligo

Co Mayo

WESTPORT ZOO PARK AND HOUSE Map L9080 Open Apr–7 Oct daily 2–5pm. Open Jun–Aug daily 10.30am–6pm. Admission to zoo park and house £1.75, children 50p. Parties of 20 and over: adults £1, children 50p.

Co Offaly

BIRR CASTLE *Demesne* Map N0000 Gardens, arboretum and telescope museum open all year 10am–1pm & 2–6pm (or dusk if earlier in winter). Admission 60p, children 30p. The 17th-C castle is not shown.

Co Roscommon

CASTLEREA, *Clonalis House* Map M6080 Open May, Jun & Sep 1–3pm Sat, Sun & Mon; Jul & Aug daily except Tue 2–6pm. Admission 50p, children 25p. Reductions for parties over 20.

BOSCOMMON CASTLE Map M8060 Open at all reasonable times. Admission free. (NM)

Co Sligo

DRUMCLIFF, *Lissadell House* (9m NW of Sligo) Map G6040 Open May–Sep daily (except Sun). 2.30–5.15pm. Admission 50p.

Co Tipperary

CAHIR CASTLE (10m W of Clonmel) Map S0020 Open mid Jun–Sep daily 10am–7pm (closed 1–2pm). Off season Mon. Tue–Sat 10am–7pm (closed 1–2pm) Sun 2–5pm. Admission 30p, children 10p, includes guided tour.

CARRICK-ON-SUIR, *Ormonde Castle* Map S4020 Open at all reasonable times; apply to resident caretaker. Admission free. (NM)

GOOLDS CROSS, *Longfield House* (6m NW of Cashel) Map S0040 Open Apr–Sep and by arrangement Sun 2–6pm. Admission 30p, children 15p.

LOUGHMORE CASTLE (6m N of Thurles) Map S1060 The castle may be seen at all reasonable times. Admission free.

NENAGH CASTLE Map R8070 Accessible at all reasonable times. Admission free.

Co Tyrone

ARBOE CROSS (9m E of Cookstown) off B73 Map H9070 May be seen at all times. Admission free. (HM)

BEAGHMORE *Stone Circles and Alignments* (NW Cookstown) Map H6884 Impressive group of prehistoric stone monuments in peat-covered upland. Guide card available. (HM)

CASTLECAULFIELD (13m S of Cookstown) Map H7060 Open 10am–4pm. (HM)

DONAGHMORE CROSS (at W end of Main St) Map H7565 Impressive figure-carved cross marks site of an early monastery. (HM)

HARRY AVERY'S CASTLE (SW of Newtownstewart) Map H3080 Hilltop castle built in 14th or 15thC. (HM)

MOUNTJOY CASTLE (10m SE of Cookstown on western slopes of Lough Meagh) Map H9060. (HM)

MOUNTJOY MELLON HOUSE and *Ulster-American Folk Park* (5m NW of Omagh) Map H4070 Open from May–Aug daily 10.30am–6.30pm; Sep–Apr daily 10.30am–4.30pm. Admission 30p, children 15p. (NT)

STRABANE, *Gray's Printing Press, Main Street* Map H3090 Open Apr–Sep daily (except Thu & Sun) 2–6pm. Admission 30p, children 15p. (NT)

TULLAGHOGE FORT (2m S of Cookstown) Map H8070 Large hilltop earthwork, treeplanted, marks a headquarters and inauguration place of the O'Neills. (HM)

WELLBROOK BEETLING MILL (Situated 2½m W of Cookstown on Omagh Road) Map H7070 Open Apr–Sep daily (except Fri but open Good Fri) 2–6pm. Admission 30p, children 15p. (NT)

Co Waterford

PORTLAW, *Curraghmore* (5m SE of Carrick-on-Suir) Map S4010 The gardens and Shell house are open each Thu & on Bank Hols 1.30–4.30pm. Admission 50p, children 25p.

WATERFORD, *Reginald's Tower* Map S6010 Open 27 Mar–13 Oct, Mon–Fri 9.30am–5.30pm, Sat 9.30am–12.30pm; at other times by appointment only. Admission 10p, children, if accompanied by an adult, admitted free.

Co Westmeath

BELVEDERE HOUSE (4m S of Mullingar) Map N4040 Open Mon–Fri 10am–5pm by prior arrangement with owner (Mr R Beaumont).

TULLYNALLY CASTLE (13m N of Mullingar) Map N4070 Open Jun–Sep, Sun 2.30–6pm. Admission to pleasure gardens 15p, to Victorian kitchens, laundries and museum in the castle courtyard 5p extra. Children half price. Tours of private rooms of the castle by previous arrangement for coach parties only. Contact the Secretary, Tullynally Castle, Castlepollard, Mullingar. ☎ Castlepollard (044) 61159.

Co Wexford

ENNISCORTHY MUSEUM Map S9030 Open from Jun–Sep daily 10am–6pm, Oct–May 2–5.30pm.

REDMONDSTOWN, *Johnstown Castle* (5m SW of Wexford) Map T0010 Grounds and gardens only, open daily 9.30am–5pm all year. Admission free, but admission to nature trails by guide book 20p. Dogs admitted on lead.

SLIEVE COILLTE, *John F Kennedy Park* (8m S of New Ross) Map S7020 Leaflet available 10p. A road leads to a high level view point of Slieve Coillte. Open May–Aug 10am–8pm, Apr–Sep 10am–6.30pm, Oct–Mar 10am–5pm. Parking charges 30p per car, £1.50 per bus.

TACUMSHANE WINDMILL (7m SW of Rosslare Harbour) Map T0000 Accessible at all reasonable times. Caretaker lives nearby.

Co Wicklow

ASHFORD, *Mount Usher Gardens* Map T2090 Open Mon–Sat 10am–5.30pm all the year, Sun 2–5.30pm May–Sep. Admission to garden 75p, children 35p.

DONARD, *Dwyer McAllister Cottage* (18m SW of Tullard) Map S9090 Open at all times. Admission and car park free.

ENNISKERRY, *Powerscourt Gardens* (4m SW of Bray) Map 02010 Gardens are open daily, Etr–Oct 10.30am–5.30pm. Admission 70p, children 45p, under 5 years free. Deer park with waterfall (398ft) open daily 10.30am–8pm all the year. The waterfall gates are 4m S of Enniskerry. Admission 40p, children 5–16 years 20p, under 5 years free.

ABBREVIATIONS AND SYMBOLS

AA   AA office

☎   telephone ⎫

    night ⎬ *unless stated, the name of the exchange is the same as the placename; at hotels the number is usually for reception only*

☎   telephone ⎭

Ec   early closing
Etr   Easter
fr   from
Map   figures and letters which follow give the service atlas page number and the national grid reference (see page 192)
Md   market day
mdnt   midnight

Hotels, guesthouses, restaurants, farmhouses

(see also pages 157, 160 and 165

*   1979 prices
☆   hotel classification (see page 116)
★   hotel classification (see page 115)
(RS)   hotel classification (see page 116)
○   newly opened hotel: no inspection yet made
♣   country-house hotel (see page 116)
×   restaurant classification (see page 157)
⌂   private bathroom/shower with own toilet
☽   night porter
⊞   air conditioning
☒   room(s) set aside for non-smokers
♨   central heating throughout
⊘   no dogs allowed overnight in hotel bedrooms
⌂   garage and/or lock-up accommodation
🚌   no coach parties accepted
⚓   garden over ½ acre
▱   indoor swimming pool
≋   outdoor swimming pool
♿9   9-hole golf course
♿18   18-hole golf course
🎾   tennis court(s)
🐟   fishing
♞   riding stables on premises
    special facilities for children
♿   hotel can accommodate disabled persons
♨   type of cooking
☕   afternoon tea
☕   morning coffee
A   annexe: figure following shows number of bedrooms, etc (see page 116)
alc   à la carte
sB&B   single room including breakfast per person per night
sB&B⌂   single room with private bath/shower and toilet and breakfast per person per night
dB&B   double room (2 persons) including breakfast
dB&B⌂   double room (2 persons) with private bath/shower and toilet and breakfast
CTV   colour television
D   dinner price
L   lunch price
Ld   latest time dinner can be ordered
Lic   licensed
nc....   no children under .... years of age
P   parking (number of cars usually stated)
₽   no parking available on premises
rm   bedrooms in main building
RS   restricted service
S%   service charge levied and included in price
T   temperance
TV   monochrome television

U   unlicensed
W   weekly terms per person
Wine   minimum price of full bottle of wine

Prices

All price information given for the Republic of Ireland is shown in Punts. Prices for Northern Ireland, comprising Counties Antrim, Armagh, Down, Fermanagh, Londonderry and Tyrone, are shown in pounds sterling. The rate of exchange between the two currencies is liable to fluctuate. The following symbols apply:

£ pound sterling   IR£ Punt

Credit cards

The numbered boxes below indicate the credit cards which the hotels and restaurants accept.

1 Access
2 American Express
3 Barclays
4 Carte Blanche
5 Diners
6 Euro

Garages

ᔭ   Breakdown Service available 7 days a week until 23.00hrs
ᔭ   Breakdown Service available Monday–Friday during normal working hours (08.00–18.00hrs) or until time shown
R   repair and servicing facilities during normal working hours or until time shown
⅏   open Sunday
n⅏   no attendance Sunday, but Breakdown Service may be available by telephone

Vehicle franchises

The garage entries throughout the gazetteer include abbreviations of the makes of vehicle for which franchises are held

AC	AC	MG	MG
AM	Aston Martin	Opl	Opel
AR	Alfa Romeo	Peu	Peugeot
Aud	Audi	PF	Polski Fiat
BL	Austin/Morris	Rel	Reliant
BMW	BMW	Ren	Renault
Cit	Citroën	RT	Rover/Triumph
Col	Colt	Sab	Saab
Dat	Datsun	Sko	Skoda
DJ	Daimler/Jaguar	Tal	Talbot (formerly
Fia	Fiat		Chrysler), Hillman,
Frd	Ford		Simca, Sunbeam
Hon	Honda		and Commer
La	Lada	Toy	Toyota
Lnc	Lancia	Vau	Vauxhall/Bedford
Lot	Lotus	Vlo	Volvo/Daf
Maz	Mazda	VW	Volkswagen
MB	Mercedes-Benz		

Camping and caravanning sites

See page 172

AA Home touring information

Attention AA members!

The AA can supply information on all aspects of touring in Ireland and Great Britain on request. All correspondence should be addressed to Dublin or Belfast offices. In addition all AA Service centres carry a comprehensive range of maps and publications of general touring interest.

Routes

Routes for any journey in Ireland are available in two forms. The AA map of **Tours and Throughroutes in Ireland** provides the motorist with recommended throughroutes, together with some suggested tours.
Prepared routes, in text form, meet such individual requirements as country routes, scenic routes, routes for caravans, high loads or routes to avoid bottlenecks. These are also available for use in Great Britain. Also available in Great Britain are **Throughroute maps,** each based on a large town or principal port, which show the AA-recommended routes, including road numbers and mileages, to over 500 destinations.

Touring information

The AA publishes valuable free information for the touring motorist, much of it in booklet or leaflet form. For Ireland, this includes useful town plans and the series of Day Drives based on the four provinces.

London Pilot Service

The AA recommends agents who will provide pilots to drive private cars in, through and round London; users of this service are normally met at certain recognised points on the outskirts of London. AA personnel no longer provide this service. Full details are available at AA offices, reference leaflet LP1.

How to obtain routes and touring information

The map of *Tours and Throughroutes in Ireland* and local leaflets can be obtained from AA Service centres. Other maps and leaflets, and all specially prepared routes are available on application to Belfast or Dublin offices. Written applications for specially prepared routes should be made at least fourteen days before the date of travel, especially at peak holiday times, stating the date of travel and full details of the required route; to avoid delay they should be kept separate from other correspondence. AA Service centres accept urgent requests by telephone.

Signs

All AA-appointed hotels, classified restaurants and camp sites are entitled to display the familiar yellow and black sign. Hotels are

denoted by star classifications in either black, white or red, but in the Republic of Ireland some establishments may still display the old-type AA sign with the word 'Hotel' on the lower panel. Restaurants are denoted by crossed knives and forks, and caravan and camp sites by pennants.

Classification of tourist accommodation

The AA's full-time and highly qualified team of inspectors regularly inspects all AA-recommended tourist accommodation in Ireland and Britain. Establishments are required to meet and constantly maintain minimum standards, details of which, together with the criteria for classification by the AA, are set out in the following booklets obtainable from Erskine and Dublin offices:

HH5   Hotels and The Automobile Association
HH12 Notes on the listing of guesthouses, private hotels, farmhouses and inns
HH62 Notes on caravan and camp site classification

Hotels

Hotels are classified by stars; each classification reflects the provision of facilities and services rather than comparative merit. The range of menus, service and hours of service are appropriate to the classification, although hotels often satisfy several of the requirements of a classification higher than that awarded.

★Good hotels and inns generally of small scale and with modest facilities and furnishings, frequently run by the proprietor himself. All bedrooms with hot and cold water; adequate bath and lavatory arrangements; main meals with a choice of dishes served to residents; menus for residents and meal facilities for non-residents may be limited, especially at weekends.

★★Hotels offering a higher standard of accommodation, more baths and perhaps a few private bathrooms/showers; lavatories on all floors; wider choice of meals (but these may be restricted, especially to non-residents).

★★★Well-appointed hotels with more spacious accommodation and at least 40% of the bedrooms with private bathrooms/

showers; full meal facilities for residents every day of the week, but at weekends service to non-residents may be restricted.

★★★★ Exceptionally well-appointed hotels offering a high standard of comfort and cooking with 80% of the bedrooms providing private bathrooms/showers. At weekends meal service to non-residents may be restricted.

★★★★★ Luxury hotels, offering very high standards of accommodation, service and comfort. All bedrooms have private bathrooms/showers.

⑩ There are no hotels within the 'Approved' category in either Northern Ireland or the Republic of Ireland.

Red stars (RS)
★ The award of red stars is based on a subjective assessment to highlight hotels considered to be of outstanding merit within their normal star ratings, offering something special in the way of welcome and hospitality. The award is normally withdrawn when the hotel undergoes a change of ownership.

White stars
☆ Purpose-built hotels, some motels, motor hotels, motor inns, posthouses and similar establishments which conform to the major requirements for black-star classification. In some cases, porterage, room service and lounge accommodation may be rather restricted. This is offset by the provision of studio-type bedrooms all with either private bath and/or shower, more parking space, and extended meal hours. It is emphasised that white stars are an indication of a type of hotel only.

Country house
🏠 Hotels which display many of the characteristics of a traditional country house, set in secluded rural surroundings. Reception and service facilities may be of a more informal nature than in conventional hotels of similar classification.

Annexes
Annexes may lack some of the amenities available in the hotel building; the exact nature of the accommodation should be checked at the time of reservation. Note the gazetteer only gives information on recommended annexes.

Children
Not all hotels accept children of all ages, and those that do vary in the special facilities provided for them. You are advised to check with a hotel before making reservations.

Disabled persons
Anyone with any form of disability should notify proprietors so that appropriate arrangements can be made to minimise difficulties, particularly in the event of an emergency.

Fire precautions
Northern Ireland The Fire Precautions Act 1971 does not apply in Northern Ireland. The

Fire Services Act 1963 covers those hotels with more than 30 bedrooms which must have a fire certificate issued by the Northern Ireland Fire Authority. Those hotels with under 30 bedrooms have to satisfy the authority that they have adequate exits.

Republic of Ireland AA officials inspect emergency notices, fire-fighting machinery and fire exits although fire safety regulations are a matter for the local authority Fire Services.

Hygiene
AA inspectors, during regular classification visits, inspect kitchens, storerooms etc to ensure that satisfactory standards of cleanliness and hygiene are being maintained.

Licensing regulations
Northern Ireland Public houses are open Monday to Saturday 11.30am to 11pm. They are closed on Sundays. Hotels are able to serve residents seven days a week without restriction. On Sundays non-residents who partake of a meal may be served from 12 noon to 2.30pm and 7pm to 10pm, and on Christmas Day from 12.30pm to 10pm. Children under 18 are not allowed in public houses, neither are they allowed to buy or consume liquor in hotels.

Republic of Ireland The general licensing hours under present legislation are, in winter, Monday to Saturday 10.30am to 11pm and in summer, 10.30am to 11.30pm. On Sundays and St Patrick's Day the times are 12.30pm to 2pm and 4pm to 10pm and there is no service on Christmas Day and Good Friday. In addition in some areas there may be no service for an hour at lunch time at any time of the year.

Meals
Residents may obtain breakfast, lunch and dinner at all AA-appointed hotels but service to non-residents at weekends, and to a lesser extent at lunch, may be restricted in all but five-star establishments.

Seeking to maintain a balance between the high cost of staff and an acceptable price to consumers some hotels have introduced an element of self-service at some meals, particularly for breakfast and at weekends.

Prices
Prices should be checked before booking as they are likely to fluctuate significantly during the currency of this guide. The effects of inflation, possible variations in the rate of VAT and other factors may influence prices over the next two years. Published prices, which have been provided by the proprietors in good faith, must therefore be accepted as indications rather than firm estimates.

Charges should be verified at the time of booking as they vary appreciably according to the time of year. There may also be an increase at public holidays and for other special events.

Hotel prices are for bed and breakfast (which includes a full breakfast unless otherwise stated), and the minimum and maximum rates for a single room (one person) and a double room (two persons). In some hotels only continental breakfast is offered and this is highlighted in the gazetteer. Minimum and maximum table d'hôte prices are given for main meals served in hotel dining rooms and restaurants. Where an à la carte menu is available, the average price of a three-course dinner and lunch is shown. In cases where establishments offer both types of menu, table d'hôte prices are the only ones given, but with an indication that à la carte is also available. Prices include any cover charge. The price of wine quoted is that of the cheapest full bottle.

Guesthouse and farmhouse prices are from minimum (out of season) to maximum (in season) per person per night. Weekly terms vary from full board to bed and breakfast only. This is shown in the text by the symbols L (no lunch) and M (no main meals).

Site charges for camping and caravanning apply to the overnight cost for: one tent or caravan, one car, two adults, one child over 12 years, one child under 12 years; OR one motor caravan, two adults, one child over 12 years, one child under 12 years. These charges are intended to indicate what an average family can expect to pay. If your group contains more or fewer persons you can expect to pay correspondingly more or less for your pitch.

Reports

The AA welcomes comments on establishments. Any criticisms should be brought to the hotel management's notice immediately so that the problem can be dealt with promptly. If a personal approach fails the AA should be informed within a week stating whether or not their name can be disclosed to the hotel, so that an investigation can be made.

Reservations

It is advisable to book early, especially during the holiday season. You should inform the hotel staff at once of any delay or change of plan, since you may be held legally responsible for part of the charge if the room booked cannot be relet.

Some hotels, especially those in short-season holiday centres, do not accept advance bookings for bed and breakfast only; others, particularly in the larger towns, find it necessary to ask for a deposit from chance visitors who are staying for one night only; others charge for dinner, bed and breakfast, whether or not dinner is taken. *En pension* terms are normally offered only for periods of three days or more. Many hotels, particularly at seaside resorts, do not take bookings from midweek to midweek and will only accept period bookings at a full board rate.

In the Republic of Ireland, as part of the registration scheme operated by Bord Failte, establishments must display tariffs; these are usually found in bedrooms, where appropriate, and may also be displayed at reception.

Telephone surcharge

To cover high equipment installation and rental costs a surcharge is usually imposed on telephone calls made through the hotel switchboard. You are advised to ascertain the rate of surcharge prior to placing a call.

Restaurants
Classification

Restaurants are inspected by the AA who classify them by knife-and-fork symbols ranging in number from one to five, reflecting comfort, service and cooking. The basic requirements for a recommendation are a high standard of cooking, prompt and courteous service, a pleasant atmosphere and value for money.

A high standard of cooking and service is expected from restaurants throughout Ireland and Great Britain but differing national and regional tastes and styles are taken into account. Details of AA-classified restaurants in Ireland appear as a special section in this guide which also gives definitions of each classification.

Rosette awards

Each year the AA presents rosette awards to hotels and restaurants where the cooking, wine and service can be particularly recommended. The award can be of one, two, or exceptionally three rosettes.

The rosette symbol is not located against gazetteer entries but on a quick-reference list of establishments awarded one or more rosettes which appears on page 189.

Camping and caravanning sites

The AA inspects camping and caravanning sites throughout Ireland and Great Britain and classifies them with between one and five pennant symbols. Each classification indicates the type of site and its range of facilities.

To provide a qualitative comparison between sites the AA has introduced an assessment taking account of three major aspects of a site: environment, sanitary installations and other equipment.

By combining both the pennant and qualitative schemes, readers are now better able to choose a site best suited to their needs. Details of AA classified sites in Ireland appear in a special section of this guide.

Guesthouses and farmhouses

These establishments are not graded by the AA but they are regularly inspected and have to maintain minimum standards and meet stipulated criteria. Details of AA-listed guesthouses and farmhouses in Ireland appear in this guide.

Picnic sites

The AA inspects and lists picnic sites, details of which appear in this guide. A picnic site is one considered worthy of a visit and must be equipped with litter bins.

Gazetteer

Explanation of entries

Abbreviations and symbols for hotels, restaurants and garages, some of which apply also to guesthouses and farmhouses, are given on page 114.
The additional symbols and abbreviations for guesthouses and farmhouses, and all those applicable to camping and caravanning sites, are given on the first page of each relevant gazetteer section (pages 160, 165 and 172).

Towns

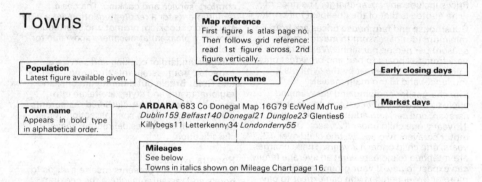

Map reference
First figure is atlas page no. Then follows grid reference: read 1st figure across, 2nd figure vertically.

Population
Latest figure available given.

County name

Early closing days

Town name
Appears in bold type in alphabetical order.

Market days

ARDARA 683 Co Donegal Map 16G79 EcWed MdTue
Dublin159 Belfast140 Donegal21 Dungloe23 Glenties6
Killybegs11 Letterkenny34 *Londonderry55*

Mileages
See below
Towns in italics shown on Mileage Chart page 16.

Atlas
The map references refer to the service atlas starting after page 192. At the beginning of the atlas section there is an explanation of symbols and other markings, and of the Irish National Grid.

Early closing days
The information can be a general guide only. Shops are now empowered to choose their own early closing day and the days shown here may be varied. Some shops close for the full day.

Mileages
Under each placename, mileages are given for the AA-recommended route to a number of other towns. These distances, which are intended as a guide only, are calculated to the nearest mile and are generally measured between the approximate centres of towns. *Italic type* is used for towns which also appear on the mileage chart on pages 16 and 17. The mileages can be used in combination with the mileage chart. For example, to find the distance from Roscommon to Kenmare: under the entry you see Athlone 20 miles, and under the Kenmare entry Killarney 21 miles; on the mileage chart Athlone ⊖ Killarney is 144 miles therefore Roscommon ⊖ Kenmare is 185 miles.

Special notes about mileages and routes are given with the mileage chart on page 16.

Population
The most up-to-date figures are given, where available, after the name of the town in each entry.

Town plans

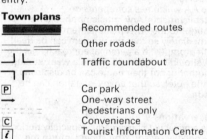

Recommended routes

Other roads

Traffic roundabout

P Car park
→ One-way street
   Pedestrians only
C Convenience
i Tourist Information Centre

The town plans in Northern Ireland are based on the Ordnance Survey maps with the sanction of the Controller of HM Stationery Office. Those of towns in the Republic of Ireland are based on the Ordnance Survey maps by permission of the Government.

Gazetteer location policy
The AA applies the following principle in deciding under which towns establishments will be listed: all establishments within three miles of a larger centre, in particular when part of a continuous urban belt, may be consolidated under that centre unless a county change is involved.

It should be remembered that the atlas highlights all AA-appointed and listed establishments. If the gazetteer does not provide the required information under one location members should refer to the atlas for alternative entries in the vicinity.

Hotels

Hotels are classified by stars ★ (black, red and white). Those with a red star classification bear the symbol (**RS**). For an explanation of these and other hotel symbols, see pages 115–116.

(fictional example)

Prices shown under individual establishments other than camping and caravanning sites are those for 1980, except where marked with an asterisk (*) which signifies 1979 prices. Camping and caravanning prices are those applicable at the time of going to press.

Garages

↳ Breakdown service available seven days a week until 23.00hrs.
↳ Breakdown service available from Monday to Friday during normal working hours (08.00–18.00hrs) or until time shown.

(fictional example)

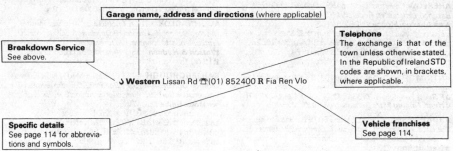

Other establishments

See page 117 for notes on classification and standards of restaurants, camping and caravanning sites, guesthouses and farmhouses, and picnic sites.

See above for a note on prices.

See pages 157, 160 and 172 for examples of gazetteer entries.
See pages 157 and 172 for details of the classification of restaurants and camping and caravanning sites.

Places with AA-listed hotels and garages

See also Restaurants (page 157), Guesthouses (page 160), Farmhouses (page 165), Camping and caravanning sites (page 172).

ABBEYFEALE 1,337 Co Limerick Map3R12 EcWed
*Dublin*162 *Belfast*241 *Cork*65 Newcastle West13
*Killarney*30 Listowel11
★**Leen's** ☎(068)31121
Closed Xmas wk; Lic; 15rm(2⇄🅿) 🚻 CTV 🅿 🚗 Ld8.30pm
👶 ⚲ sB&B IRE5.50–IRE6.50 dB&B IRE10–IRE12
dB&B IRE11–IRE13 LIRE2.75–IRE3 Tea50–75p
High Tea IRE5 D IRE6 Wine IRE3

ABBEYLEIX 1,033 Co Laois Map8S48 EcWed MdSat
*Dublin*62 *Belfast*166 Carlow20 Cashel38 Cork99
Durrow6 *Kilkenny*23 Port Laoise9 Roscrea22 Thurles30
⚲*Abbeyleix Mtr Wks* ☎(0502)31226 R n🚗

ACHILL ISLAND Co Mayo Map1OF&L EcThu *Dublin*191
Achill Sound to Doogort7 Keel10 Mulrany9
★**Achill Head** Keel ☎Keel31
Closed Sep–May; Lic; 24rm4⇄🅿 𝔇 CTV 👷 100P 🚶(hard)
Live music 6nights'wkly 🍷English & French Ld8.30pm
👶 ⚲
★**McDowell's** Doogort ☎Doogort5
Closed 16 Sep–May except Etr; Lic; 10rm(2🅿) CTV 👷
20P Ld8.30pm 👶 ⚲ sB&B IRE4.75–IRE5.50
dB&B IRE9.50–IRE10.50 dB&B🅿 IRE15–IRE17 Tea60p
D IRE5 Wine IRE3 🏠

ADARE 545 Co Limerick Map7R44 EcThu *Dublin*133
*Cork*55 *Killarney*58 Limerick11 Newcastle West15
★★★**Dunraven Arms** ☎(061)94209
Lic; 22rm(15⇄🅿) 𝔇 🚻 CTV 👷 50P 🚗🚶 🐕🐈 🕄 ∩
Ld9.15pm 👶 ⚲ *sB&B IRE9.35–IRE11.35
sB&B⇄🅿 IRE9.85–IRE11.85 dB&B IRE18.70
dB&B⇄🅿 IRE20.70 LIRE3.75 Tea45p D IRE6.85
Wine IRE3.50 Credit cards 🏧②③⑥

AHERLOW Co Tipperary Map4R93 *Dublin*123 *Cork*51
Bansha6 Limerick34 *Tipperary*11
★★★**Aherlow House** ☎(062)56153
Lic; 11⇄🅿 🚻 CTV 👷 100P 🚶 Ld9.15pm 👶 ⚲ S%
sB&B⇄🅿 IRE11–IRE13.50 dB&B⇄🅿 IRE18.50–IRE26
LIRE3.75–IRE4.50 D IRE7–IRE8 Wine IRE4
Credit cards ②③⑤

ANTRIM 7,320 Co Antrim Map15J18 EcWed *Belfast*18
*Armagh*42 *Dublin*116 Lisburn18 *Londonderry*55 Newry50
⚲*F Scott* Fountain St ☎3340 ⚲Temple Patrick32721 R
⚲*Hugh Tipping Mtrs* Randalstown Rd ☎2225

ARDARA 683 Co Donegal Map16G79 EcWed MdTue
*Dublin*159 *Belfast*140 Donegal21 Dunglow23 Glenties6
Killybegs11 Letterkenny34 *Londonderry*55
★**Nesbitt Arms** ☎3
Closed Xmas; Lic; 30rm 🚻 TV 👷🅿 Credit cards 🏧②③

ARDEE 3,096 Co Louth Map13N99 EcThu MdTue
*Dublin*42 Bailieborough21 *Belfast*65 Carrickmacross13
Cavan42 Cork189 Navan21
★**Brophy's** ☎(041)53331
Closed Xmas; Lic; 10rm TV 3P 🚗 Ld7.30pm 👶 ⚲
sB&B IRE6 dB&B IRE11.50 LIRE2.75 Tea75p
High Tea IRE2.50 Wine IRE2

ARDMORE 233 Co Waterford Map4X17 EcThu
*Dublin*143 *Belfast*247 *Cork*40 Dungarvan15 *Waterford*44
Youghal10
★★**Cliff House** ☎(024)41106
Closed Oct–3 Apr; Lic; 21rm 🚻 CTV 🚗🚶 Ld8.30pm 👶
*sB&B IRE7.20–IRE9.80 dB&B IRE14.40–IRE19.60
(Continental breakfast) LIRE4.80 D IRE7.20&alc
Credit cards ②⑧

ARKLOW 6,948 Co Wicklow Map9T27 EcWed
*Dublin*46 *Cork*144 Gorey11 Rosslare Harbour50
★★**Arklow Bay** (Inter-Hotel) ☎(0402) 2289
Telex no.4858
Lic; 28rm(18⇄🅿) 𝔇 🚻 CTV 100P 🚶 🐈 Ld8.30pm 👶

sB&B IRE10.73–IRE12.38 sB&B⇄🅿 IRE12.38–IRE14.03
dB&B IRE19.80–IRE23.10 dB&B⇄🅿 IRE23.10–IRE26.40
LIRE4.40 D IRE7.70 Wine IRE3 Credit cards ②⑥

The Royal School, Armagh

ARMAGH 12,297 Co Armagh Map14H84 EcWed MdTue
*Belfast*40 Banbridge20 Cookstown24 *Dublin*81
*Dundalk*28 Dungannon13 *Enniskillen*52 *Londonderry*70
Lurgan16 Monaghan17 *Omagh*36 Portadown11
⚲*Joshua White Ltd* College St ☎522467 R n🚗 BL

ATHLONE 11,611 Co Westmeath Map12N04 EcThu
MdTue/Sat *Dublin*78 Athenry41 Ballinasloe16
Ballymahon15 *Belfast*141 Birr28 Cavan54 *Cork*136
*Galway*58 Limerick75 Longford29 Loughrea35 Moate10
*Mullingar*32 Roscommon20 *Sligo*73 Tuam42 *Tullamore*25
★★**Royal** ☎2924
Lic; 41rm 19⇄🅿 Lift 𝔇 🚻 CTV 👷 50P 🚶 🍷Irish, English &
French Ld9.15pm 👶 ⚲ 🏠 Credit cards ②④⑥
⚲20.00 *Bigley's* Cornafulla ☎(0902)37103 R 🚗

AUGHNACLOY 732 Co Tyrone Map14H65 EcThu
MdWed *Belfast*58 *Armagh*18 *Dundalk*43 Dungannon10
*Enniskillen*34 Monaghan12 Omagh20
Watson & Hadden 138/144 Moore St ☎281 ☎220
R19.00 Toy

BAILIEBOROUGH 1,293 Co Cavan Map12N69 EcWed
MdMon *Dublin*54 Ardee21 *Belfast*82 Carrickmacross16
Cootehill14 *Cork*185 Kingscourt8 Virginia8
★★**Hotel Bailie** ☎(042)65334
Lic; 21rm(3⇄🅿) 🎿 🚻 CTV 👷 25P Disco Sat
Ld9.30pm 👶 ⚲ sB&B IRE8.80 sB&B⇄🅿 IRE9.90
dB&B IRE15.40 dB&B⇄🅿 IRE16.50 LIRE3.30 Tea82p
High tea IRE6.60 D IRE6.60 Wine IRE3.52 🏠 Credit card ②

BALLINA 6,369 Co Mayo Map10G22 EcThu MdMon
*Dublin*153 Athlone86 Ballycastle16 *Belfast*165 Belmullet40
Boyle40 Castlebar25 *Cork*193 Foxford10 *Galway*73
Longford75 Pontoon12 *Sligo*37 Swinford19 Tobercurry20
★★★**Downhill** ☎(096)21033
Closed Xmas; Lic; 57rm(42⇄🅿) 𝔇 🚻 CTV 👷 100P 🚶
📺(heated) 🚶(hard) 🏓 squash billiards sauna bath Disco Tue
Live music & dancing Mon, Tue & Thu 🍷Irish & French
Ld9pm 👶 ⚲ S% sB&B IRE10–IRE11.50 sB&B⇄🅿 IRE16–
IRE22 dB&B IRE19.50–IRE22.50 dB&B⇄🅿 IRE25–IRE32
LIRE4–IRE5 Tea IRE3–IRE4 High Tea fr IRE4
D IRE7.70–IRE9 Wine IRE5 🏠 Credit cards ②③⑤⑥⑧
⚲*Judges Mtr Wks* "Camelot", Castlehill ☎(096)31397
R 🚗 AR BL Frd Ren Toy Vau Tal
⚲*McAndrews Motors* ☎(096)21444 R n🚗 Aud Maz
MB VW

BALLINASCARTY Co Cork Map3W44 *Dublin*190
Bandon9 *Belfast*293 Clonakilty4 *Cork*29
★★★**Ardnavaha House** ☎(023)49135
Closed Oct–Apr; Lic; 24⇄🅿 🚻 TV 20P 🚗🚶 📺(heated)
🚶(hard) ∩ sauna bath nc3 🍷French Ld8pm 👶 ⚲
*sB&B⇄🅿 IRE13–IRE15 dB&B⇄🅿 IRE20–IRE24
Tea IRE1.75 D IRE7.50 Wine IRE2.50

BALLINASLOE 5,969 Co Galway Map7M83 EcThu
MdSat Dublin94 Athenry25 Athlone16 Belfast157 Birr26
Cork128 Ennis53 Galway42
★★★**Hayden's** Dunloe St (Inter-Hotel) ☎(0905)2347
Closed 3 days Xmas; Lic; 56rm30⇨▥ Lift ⊥ ♚ CTV ⊛ 150P
⊥ ♥English Ld9.15pm ✿ ⊈ ♠ Credit cards ① ② ③ ⑤ ⑥

BALLINROBE 1,272 Co Mayo Map10M16 EcMon
Dublin140 Athlone63 Ballina43 Ballinasloe53 Belfast183
Castlebar18 Claremorris14 Clifden47 Cong7 Cork160,
Galway30 Headford14 Leenane29 Mulrany39 Tuam20
Westport21
★**Lakelands** ☎20
Closed 23–31 Dec; Lic; 18rm(5⇨▥) ▥ CTV 9P ♨
Ld8.30pm ✿ ⊈ sB&B IR£8–IR£9 sB&B⇨▥IR£10
dB&B IR£16–IR£18 dB&B⇨▥IR£21 LIR£3.50
Tea IR£1.20–IR£1.50 High Tea IR£2.50–IR£6.50
D IR£4.75–IR£7.75 ♠

BALLINSKELLIGS Co Kerry Map2V46 Dublin233
Cork107 Limerick110 Killorglin37 Waterville9
★**Sigerson Arms** ☎4
RS Oct–Apr; Lic; 10rm ▥ CTV 80P ⊥ Disco Fri
Live music & dancing Wed ♥ French Ld8.45pm ✿ ⊈
SB&B IR£6.50–IR£7.50 dB&B IR£13–IR£15
High Tea IR£1 80–IR£3.50 D IR£6–IR£7.50 Wine IR£3.55
Credit cards ③ ⑥

BALLINSPITTAL Co Cork Map3W55 EcThu Dublin186
Cork25 Bandon12 Kinsale7
❧**O'Regans** ☎(021)73120 ♠

BALLYBRITTAS Co Laois Map8N51 Dublin44 Cork118
Kildare11 Naas23 Port Laoise9
❧**O'Reilly's** ☎(0502)26138 **R** n♠

BALLYBUNION 1,287 Co Kerry Map6Q84 EcWed
Dublin174 Abbeyfeale20 Belfast253 Cork85 Glin20
Limerick52 Listowel10 Tralee21
★★**Marine** ☎(068)27139 Telex no.8225
Closed 21 Oct–9 Nov; Lic; 20rm ♪ CTV Cabaret Fri & Sat
♥Irish & French Ld10pm ✿ ⊈ sB&B IR£6.60–IR£8.25
dB&B IR£13.20–IR£16.50 Tea IR£1.50 D IR£7 alc
Wine IR£4 ♠

BALLYCASTLE 2,895 Co Antrim Map15D14 EcWed
MdTue Belfast55 Antrim40 Ballymena28 Ballymoney16
Bushmills12 Coleraine19 Cushendall17 Dublin154
Larne43 Londonderry50 Portrush18
❧**J W McCaughan & Sons Ltd** Market St ☎62517 **R**
n♠ BL
Starrs Coleraine Rd ☎62460 **R**20.00 ♠

BALLYCOTTON 389 Co Cork Map4W96 Dublin171
Cork26 Rosslare Harbour120 Youghal20
★★**Bay View** ☎(021)62746
Lic; 23rm(5⇨▥) CTV ⊛ 40P 3▥ ⊥ Ld8.30pm ✿ ⊈ S%
sB&B IR£6.50–IR£7 dB&B IR£12.50–IR£13.50
dB&B⇨▥IR£15–IR£16 LIR£3–IR£4.50 Tea60p–IR£1.50
D IR£6–IR£7 Wine IR£3.20 ♠

BALLYDEHOB 253 Co Cork Map2V03 Cork64
Dublin224 Bantry10 Skibbereen10
★**Audley House** ☎74
Closed Jan & Feb; Lic; 10⇨▥ ▥ CTV 40P ♨ ⊥ ♥Dutch & French Ld10pm ✿ ⊈ S% sB&B⇨▥IR£11
dB&B⇨▥IR£18 LIR£5 Tea IR£1 High Tea IR£3 D IR£6
Wine IR£3.25

BALLYDUFF Co Waterford Map4W99 Dublin148 Cork33
Dungarvan20 Fermoy11 Waterford50
★★**Blackwater Lodge** ☎35
Closed Oct–Jan; Lic; 10⇨▥ ▥ TV ⊛ 50P ♙ squash
sauna bath Ld8pm ✿ ⊈ sB&B⇨▥IR£8–IR£9
dB&B⇨▥IR£15–IR£17 Tea IR£1–IR£1.50
High Tea IR£2–IR£3 D IR£5–IR£8&alc Wine IR£2.50

BALLYGALLY 487 Co Antrim Map15D30 EcMon/Thu
MdTue/Fri Belfast27 Cushendall1 Dublin131
Glenarm8 Larne5

★★★**Ballygally Castle** 274 Coast Rd ☎212
29⇨▥ ♪ ▥ CTV in bedrooms ⊛ 50P ⊥ ♚ (hard) ♙
Disco Sat Live music & dancing Mon Cabaret Sat
♥English & French Ld9.15pm ✿ ⊈ S%
*sB&B⇨▥lfr £16.10 dB&B⇨▥lfr £20.70 Lfr £3.50 Tea £1
High Tea £2.10–£4.45 D £7.90 alc Wine £2.95 ♠ Xmas
Credit cards ① ② ③ ⑤

★★**Coastway** Antrim Coast Rd ☎265
14rm(4⇨▥) ♪ ▥ CTV 100P ⊥ Disco wkly Live music &
dancing wkly Cabaret wkly Ld9.30pm ✿ ⊈ *sB&B£9
sB&B⇨▥£9.50 dB&B£12 dB&B⇨▥£13 L£1.50–£4
Tea50p–£1.15 High Tea£2.25–£5 D£3.50–£7&alc
Wine£2.95 ♠ Xmas Credit cards① ⑤'

BALLYGAR 359 Co Galway Map11M75 Dublin97
Belfast150 Galway40 Roscommon11 Sligo64 Tuam27
❧19.00 **Flynn Bros** ☎(0903)4583 **R**19.00 n♠

BALLYGAWLEY 572 Co Tyrone Map14H65 EcWed
MdTue/Fri Belfast57 Armagh36 Dublin97 Dungannon13
Enniskillen31 Fivemiletown13 Londonderry50
Monaghan16 Omagh16 Portadown30
❧**J Loughran & Sons Ltd** 11 Main St ☎225 **R** ♠ VW

BALLYHAUNIS 1,093 Co Mayo Map11M47 EcThu
MdTue Dublin123 Belfast159 Castlebar28 Roscommon32
Sligo44 Tobercurry22 Tuam20
★**Central** ☎30
Lic; 16rm ▥ ♨ ♥Irish, English & French Ld8.30pm
✿ ⊈ sB&B IR£8.03–IR£9.13 dB&B IR£16.06–IR£18.26
L IR£3–IR£3.50 Tea IR£1 D IR£5–IR£6.50
Wine IR£1.50

BALLYLICKEY Co Cork Map2W05 Dublin217 Bantry4
Belfast320 Cork56 Glengarriff8 Killarney46 Macroom31
★★★▟♨ **Ballylickey House** ☎Bantry71
Closed Oct–Mar; Lic; 25⇨▥ ▥ ⊛ 35P ▥ ⊇(heated) ♙
♥French Ld9pm ✿ ⊈ S% *sB&B⇨▥IR£15.85
dB&B⇨▥IR£30.20 (Continental breakfast) LIR£5.50
D IR£8 Wine IR£3.50 Credit cards ② ⑤ **(RS)**
★★▟♨ **Sea View** ☎Bantry73
Closed Nov–Mar; Lic; 12rm(4⇨▥) Annexe: 3rm ▥
CTV P ▥ ⊥ Ld9pm ✿ ⊈ S% sB&B IR£6.87–IR£8.25
dB&B IR£16.50 dB&B⇨▥IR£18.50 LIR£4 Tea75p
D IR£8.25 Wine IR£3.50 **(RS)**

BALLYLIFFEN 808 Co Donegal Map14C34 Dublin176
Belfast98 Cardonagh6 Letterkenny38 Londonderry25
★★**Strand** ☎Clonmany7
Closed Xmas eve–26 Dec; Lic; 10⇨▥ ▥ CTV
TV available in bedrooms ⊛ P ▥ ⊥ Live music &
dancing Sat Ld9pm ✿ ⊈ *sB&B⇨▥IR£8–IR£11
dB&B⇨▥IR£14–IR£18 LIR£3.25 Tea75p D IR£6 ♠

An early grave slab, Ballymena

BALLYMENA 16,487 Co Antrim Map15D10 EcWed
MdSat Belfast23 Antrim11 Ballycastle28 Ballymoney19
Coleraine27 Cookstown29 Cushendall18 Dublin127
Larne22 Londonderry51

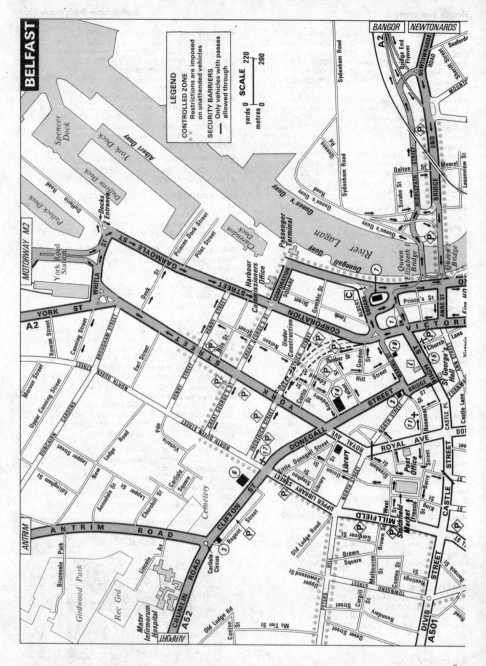

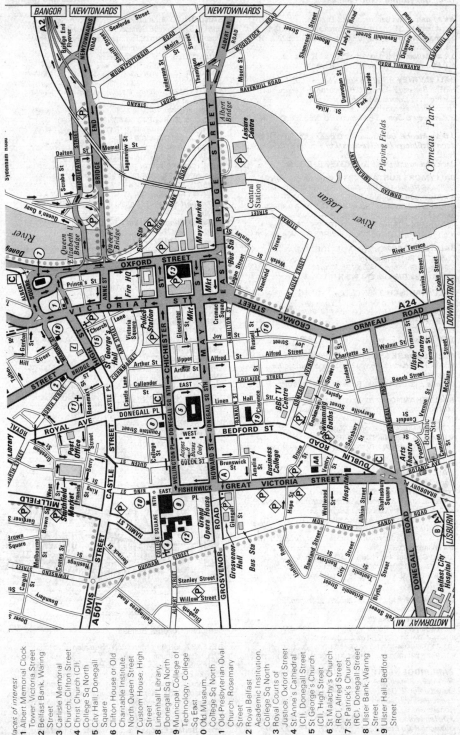

places of interest
1 Albert Memorial Clock Tower, Victoria Street
2 Belfast Bank, Waring Street
3 Carlisle Memorial Church, Clifton Street
4 Christ Church (CI), College Sq North
5 City Hall, Donegall Square
6 Clifton House or Old Charitable Institute, North Queen Street
7 Custom House, High Street
8 Linenhall Library, Donegall Sq North
9 Municpal College of Technology, College Sq East
10 Old Museum, College Sq North
11 Old Presbyterian Oval Church, Rosemary Street
12 Royal Belfast Academical Institution, College Sq North
13 Royal Courts of Justice, Oxford Street
14 St Anne's Cathedral (CI), Donegall Street
15 St George's Church (CI), High Street
16 St Malachy's Church (RC), Alfred Street
17 St Patrick's Church (RC), Donegall Street
18 Ulster Bank, Waring Street
19 Ulster Hall, Bedford Street

★★★**Adair Arms** Ballymoney Rd ☎3674
Lic; 41⇌🛏 CTV 160P Ld9 45pm Credit cards 2️⃣5️⃣
⑂*General Mtr Wks Ltd* 197 Ballymoney Rd ☎2171 **R**
n🅰 RT Vau
⑂*R McMillan* 56 Balee West ☎3747 **R**24hrs🅰
⑂*J J Smith* Waveney Av ☎3557 **R** n🅰 BL

BALLYMONEY 3,757 Co Antrim Map14C92 EcMon
MdThu·*Belfast47 Antrim30* Ballycastle16 Ballymena19
Bushmills11 Coleraine8 *Dublin146 Larne41*
Londonderry39 Maghera21 Portrush14
R Kennedy & Son 23 Ballymena Rd ☎63388 ☎63377
R🅰 Frd
J B McAteer & Son Queen St ☎62221 ☎62019 **R**🅰
John McElderry (Mtr Tractors) Ltd Victoria St ☎63324
R BL
Jack McLaughlin Café Ln ☎63182 **R**18.30🅰

BALLYMORE EUSTACE 433 Co Wicklow Map9N91
Dublin25 Belfast129 Blessington5 *Cork143* Kilcullen7
★★**Ardenode** ☎(045)64198
Closed Sep–May; Lic; 10rm(4⇌🛏) 🍴 CTV 🅰 130P 🖈
🖈 🛏 Disco Sun Ld9pm ☝ 🔄 sB&B IRE7.50
dB&B IRE14 dB&B⇌🛏IRE17 Lfr IRE4.50 Tea fr 75p
High Tea fr IRE3 D fr IRE6.50 Wine IRE3 🍷 Credit card 2️⃣

BALLYMOTE 952 Co Sligo Map11G61 EcMon
Dublin123 Ballaghaderreen12 *Belfast138* Boyle12
Carrick-on-Shannon22 *Cork195* Sligo12
⑂19.00 *Alex Gilmore* ☎3343 **R**19.00 n🅰

BALLYNAHINCH 3,485 Co Down Map15J35 Ec Mon/
Fri MdThu *Belfast15* Banbridge18 Bangor23
Downpatrick10 Dublin96 Lisburn11 *Londonderry84*
Lurgan20 Newcastle15 Newry28 Newtownards17
Portadown25
⑂*J G Walsh* 12 Downpatrick Rd ☎2958 **R**

BALLYSADARE Co Sligo Map11G62 EcWed *Dublin130*
Ballina32 Belfast134 Boyle21 *Galway81* Roscommon48
Sligo5
⑂*Parke's* ☎(071)71291 **R** n🅰 Aud Maz MB VW

BALLYSHANNON 2,325 Co Donegal Map16G86 EcWed
MdThu/Sat *Dublin130 Belfast114* Belleek4 Bundoran5
Donegal14 Enniskillen28 *Londonderry57*
Manorhamilton20 *Omagh41 Sligo27*
★*Dorrian's Imperial* ☎(072)65147
Lic; 17rm 12⇌🛏 🍴 CTV 🅰 10P 🅿 English Ld8.30pm
☝ 🔄 S%🍷 Credit cards 3️⃣

BALLYVAUGHAN Co Clare Map6L20 *Dublin147*
Ennis34 *Galway31* Limerick57
★★**Gregan's Castle** ☎5 Telex no.8110
Closed 2 Nov–13 Mar; Lic; 14rm(10⇌🛏) 🍴 CTV 🅰 40P
🚗 🖈 Cabaret wkly 🅿 French Ld8pm ☝ 🔄
sB&B IRE9.50–IRE15 sB&B⇌🛏IRE10.50–IRE16.50
dB&B IRE14–IRE19 dB&B⇌🛏IRE18–IRE26 Tea75p alc
D IRE6.50–IRE11 Wine IRE3.60 🍷 Credit cards 2️⃣3️⃣ **(RS)**
★★**Hyland's** ☎37
Closed Oct–Mar; Lic; 12rm(9⇌🛏) 🍴 CTV 🅰 100P 🖈
Disco Sat Ld8.30pm ☝ 🔄 S% sB&B IRE8 sB&B⇌🛏IRE9
dB&B IRE16 dB&B⇌🛏IRE18 Tea IRE1 D IRE6
Wine IRE2.50

BALTIMORE 200 Co Cork Map3W02 *Dublin223*
Belfast327 Cork62 Skibbereen8
★★**Baltimore House** ☎27
Closed Jan & Feb; RS Oct–Dec; Lic; 15rm(4⇌🛏)
Annexe: 4rm 🍴 CTV 28P 🚗 🖈 Ld9pm ☝ 🔄 S%
sB&B IRE6.50–IRE7.50 sB&B⇌🛏IRE8.50–IRE9.50
dB&B IRE13–IRE15 dB&B⇌🛏IRE15–IRE17 D fr IRE6.50

BANBRIDGE 6,864 Co Down Map15J14 EcThu
MdThu/Fri *Belfast25 Antrim37 Armagh20* Ballynahinch18
Downpatrick28 Dublin79 Dundalk27 Lisburn16
Londonderry91 Lurgan9 Newcastle21 Newry13
Portadown11
J J Henderson Scarva Rd ☎22655 ☎23307 **R**🅰 Tal
⑂*Wright & Co Ltd* 27 Dromore St ☎23641 ☎22377
R Frd

BANDON 4,071 Co Cork Map3W45 EcThu MdSat
Dublin181 Bantry38 *Belfast284* Clonakilty14 *Cork20*
Kinsale12 Macroom19 Dunmanway17 *Glengarriff48*
Ross Carberry22 Skibbereen34
⑂*Star* ☎(023)41514 **R** n🅰 Fia Lnc

BANGOR 35,178 Co Down Map15J58 EcThu MdWed
Belfast13 Ballynahinch23 Donaghadee5 Downpatrick28
Dublin117 Londonderry86 Newtonards6 Portaferry24
★★★**Royal** ☎3866
32⇌🛏 Lift 🕉 🍴 CTV TV in bedrooms 🅰 P Disco twice wkly
Ld10pm ☝ 🔄 sB&B IRE13.50 dB&B IRE19 L £3.50
alc Tea75p alc High Tea £3.75 D £6 alc Wine£2 🍷
Credit cards 1️⃣2️⃣3️⃣4️⃣5️⃣6️⃣
★★**Winston** 19-23 Queens Pde ☎4575
Closed 25 & 26 Dec; Unlicensed;
30rm(12⇌🛏) 🍴 CTV TV available in bedrooms 4P
Ld11pm ☝ 🔄 S% sB&B IRE8.63 sB&B⇌🛏IRE12.65
dB&B IRE15.53 dB&B⇌🛏IRE19.55 Lunch fr £3
Dfr £5 🍷 Credit cards 1️⃣
Ballyrobert S/sta 402 Belfast Rd ☎Helensbay2262
R Vau
⑂*Charles Hurst (Mtrs) Ltd* 71/79 Newtonards Rd ☎4312
☎Groomsport288 **R**🅰 BL RT
⑂*Gael Mtrs Ltd* 62 Groomsport Rd ☎4211 **R**🅰 Frd
⑂*P W Gethin & Sons* 118 Main St ☎65235 ☎3773 **R**
Dat
⑂*S C Taylor Ltd* 2 Ballyholme Rd ☎65307 **R**🅰

BANGOR-ERRIS 165 Co Mayo Map10F82 *Dublin179*
Ballina28 Belfast193 Belmullet12 *Cork221* Mulrany20
⑂*Erris Mtrs* ☎3 **R**🅰 Frd

BANTRY 2,579 Co Cork Map2V94 EcWed MdSat
Dublin219 Bandon38 *Belfast323 Cork59* Dunmanway20
Glengarriff11 Kenmare38 *Killarney49* Macroom34
Skibbereen18
★★★**Westlodge** ☎360 Telex no. 8477
Lic; 60⇌🛏 🕉 🍴 CTV TV available in bedrooms 500P 🖈
🏊(heated) 🖈 (hard) squash billiards sauna bath
Disco twice wkly Live music & dancing five nights wkly
Cabaret twice wkly ♨ Ld9pm ☝ 🔄 sB&B⇌🛏IRE15–IRE17
dB&B⇌🛏IRE18–IRE22 L IRE4–IRE4.50 Tea90p
High Tea IRE3.95–IRE4.95 D IRE7–IRE8.50
Wine IRE3.80 🍷 Credit cards 1️⃣2️⃣3️⃣6️⃣
⑂*O'Leary's* ☎127 **R** n🅰

Campbell College, Belfast

BELFAST 358,991 Map 15J37 **See plan**
🅰🅰 Fanum House
108–110 Great Victoria Street Belfast BT2 7AT
☎26242 EcWed/Sat MdFri see also Holywood,
Newtownabbey, and Dunmurry *Antrim78 Armagh40*
Ballymena29 Ballynahinch15 Bangor13 Carrickfergus10
Coleraine55 Donaghadee19 *Downpatrick22 Dublin104*
Larne22 Lisburn9 *Londonderry72* Lurgan25
Newcastle31 Newry38 Newtownards10 Portadown32
☆☆☆☆**Belfast Europa** Great Victoria St (Grand Met)
☎45161

210⊆🛏 Lift ♪ 📺 CTV available in bedrooms 180P
Disco Tue ♀English & French Ld10.30pm ♦ ⚼ S%
*sB&B⊆🛏£16 dB&B⊆🛏£26 (Continental breakfast)
&alc 🍽 Credit cards ①②③④⑤⑥
★★Cavalier Hotel 149 Upper Newtownards Rd
☎658579
15rm(3⊆🛏) ♪ 📺 CTV 40P Disco wkly Ld9pm ♦ ⚼ S%
*sB&B£9 sB&B⊆🛏£11 dB&B£13 dB&B⊆🛏£14 L£2.50
Tea60p High Tea£1.75–£3 D£3–£6
♪**W H Alexander Ltd** 62–64 Great Victoria St ☎28424
☎669491 **R** BL
♪**A S Baird Ltd** Annadale Embankment, Ormeau Rd
☎642972 ☎667870 **R** n♠ Tal
♪**Connsbrook F/sta** 125 Connsbrook Av ☎653000
☎652980 **R**♠
♪**Daly's** 249–255 Falls Rd ☎26037 **R** n♠ Dat
♪**Dick & Co Ltd** 112 Donegal St ☎28551 **R** Fia
Gowan 133 Lisburn Rd ☎661911 **R** Peu
Hills Engineering Wks Holywood Rd ☎656241 **R**♠ Maz
♪**Charles Hurst (Mtrs) Ltd** 10 Adelaide St ☎30566 **R** BL
DJ RT
Loughside S/sta 809 Shore Rd ☎76951 **R**♠
♪**Maguires** 534 Falls Rd ☎613141 **R** BL
♪**McLean & Bryce Ltd** Prince Regent Rd ☎51111
☎Comber872670 **R** BL
W J McCrum Ltd 38/44 Clifton St ☎23065 **R**♠ Rel
♪**Orchard S/sta** 214 Holywood Rd ☎659197 ☎644683
R Tal
Speedline Kennedy Way ☎613499
♪**Stanley Mtr Wks** 27 Pakenham St ☎29399 **R**♠ Dat

BERAGH 362 Co Tyrone Map 14H57 EcThu *Belfast62*
Armagh33 Cookstown20 *Dublin108* Dungannon20
Enniskillen30 Londonderry41
♪**J J Keenan** 51 Cooley Rd ☎317 **R**♠ Tal

BIRR 3,881 Co Offaly Map8N00 EcThu MdMon
Dublin80 Athlone28 Ballinasloe26 *Belfast155 Cork108*
Galway58 Limerick47 Loughrea35 Mountmellick28
Nenagh22 *Port Laoise35 Portumna16* Roscrea12
Tullamore23
★★County Arms ☎193
Lic; 24rm2⊆🛏 ♪ 📺 CTV 300P ⚓ billiards Music Sat
Cabaret Thu ♨ Ld9.30pm ♦ ⚼ Credit card ②
♪**A Bridge Ltd** Railway Rd ☎10 **R** n♠ Frd
♪18.30 **P L Dolan & Sons** ☎6 **R**18.30 n♠

BLANCHARDSTOWN Co Dublin Map9O03 *Dublin6*
Athlone75 Lucan5 *Galway133*
♪21.00 **Ryan's** ☎(01)213945 **R**♠

BLARNEY 1,128 Co Cork Map3W67 *Cork6 Mallow17*
Macroom21 *Limerick60*
★★★Hotel Blarney ☎(021)85281
Lic; 76⊆🛏 ♪ 🍴 📺 CTV 150P ⚓ Disco 3 nights wkly
Live music & dancing wkly sB&B⊆🛏IRE14.40–IRE17.40
dB&B⊆🛏IRE31–IRE34.60 LIRE4.50 DIRE7.50 Wine IRE4
🍽 Credit cards ②③⑤

BLESSINGTON 637 Co Wicklow Map9N91 EcWed
Dublin19 Belfast123 Carlow36 Cork152
★★★Downshire House ☎(045)65199
Closed 23 Dec–11 Jan; Lic; 25⊆🛏 ♪ 📺 CTV ⊛ 25P ⚓
🌜(hard) ⇘ ♨ Ld9.30pm ♦ ⚼ sB&B⊆🛏IRE15–IRE17
dB&B⊆🛏IRE26–IRE28 LIRE4–IRE5 Tea IRE1.50 alc
High Tea IRE4.50 alc DIRE7–IRE8 Wine IRE3
♪**Hughes** ☎(045)65156 **R**18.30♠

BOARDMILLS Co Down Map15J36 *Belfast11 Dublin99*
Lisburn6 Saintfield4
Temple S/sta 82 Carrdyduff Rd ☎Bailliesmills228 **R**♠

BORRIS-IN-OSSORY 276 Co Laois Map8S28
Dublin70 Cork108 Limerick53 Roscrea7
★Leix County ☎26
Lic; 16⊆🛏 ♪ 📺 CTV 100P ⚓ ♀French Ld9pm ♦ ⚼ S%
sB&B⊆🛏IRE8–IRE9 dB&B⊆🛏IRE15–IRE17
LIRE2.95–IRE3.50 Tea75–95p High Tea IRE1.25–IRE3.25
DIRE4.50–IRE6 Wine IRE2.95 Credit cards ②③

BORRISOKANE 769 Co Tipperary Map7R99 EcWed
MdTue *Dublin95 Belfast167* Birr13 *Cork99 Limerick34*
Nenagh9 *Portumna10 Tullamore36*
♪22.00 **Henderson & Bailey** ☎(067)27111
☎(067)27164 **R**♠

BOYLE 1,339 Co Roscommon Map11G80 EcWed
MdWed/Sat *Dublin109 Athlone48* Ballaghaderreen15
Ballina40 Belfast132 Carrick-on-Shannon10 Castlerea19
Cork183 Elphin12 Longford33 *Roscommon27 Sligo26*
Tobercurry20
★Royal Bridge St ☎16
Closed Xmas Day; Lic; 20rm(5⊆🛏) 📺 CTV ⊛ 200P
Disco Sat Live music & dancing Sun Cabaret Wed
♀Irish & French Ld9pm ♦ ⚼ sB&B IRE6.10–IRE7.10
sB&B⊆🛏IRE7.20–IRE8.10 dB&B IRE10 dB&B⊆🛏IRE11.80
LIRE3–IRE4.95 Tea IRE1.50–IRE3 DIRE3.50–IRE5.50
Wine IRE3.95 Credit cards ①②③⑥
♪18.15 **W Roe & Sons Ltd** ☎22 **R**18.15 n♠ Frd

BRAY 15,841 Co Wicklow Map9O21 EcWed MdSat
Dublin14 Arklow33 *Belfast118 Cork175* Dun Laoghaire8
Glendalough19 Rathdrum25 *Wexford75 Wicklow19*
♪**Bray Mtr Engineers Ltd** Vevay Rd ☎(01)863693 **R** n♠
Peu

BUNDORAN 1,337 Co Donegal Map1G85 EcThu
Dublin135 Ballyshannon5 *Belfast118* Belleek8
Donegal18 Enniskillen32 *Londonderry61* Manorhamilton16
Omagh46 *Sligo22*
★Maghery House ☎(072)41234
Lic; 31rm6⊆🛏 TV ⊛ 25P ♨ Ld9pm
♪**T P O'Connell Mtrs** East End ☎(072)41300 **R** n♠ Aud
Maz MB VW

BUNRATTY Co clare Map7R46 *Dublin132 Belfast210*
Cork74 Ennis15 *Limerick9 Shannon Airport7*
★★★Fitzpatrick's Shannon Shamrock ☎(061)61177
Telex no.6214
Lic; 100⊆🛏 ♪ 📺 CTV CTV available in bedrooms 200P ⚓
⊒(heated) sauna bath ♨ ♀ Irish & French Ld9.30pm ♦ ⚼
sB&B⊆🛏IRE23.80–IRE28.80 dB&B⊆🛏IRE39.65–
IRE47.10 LIRE5&alc Tea IRE1.50&alc
High Tea IRE6.50&alc DIRE8.50&alc Wine IRE3.50 🍽
Xmas Credit cards ①②③④⑤⑥

CAHERDANIEL Co Kerry Map2V65 *Dublin241 Belfast 319*
Cork90 Kenmare30 *Waterville9*
★★★Derrynane ☎36
Closed Nov–26 May; Lic; 62⊆🛏 ♪ 📺 CTV
CTV available in bedrooms 100P ⚓ ⊒(heated) 🌜(hard)
Live music & dancing 4–6 nights wkly ♨ Ld9pm ♦
sB&B⊆🛏IRE11.80–IRE14.90 dB&B⊆🛏IRE18.80–
IRE22.60 LIRE4.15 DIRE7.50 Wine IRE3.50 🍽
Credit cards ①②⑥⑥

CAHIR 1,747 Co Tipperary Map4S02 EcThu MdFri
Dublin111 Belfast215 Cashel11 Clonmel10 *Cork50*
Fermoy28 *Kilkenny42 Limerick55 Mallow39*
Mitchelstown18 *Port Laoise59* Thurles24
★★★Kilcoran Lodge ☎261
Lic; 24rm(9⊆🛏) 2⊟ ♪ 🍴 📺 CTV TV available in bedrooms
⊛ 300P 🅿 ⚓ ⇘ ♨ Ld9.15pm ♦ ⚼ S%
sB&B IRE10–IRE11 sB&B⊆🛏IRE10–IRE12
dB&B IRE20–IRE23 dB&B⊆🛏IRE23–IRE25 LIRE4 alc
Tea85p alc High Tea IRE3 alc DIRE7.50 alc Wine IRE3 🍽
Credit cards ②③
♪**Barry's** ☎270 **R** n♠ BL

CAHIRCIVEEN 1,547 Co Kerry Map2V47 EcThu MdWed
Dublin222 Belfast300 Cork109 Glenbeigh18
Kenmare49 *Killarney39* Killorglin26 *Limerick99*
Parknasilla34 *Tralee43* Valentia10 *Waterville11*
★★Evan's O'Connel St ☎10
Closed Oct–Apr; RSEtr & Sep; Lic; 12rm(1⊆🛏) 🍴 ⊛
8🅿 ♀French Ld8pm ♦ ⚼ sB&B⊆🛏IRE5–IRE6.50
dB&B IRE10–IRE13 dB&B⊆🛏IRE11.50–IRE15
LIRE2–IRE3&alc Tea80p–IRE1.50&alc High Tea IRE2.85–
IRE9.50&alc DIRE6.50–IRE9.50&alc Wine IRE3
Credit cards ①③

A view of Camlough Mountains

CAMLOUGH Co Down Map13J02 *Belfast42 Dublin69* Newry4
♪*Charles Doyle Auto Engineer* ☎Bessbrock257 **R**

CARLOW 10,399 Co Carlow Map9S77 EcThu MdMon/ Tue *Dublin52* Arklow43 *Athlohe70* Athy12 Baltinglass15 *Belfast155* Clonmel56 *Cork120* Enniscorthy33 Kilkenny24 Muine Bheag11 Naas31 New Ross36 *Port Laoise24* Tullow10 *Waterford47* Wexford48 *Wicklow54*
★★**Royal** Dublin St ☎(0503)31621 Telex no.4858
Closed 25–27 Dec; RS28 Dec–1 Jan; Lic;
37rm(20⇔fil) ♪ ㎜ CTV TV available in bedrooms ✿ 30P 7♨ ♨ ♀ Irish & English Ld9.15pm ♥ ♨ S%
sB&B IR£8.95–IR£9.75 sB&B⇔filIR£10.95–IR£11.95 dB&B IR£16.50–IR£16.95 dB&B⇔filIR£18.75–IR£19.75 LIR£3–IR£4.95 Tea75p–IR£1.75 High Tea IR£2.25–IR£3.25&alc DIR£5.50–IR£6.60 Wine IR£2.95 🏴 Credit cards ② ③

CARNLOUGH 1,385 Co Antrim Map15D21 EcThu *Belfast38 Antrim28* Ballycastle27 Ballymena17 Cushendall11 *Dublin142* Larne15 *Londonderry68 Maghera36*
★★**Londonderry Arms** ☎85255
10rm(2⇔fil) ㎜ CTV ✿ ♣6P ♨ ♨ Children under 12yrs not accommodated Ld8.45pm (7.45pm Sun) ♥
sB&B£7.95–£8.95 sB&B⇔filIR£9.50–£10.75 dB&B£15.90–£17.90 dB&B⇔filIR£19–£21.50 Lfr£3.50 High Teafr£3.50&alc D £6.50–£9&alc Wine £2.95 Credit cards ① ② ③ ④ ⑤ ⑥

CARRAROE Co Galway Map10L92 *Dublin164 Galway28 Clifden38 Limerick92*
★★**Ostan Cheathru Rua** ☎(091)72105 Telex no.8871
Closed 2 Oct–14 May; Lic; 24rm(17⇔fil) ♪ ㎜ CTV TV available in bedrooms 150P ♨ ♨ ➤ Live music & dancing 6 nights wkly Cabaret 6 nights wkly ♨ Ld9pm ♥ ♨ sB&B IR£9.40–IR£11.30
sB&B⇔filIR£9.40–IR£11.30 dB&B IR£18.80–IR£22.60 dB&B⇔filIR£18.80–IR£22.60 LIR£4.15&alc Tea IR£1.75&alc High Tea IR£3&alc DIR£7.50&alc Wine IR£4.50 🏴 Credit card ②

CARRICKFERGUS 15,162 Co Antrim Map15J48 EcWed/Sat *Belfast10 Antrim20 Dublin114 Larne15 Londonderry75* Whitehead5
★★**Coast Road** ☎61021
Closed Xmas Day; 20rm(15⇔fil) ♪ ㎜ CTV TV in bedrooms ✿ Ld9.15pm ♥ L £1.80–£3.80 High Tea £1.85–£3.90 D £3–£4&alc Wine £2.45 Credit cards ② ④ ⑥
★**Dobbins Inn** 6–8 High St ☎63905
Closed Xmas Day; 14rm(2⇔fil) ♪ CTV ♀ Mainly grills Ld8.45pm ♥ ♨ *sB&B £7.56 sB&B⇔filIR£8.64 dB&B £14.04 dB&B⇔filIR£18.36 Lfr £1.95 Teafr 50p High Tea £2–£3.50 D £5 alc Wine £2.20 Credit card ⑥

CARRICKMORE 398 Co Tyrone Map14H67 MdFri *Belfast58 Dublin109 Omagh11*
♪*J McElduff* ☎224 **R** ☆
♪*Rockview S/sta* ☎244

CARRICK-ON-SHANNON 1,854 Co Leitrim Map12M99 EcWed MdThu *Dublin100 Athlone52* Ballaghaderreen23 *Ballina49* Ballinamore17 *Belfast121* Boyle10 Castlerea24 *Cork183* Drumshanbo8 *Enniskillen41* Longford23 *Mullingar49 Roscommon26 Sligo35*
★★**Bush** ☎14 Telex no.4394
Closed Dec–mid Jan; RSmid Jan–May & Oct–Nov; Lic; 26rm(20⇔fil) ♪ ㎜ CTV 25P ♨ Ld8.45pm ♥ ♨
sB&B IR£8.80–IR£11 sB&B⇔filIR£11–IR£13.75 dB&B IR£16.50–IR£19.50 dB&B⇔filIR£19–IR£23.50 LIR£2.25–IR£6.60&alc Tea IR£1.10 alc High Tea IR£4.75 alc DIR£6.60–IR£7.70 Wine IR£3 🏴 Credit cards ① ② ③ ⑤ ⑥
★★**County** ☎42
Closed 25 & 26 Dec; Lic; 19rm(9⇔fil) TV ✿ ♨
Ld9pm ♥ sB&B IR£8.50–IR£9.50 sB&B⇔filIR£9.50–IR£10.50 dB&B IR£17–IR£19 dB&B⇔filIR£19–IR£21 LIR£2.95–IR£3.50 DIR£6–IR£7.50 Wine IR£3.25 Credit cards ② ⑥
♪*Wm Cox & Sons* Main St ☎217 ☎63 **R**18.30 ☆

CARRYDUFF 2,279 Co Down Map15J36 EcWed *Belfast7*
♪*Jamison of Carryduff Ltd* 636 Saintfield Rd ☎812204 ☎813314 **R** n☆ Frd Maz

CASHEL Co Galway Map10L84 *Dublin178 Belfast231 Clifden15 Galway41*
★★★♨♨ **Cashel House** ☎9 Telex no.8812
Closed Nov–Feb; Lic; 23rm(20⇔fil) ♪ ㎜ 40P ♨ ♨ ➤ (hard) nc5 Ld8.30pm ♥ ♨ sB&B IR£8.50–IR£12
sB&B⇔filIR£10–IR£14 dB&B IR£17–IR£24 dB&B⇔filIR£20–IR£28 LIR£6.50 Tea80p DIR£8–IR£8.50 Wine IR£2.90 🏴 Credit card ③ **(RS)**
★★★**Zetland** ☎8 Telex no.8853
Closed Oct–Mar; Lic; 18rm(10⇔fil) ⊞ ✗ ㎜ CTV P ♨ ➤ billiards ♨ Ld9pm ♥ ♨ sB&B IR£8.70–IR£10.65 sB&B⇔filIR£13.45–IR£16.75 dB&B IR£17.40–IR£21.30 dB&B⇔filIR£20.90–IR£27.50 Tea50p–IR£2 DIR£6.75–IR£8 Wine IR£3 Credit cards ① ② ③ ⑤ ⑥

CASHEL 2,692 **Co Tipperary** Map4S04 EcWed *Dublin99 Cork61 Rosslare97* Cahir11
☆☆**Cashel Kings** ☎(062)61477
Lic; 40⇔fil ♪ ㎜ CTV 150P Disco Fri Live music & dancing Sun ♥ ♨ S% sB&B⇔filIR£12.38–IR£14.63 dB&B⇔filIR£22.50–IR£25.88 LIR£3.50–IR£4.75 Tea IR£1.50–IR£2.50 High Tea IR£3–IR£5 DIR£6.50–IR£7.50 Wine IR£3 🏴 Credit cards ① ② ③ ⑤
♪$20.00 *O'Doherty & O'Dwyer* ☎(062)61544 **R** ☆ Frd

CASTLEBAR 5,979 Co Mayo Map10M19 EcThu MdSat *Dublin151* Ballaghaderreen35 *Ballina25* Ballinrobe18 *Belfast181* Claremorris17 *Clifden52* Foxford15 *Galway48* Mulrany23 Pontoon10 *Roscommon60 Sligo53* Swinford17 Tuam35 Westport11
★★★**Breaffy House** ☎(094)22033 Telex no.4404
Closed Xmas; Lic; 41⇔fil Lift ♪ ㎜ CTV ♨ Disco Mon Live music & dancing wkly in summer Cabaret wkly in summer ♨ ♨ Irish, English & French Ld9pm ♥ ♨ S% sB&B⇔filIR£13–IR£18.50 dB&B⇔filIR£19–IR£30 LIR£2–IR£5 Tea IR£2 DIR£8.75 Wine £3.60 🏴 Credit cards ① ② ③ ⑤ **(RS)**

★**Travellers Friend** ☎(094)21919
Lic; 20rm ⅅ ▥ CTV 200P Cabaret Wed & Fri
Ld8.45pm ♨ ⵣ sB&B IR£9–IR£10 dB&B IR£18–IR£20
L IR£2.75–IR£4 Tea75p–IR£1 High Tea IR£4.50 alc
D IR£6–IR£7.50 Wine IR£3.25 🏠 Credit card ③
★**Welcome Inn** ☎(094)22054
Closed Xmas; Lic; 28rm(6⇔🛏) ⅅ ▥ CTV ✿ 100P
Disco Thu & Sat Live music & dancing Sat & Sun
Ld8.30pm ♨ ⵣ S% *sB&B IR£7.20–IR£7.90
sB&B⇔🛏IR£8.80–IR£9.40 dB&B IR£12.65–IR£13.85
dB&B⇔🛏IR£14.15–IR£15.35 L IR£2.50 alc
Tea IR£1 alc High Tea IR£3.alc D IR£4 alc
Wine IR£3.75

CASTLECAULFIELD 678 Co Tyrone Map14H76 EcWed
Belfast46 Armagh17 Aughnacloy9 Portadown21
⛟**Fred Martin** Ballygawley Rd ☎Donaghmore219 **R** ⵠ

CASTLEDAWSON 1,161 Co Londonderry Map14H99
EcMon *Belfast34 Antrim17* Ballymena17 Cookstown12
Dublin116 Londonderry40 Maghera8
Boyle Bros Magherafelt Rd ☎237 **R** Frd

CASTLEDERG 1,684 Co Tyrone Map14H28 EcWed MdFri
*Belfast88 Dublin130 Enniskillen33 Londonderry26
Omagh17* Strabane12
⛟**Sharkeys** Main St ☎278 **R** ⵠ Frd

CASTLEDERMOT 583 Co Kildare Map9S78 EcWed
MdSat *Dublin45* Athy9 Baltinglass7 *Belfast149 Carlow7
Cork123* Kilcullen17 Naas24 Tullow9
⛟**M Hennessy & Sons Ltd** ☎(0503)44114 **R** nⵠ

CASTLEFREKE Co Cork Map3W33 *Dublin199 Cork39*
Clonakilty5 Ross Carberry3
☆☆**Castlefreke** ☎(023)48106
Closed Oct–Mar; Lic; 15⇔🛏 ▥ ▦ ▥ CTV 40P ⥻ (hard) ⥺ ∩
🇾International Ld8.30pm

CASTLEGREGORY 216 Co Kerry Map2Q61 *Dublin204*
Dingle15 *Cork 91 Killarney36 Tralee15*
★★**Tralee Bay** ☎(066)39138
Closed Oct–Mar; Lic; 13rm(6⇔🛏) ▥ CTV ✿ 60P ⥻
Live music & dancing twice wkly Ld9.30pm ♨
sB&B IR£11 sB&B⇔🛏IR£14 dB&B IR£22 dB&B⇔🛏IR£27
D IR£8–IR£15 Wine IR£3.50

CASTLEPOLLARD 693 Co Westmeath Map12N47
Dublin54 Belfast104 Ceanannus Mor21 Longford25
Mullingar13
⛟19.00 **Doran's** ☎(044)61145 ☎(044)61295 **R**19.00 ⵠ

CASTLEREA 1,752 Co Roscommon Map11M68 EcThu
Dublin110 Belfast146 Roscommon19 Tuam30
⛟**Lavin's** ☎96 **R**18.30 ⵠ Frd

CHARLESTOWN 677 Co Mayo Map11G40
Dublin126 Ballaghaderreen11 *Belfast157 Limerick114
Sligo29* Swinford7
⛟21.00 **Walsh's Auto Service** ☎16 **R**21.00 ⵠ

CLAUDY 513 Co Londonderry Map14C50 EcWed
Belfast63 Coleraine28 *Dublin140* Dungiven10
Limavady14 *Londonderry10 Maghera25* Strabane16
⛟**Browne & Day** Hill Top Gar ☎234 **R** Frd

CLIFDEN 790 Co Galway Map10L65 EcThu *Dublin185*
Ballynahinch13 *Belfast226* Castlebar52 Cong40 *Cork179
Galway49* Leenane21 Mulrany59 Oughterard32
Renvyle14 Westport41
★★★**Abbeyglen** ☎33 Telex no.8366
Closed 5 Nov–Mar except Xmas; Lic; 35rm(28⇔🛏) ▥
CTV 50P ⥻ ⥺ ⥺ ∩ (hard) Ld8.30pm ♨ ⵣ
sB&B IR£8–IR£12 sB&B⇔🛏IR£10–IR£15
dB&B IR£15–IR£24 dB&B⇔🛏IR£19–IR£28 L IR£5
Tea IR£1 D IR£7.80 Wine IR£4 🏠 Credit card⑨
★★★**Alcock & Brown** ☎134
Closed Oct–Mar; Lic; 20⇔🛏 ⅅ ▥ CTV TV available in
bedrooms ✿ 20P ⥻ 🇾International Ld9pm ♨ ⵣ
*sB&B⇔🛏IR£9.30–IR£10.80 dB&B⇔🛏IR£18.60–
IR£21.60 L IR£3.40 D IR£6.60 Wine IR£3.90
Credit cards ② ⑤
★★**Celtic** Main St ☎115 Telex no.8313

Closed 16–27 Dec; Lic; 20⇔🛏 Lift ⅅ ⵡ CTV ⥻ ⤵
Live music 6 nights wkly in summer Ld8.45pm S%
*sB&B⇔🛏IR£7–IR£8 dB&B⇔🛏IR£14–IR£16
(Continental breakfast) L IR£3.50 Tea IR£2 alc
D IR£5.75 alc Wine IR£3.20 🏠

CLOGHER 429 Co Tyrone Map14H55 EcThu MdSat
Belfast62 Armagh27 Aughnacloy10 Fivemiletown7
Londonderry50 Monaghan22 *Omagh16* Portadown37
⛟**Armstrong Bros** Augher Rd ☎661 **R** nⵠ
⛟21.00 **McKenna Bros** Main St ☎613 **R** ⵠ Frd

CLONAKILTY 2,430 Co Cork Map3W34 EcWed MdFri
Dublin194 Bandon14 *Belfast299 Cork33* Dunmanway15
Kinsale20 Ross Carberry8 Skibbereen20
★**Emmet** ☎(023)43394
Lic; 11rm(4⇔🛏) ▥ CTV ✿ P ⤵ Disco wkly
Live music & dancing wkly Cabaret wkly Ld8.30pm
♨ ⵣ S% *sB&B IR£5.50–IR£6.50 sB&B⇔🛏IR£6.75–
IR£7.75 dB&B IR£13.50–IR£15.50 dB&B⇔🛏IR£13.50–
IR£15.50 L IR£2.75 Tea IR£2–IR£3 High Tea IR£2–IR£6
Wine IR£2.75 Credit cards ③
⛟22.00 **Western** Western Rd ☎(023)43327 **R** ⵠ BL

Clonmel tower and old town walls

CLONMEL 12,291 Co Tipperary Map4S22 EcThu MdSat
Dublin105 Belfast209 Cahir10 Callan22 Carrick-on-
Suir13 Cashel15 *Cork60* Dungarvan26 Fermoy38
Fethard9 *Kilkenny32 Limerick50 Mallow49* Thurles28
Tipperary25 Waterford30 Youghal39
★★★**Clonmel Arms** ☎(052)21233
Closed 24–26 Dec; Lic; 40rm(20⇔🛏) Lift ⅅ ▦ ▥ CTV
TV available in bedrooms ✿ 50P Disco twice wkly
Live music & dancing wkly Cabaret wkly Ld10.15pm ♨ ⵣ
S% sB&B IR£12.75–IR£13.75 sB&B⇔🛏IR£13.75–
IR£14.75 dB&B IR£23.50–IR£25.50 dB&B⇔🛏IR£25.50–
IR£27.50 L IR£3.50–IR£4 Tea IR£1 High Tea IR£3.50 alc
D IR£6–IR£6.50 Wine IR£3.50 🏠 Credit cards ① ② ③ ④ ⑤ ⑥
★★★**Minella** ☎(052)22388
Lic; 41⇔🛏 ⅅ ▥ CTV TV available in bedrooms 300P
⤵ ⤾ Ld9pm ♨ S% sB&B⇔🛏IR£13 dB&B⇔🛏IR£23 🏠
Credit cards ① ③ ⑤
★★**Hearns** ☎(052)21611
Closed 23–31 Dec; Lic; 28rm15⇔🛏 ⅅ ▥ CTV ✿ 40P ⥻
Ld8.45pm ♨

CLOUGHEY 767 Co Down Map15J65 EcThu
Belfast27 Portaferry5 Newtonards17 Dongahadee18
★★**Roadhouse** 204–208 Main Rd ☎Portavogie500
11rm(3⇔🛏) ▥ CTV ✿ 123P Ld9.30pm ♨ S%
sB&B £8.50–£10 sB&B⇔🛏£9.50–£11 dB&B £17–£20
dB&B⇔🛏£19–£22 L £2.70–£3.50 High Tea £3.50–£5.50
D £5.50–£7.50&alc Wine £3

CORK

DUBLIN

Blackpool

Gurranebraher

SCALE

440
400

220
200

0   0
yds mtrs

Gardiners Hill
L188
BALLYHOOLY NEW ROAD
St Luke's Cross
Old Youghal Road
Millrd
Hospital
A
Rathmore Road
Glen Avenue
Glen Avenue
Assumption Road
Pope's Road
Cemetery
Camp Field
Sports Ground
Rathmore Park
Audley Place
Richmond Hill
St Patrick's Hill
York Street
Wellington Road
AA
N8[T11] LOWER GLANMIRE ROAD
To B & I Car Ferry
G
Station
Railway Street
Alfred Street
PENROSE'S QUAY
Custom House
HORGAN QUAY
Anderson Quay
Pine Street
LEITRIM STREET
John Street
JOHN STREET UPPER
Camden Place
MACCURTAIN STREET
St Patrick's Quay
P.O.
St Patrick's Bridge
Police Station
Coburg St
COAL QUAY
Merchant Quay
Parnell Place
Maylor Street
Smith St
Plunkett St
Lavitt Quay
Emmet Place
City Hall
ANGLESEA ST
Kennedy Quay
VICTORIA ROAD
Albert Street
Albert Road
City Works Road
P
Parliament ST
SOUTH MALL
Cook St
Marlborough St
Princess St
PARADE
GRAND
ST PATRICK ST
Academy Street
St Paul's Av
Paul St
Brown St
Opera House
Eason's Hill
Coburg St
10
Id.
P.O.
e
i
4
Corn Market St
Dominick Street
J Redmond St
Hospital
16
18
Church Street
SHANDON STREET
GREAT WILLIAM O'BRIEN STREET
GERALD GRIFFIN STREET
3
Commons Road
L69
N20[T11]
BLARNEY
LIMERICK
THOMAS DAVIS STREET
WATERCOURSE ROAD
Lover's Walk
Seminary Walk
Seminary Road
Redemption Road
St Mary's Road
Old Market Place
Wolfe Tone Street
Gerald Griffin Avenue
Farranferris Avenue
Sports Ground
Fair Hill
Valley Drive
Knockpogue Ave
Fairfield Avenue
Upper Fair Hill
Knockfree Avenue
St Colville's Road
Gurranebraher Road
St Anthony's Road
Glen Ryan Road
BLARNEY STREET
CATHEDRAL ROAD
Roman Street
NORTH MAIN STREET
NORTH MALL
SUNDAY'S WELL ROAD
Sheares Street
Grattan Street
N WASHINGTON ST
Liberty St
Henry Street
7
Hospital
1
P
GRENVILLE PLACE
Footbridge
LANCASTER QUAY
WESTERN ROAD
CASTLE WHITE ROAD
MARDYKE WALK
SAWMILL STREET
SHEARES ST

AA Office. 9 Bridge
Street ☎(021)505 155

A ★★★ Arbutus Lodge
C ★★ Glengarriffe
D ★★★ Jury's
E ★★★★ Metropole
F ★★★ Moore's
G ★★★ Silver Springs

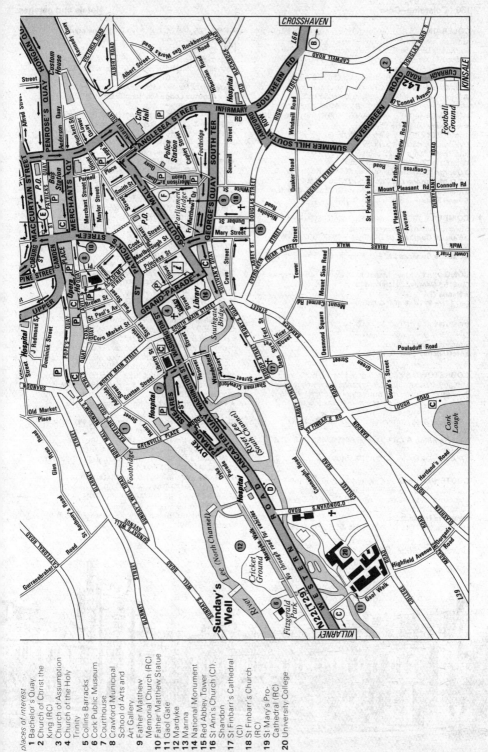

places of interest

1 Bachelor's Quay
2 Church of Christ the King (RC)
3 Church of Assumption
4 Church of the Holy Trinity
5 Collins Barracks
6 Cork Public Museum
7 Courthouse
8 Crawford Municipal School of Arts and Art Gallery
9 Father Matthew Memorial Church (RC)
10 Father Matthew Statue
11 Gaol Gate
12 Mardyke
13 Marina
14 National Monument
15 Red Abbey Tower
16 St Ann's Church (Cl). Shandon
17 St Finbarr's Cathedral (Cl)
18 St Finbar's Church (RC)
19 St Mary's Pro-Cathedral (RC)
20 University College

COLERAINE 14,871 Co Londonderry Map14C83 EcThu
MdMon/Tue/Wed *Belfast55 Antrim38 Armagh61*
Ballycastle19 Ballymena27 Ballymoney8 Bushmills8
Dublin141 Kilrea15 *Larne49* Limavady14 *Londonderry31*
Maghera21 Portrush6
☆☆☆**Bohill Auto Inn** Bushmills Rd ☎4406
30rm(24⇌🚿) 🄳 🎜 CTV CTV available in bedrooms 100P
⚓ ♀English & French Ld9 15pm ♥ *sB&Bfr £9.50
sB&B⇌🚿fr £15 dB&Bfr £22 dB&B⇌🚿fr £22 L £3.75
High Tea £4 alc D £5 alc Wine £3.20 ➡ Credit cards ① ④ ⑤ ⑥
★★★**Lodge** Lodge Rd ☎4848
15⇌🚿 🄳 🎜 CTV TV available in bedrooms 150P ⚓
Live music & dancing Sat Ld9.15pm ♥ sB&B⇌🚿fr £12
dB&B⇌🚿fr £18 Lfr £3.25 High Tea fr £1.80 D £5 alc
Wine £1.80 ➡ Credit cards ① ③ ⑤ ⑥
🛪*George McAlister* Glenlearey ☎4704 **R** 24hrs ✿
🛪*T D McFarlane Ltd* Church St ☎2361 **R** ✿ Frd
🛪*MacFarlane Mtrs Ltd* Kingsgate St ☎2718 **R** ✿ BL
Strand S/sta 7–13 Strand Rd ☎3561

COMBER 5,193 Co Down Map15J46 EcWed MdTue
Belfast9 Dublin107 Newtownards4
🛪*Kane of Comber Ltd* The Square ☎872302 **R** n✿
BL RT
🛪*Lisbane Services Ltd* 175 Killinchy Rd ☎541396 **R** ✿

CONG 233 Co Mayo Map10M15 *Dublin143* Ballinrobe7
Cork155 Galway27 Headford11
★**Ryans** ☎4
Lic: 17rm 🍴 TV ✿ 40P ⚓ Ld8pm

CONVOY 654 Co Donegal Map16C20 *Dublin143*
Belfast101 Donegal24 Letterkenny15 *Londonderry19*
Strabane6 Stranorlar6
🛪*McGlinchey* ☎36 **R** n✿

COOKSTOWN 6,673 Co Tyrone Map14H87 EcWed
MdSat *Belfast51 Antrim29 Armagh24* Ballymena29
Coleraine37 *Dublin105* Dungannon11 *Enniskillen55*
Larne51 Londonderry49 Maghera16 Magherafelt10
Omagh27 Portadown25
🛪*Bradford Bros* Northern Gar, Lissan Rd ☎63667
R VW
🛪*T J Hamilton & Co* 50 Union St ☎62488 **R** 18.30 ✿
Peu Toy
🛪*R A Patrick* Orritor St ☎63601 **R** ✿ Frd

COOTEHILL 1,542 Co Cavan Map12H61 EcTue
MdFri/Sat *Dublin73* Bailieborough14 *Belfast73*
Carrickmacross18 Castleblayney17 *Cavan15* Clones11
Cork203 Monaghan16
★★**White Horse** ☎24
Lic: 33rm3⇌🚿 🎜 CTV ✿ 50P 8🏠 ⚓ Ld9.30pm ➡

University College, Cork

CORK 128,645 Co Cork Map3W67 **See plan**
9 Bridge Street
AA ☎(021)505155
Dublin160 Bandon20 Bantry59 *Belfast264* Blarney6
Cashel61 Cobh16 Fermoy23 *Glengarriff63 Killarney56*
Kinsale18 *Limerick65* Macroom25 *Mallow22* Midleton14
Tipperary53 Tralee75 Waterford78 Youghal30
★★★**Arbutus Lodge** Montenotte ☎(021)501237
Telex no.32079
Closed 24–31 Dec; Lic; 20⇌🚿 🄳 🎜 CTV in bedrooms
✿ 25P 🚗 ⚓ ♀Irish & French Ld9.30pm S%
sB&B⇌🚿fr IRE20.50–IRE23.50 dB&B⇌🚿fr IRE32.50–
IRE35.75 L IRE7.95&alc D IRE10.65&alc
Wine IRE3.45 ➡ Credit cards ② ③ ⑤
★★★**Jury's** Muskerry Island, Lancaster Quay,
Western Rd ☎(021)26651 Telex no.6073
Lic; 150⇌🚿 🄳 🎜 CTV in bedrooms 200P ⚓
♀International Ld11pm ♥ ⚓ sB&B⇌🚿fr IRE23.92–
IRE31.62 dB&B⇌🚿fr IRE31.90–IRE46.64 L IRE5&alc
D IRE7.75–IRE8.50&alc Wine IRE3.50 ➡
Credit cards ① ② ③ ④ ⑤ ⑥
★★★**Metropole** McCurtain St ☎(021)508122
Telex no.32077
Lic; 125rm(83⇌🚿) Lift 🄳 🎜 CTV CTV available in
bedrooms ✿ 70🏠 Disco 5 nights wkly Live music &
dancing wkly Cabaret nightly ♀International Ld9.45pm
♥ ⚓ S% sB&B IRE19.25–IRE20.90 sB&B⇌🚿fr IRE23.10–
IRE24.75 dB&B IRE26.40–IRE28.60 dB&B⇌🚿fr IRE31.35–
IRE35.75 L IRE3–IRE4.40 Tea75p–IRE1.25
High Tea IRE3.75–IRE5&alc D IRE8&alc Wine IRE3.75 ➡
Credit cards ① ② ③ ④ ⑤ ⑥
★★★**Silver Springs** Lower Glenmire Rd, Tivoli
☎(021)507533 Telex no.6111
Closed 24 & 25 Dec; Lic; 72⇌🚿 Lift 🄳 🎜 CTV in
bedrooms 300P ⚓ Disco twice wkly Live music &
dancing 3 nights wkly Cabaret twice wkly ♪ ♀Irish &
French Ld10pm ♥ ⚓ S% sB&B⇌🚿fr IRE20–IRE24
dB&B⇌🚿fr IRE27–IRE33 L IRE3–IRE5.50 Tea40–50p
High Tea IRE4 20 alc D IRE8.50 Wine IRE3.30 ➡
Credit cards ① ② ③ ⑤
★★**Glengarriffe** Orchard Rd, Victoria Cross
☎(021)41785
Closed 23 Dec–16 Jan; Lic; 12rm(2⇌🚿) 🎜 CTV ✿ 30P
🚗 ⚓ ✦(hard) sauna bath Ld7pm ♥ ⚓
sB&B IRE14–IRE15 sB&B⇌🚿fr IRE17–IRE18
dB&B IRE28–IRE30 dB&B⇌🚿fr IRE34–IRE36
L IRE4–IRE4.50 Tea70p–IRE1.30 High Tea IRE4–IRE5
D IRE6–IRE7 Wine IRE3.50
★★**Moore's** Morrison's Island ☎(021)20068
Lic; 38rm(15⇌🚿) 🄳 🎜 CTV ✿ 🅿 Ld8.30pm ♥ ⚓ S%
sB&B IRE13.50 sB&B⇌🚿fr IRE15 dB&B IRE26.50
dB&B⇌🚿fr IRE29.50 L IRE4 alc Tea90p alc
High Tea IRE1.80&alc D IRE6 alc Wine IRE2.25 ➡
Credit cards ① ③

University College, Cork

Parliament Bridge, Cork

>*W M Canty & Sons* Anglesea St ☎(021)21285 **R** n⊜
>*Dennehy's* Dennehy's Cross ☎(021)42846 **R** n⊜ Frd
>*Johnson & Perrott Ltd* Emmet Pl ☎(021)23295 **R** n⊜
Peu Toy
>*P J O'Hea & Co Ltd* St Patrick's Quay
☎(021)26657 **R** n⊜ Opl
>*Pope Bros Ltd* Victoria Cross ☎(021)41851 **R** n⊜ BL

COURTMACSHERRY 210 Co Cork Map3W54
Dublin192 Cork31 Clonakilty9 Kinsale19
★★**Courtmacsherry** ☎(023)46198
Closed Oct–Mar; Lic; 16rm(5⇔ffl) ₪ CTV 50P ⇔ ⊥ ∩
♀ International Ld9.30pm ७ ⌂ S% sB&B IRE9.99–IRE12.10
dB&B IRE19.80–IRE24.20 dB&B⇔ffllRE23.10–IRE27.50
D IRE6–IRE7.50 Wine IRE3 **(RS)**

COURTOWN HARBOUR 291 Co Wexford Map9T15
Dublin70 Arklow15 *Belfast74 Cork137* Gorey4
Rosslare Harbour43 Wicklow35 Wexford30
★★**Bay View** ☎(055)25307
Closed Oct–16 Mar; Lic; 20rm(3⇔ffl) ₪ CTV ⊗ 30P
squash Ld8 45pm ७ ⌂ S% sB&B IRE7.70–IRE8.25
sB&B⇔ffllRE9.35–IRE9.62 dB&B IRE15.40–IRE16.50
dB&B⇔ffllRE18.70–IRE19.24 LIRE3.50–IRE4
Tea90p High Tea IRE4 alc D IRE6.50–IRE8.50
Wine IRE3 ➒ Credit cards ③
★★**Courtown** ☎(055)25108
Closed 28 Oct–3 Apr; Lic; 30rm(13⇔ffl) ₪ CTV ⊗ 20P
◪(heated) Live music & dancing Sat in season
♀Irish & French Ld9.30pm ७ ⌂ sB&B IRE9–IRE10.50
sB&B⇔ffllRE10.50–IRE12 dB&B IRE18–IRE21
dB&B⇔ffllRE20–IRE23 LIRE4–IRE4.50
D IRE3.50–IRE10 Wine IRE3.50 ➒ Credit cards ② ③ ⑤
>*Doyle's* Askigarron ☎(055)27366 **R** n⊜

CRAIGAVON 55.500 (with Lurgan and Portadown)
Co Armagh Map15J05 *Belfast30 Armagh12* Newry26
Dublin90
>*Irish Road Mtrs Ltd* Highfield Heights, Highfield Rd
☎42424 ☎33751 **R** Frd

CRAWFORDSBURN 487 Co Down Map15J48
EcThu/Sat *Belfast10* Bangor3 Donaghadee8
Downpatrick27 Dublin114 Newtownards5
★★★**Old Inn** ☎Helen's Bay853255
Closed Sun; 17rm(13⇔ffl) 1◻ ∫ ₪ CTV TV available in
bedrooms ⊗ 70P ⇔ ⊥ Ld9pm ७ S% sB&B £11.31
sB&B⇔ffl£11.98 dB&B £21.98 dB&B⇔ffl£29.40
L£3.85 D£4.85–£5.75&alc Wine £2.48

CREESLOUGH 269 Co Donegal Map16C03 EcMon
Dublin166 Belfast110 Carrigart8 *Donegal47*
Dunfanaghy6 Letterkenny17 *Londonderry38*
>*Friel Bros* ☎7 **R** n⊜ Frd

CROSSHAVEN 1.222 Co Cork Map4W76 *Dublin173*
Bandon23 Carrigaline5 *Cork13* Kinsale18
★**Helm** ☎(021)831400
Closed Sep–29 May; Lic; 19rm(1⇔ffl) ∫ ₪ TV ⊗ 75P ⊥
Live music & dancing twice wkly ♀Irish & French
Ld9pm ७ ⌂ *sB&B IRE7.40 sB&B⇔ffllRE8.90
dB&B IRE14.80 dB&B⇔ffllRE16.80 LIRE3.50 Tea90p
High Tea IRE4.50 alc D IRE5.75 Wine IRE2.50

CROSSMAGLEN 1.145 Co Armagh Map13H81
EcTue/Wed/Thu MdFri *Belfast54 Armagh21*
Castleblayney8 *Dublin66* Dundalk13 Newry16
>*Donaghy Bros* Newry St ☎228 **R** n⊜ Frd

CULLYBACKEY 1.642 Co Antrim Map15D00 EcWed
Belfast32 Ballymena4 *Dublin131*
>*Albert Wylie* Kilrea Rd ☎554 **R**

DERRYGONNELLY 383 Co Fermanagh Map16H15
EcThu *Belfast96 Dublin112* Enniskillen10
>*Derrygonnelly Autos* Main St ☎217 **R** ⊜ Lad

DERVOCK 600 Co Antrim Map15C93 EcSat *Belfast52*
Ballymena24 Bushmills7 *Dublin151*
>*A Chestnut & Son* Ballymoney Rd ☎387 ☎314 **R**

DINGLE 1.401 Co Kerry Map2O40 EcThu *Dublin220*
Belfast298 Cork97 Tralee31
★★★**Sceilig** ☎104 Telex no. 6900
Closed Dec–Feb; Lic; 80⇔ffl ∫ ₪ 100P ⊥ ◪(heated)
◪(hard) Live music & dancing twice wkly ⚭ Ld8.30pm
७ ⌂ sB&B⇔ffllRE9.70–IRE20.20 dB&B⇔ffllRE19.40–
IRE28.40 LIRE4.50 Tea IRE1.20 D IRE7.95 Wine IRE4
Credit cards ① ② ③ ⑤ ⑥
>*O'Connor's* ☎38 **R** ⊜

DOAGH 611 Co Antrim Map15J29 EcSat *Belfast11*
Ballymena15 *Larne13 Antrim9 Londonderry64 Dublin114*
Ballyclare2
>*Fortfield Mtrs* Belfast Rd ☎310 ☎215 **R** n⊜

DONAGHADEE 3.687 Co Down Map15J58 EcThu
Belfast19 Bangor6 *Downpatrick30 Dublin123*
Newtownards8 Portaferry23
★★**Imperial** The Parade ☎882661
24⇔ffl ∫ CTV TV available in bedrooms ⊗ ᵽ ⇔
Live music & dancing Sat Ld9.30pm ७ ⌂ L£3–£4&alc
Credit cards ① ② ⑤
Hightrees 28 New Rd ☎883363 **R**

DONEGAL 1.725 Co Donegal Map16G97 EcWed MdSat
Dublin138 Ballyshannon14 *Belfast122* Bundoran18
Cork250 Enniskillen36 Glenties17 Killybegs17
Londonderry43 Pettigo17 *Sligo40* Strabane32
Stranorlar18
★★★**Central** The Diamond ☎27 Telex no 33522
Closed Xmas; Lic; 48⇔ffl Lift ∫ ₪ CTV ᵽ ⊥ billiards
Live music & dancing Sat Ld9pm ७ ⌂ sB&B⇔ffllRE9–
IRE13.50 dB&B⇔ffllRE18–IRE27 LIRE4–IRE4.50
Tea IRE1–IRE1.25 D IRE7–IRE7.50 Wine IRE3 ➒
Credit cards ② ③ ⑥
★★**Abbey** ☎14
Closed Xmas; Lic; 40rm(26⇔ffl) Lift ∫ ₪ CTV TV available
in bedrooms P Ld9pm ७ ⌂ *sB&B IRE7.50–IRE8.50
sB&B⇔ffllRE8.25–IRE9.25 dB&B IRE15–IRE17
dB&B⇔ffllRE16.50–IRE18.50 LIRE3.25–IRE3.50
Tea IRE1 High Tea IRE3–IRE4.50 D IRE6 Wine IRE2.75
➒ Credit cards ① ② ③ ⑥
>*R E Johnston* ☎39 **R** n⊜ BL

DONEMANA 610 Co Tyrone Map14C40 EdWed MdSat
Belfast72 Dublin137 Dungiven19 Limavady22
Londonderry11
>23.00 *J L Cochrane & Son* ☎252 **R** Opl

DOUGLAS Co Cork Map3W66 *Dublin165 Cork3*
>*O'Mahony Bros Ltd* ☎(021)961321 **R** n⊜ Ren

DOWNINGS Co Donegal Map16C14 *Dublin181*
Dunfanaghy17 Letterkenny26 Milford13

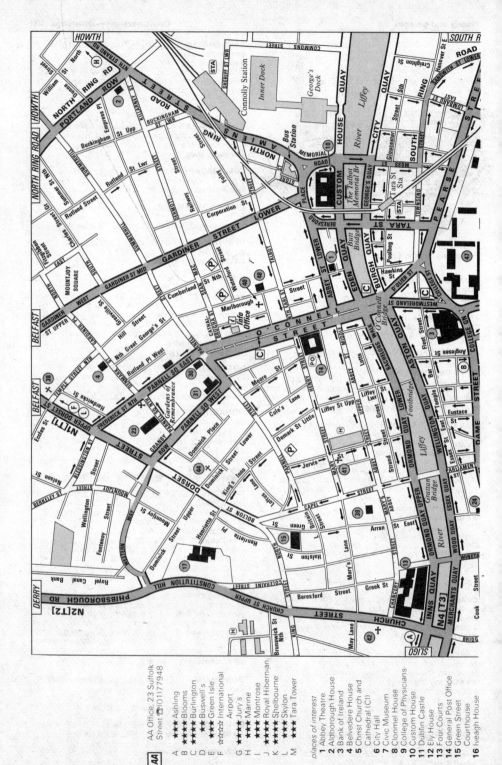

AA Office, 23 Suffolk Street ☎ 0117794B

A ★★★★ Ashling
B ★★★★ Blooms
C ★★★★ Burlington
D ★★ Buswell's
E ★★★★★ Green Isle
F ★★★★★ International Airport
G ★★★★ Jury's
H ★★★ Marine
J ★★★ Montrose
K ★★★★ Royal Hibernian
L ★★★★★ Shelbourne
M ★★★ Skylon
    ★★★ Tara Tower

places of interest
1 Abbey Theatre
2 Aldborough House
3 Bank of Ireland
4 Belvedere House
5 Christ Church and Cathedral (CI)
6 City Hall
7 Civic Museum
8 Clonmel House
9 College of Physicians
10 Custom House
11 Dublin Castle
12 Ely House
13 Four Courts
14 General Post Office
15 Green Street Courthouse
16 Iveagh House

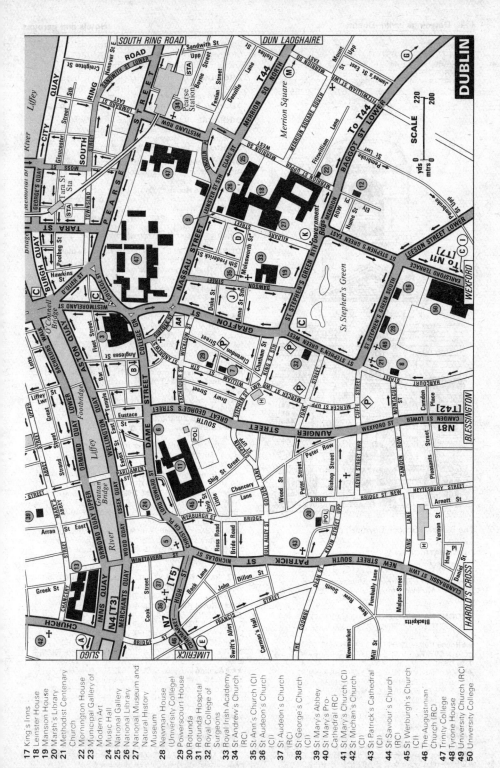

DUBLIN

17 King's Inns
18 Leinster House
19 Mansion House
20 Marsh's Library
21 Methodist Centenary
   Church
22 Mornington House
23 Municipal Gallery of
   Modern Art
24 Music Hall
25 National Gallery
26 National Library
27 National Museum and
   Natural History
   Museum
28 Newman House
   (University College)
29 Powerscourt House
30 Rotunda
31 Rotunda Hospital
32 Royal College of
   Surgeons
33 Royal Irish Academy
34 St Andrew's Church
   (RC)
35 St Ann's Church (CI)
36 St Audeon's Church
   (CI)
37 St Audeon's Church
   (RC)
38 St George's Church
   (CI)
39 St Mary's Abbey
40 St Mary's Pro-
   Cathedral (RC)
41 St Mary's Church (CI)
42 St Michan's Church
   (CI)
43 St Patrick's Cathedral
   (CI)
44 St Saviour's Church
   (RC)
45 St Werburgh's Church
   (CI)
46 The Augustinian
   Church (RC)
47 Trinity College
48 Tyrone House
49 University Church (RC)
50 University College

★★**Beach** 🏠5
Closed 21 Dec–Mar; RS15 Oct–20 Dec; Lic;
22rm(4⇌🛏) TV 60P 🚗 Ld10.30pm ✿ ⚓ S%
sB&B IRE6.75–IRE7.75 sB&B⇌🛏IRE8–IRE9
dB&B IRE12.50–IRE14.50 dB&B⇌🛏IRE15–IRE17
Tea IRE1.75–IRE2.25 High Tea IRE3.50–IRE4.25&alc
D IRE6–IRE6.50 Wine IRE2.75 🍴 Credit card ②

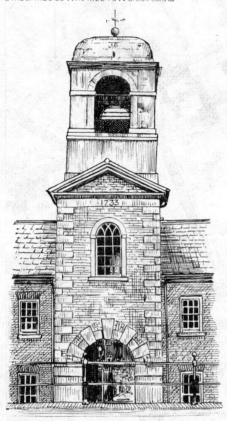

The Bluecoat School, Downpatrick

DOWNPATRICK 7,403 Co Down Map15J44 EcWed
MdTue/Sat *Belfast22* Ballynahinch10 Bangor28 *Dublin96*
Londonderry94 Lurgan29 Newcastle13 Newry30
Newtownards22 Saintfield11 Strangford9
⤳*Stewart Mtr Wks Ltd* 23 St Patricks Av ☎2215 **R** 🔧
BL RT

DROGHEDA 19,762 Co Louth Map13O07 EcWed
Dublin30 Dundalk22 Belfast73 Ceanannus Mor24
Navan17 Ardee15
★★**Boyne Valley** ☎(041)7737 Telex no.31334
Lic; 20⇌🛏) 🍴 CTV TV available in bedrooms 200P 4🏠
⚓ 🐟 Disco 4 nights wkly Live music & dancing 4 nights wkly
♨ ♀International Ld10.30pm ✿ ⚓ sB&B⇌🛏IRE13.50–
IRE14.50 dB&B⇌🛏IRE27–IRE29 L IRE3 Tea IRE1.50
High Tea IRE4.50 D IRE6.50 Wine IRE2.80
Credit cards ② ③ ⑤

⤳**DROMINEER** Co Tipperary Map7R88 *Dublin104*
Nenagh6 *Limerick31*
★★**Sail Inn** ☎Puckane3
Lic; 12rm(8⇌🛏) 2◫ Lift 🍴 CTV TV available in bedrooms
P ⚓ 🐟 Disco wkly Live music & dancing wkly Cabaret wkly
♨ ♀French Ld11pm ✿ ⚓ sB&B IRE7.15–IRE8.25

sB&B⇌🛏IRE9.15–IRE10.25 dB&B IRE14.30–IRE16.50
dB&B⇌🛏IRE17–IRE19.50 L IRE3.50 Tea IRE1.50
D IRE7–IRE8 🍴 Credit cards ② ③ ⑤ ⑥

DROMORE 2,303 **Co Down** Map15J25 EcThu MdWed/
Sat *Belfast18* Ballynahinch11 Banbridge7 *Downpatrick20*
Dublin86 Dundalk34 Lisburn9 Lurgan9 Newry20
⤳*Dominic McClure* Hillsborough Rd ☎692325 **R** n🔧

DROMORE 703 **Co Tyrone** Map14H36 EcWed
Belfast79 Dublin120 Enniskillen18 Fintona7 Irvinestown8
Londonderry43 Omagh9
⤳*McGlones* Omagh Rd ☎228 **R** 19.00 Dat

DRUMCONRATH Co Meath Map13N88 *Dublin45*
Ardee5 *Belfast70* Carrickmacross10 Cavan36 Drogheda18
Dundalk18 Slane12
★★🍴 **Aclare House** ☎(041)54101
Closed Nov–14 Mar; Lic; 16rm(9⇌🛏) ⚔ 🍴 TV ⊗ ⚓ ⚓ 🐟
♨ ♀Irish & German Ld9pm ✿ ⚓ sB&B IRE8.80
sB&B⇌🛏IRE10.15 dB&B IRE17 dB&B⇌🛏IRE19.20
L IRE3.05 Tea IRE1.10 High Tea IRE2.75–IRE6.60
D IRE3.85 Wine IRE2.50 🍴 Credit card ②

DUBLIN 679,748 Co Dublin Map 9O13 **See plan**
AA 23 Suffolk Street, Dublin 2 ☎(01)779481 EcWed/Sat
MdTue/Thu/Fri Arklow46 *Athlone78* Athy43
Balbriggan20 *Belfast104* Bray14 *Carlow52 Cork160*
Drogheda31 *Dundalk53* Dun Laoghaire7 Howth9 Lucan9
Mullingar51 Naas21 Navan29 *Port Laoise53* Skerries19
Slane29 *Trim28 Tullamore61 Wicklow32*
★★★★**Shelbourne** St Stephen's Green (Trusthouse
Forte) ☎(01)766471 Telex no.5184
Lic; 172⇌🛏 Lift) 🍴 TV available in bedrooms 60🏠
Ld10.30pm ✿ ⚓ *sB&B⇌🛏IRE25.75–IRE37.60
dB&B⇌🛏IRE39.15–IRE57.70 L IRE6.50 D IRE8.25
Wine IRE4 🍴 Credit cards ① ② ③ ④ ⑤ ⑥ **(RS)**
★★★★**Blooms** Anglesea St ☎(01)715622 Telex no.31688
Lic; 86⇌🛏 Lift) 🍴 CTV CTV in bedrooms ⊗ 50P
♀International Ld10.45pm ✿ ⚓ sB&B⇌🛏IRE35.50–
IRE41.25 dB&B⇌🛏IRE48–IRE56.50 L IRE7.50
Tea IRE1.80 D IRE9–IRE10 Wine IRE3.50 🍴
Credit cards ① ② ③ ④ ⑤ ⑥
★★★★**Burlington** Leeson St ☎01-785711
Telex no.5517
Lic; 420⇌🛏 Lift) ⊞ 🍴 CTV ⊗ P ⟨heated⟩
sauna bath ♀English & French Ld10.15pm ✿ ⚓ S%
Credit cards ① ② ③ ④ ⑤
☆☆☆☆**International Airport** Dublin Airport (5m N on N1)
(Trusthouse Forte) ☎(01)379211 Telex no.4612
Closed 25 Dec; Lic; 150⇌🛏) ⊞ 🍴 TV in bedrooms
200P ⚓ ⟨heated⟩ sauna bath Disco Sat Ld10.20pm ✿ ⚓
sB&B⇌🛏IRE20.13–IRE24.63 dB&B⇌🛏IRE28.44–
IRE38.57 L IRE4.05&alc
D IRE6.18&alc Wine IRE2.80 🍴 Credit cards ① ② ③ ④ ⑤ ⑥
★★★★**Jury's** Ballsbridge ☎(01)767511 Telex no.5304
Lic; 314⇌🛏 Lift) ⊞ 🍴 CTV in bedrooms 300P ⚓
◫ & ⟨heated⟩ Live music & dancing Tue–Sat
Cabaret Tue–Sun (Apr–Oct) ♀International Ld11pm
✿ ⚓ sB&B⇌🛏IRE32.50–IRE36.50 dB&B⇌🛏IRE42.50–
IRE54 L IRE5.50–IRE6.50&alc D IRE6.50–IRE8.50&alc
Wine IRE3.25 🍴 Credit cards ① ② ③ ④ ⑤ ⑥
★★★★**Royal Hibernian** Dawson St (Trusthouse Forte)
☎(01)772991 Telex no.5220
109⇌🛏 Lift) ⊞ 🍴 CTV in bedrooms ♀French
Ld11pm ✿ ⚓ S% sB&B⇌🛏IRE25.37–IRE34.31
dB&B⇌🛏IRE31.56–IRE48.38 L IRE5.75–IRE6.50
Tea IRE2–IRE2.25 D IRE7–IRE8.25 🍴 Credit cards ① ② ③ ④
⑤ ⑥
★★★**Ashling** Parkgate St ☎(01)772324 Telex no.5891
Lic; 42⇌🛏) 🍴 CTV CTV available in bedrooms ⊗ 30P
12🏠 Ld10pm ✿ ⚓ S% sB&B⇌🛏IRE17 dB&B⇌🛏IRE29
L IRE5.40 Tea IRE1.20 High Tea IRE5.40 D IRE8
Wine IRE3.90 Credit card ②
★★★**Green Isle** Crondalkin ☎(01)593406 Telex no.5517
Lic; 65⇌🛏) 🍴 TV ⊗ 250P ⚓ Ld11pm S%
Credit cards ① ② ③ ④ ⑤
★★★**Marine** Sutton ☎(01)322613 Telex no.4858
Closed Xmas; Lic; 23⇌🛏) 🍴 CTV in bedrooms ⊗ 100P
🚗 ⚓ ⟨heated⟩ sauna bath Ld11.15pm ✿ S%

Oscar Wilde's Birthplace, Dublin

No. 33 Synge Street, Dublin

BERNARD SHAW
AUTHOR OF MANY PLAYS
WAS
BORN IN THIS HOUSE
26 JULY 1856

Kilmainham Royal Hospital, Dublin

sB&B⇔fIRE17–IRE18 dB&B⇔fIRE30–IRE32
LIRE4.50–IRE5&alc DIRE6.50–IRE7.50&alc
Wine IRE3.50 Credit cards ①②③⑤⑥
★★★**Montrose** Stillorgan Rd ☎(01)693311
Telex no. 5517
Lic; 179⇔fi Lift 🅳 ♨ CTV ⊘ 200P sauna bath
Ld9.45pm ⚓ 🄛 sB&B⇔fiIRE13.02–IRE15.02
dB&B⇔fiIRE19.34–IRE22.24 LIRE2.60–IRE3.95 Tea75p
DIRE3.70–IRE6.50🄬 Credit cards ①②③④⑤⑥
★★★**Royal Dublin** O'Connell St ☎(01)749351
Telex no. 4288
Lic; 101⇔fi Lift 🅳 🎔 ♨ CTV available in bedrooms ⊘
50🏠 ♥ Irish & French Ld10.15pm ⚓ 🄛
*sB&B⇔fiIRE21.50–IRE28 dB&B⇔fiIRE29.50–IRE36
LIRE5.50 High Tea IRE4 DIRE6–IRE9 Wine IRE4.65🄬
Credit cards ①②③④⑤⑥

★★★**Skylon** Drumcondra Rd ☎379121
Lic; 88⇔fi Lift 🅳 🎔 ♨ CTV ⊘ 200P 20🏠 Ld10.30pm
⚓ 🄛 S% Credit cards ①②③④⑤⑥
★★★**Tara Tower** Merrion Rd ☎(01)694666 Telex no. 5517
Lic; 83⇔fi Lift 🅳 🎔 CTV TV in bedrooms ⊘ 100P
Ld10.30pm ⚓ 🄛 sB&B⇔fiRfr IRE14.02
dB&B⇔fiRfr IRE19.34 LIRE3.15–IRE4.95 Tea 75p
DIRE4.85–IRE6.90🄬 Credit cards ①②③④⑤⑥
★★**Buswell's** 25 Molesworth St (Inter-Hotel)
☎(01)764013 Telex no. 4858
Lic; 60⇔fi Lift 🅳 🎔 CTV 🏍 Ld8.15pm S% Credit card ②
⚡**R W Archer & Co Ltd** Sandwith St. 2 ☎(01)764131
R n⚓ Frd
⚡**Donore** Cork St. 8 ☎(01)751768 **R**
⚡**Walden Mtr Co Ltd** 173/4 Parnell St. 1 ☎(01)747831
R n⚓ Frd

DUNADRY Co Antrim Map15J28 *Belfast14 Antrim4 Dublin117*
★★★★**Dunadry Inn** ☎Templepatrick32474
Telex no.747245
Closed 25–27 Dec; 78⇌⋒ ☽ Ⅲ CTV in bedrooms ⊘ 250P ⚓ ∽ Live music & dancing Sat ♛ International Ld10.15pm ✿ ♆ S% sB&B⇌⋒£17.50–£22 dB&B⇌⋒£34 L£3.50–£4&alc Tea£1.50–£2.50 D£10 Wine£3 ⊟ Credit cards [1] [2] [3] [5]

The ancient keep of Dundalk

DUNDALK 23,816 Co Louth Map13J00 EcThu MdMon/Wed *Dublin53* Ardee13 *Armagh28 Belfast52* Carrickmacross14 Castleblayney17 *Cavan51* Ceanannus Mor32 Clones41 *Cork213* Drogheda22 Greenore15 Monaghan31 *Mullingar58* Navan34 Newcastle34 Newry13 Portadown33
★★★**Ballymascanlon House** ☎(042)71124
Telex no.33860
Closed Xmas Day; Lic; 44rm(24⇌⋒) ☽ Ⅲ TV 200P ⚓ ▭(heated) squash ∩ sauna Live music & dancing Sat & Sun Cabaret Thu ♣ Ld9.15pm ✿ ♆ LIR£3–IR£4 Tea IR£1–IR£2 D IR£5.50–IR£7 Wine IR£3 ⊟ Credit cards [1] [2] [3] [4] [5] [6]
★★★**Imperial** (Inter-Hotel) ☎(042)32241 Telex no.4858
Lic; 50⇌⋒ Lift ☽ Ⅲ CTV 100P 5⌂ Disco wknds Live music & dancing wknds Cabaret twice wkly ♛English & French Ld11pm ✿ ♆ ⊟ Credit cards [1] [2] [3] [5]
★★**Fairways** Dublin Rd ☎(042)35425
Lic; 46⇌⋒ ☽ Ⅲ CTV 300P ⚓ squash billiards sauna bath Disco wkly Live music & dancing 4 nights wkly Ld9.30pm ✿ ♆ sB&B⇌⋒IR£11–IR£13 dB&B⇌⋒IR£20–IR£22 LIR£3–IR£4 D IR£4.50–IR£5.50 Wine IR£2.50 ⊟ Credit cards [2] [3] [5]
⚒***Byrne & Maguire Ltd*** Dublin St ☎(042)31171 **R** n✲ Frd
⚒***Meehan's Ltd*** Dublin Rd ☎(042)34256 **R** n✲ Tal
⚒***Smith's*** ☎(042)4604 **R** n✲ Ren

DUNDONALD 7,978 Co Down Map15J47 EcThu *Belfast5* Ballynahinch18 Bangor11 *Downpatrick22 Dublin109* Killyleagh17 Newtownards5
T G Tinsley 763 Up Newtownards Rd ☎2651 **R** ✲ BL

DUNDRUM 807 **Co Down** Map13J43 EcThu *Belfast27* Ardglass15 Ballynahinch12 Castlewellan6 *Downpatrick6 Dublin89* Newcastle4
⚒20.00 ***William Graham & Sons*** Main St ☎250 **R**20.00 ✲

DUNDRUM Co Tipperary Map4R94 EcThu *Dublin10 Belfast211* Cashel9 *Cork70 Tipperary8*
⚒***Kennedy's*** ☎(062)71126 **R** n✲

DUNFANAGHY 303 Co Donegal Map16C03 EcWed *Dublin172 Belfast116 Carrigart14*
★★**Arnold's** ☎7
Closed 6 Oct–Mar; Lic; 37rm(15⇌⋒) ⚔ CTV 50P ⚓ ⚫(hard) ∽ ∩ ♣ Ld8.45pm ✿ ♆ sB&B IR£6.60–IR£7.90 sB&B⇌⋒IR£7.95–IR£9.30 dB&B IR£13.20–IR£18.80 dB&B⇌⋒IR£19.70–IR£29 L IR£3.30–IR£3.50 Tea IR£1–IR£1.20 High Tea IR£4 D IR£5–IR£5.30 ⊟ Credit card [5]
★★**Carrig Rua** ☎14
Closed Oct–Mar; RS Etr–Spring Bank Hol; Lic; 9rm(6⇌⋒) CTV ⊘ 16P Ld8.15pm ✿ ♆ sB&B IR£6.60–IR£7.80 sB&B⇌⋒IR£8–IR£9.35 dB&B IR£13.20–IR£15.60 dB&B⇌⋒IR£16–IR£18.70 L IR£3.60 Tea IR£2 High Tea IR£2.50–IR£6 Wine IR£4.50 ⊟ Credit card [2]

DUNGIVEN 1,479 Co Londonderry Map14C60 EcThu MdFri/Sat *Belfast54 Antrim36* Coleraine20 *Dublin133* Garvagh12 Limavady10 *Londonderry20 Maghera13* Strabane26
⚒***Dungiven Mtrs*** Railway Pl ☎342 **R**

DUNGLOE 940 Co Donegal Map16B71 EcWed *Dublin72 Belfast24 Carrigart43 Cork284 Donegal34* Dunfanaghy28 Glenties17 Gweedore10 Letterkenny32 *Londonderry56* Rosapenna45 Strabane45 Stranorlar31
★★**Ostan Na Rosann** ☎91
50⇌⋒ ☽ Ⅲ CTV ⊘ 200P ⚓ ▭(heated) Live music & dancing nightly ♣ Ld9pm ✿ ♆ sB&B⇌⋒IR£7.50–IR£9.50 dB&B⇌⋒IR£14–IR£18 L IR£2.65 Tea IR£1.20 High Tea IR£5–IR£6 alc D IR£5.50 ⊟ Xmas Credit cards [2] [5]
⚒***Greene's*** ☎14 **R** ✲ Frd

DUN LAOGHAIRE 98,379 Co Dublin Map9O22 EcWed *Dublin7 Belfast111 Cork168* Bray8 Wicklow27
★★★**Royal Marine** ☎(01)801911
Lic; 115rm100⇌⋒ Lift ☽ Ⅲ CTV ⊘ 200P 10⌂ ✲ ⚓ ⚫ sauna bath ♛International Ld9.30pm ✿ ♆ S% ⊟ Credit cards [1] [2] [3] [5]
★★**Hotel Victor** Rochestown Av ☎(01)853555
Telex no.4404
Lic; 45⇌⋒ Lift ☽ Ⅲ CTV CTV available in bedrooms ⊘ P ⚓ billiards sauna bath ♣ ♛English & French Ld10.15 ✿ ♆ S% sB&B⇌⋒IR£12.50 dB&B⇌⋒IR£20 L IR£3.50–IR£4.50 Tea IR£2–IR£3 High Tea IR£3.50–IR£5.50 D IR£6–IR£7.50 Wine IR£3.60 ⊟ Credit cards [2] [3] [5]
★**Abbey** ☎(01)805156
Lic; 11rm Ⅲ TV ⊘ ♛English Last High Tea7.30pm S% ⊟ Credit cards [2] [3] [6]

DUNMORE EAST 656 Co Waterford Map5S60 EcThu *Dublin108 Belfast211 Cork87* Tramore9 *Waterford9*
★★**Haven** ☎(051)83150
Closed Oct–Mar; Lic.; 17rm(8⇌⋒) ☽ Ⅲ CTV ⊘ 40P ⚓ Disco twice wkly Carbaret 5 nights wkly ♣ Ld10pm ✿ sB&B IR£11–IR£16.50 sB&B⇌⋒IR£12.10–IR£17.60 dB&B IR£22–IR£33 dB&B⇌⋒IR£24.20–IR£35.20 D IR£7 Wine IR£2 ⊟ Credit cards [1] [2] [3] [5]

DUNMURRY 6,078 Co Antrim Map15J26 EcWed/Sat *Belfast5 Dublin99*
★★★★**Conway** (Trusthouse Forte) ☎Belfast612101
Lic; 78⇌⋒ Lift ☽ Ⅲ TV available in bedrooms 200P ⚓ ⌒(heated) Ld9.45pm ✿ ♆ sB&B⇌⋒£18.50 dB&B⇌⋒£26 Credit cards [1] [2] [3] [4] [5] [6]

DURROW 596 Co Laois Map8S47 EcWed *Dublin68 Belfast171 Cork94 Kilkenny17* Roscrea22
★★**Castle Arms** ☎(0502)36117
Lic; 15rm(5⇌⋒) ⚔ Ⅲ CTV ⚓ ∽ Disco Sat Live music & dancing Sat & Sun ♣ Ld8.45pm ✿ ♆ sB&B IR£7–IR£8.25 sB&B⇌⋒IR£7–IR£8.25 dB&B IR£13.75–IR£15.95 dB&B⇌⋒IR£13.75–IR£15.95

EDERNEY Co Fermanagh Map16H26 EcWed *Belfast88 Bundoran29 Donegal25 Dublin117 Enniskillen15 Omagh17* Strabane26
⚒***John James McElhill*** Market St ☎Kesh294 ☎Kesh348 **R** Lad

EDGEWORTHSTOWN 546 Co Longford Map12N27 *Dublin68 Athlone27 Belfast112 Cavan26* Longford8
★**Edgeworth** ☎18
RS25 & 26 Dec; Lic; 16rm(4⇌⋒) 2⊟ ☽ Ⅲ CTV 15P 6⌂

♀Irish & French Ld9pm ✿ ⚘ sB&B IRE9–IRE10
sB&B🖨IRE11–IRE12 dB&B IRE18–IRE19
dB&B🖨IRE20–IRE22 L IRE3 Tea IRE1.50
High Tea IRE3alc D IRE5–IRE6.50&alc Wine IRE3.50
Credit card ②

ENNIS 10,840 Co Clare Map7R37 *Dublin 146*
Ballyvaughan39 *Belfast211 Cork88* Ennistymon16
Galway42 Gort19 Kilkee35 Killaloe31 Kilrush27
Lahinch19 *Limerick23* Loughrea34 *Portumna46*
Shannon Airport14
★★★**Old Ground** (Trusthouse Forte) ☎(065)21127 **(RS)**
Telex no.8103
Lic; 63rm(61🖨🛏) 𝒟 ㎜ CTV CTV in bedrooms 100P ⚓
Cabaret Mon in season ♀French Ld10.45pm ✿ ⚘
sB&B🖨IRE17.50–IRE22 dB&B🖨IRE22.50–IRE31.50
L IRE4.40–IRE5&alc Tea IRE1.20–IRE1.50
High Tea IRE5.50alc D IRE8&alc 🍴 Credit cards ①②③④⑤⑥
★★★**Auburn Lodge** Galway Rd ☎(065)21247
Closed Xmas Day; Lic; 23rm(17🖨🛏) 𝒟 ㎜ CTV
CTV available in bedrooms ⊗ P ⚓ ♀European
Ld9.30pm ✿ ⚘ S% sB&B IRE9.35–IRE11
sB&B🖨IRE11–IRE13.20 dB&B IRE17.60–IRE18.70
dB&B🖨IRE19.25–IRE22 L IRE4 Tea IRE1.15
High Teafr IRE4 D IRE6 Wine IRE3.50 Credit card ②
★★★**West County Inn** ☎(065)21421
Lic; 50🖨🛏 𝒟 ㎜ CTV 350P ⚓ ♨ sauna bath Music nightly
Music & dancing Sat ⚘ ♀English & French Ld10.30pm ✿ ⚘
Credit cards ①②③⑤
🔧*T Shiels & Co Ltd* ☎(065)21035 **R** n☢ Frd

ENNISCORTHY 5,704 Co Wexford Map5S93 EcThu
MdWed/Fri *Dublin81* Arklow30 *Belfast185* Borris19
Bunclody13 *Carlow33 Cork114* Gorey19 *Kilkenny36*
Muine Bheag30 New Ross21 *Rosslare Harbour27*
Wexford15 Wicklow46
★**Murphy-Flood's** Town Centre ☎(054)2413
Telex no.8586
Closed Xmas Day & Good Fri; Lic; 25rm(5🖨🛏) ㎜ CTV ⊗
3🏠 Disco twice wkly Live music & dancing twice wkly
♀Irish & French Ld8.45pm ✿ ⚘ S% sB&B IRE9.65–IRE9.90
sB&B🖨IRE11.15–IRE11.40 dB&B IRE17.15–IRE17.60
dB&B🖨IRE20.15–IRE20.60 L IRE3.50 Tea IRE1
High Tea IRE4–IRE5alc D IRE5.50–IRE6&alc
Wine IRE2.50 🍴 Credit cards ①②

ENNISCRONE 582 Co Sligo Map11G22 *Dublin163*
Ballina8 *Belfast163 Cork201 Sligo35*
★**Killala Bay** ☎(096)36239
Lic; 17rm(5🖨🛏) ㎜ CTV P billiards Disco wkly Live music &
dancing 3 nights wkly Ld8pm ✿ ⚘ *sB&B IRE6–IRE7
dB&B IRE11–IRE13 dB&B🖨IRE13.50–IRE15.50
L IRE3.50 Tea IRE1alc High Tea IRE3–IRE4&alc
D IRE6&alc Wine IRE2.85 🍴 Credit cards ①②③⑤

ENNISKILLEN 6,553 Co Fermanagh Map12H24 EcWed
MdTue/Thu *Belfast86 Armagh52* Athlone80 Ballyshannon28
Belcoo12 Belleek24 Carrick-on-Shannon41 *Cavan32*
Clones11 *Cork216* Donegal36 *Dublin102* Dungannon44
Kesh14 *Londonderry60* Longford52 Manorhamilton26
Monaghan34 Omagh27 Sligo42
★★★**Killyhevlin** *Dublin Rd* ☎3481
Closed Xmas; 27rm(17🖨🛏) 𝒟 ㎜ CTV TV available in
bedrooms ⊗ 200P ⚓ Live music & dancing Sat
Ld9pm ✿ ⚘ *sB&Bfr IRE8.64 sB&B🖨IRE fr IRE13.50
dB&Bfr IRE16.20 dB&B🖨IRE fr IRE23.76 Lfr IRE3.51 Tea IRE1alc
High Tea IRE3.50alc D IRE5alc Wine IRE2.80 🍴
Credit cards ①③⑤
★**Railway** ☎22084
Closed Sun; 17rm(14🖨🛏) A6rm 𝒟 ㎜ CTV ⊗ P 🚗 ♿
Ld8.30pm ✿ ⚘ sB&B IRE7–£8 sB&B🖨IRE8–£9
dB&B IRE14–£16 dB&B🖨IRE16–£18 L£2.75–£3.90
High Tea £4alc D £4.50–£6.50 Wine £3.50 🍴
🔧23.00 *T P Topping & Co Ltd* Dublin Rd ☎3475
☎3311 **R** BL RT

ENNISTYMON 1,013 Co Clare Map6R18 EcThu MdTue/
Sat *Dublin165* Ballyvaughan18 *Belfast227 Cork104*

Ennistymon and the River Cullinagh

Ennis16 Galway49 Kilkee29 Lahinch3 *Limerick39*
Lisdoonvarna8
★★**Falls** ☎4
Lic; 38rm(16🖨🛏) CTV 30P 🚗 ⚓ ⚘ Ld9pm ✿ ⚘
sB&B IRE8.25 sB&B🖨IRE9.08 dB&B IRE16.50
dB&B🖨IRE17.33 L IRE2.50 Tea60P High Tea IRE4
D IRE5 Wine IRE2.40 Credit cards ②③

FERMOY 4,033 Co Cork Map4W89 EcWed MdSat
Dublin139 Belfast242 Cahir28 Cappoquin20 Cashel39
Clonmel38 Cobh32 *Cork23* Dungarvan32 *Killarney61*
Kilmallock24 *Limerick45* Lismore17 *Mallow19* Midleton20
Mitchelstown10 *Tipperary30 Waterford59* Youghal27
🔧*Patrick O'Connor (Mtrs) Ltd* Dublin Rd ☎(025)31700
R n☢ Toy
🔧*O'Sullivan's* McCurtain St ☎(025)31797 **R** n☢
Aud Maz VW

FINAGHY 4,919 Co Antrim Map15J37 EcWed *Belfast4*
Armagh37 Dublin100 Dungannon38 Dunmurry1
Lisburn5 Newry34
🔧*Finaghy* 87–89 Upper Lisburn Rd ☎Belfast610196
R ☢

FINTONA 1,216 Co Tyrone Map14H46 EcWed MdTue
Belfast71 Dublin103 Enniskillen21
🔧*Coulters Auto Engineers* 12–14 King St ☎208 **R** ☢

FIVEMILETOWN 936 Co Tyrone Map14H41 EcWed
MdFri *Belfast70 Armagh34* Aughnacloy16 *Dublin109*
Dungannon26 *Enniskillen18* Fintona9 *Londonderry52*
🔧*R M Smith & Sons* Clogher Rd ☎238 **R** ☢
🔧*Wesley Irvine* Clabby ☎206 **R** ☢ Tal

FOXFORD 868 Co Mayo Map11G20 EcWed MdThu
Dublin141 Ballina10 Belfast171 Castlebar15 *Cork183*
Pontoon5 Swinford9
★★★**Pontoon Bridge** ☎20
Closed 15 Oct–14 Apr; Lic; 24rm10🖨🛏 ㎜ CTV 40P ⚓ ♨
♨ ⚘ Ld9pm ✿ ⚘ Credit cards ②⑥
🔧23.59 *Reape's Auto Service* ☎19 **R** 18.30 ☢ Frd Tal

GALWAY 29,375 Co Galway Map7M22 EcMon MdWed/
Sat *Dublin136* Athenry15 *Athlone58* Ballinasloe42
Ballinrobe30 Ballyvaughan31 *Belfast190* Castlebar48
Clifden49 Cork129 Cong26 *Ennis42* Gort23 Headford16
Leenane41 *Limerick64* Loughrea23 Oughterard17
Portumna42 Roscommon51 Sligo85 Tuam21 Westport51
★★★★**Great Southern** Eyre Sq ☎(091)64041
Telex no.8364
Lic; 120🖨🛏 Lift 𝒟 ㎜ CTV CTV available in bedrooms ⊗
50P 🅿(heated) sauna bath Disco 5 nights wkly
Cabaret 6 nights wkly ♀International Ld10pm ✿ ⚘
sB&B🖨IRE18.20–IRE28.70 dB&B🖨IRE27.45–
IRE48.55 L IRE4.60 Tea IRE2 High Tea IRE4 D IRE8&alc
Wine IRE3 🍴 Credit cards ①②③⑤
★★★**Ardilaun House** Taylor's Hill ☎(091)21433
Telex no.8873
Closed 24–27 Dec; Lic; 73🖨🛏 Lift 𝒟 ㎜ CTV CTV available
in bedrooms 150P ⚓ Live music & dancing Sat ⚘

♡Irish & French Ld9pm ✿ ⬜ sB&B⇴🏠IRE1·1–IRE17
dB&B⇴🏠IRE18–IRE27 LIRE4–IRE4.50&alc
DIRE7–IRE8.25&alc Wine IRE3 Credit cards ①②③④⑤⑥
★★★**Corrib Great Southern** ☎(091)65281
Lic; 117rm115⇴🏠 Lift ♪ 🐎 CTV ⬛(heated) billiards
sauna bath Live music Sat Live music & dancing Sat
(Nov–Apr) ✿ ⬜ S% Credit cards ①②③⑥
☆☆☆**Flannery's** Dublin Rd ☎(091)65111
Telex no 4404
Lic; 72⇴🏠 Lift ♪ ⊞ 🐎 CTV ✷ 200P ♡English
Ld8.45pm ✿ ⬜ S% 🏱 Credit card ②
★★★**Odeon** Eyre Sq ☎(091)62041
Lic; 60rm30⇴🏠 Lift ♪ 🐎 CTV ✷ 30P ♡English & French
Ld9.30pm ✿ ⬜ S% Credit cards ①②③④⑤⑥
★★★**Warwick** Salthill ☎(091)64325

Closed Xmas; Lic; 50rm(30⇴🏠) ♪ 🐎 CTV 50P ⚓
Cabaret 3 nights wkly Ld8.45pm ✿ sB&B IRE8–IRE10
sB&B⇴🏠IRE9.50–IRE11.50 dB&B IRE15–IRE20
dB&B⇴🏠IRE18–IRE23 LIRE3.50 DIRE7 Wine IRE3.50
Credit cards ②③
★★**Anno Santo** Threadneedle Rd, Salthill ☎(091)22110
Lic; 16⇴🏠 ♪ 🐎 CTV TV available in bedrooms ✷ 10P ♠
Ld8.30pm ✿ ⬜ sB&B IRE7.50–IRE13 20
sB&B⇴🏠IRE8.95–IRE14.65 dB&B IRE13.50–IRE17
dB&B⇴🏠IRE16.40–IRE19.95 LIRE4–IRE7.50
Tea IRE2–IRE3.50 DIRE6–IRE8.50 Wine IRE3 🏱
Credit card ⑥
★★**Galway Ryan** Dublin Rd ☎(091)63181
Telex no 8349
Lic; 96⇴🏠 Lift 🐎 TV 200P ⚓ Ld9pm ✿ ⬜

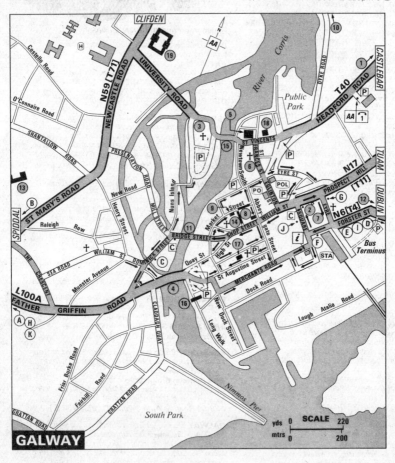

GALWAY

```
                                        SCALE
                            yds  0          220
                            mtrs 0        200
```

AA Road Service Centre ☎(091)64438

		places of interest		
A	★★ Anno Santa	**1** Ballindooly Tower	**11** O'Brien's Bridge
B	★★★ Ardilaun House	**2** Browne's Gateway	**12** Roscam Round Tower
C	★ Atlanta	**3** Cathedral of St Nicholas and Our	**13** St Mary College
D	★★★ Corrib Great Southern	Lady Assumed into Heaven	**14** St Nicholas Church (CI)
E	★★ Galway Ryan	**4** Claddagh Bridge	**15** Salmon Weir Bridge
F	★★★★ Great Southern	**5** Courthouse	**16** Spanish Arch
G	★★★ Odeon	**6** Franciscan Friary	**17** Taebhdhearc Theatre
H	★★ Rockbarton Park	**7** J F Kennedy Memorial Garden	**18** Town Hall
I	☆☆☆ Flannery's	**8** Lynch's Castle	**19** University College
J	★★ Skeffington Arms	**9** Lynch Stone	
K	★★★ Warwick	**10** Menlough Castle	

O'Brien Bridge, Galway

sB&B⇨🏠ﬁIR£16–IR£20 dB&B⇨🏠ﬁIR£24–IR£30 🅿
Credit cards 1 2 3 4 5 6
★★Rockbarton Park Salthill ☎(091)61717
Closed 24–27 Dec; Lic; 11rm(9⇨ﬁ) 🍴 CTV 11P
Ld9.15pm ⚹ ⫴ S% sB&B IR£7.45–IR£11.55
sB&B⇨🏠ﬁIR£8.10–IR£12.20 dB&B IR£12.35–IR£19.80
dB&B⇨🏠ﬁIR£13.50–IR£21 LIR£4.65 Tea IR£1.20
High Tea IR£2.60–IR£5.50 D IR£6.60 Wine IR£4.30
★★Skeffington Arms Eyre Sq ☎(091)63173
Closed 23–31 Dec; Lic; 22rm(13⇨ﬁ) 𝄞 🍴 CTV ⚹ 20P
♿ Irish & French Ld9pm ⚹ ⫴ sB&B IR£10–IR£11
sB&B⇨🏠ﬁIR£11–IR£12 dB&B IR£17.50–IR£19
dB&B⇨🏠ﬁIR£19.50–IR£21 LIR£4 High Tea IR£5alc
D IR£6.50 Wine IR£3.20 Credit card 3
★Atlanta Dominick St ☎(091)62241
Lic; 20rm 🍴 CTV ⚹ 4P 🚐 Ld8pm ⚹ ⫴ sB&B IR£7.50–
IR£8.50 dB&B IR£14–IR£16 Tea75p–IR£1&alc
D IR£6.50–IR£8&alc Wine IR£2.50

GARRISON 119 Co Fermanagh Map16G95 EcThu
Belfast111 •
⟋Melvin (A & S Rasdale) ☎Belleek246 **R**19.00 n🚍

GARRYVOE Co Cork Map4W96 *Dublin159 Cork22*
Ballycotton6 Midleton9
★★Garryvoe ☎(021)62718
Closed Xmas Day; Lic; 20rm(11⇨ﬁ) 🍴 CTV ⚹ 🅿 🚐 👶
Cabaret twice wkly ♫ Ld8.45pm ⚹ ⫴ S%
*sB&B IR£6.25–IR£6.75 sB&B⇨🏠ﬁIR£7.50–IR£8
dB&B IR£12–IR£13 dB&B⇨🏠ﬁIR£14.50–IR£15.50
LIR£3.30–IR£4 Tea90p–IR£1.15 High Tea IR£1.90–
IR£4.80 D IR£2.50–IR£7 Wine IR£3 Credit cards 1 2 3 4
5 6

GLENBEIGH 266 Co Kerry Map2V69 *Dublin204
Belfast282* Cahirciveen18 *Cork78 Killarney22*
Killorglin8 *Limerick81* Tralee25 Waterville28
★★Falcon Inn ☎56
Lic; 17rm 🍴 CTV 40P ⚓ ⚓ ∩ Live music nightly (in season)
nc3 ♿ English, American, Continental Ld9pm ⚹ ⫴ S% 🅿
Credit cards 2 3 5 6
★★Glenbeigh ☎4
Closed Oct–Mar; Lic; 21rm(9⇨🏠ﬁ) 𝄞 🍴 CTV 100P ⚓
Ld9pm ⚹ ⫴ sB&B IR£9.50–IR£11 sB&B⇨🏠ﬁIR£13.50–
IR£16 dB&B IR£18–IR£21 dB&B⇨🏠ﬁIR£23–IR£27
Tea IR£1.50alc D IR£7.50alc 🅿 Credit cards 1 2 3 5
★★Towers ☎12
Closed mid Oct–mid Nov; Lic; 21rm(4⇨🏠ﬁ) 𝄞 🍴 200P
⚓ ⫴ Live music & dancing Sat Cabaret nightly
♿ Irish & Continental Ld8.30pm ⚹ ⫴ sB&B IR£10.50–IR£12
sB&B⇨🏠ﬁIR£15.50–IR£17 dB&B IR£20–IR£22
dB&B⇨🏠ﬁIR£25–IR£27 LIR£4.95–IR£6.50 D IR£11.50
Wine IR£5.95 🅿 Credit cards 2 3 5 6
⟋£21.00 *John O'Sullivan* ☎7 **R**19.00 🚍 Frd

GLENDALOUGH Co Wicklow Map9T19 *Dublin31*
Arklow22 Bray19 *Cork165* Naas26 Rathdrum9 *Wicklow20*
★★Royal ☎(0404)5135
Closed Oct–Mar; Lic; 28rm(16⇨🏠ﬁ) Lift 🍴 20P 4🏠 ⚓
Ld8pm ⚹ S% sB&B IR£10.95 sB&B⇨🏠ﬁIR£15
dB&B IR£21.90 dB&B⇨🏠ﬁIR£27.58 LIR£5.23
D IR£8.75 Wine IR£4.10 🅿

GLENGARRIFF 244 Co Cork Map2V95 *Dublin223*
Bandon48 Bantry11 *Belfast309* Castletownbere21 *Cork63*
Kenmare18 *Killarney38* Macroom38 Parknasilla32
Skibbereen29
★★Eccles ☎3
RSJan–Mar; Lic; 60rm(31⇨🏠ﬁ) 𝄞 🍴 CTV 60P ⚓
billiards Disco twice wkly Live music & dancing twice
wkly Cabaret wkly Ld9.15pm ⚹ ⫴ sB&B IR£9–IR£11
sB&B⇨🏠ﬁIR£10–IR£12 dB&B IR£18–IR£20
dB&B⇨🏠ﬁIR£14–IR£22 LIR£3.50–IR£4
Tea IR£1–IR£2 High Tea IR£3–IR£5 D IR£6–IR£8
Wine IR£2.75 🅿 Credit card 2

GLOUNTHAUNE 432 Co Cork Map4W77 *Dublin160
Belfast265 Cork6* Midleton7
★★Ashbourne House ☎(021)821230
Closed 23–30Dec; Lic; 26⇨🏠ﬁ 𝄞 🍴 CTV
TV available in bedrooms 100P ⚓ ⌸(heated) ⌁(hard)
sauna bath croquet Ld9pm ⚹ ⫴ S% *sB&B⇨🏠ﬁIR£16.50–
IR£18 dB&B⇨🏠ﬁIR£28.50–IR£33 LIR£3.90–IR£4.50
D IR£6.75–IR£8 Wine IR£3.35 🅿 Credit cards 1 2 3 5 6

GOREY 3,024 Co Wexford Map9T15 EcWed MdSat
Dublin62 Arklow11 *Belfast166* Carlow37 *Cork133*
Enniscorthy19 New Ross40 Rosslare Harbour39
Shillelagh16 Waterford55 Wexford26 Wicklow27
★★★⚑⫴Marlfield House ☎(055)21124
Closed 10 Dec–14 Feb; Lic; 11⇨🏠ﬁ2⌸ 🍴 CTV ⚹ 50P 🚐
⚓ English, Irish & French Ld8.30pm ⚹ ⫴
sB&B⇨🏠ﬁIR£14–IR£15 dB&B⇨🏠ﬁIR£23–IR£28
LIR£4alc Tea IR£1.40alc Wine IR£3.50 🅿
Credit card 3
⟋R H Nixon Ltd ☎(055)21285 **R** n🚍

GORTAHORK Co Donegal Map16B93 *Dublin182
Belfast126* Carrigart24 Dunfanaghy10 Dungloe18
Letterkenny33
★★McFadden's ☎Falcarragh17
Lic; 35rm(7⇨🏠ﬁ) 🍴 CTV ⚹ 50P 🚐 Disco wkly
Live music & dancing twice wkly ♿ French Ld9pm
⚹ ⫴ S% sB&B IR£7.25–IR£8.40 sB&B⇨🏠ﬁIR£8.75–
IR£9.90 dB&B IR£15.50–IR£16.80 dB&B⇨🏠ﬁIR£17.50–
IR£19.80 LIR£3.50–IR£3.90 Tea80p–IR£1.20
High Tea IR£6alc D IR£7–IR£7.70 Wine IR£3.50 🅿
Credit cards 2 3 5

GORTEEN 165 Co Sligo Map11G60 *Dublin119 Cork193
Sligo22* Tobercurry11

꙰*Sherlock's* ☎25 ☎500 **R**

GORTIN 261 Co Tyrone Map14H48 EcThu *Belfast81*
Carrickmore17 *Dublin123 Londonderry25*
Newtownstewart7 *Omagh10* Strabane15
꙰*G G Pentland & Sons* Main St ☎201 **R**

GOUGANE BARRA Co Cork Map3W06 *Dublin205*
Bantry15 *Belfast309 Cork45 Glengarriff29* Macroom20
★★**Gougane Barra** ☎Ballingeary31
Closed 8 Oct–Mar; Lic; 33rm(18⇨fl) ♨ CTV ⚘ 30P ⇔ ⑁
Live music & dancing Sat nc8 Ld8pm ♦ ⚲ S%
sB&B IRE7.50–IRE8.50 sB&B⇨fl IRE8.50–IRE9.50
dB&B IRE14.50–IRE16 dB&B⇨fl IRE16–IRE18
Tea IRE1.50 D IRE6.50 Wine IRE2.75 ☐ Credit card ③

GREYSTONES 3,292 Co Wicklow Map9O21 EcWed
Dublin20 Bray6 Dun Laoghaire13 *Wicklow13*
★★★**La Touche** ☎(01)874401
Lic; 44rm(17⇨fl) A11rm(4⇨fl) CTV ⚘ 80P ⚲
⚲ (hard & grass) Live music & dancing Wed ♨
⚑Irish & French Ld10pm ♦ ⚲ sB&B IRE10–IRE14
sB&B⇨fl IRE12–IRE17 dB&B IRE18–IRE26
dB&B⇨fl IRE24–IRE34 LIRE4–IRE6 Tea IRE1.50–
IRE2.50 High Tea IRE2.50–IRE5 DIRE7–IRE10&alc
Wine IRE3.50 ☐ Credit cards ①②③⑤

HEADFORD 673 Co Galway Map 11M24 EcThu
Dublin133 Belfast189 Cork145 Galway16
★**Angler's Rest** ☎(093)21528
Lic; 14rm3⇨fl ♨ CTV 50P Ld8.30pm ♦ ⚲

HELEN'S BAY 799 Co Down Map15J48 EcThu *Belfast11*
Bangor4 *Dublin115*
꙰18.30 (13.00 Sat) *Marshall Pritchard* Helen's Bay
Garage, Bridge Rd ☎3634 **R**18.30 (13.00 Sat)

HILLTOWN 597 Co Down Map13J22 EcThu *Belfast36*
Castlewellan10 *Downpatrick21* Kilkeel13
Newcastle12 Newry9 Rathfriland3 Rostrevor9
꙰*Mathews Mtrs* ☎Rathfriland326 **R**22.00 ⚘

HOLYWOOD 7,980 Co Down Map15J22 EcWed
Belfast6 Dublin110
★★★★**Culloden** ☎5223
34⇨fl 1☐ Lift ♪ ♨ CTV CTV in bedrooms 400P ⚲
Live music & dancing Thu ⚑French Ld9.30pm ♦ ⚲ S%
sB&B⇨fl fr£20.70 dB&B⇨fl fr£29.90 Lfr£5.75 Dfr£5.75
Wine £3.80 Credit cards ①②③⑤
꙰*R Henderson* Redburn Square ☎3795 **R**18.30 ⚘
꙰*Leslie Innes* 131 High St ☎3044 **R**21.00 (Sat & Sun
18.00) ⚘
꙰*J E Meneely & Son* 69/75 High St ☎3132 **R** ⚘ BL

INCHIGEELA Co Cork Map3W26 *Dublin195 Belfast299*
Cork35 Glengarriff28
★**Creedon's** ☎12
Closed 20–28 Dec; Lic; 20rm(5⇨fl) ✗ ♨ CTV
CTV available in bedrooms 20P ⚲ ○ Ld8pm ♦ ⚲ S%
sB&B IRE5.75 sB&B⇨fl IRE6.75 dB&B IRE11.50
dB&B⇨fl IRE13.50 LIRE2.75–IRE3&alc Tea IRE1&alc
High Tea IRE3–IRE4&alc DIRE4–IRE6&alc Wine IRE3 ☐
Credit cards ①②③④⑤⑥
★**Lake** ☎10
Lic; 15rm(2⇨fl) CTV ⚘ P 2🏠 nc12 Ld6pm ♦ ⚲
sB&B IRE5 sB&B⇨fl IRE6 dB&B IRE10 dB&B⇨fl IRE11
LIRE3 Tea IRE1 High Tea IRE4 DIRE5 Wine IRE4

INNISHANNON 190 Co Cork Map4W96 *Dublin176*
Cork15 Bandon5 Kinsale8
★★**Innishannon** ☎(021)75121
Closed 24&25 Dec; Lic; 13⇨fl ♨ CTV 50P ⇔ ⚲ ⑁
Live music & dancing Sat ⚑Irish & French Ld 9.45pm ♦ ⚲
S% ☐ Credit cards ②③⑥

IRVINESTOWN 1,286 Co Fermanagh Map16H25 EcThu
MdWed *Belfast96* Ballyshannon27 *Bundoran32 Dublin112*
Enniskillen10 Kesh6 *Londonderry51 Omagh17*
★★**Mahons** ☎656
20rm(7⇨fl) 2☐ ♨ CTV CTV available in bedrooms 40P
20🏠 ♨ Ld9pm ♦ ⚲ sB&B&fr£8 sB&B⇨fl fr£8.50

dB&Bfr£16 dB&B⇨fl fr£17 Lfr£3.50 Teafr£1.20
Dfr£6.50 ☐ Credit card ③
꙰*Lawders* ☎228 **R** n⚘

Old Court Castle, Kanturk

KANTURK 2,063 Co Cork Map3R30 EcWed *Dublin162*
Belfast252 Cork35 Killarney32 Listowel40 *Mallow13*
꙰*Kanturk Mtr Wks* O'Brien St ☎12 **R** n⚘ Aud Maz VW

KEEL Co Mayo see **ACHILL ISLAND**

KENMARE 903 Co Kerry Map2V97 EcThu MdWed
Dublin213 Bantry28 *Belfast 291* Castletownbere29 *Cork60*
Glengariff18 *Killarney21* Macroom35 Parknasilla15
Waterville39
★★★**Kenmare Bay** ☎(064)41300 Telex no.8180
Closed 20 Nov–Feb; Lic; 50⇨fl ♪ ♨ CTV 300P ⚲ ♨
⚑International Ld9.30pm ♦ ⚲ *sB&B⇨fl IRE11.70–
IRE17 dB&B⇨fl IRE17.40–IRE28 LIRE4.25
Tea IRE1.50 High Teafr IRE2.50 DIRE7.50
Wine IRE3.70 ☐ Credit cards ①②③④⑤⑥
★★★**Riversdale** ☎(064)41299
Lic; 40⇨fl ♨ CTV 100P Ld9.30pm
꙰22.00 *Randle Bros* Shelbourne St ☎(064)41355 **R** ⚘
BL

KESH 311 Co Fermanagh Map16H16 EcThu *Belfast90*
Bundoran26 *Donegal122 Dublin116* Enniskillen14
Londonderry43 Omagh19 Strabane29
★★**Lough Erne** Main St ☎275
Closed Xmas Day; Lic; 14rm(4⇨fl) ♪ ✗ ♨ CTV
TV available in bedrooms 90P ⚲ ⑁ billiards Disco wkly
Live music & dancing twice wkly Ld8.30pm ♦ ⚲ S%
sB&B £5 sB&B⇨fl £7 dB&B £10 dB&B⇨fl £14
L£3 High Tea £3.50&alc D £4&alc Wine £2.50 ☐
Credit card ②

KILCOCK 827 Co Kildare Map13N83 EcThu *Dublin19*
Athlone59 *Belfast108 Cork154* Edenderry20 Enfield8
Kinnegad20 Lucan11 *Mullingar32* Naas14 *Trim14*
Tullamore42
꙰*Dermot Kelly Ltd* ☎(01)287311 **R** n⚘ Frd

KILDARE 3,137 Co Kildare Map9N71 EcWed MdThu
Dublin33 Athy15 *Belfast137* Carlow26 *Cork127*
Droichead Nua6 Edenderry16 Kilcullen8 *Kilkenny45*
Monasterevin7 Naas12 *Port Laoise20* Rathangan7
Tullamore30
꙰*Robert Chapman & Son* ☎(045)21203 **R** n⚘ BL
BMW Vlo

KILKEEL 2,884 Co Down Map13J31 EcThu MdWed
Belfast44 Ballynahinch29 *Downpatrick26 Dublin85*
Londonderry102 Newcastle13 Newry18 Rostrevor10
Warrenpoint12

★★**Kilmorey Arms** ☎62220
Lic; 12rm ♪ ♛ CTV P 12⋒ Ld8.45pm Credit card ①
⑤*D McAtee & Sons* 17–19 Greencastle St ☎62217 **R**

KILKENNY 13,306 Co Kilkenny Map8S55 EcThu *Dublin73*
Athy30 *Belfast177* Borris17 Callan10 *Carlow24*
Carrick-on-Suir26 Cashel35 Castlecomer13 Clonmel32
Cork92 Durrow17 Enniscorthy36 Muine Bheag14
New Ross27 *Port Laoise32* Roscrea39 Thomastown11
Thurles30 *Waterford30 Wexford50*
★★★**Newpark** ☎(056)22122
Lic; 46rm(40⇌🏢) ♪ ♛ CTV TV available in bedrooms ❀
150P ♣ ♨ (grass) & Ld11.30pm ✧ ⚗ sB&B⇌🏢IR£14.50–
IR£17.50 dB&B⇌🏢IR£24–IR£30 🍴 Credit cards ①②③⑤
★★**Rose Hill House** ☎(056)22603
Closed 24–26 Dec; Lic; 20⇌🏢 ♛ CTV CTV in bedrooms
❀ 100P ♣ Disco 3 nights wkly ♀ Irish & French
Ld9.30pm ✧ ⚗ sB&B⇌🏢IR£13.20–IR£14.80
dB&B⇌🏢IR£19.80–IR£22 (Continental breakfast)
L IR£2.20 Tea50p High Tea IR£3.70–IR£5&alc
D IR£6.05 Wine IR£3.30 🍴 Credit card ③
⑤*Statham (1974) Ltd* 12 Patrick St ☎(056)21016 **R** n♨
Frd

An inscribed granite cross-shaft, Killaloe

KILLALOE 871 Co Clare Map7R77 EcWed *Dublin111
Belfast196 Cork79 Ennis31 Limerick15*
★★**Lakeside** ☎(061)76122 Telex no.8232
Closed 16 Dec–6 Mar; Lic; 29rm(16⇌🏢) ♪ ♛ CTV
100P ♣ Live music wkly Cabaret wkly ♙ ♀ French
Ld9.30pm ✧ ⚗ S% sB&B IR£9.35–IR£10.45
sB&B⇌🏢IR£10.45–IR£11.55 dB&B IR£18.70–IR£20.90
dB&B⇌🏢IR£20.90–IR£23.10 L IR£3–IR£3.50
Tea50p–IR£1 D IR£7.50–IR£8.50&alc Wine IR£3.50 🍴
Credit cards ①②③④⑤⑥

KILLARNEY 7,541 Co Kerry Map2V99 EcMon MdSat
Dublin192 Adare58 Bantry49 *Belfast271* Cahirciveen39
Castleisland15 *Cork56* Dingle41 Kenmare21 Killorglin14
Limerick69 Macroom31 *Mallow42* Newcastle West43
Parknasilla35 Sneem37 *Tralee20 Waterville51*

★★★★**Dunloe Castle** ☎(064)32118 Telex no.8233
Closed 16 Oct–Apr; Lic; 140⇌🏢 Lift ♪ ♛ CTV ❀ 350P
♣ 🔳(heated) ♨ (hard) ♙ Ω billiards sauna bath ♀French
Ld9.30pm ✧ ⚗ S% Credit cards ②③
★★★★**Hotel Europe** ☎(064)31900 Telex no.8213
Closed Dec–Feb; Lic; 175⇌🏢 Lift ♪ ♛ CTV
CTV available in bedrooms ❀ 300P ♣ 🔳(heated) ♨ ♨ Ω
billiards sauna bath Disco wkly Live music & dancing
3 nights wkly Cabaret twice wkly ♀European Ld9.30pm
✧ ⚗ S% sB&B⇌🏢IR£15–IR£40 dB&B⇌🏢IR£30–IR£48
Lfr IR£7 D IR£10.50 Credit cards ②③⑤
★★★★**Great Southern** ☎(064)31262 Telex no.6998
Lic; 180⇌🏢 Lift ♪ ♛ CTV CTV available in bedrooms ❀
250P ♣ 🔳(heated) ♨ (hard) Cabaret 6 nights
wkly ♀International Ld10.30pm ✧ ⚗ sB&B⇌🏢IR£18.20–
IR£28.70 dB&B⇌🏢IR£27.45–IR£48.35 L IR£4.60
Tea IR£2 High Tea IR£4 D IR£8&alc Wine IR£3 🍴
Credit cards ①②③⑤
★★★**Aghadoe Heights** ☎(064)31766 Telex no.6942
Closed Dec–15 Jan; Lic; 46⇌🏢 ♪ ♛ CTV
CTV in bedrooms 300P ♣ ♨ (hard) Live music & dancing
6 nights wkly ♙ ♀ Irish & French Ld9pm ✧ ⚗
sB&B⇌🏢IR£14–IR£20.20 dB&B⇌🏢IR£25.70–IR£32.70
L IR£4.25 D IR£7.50–IR£9&alc Wine IR£3.50 🍴
Credit cards ①②③⑤⑥
★★★**Castlerosse** ☎(064)31144 Telex no.4404
Closed 24 Dec–Feb; Lic; 40⇌🏢 ♪ ♛ CTV 50P 30⋒ ♣ ⌣
δ ♨ (hard) ♀ Irish, English & French Ld9pm ✧ ⚗
*sB&B⇌🏢IR£13–IR£18.60 dB&B⇌🏢IR£20–IR£31.20
D IR£7.30 Wine IR£3.75 Credit cards ①②③⑤
★★★**Lake** Muckross Rd ☎(064)31035
Closed Dec–Feb; Lic; 79rm(44⇌🏢) ♪ ♛ CTV 100P 2⋒ ♣ ♨
♨ Ld8pm ✧ ⚗ *sB&B IR£11–IR£12.10 sB&B⇌🏢IR£13.20–
IR£14.30 dB&B IR£19–IR£22 d B&B⇌🏢IR£24.20–IR£26.40
D IR£6.60 Wine IR£3.50 🍴 Credit cards ①②
★★★**Torc Great Southern** ☎(064)31611
Lic; 92⇌🏢 ♪ ♛ ♛ CTV TV available in bedrooms 100P ♣
🔳(heated) ♨ sauna bath Live music & dancing 4 nights
wkly Cabaret 6 nights wkly ♀French Ld9pm ✧ ⚗
*sB&B⇌🏢IR£15.05–IR£21.50 dB&B⇌🏢IR£22.10–IR£35
Tea IR£1.50alc D IR£6.60alc Wine IR£3.25
Credit cards ①②③④⑤⑥
★★**Arbutus** ☎(064)31037
Closed Xmas wk; Lic; 35rm21⇌🏢 ♪ ♛ CTV P Ld9pm
✧ ⚗ S% Credit card ③
★★**Glen Eagle** ☎(064)31870
Lic; 100⇌🏢 ♪ ♛ CTV 150P ♣ δ18 ♨ (hard) ♨ squash
billiards Ld9pm ✧ ⚗ S% sB&B⇌🏢IR£10.30–IR£16.50
dB&B⇌🏢IR£17–IR£27.50 L IR£3.50–IR£4.25&alc
Tea IR£1alc High Tea IR£2.50–IR£3.50&alc
D IR£5.85–IR£7.30&alc Wine IR£3.85 🍴
Credit cards ①②③④⑤⑥
★★**Grand** ☎(064)31159
Lic; 28rm(3⇌🏢) ♪ ♛ CTV P Ld8.45pm ⚗ S%
sB&B IR£7.15–IR£8.80 sB&B⇌🏢IR£8.80–IR£10.45
dB&B IR£15.40–IR£17.60 dB&B⇌🏢IR£17.05–IR£19.25
L IR£3.50 High Tea IR£3&alc D IR£5 🍴 Credit cards ②④⑥
★★**Killarney Ryan** ☎(064)31555 Telex no.6950
Lic; 168⇌🏢 Lift ♛ TV 200P ♣ Ld9pm ✧ ⚗
sB&B⇌🏢IR£16–IR£20 dB&B⇌🏢IR£24–IR£30 🍴
Credit cards ①②③④⑤⑥
★★**Scotts** College St ☎(064)31060
Closed Dec & Jan; Lic; 27rm5⇌🏢 ♛ CTV 50P ♣
Ld8.30pm ✧ ⚗
⑤18.00 *Randle Bros.* Muckross Rd ☎(064)31237 **R** n♨ BL

KILLINEY Co Dublin Map9Q22 *Dublin12 Belfast116*
Bray4 Rosslare91
★★★★**Fitzpatrick's Castle** ☎(01)851533
Telex no.30353
Lic; 48⇌🏢 ♪ ♛ CTV TV available in bedrooms 400P ♣
🔳(heated) ♨ (hard) squash sauna bath Live music &
dancing Sat Cabaret nightly in season Ld11.45pm ✧ ⚗
sB&B⇌🏢IR£19.50–IR£25.50 dB&B⇌🏢IR£30.25–IR£40
L IR£5&alc Tea IR£1.50 High Tea IR£4 D IR£7.50&alc
Wine IR£3.40 🍴 Credit cards ①②③④⑤⑥
★★★**Court** Killiney Bay ☎(01)851622 Telex no.33244
Lic; 34⇌🏢 Lift ♪ ♛ CTV CTV in bedrooms 120P ⊞ ♣ squash

Disco wkly ♀French Ld10pm ❀ sB&B ⇔🍴IR£10–IR£20
dB&B⇔🍴IR£20–IRE30 LIRE4–IRE4.95&alc
High Tea IRE4.50&alc D IRE10&alc Wine IRE3.60 🍴
Credit card ②

KILLYBEGS 1,094 Co Donegal Map16G77 EcWed
Dublin156 Ardara11 *Belfast139 Donegal17 Sligo58*
★★★**Killybegs** ☎120
Closed Sep–13 Jun; Lic; 31rm(20⇔🍴) ♪ 📺 CTV 50P
➷(hard) billiards ♨♀Irish & French Ld9.30pm ❀ ⚏

sB&B IRE11.50 sB&B⇔🍴IRE12.50 dB&B IRE22
dB&B⇔🍴IRE24 LIRE4 D IRE6.75–IRE8 Wine IRE3.10 🍴
Credit cards ②③⑤
★**Bay View** ☎78
Closed 24–26 Dec; Lic; 19rm 📺 CTV 🅿 ⇔ Ld9pm ❀ ⚏
S% *sB&B IRE7.10–IRE8.20 dB&B IRE13.47–IRE15.56
LIRE3.52 D IRE4.25alc Wine IRE1.85

KILLYLEAGH 2,348 Co Down Map15J55
EcThu *Belfast20* Ballynahinch11 Comber12

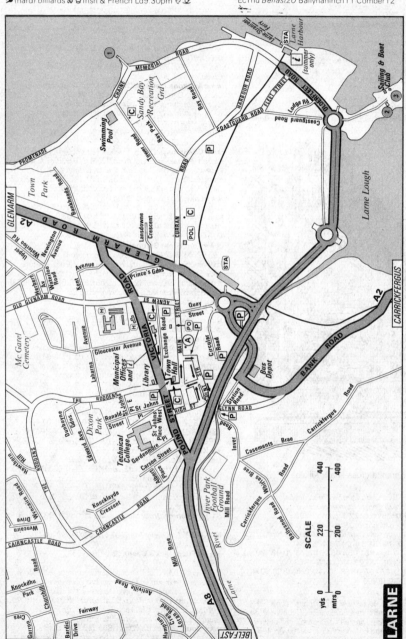

places of interest
1 Chaine Memorial Tower
2 Olderfleet Castle (Curran Castle)
3 The Curran

AA Road Service Centre ☎3958

A ★★★ Kings Arms

LARNE

Downpatrick6 Dublin102 Newtownards16
★**Dunmore** ☎258
10rm(1⇔🛏) ♪ CTV ⊗ 80P 🛝 Live music & dancing
Wed & Sat Ld9.30pm ♥ 🌄 sB&B£6 sB&B⇔🛏£6.50
dB&B£12 dB&B⇔🛏£13 L£3.75alc High Tea£3alc
D£5alc Wine£2.75 Credit cards①②
♪*T M Martin & Son* Dufferin Garage ☎203 **R** n❈ BL

KILMEADEN Co Waterford Map5S50 *Dublin106*
Dungarvan22 New Ross23 *Waterford8*
♪22.00 *Hennessy's* ☎(051)84129 ☎(051)84167 **R** ❈

KILREA 1,034 Co Londonderry Map14C91 EcThu
MdWed *Belfast41 Antrim23* Ballymena14 Ballymoney11
Coleraine15 *Dublin129* Garvagh6 *Londonderry37
Maghera9* Magherafelt18 *Portrush20*
♪*J T Proctor & Sons* 36–40 Bridge St ☎455 **R** Frd

KILRUSH 2,671 Co Clare Map6Q95 EcThu MdWed/Sat
*Dublin172 Belfast238 Cork85 Ennis27 Galway68 Kilkee8
Limerick49*
♪*Kilrush Mtr Co* ☎48 **R** n❈

KINAWLEY 531 Co Fermanagh Map12H23 *Belfast97
Enniskillen11* Carrick-on-Shannon32 *Londonderry71*
♪*V G Brennan* Rockview Mtrs ☎Derrylin314 **R**19.30

KINGSCOURT 1,016 Co Cavan Map13N79 EcWed
Dublin150 Baileborough8 Ceanannus Mor14 *Cork185*
Drogheda28 *Dundalk23*
★**Mackin's** ☎18
Closed Xmas; Lic; 14rm(2⇔🛏) 🍴 TV Ld8.30pm ♥
Credit cards ②③

Desmond Castle, Kinsale

KINSALE 1,989 Co Cork Map3W65 EcThu *Dublin179
Cork18* Dunmanway29
★★★**Acton's** (Trusthouse Forte) ☎(021)72135
Lic; 59rm(46⇔🛏) Lift ♪ CTV 90P 🛝 Live music &
dancing Sat ♀Irish, English, French & German
Ld9.30pm ♥ 🌄 S%🍴 Credit cards ①②③④⑤⑥

KINVARRA 293 Co Galway Map7M30 EcThu *Dublin132*
Ballyvaughan13 *Belfast194 Cork115 Ennis28 Galway18*
Gort9 Loughrea18
★**Winkles** ☎4

Dunguaire Castle, Kinvarra

Lic; 8rm CTV available in bedrooms 🛝 ♥ sB&B IR£6
dB&B IR£12 Wine IR£2.80

KIRCUBBIN 1,084 Co Down Map 15J56 EcThu *Belfast21*
Bangor17 Greyabbey4 Newtownards11 Portaferry8
♪*James Boyd* The Garage, 4 Main St ☎223 **R** n❈

LAHINCH 455 Co Clare Map6R18 EcThu *Dublin164*
Ballyvaughan20 *Belfast228 Cork106 Ennis19
Ennistymon3 Galway51 Kilkee27 Limerick41* Lisdoonvarna10
★★★**Aberdeen Arms** (Inter-Hotel) ☎20 Telex no.6872
Closed 15 Oct–Mar; Lic; 55rm(46⇔🛏) ♪ 🍴 CTV 46P ⊛
♀Irish & French Ld8.45 sB&B IR£8.20–IR£10.15
sB&B⇔🛏IR£9.50–IR£11.40 dB&B IR£15.20–IR£17.75
dB&B⇔🛏IR£17.76–IR£20.25 L IR£3–IR£6 D IR£6–IR£10
Wine IR£2.30 Credit cards②③⑤

LARNE 22,817 Co Antrim Map15D30 EcTue MdWed
Belfast22 Antrim22 Ballyclare2 Ballymena22
Carrickfergus15 Coleraine49 Cushendall26 *Dublin126*
Glenarm13 *Londonderry73* Portrush54 Whitehead9
★★★**King's Arms** Broadway ☎3322
49rm(33⇔🛏) Lift ♪ 🍴 CTV TV available in bedrooms 40P
Live music & dancing twice wkly Cabaret twice wkly ⚬
♀English & French Ld9pm ♥ 🌄 S% sB&B £8–£9
sB&B⇔🛏£12–£14 dB&B£13–£15 dB&B⇔🛏£16–£18
L£3.75–£5&alc Tea£1–£1.50&alc High Tea£3–£5&alc
D£5–£7&alc Wine£3🍴 Credit cards①②③④⑤⑥
♪*Gael Motors Ltd* Glynn Rd ☎5411 **R** ❈ Frd
♪*Harbour Eng Co* 104/106 Curran Rd ☎2071 **R** ❈ BL

LETTERFRACK Co Galway Map10L75 *Galway59
Dublin195* Westport32 Clifden9
★★★**Rosleague Manor** ☎Moyard7 Telex no.8313
Closed Nov–Mar; Lic; 16rm(14⇔🛏) 🍴 ⊗ 25P ⊛ 🛝
♀Irish & French Ld9.30pm ♥ 🌄 sB&B IR£9.35–IR£10.45
sB&B⇔🛏IR£11–IR£12.10 dB&B IR£18.70–IR£20.90
dB&B⇔🛏IR£22–IR£24.20 Tea IR£1.20&alc
High Tea IR£5.50–IR£6.60&alc D IR£7.70–IR£8.25&alc
Wine IR£2.90 🍴

LETTERKENNY 5,207 Co Donegal Map16C11 EcMon
Dublin150 Belfast97 Carrigart23 Cork281 Donegal31
★★★**Ballyraine** (Inter-Hotel) ☎411 Telex no.33406
Lic; 56⇔🛏 ♪ 🍴 TV 200P 🛝 Disco twice wkly Ld9.30pm
♥ 🌄 S%🍴 Credit cards②③⑤
★★**Gallagher's** ☎8
Closed Xmas Day; Lic; 20rm(3⇔🛏) 4⇔ ♪ 🍴 🍴 CTV ⊗ 20P
⚬ Ld9pm ♥ 🌄 sB&B IR£6 sB&B⇔🛏IR£7.50
dB&B IR£11.50 dB&B⇔🛏IR£13 L IR£3&alc Tea IR£1.25&
alc High Tea IR£4.50&alc D IR£5&alc Wine IR£2.75
★**McCarry's** ☎61
Lic; 16rm ♪ 🍴 CTV ⊗ 14P 3🏠 Ld8.30pm 🌄 S%
♪19.00 *Hegarty's Auto Service* ☎256 **R** n❈ Frd

LIMAVADY 5,555 Co Londonderry Map14C62 EcThu
MdMon *Belfast61*
♪*Roe Mtrs Ltd* Catherine St ☎2322 ☎2409 **R**
William Canning Mtr Engineers Ballyclose St ☎2560

LIMERICK 63.002 Co Limerick Map7R55 **See plan** EcThu
MdWed/Sat *Dublin123* Adare11 *Athlone75* Belfast201
Cork65 Croom13 Ennis23 Fermoy45 *Galway64* Killaloe15
Killarney69 Kilmallock21 Listowel47 Mitchelstown35
Nenagh25 Newcastle West27 *Port Laoise71* Rath Luirc25
Shannon Airport14 Thurles40 *Tipperary25 Tralee66*
Tulla20 *Waterford80*

★★★**Jury's** Ennis Rd ☎(061)47266 Telex no 8266
Lic; 96⇌🏠 🌙 🎬 CTV ⚲ ⚓ Ld11pm ⚲ ⚑ S%
🏳 Credit cards ①②③④⑤⑥

☆☆**Green Hills** Caherdavin ☎(061)53033
Closed Xmas Day; Lic; 56⇌🏠 🍴 🎬 CTV CTV available in
bedrooms ⚲ 200P ⚓ Live music & dancing nightly
Ld9.30pm ⚲ ⚑ S% *sB&B⇌🏠IRE12 65–IRE15 62
dB&B⇌🏠IRE20 90–IRE27 50 LIRE4 TeaIRE1 50
High Tea IRE4 D IRE7 50 Wine IRE3 50
Credit cards ①②③④⑤⑥

★★**Limerick Ryan** Ennis Rd ☎(061)53922 Telex no 6920

Lic; 184⇌🏠 Lift 🍴 TV 200P ⚓ Ld9pm ⚲ ⚑
sB&B⇌🏠IRE16–IRE20 dB&B⇌🏠IRE24–IRE30 🏳
Credit cards ①②③④⑤⑥

☆☆**Parkway** Dublin Rd ☎(061)47599 Telex no 6850
Closed Xmas Day; Lic; 103⇌🏠 🍴 🎬 CTV 1000P
Live music & dancing Sun Cabaret Sat Ld11pm ⚲ ⚑ *
sB&B⇌🏠IRE13.20–IRE15 70 dB&B⇌🏠IRE21.70–
IRE25.65 Wine IRE3 50 Credit cards ①②③⑥

★★**Royal George** O'Connell St ☎(061)44566
Telex no 6910
Closed Xmas Day; Lic; 70⇌🏠 Lift 🌙 🍴 CTV Disco twice wkly
Cabaret 3 nights wkly ♀ International Ld10 45pm ⚲ ⚑
sB&B⇌🏠IRE12 25–IRE14 15 dB&B⇌🏠IRE23.05–
IRE26 55 LIRE3 50–IRE4 Tea60–80p D IRE6 50–IRE7 50
&alc Wine IRE2 75 🏳 Credit cards ①②③④⑤⑥

☆☆**Two Mile Motor Inn** Ennis Rd ☎(061)53122
Lic; 47⇌🏠 🌙 🍴 CTV 150P ⚓ Disco 4 nights wkly
Live music & dancing nightly Cabaret nightly

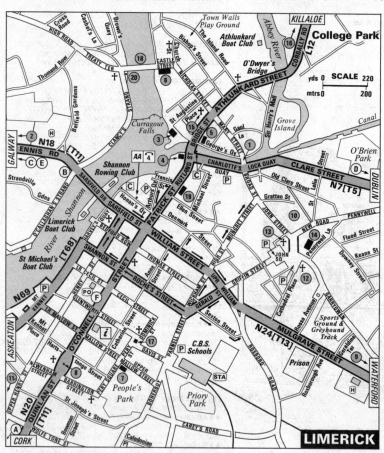

LIMERICK

AA Road Service Centre ☎(061)48241

A	☆☆ Green Hills
B	★★★ Jury's
C	★★ Limerick Ryan
D	☆☆ Parkway Motel
E	☆☆ Two Mile Motor Inn
F	★★ Royal George

places of interest
1 Ball's Bridge
2 Church of Our Lady of the Rosary
3 County Courthouse and City Court
4 Custom House
5 Gerald Griffin Memorial School
6 King John's Castle
7 Library, Art Gallery and Museum
8 O'Connell Monument
9 O'Grady Memorial
10 Old Town Walls

11 St Alphonsus' Church (RC)
12 St John's Cathedral (RC)
13 St John's Church
14 St John's Hospital
15 St Mary's Cathedral (CI)
16 St Munchin's College (Perry House)
17 Sir Peter Tait Memorial Clock Tower
18 Thomond Bridge
19 Town Hall
20 Treaty Stone

Old City Court House, Limerick

♡Irish & French Ld11.45pm ♁ Ⅎ sB&B⇐⋒IR£13.20–IR£16.50 dB&B⇐⋒IR£20.90–IR£26.40 L IR£2–IR£4 Tea IR£1.50 High Tea IR£4 D IR£7&alc Wine IR£2.50 ⊟ Credit cards 1 2 3 5 6
ↄ ***Gleeson Bros*** Ellen St ☎(061)45567 **R** n⊕

LISBURN 27 405 Co Antrim Map15J26 EcWed MdTue *Belfast9 Antrim18 Armagh32 Dublin95 Londonderry73* Lurgan18
★★★**Woodlands** 3 Belfast Rd ☎2741
Closed Xmas Day; 26rm(18⇐⋒) ⅅ ⅏ CTV TV available in bedrooms 300P ⚓ billiards Disco wkly Live music & dancing wkly Ld9.15pm ♁ Ⅎ sB&Bfr£13.07 sB&B⇐⋒fr£14.26 dB&Bfr£24.95 dB&B⇐⋒fr£26.14 L£3.50–£4&alc Teafr£1.50 High Tea £3.50alc Dfr£6&alc Wine £2.50 Credit cards 1 2 3 5
ↄ ***Marsden Tailored Panels*** 17A Chapel Hill ☎6945 ☎70368 **R** (Body repairs only)
ↄ ***John McLean & Son Ltd*** Hillsboro Rd & Longstone St ☎3201 **R** ⊕ BL
ↄ ***P & M Garages*** 13A Cross Ln, Magheragall ☎Maze494 **R**
ↄ ***Stevenson Bros Ltd*** Seymour St ☎2214 **R** ⊕ BL

The 'Spectacle' Bridge, Lisdoonvarna

LISDOONVARNA 459 Co Clare Map6R19 EcWed *Dublin155* Ballyvaughan10 *Belfast214 Cork111 Ennis24* Ennistymon8 *Galway41* Lahinch10 *Limerick47*
★★**Keane's** ☎11
Closed Oct–Mar; RSApr–14 May; Lic; 12rm(7⇐⋒) ⅏ CTV ⊗ ⛟ Ld8pm ♁ Ⅎ S% sB&B IR£7.20–IR£8.40 sB&B⇐⋒IR£8.45–IR£9.65 dB&B IR£14.40–IR£16.80 dB&B⇐⋒IR£16.90–IR£19.30 High Tea IR£1.25–IR£5&alc D IR£5.50–IR£7&alc W IR£2.50
★★**Lynch's** ☎10
Closed 5 Oct–May; Lic; 18rm(6⇐⋒) Lift ⅅ ⅏ CTV 20P ⛟ Ld8.30pm ♁ Ⅎ sB&Bfr IR£7.50 sB&B⇐⋒fr IR£8.50 dB&Bfr IR£15 dB&B⇐⋒fr IR£17 Dfr IR£6 Wine IR£2.20
★★**Spa View** ☎26 Closed Nov–Feb RSMar–May; 15rm(4⇐⋒) ⅏ CTV ⊗ 30P ⌂ ⚓ ⚘ ⥁ Ld8pm ♁ Ⅎ sB&B IR£7–IR£8 sB&B⇐⋒IR£8–IR£8.50 dB&B IR£14–IR£16 dB&B⇐⋒IR£16–IR£17 Credit card 2

LISMORE 1,041 Co Waterford Map4X09 EcThu *Dublin134 Cork38* Fermoy17 *Waterford42*
★★♣**Ballyrafter House** ☎(058)54002
Closed Oct–Mar; Lic; 14rm4⇐⋒ ⅏ CTV ⊗ 20P 2⌂ ⛟ ⚓ Ld7.30pm ♁ Ⅎ

LISNASKEA 1,443 Co Fermanagh Map 12H33 EcThu MdSat *Dublin99 Belfast82 Cavan29 Enniskillen12*
★★**Ortine** Main St ☎21206
Closed Xmas Day; 26rm(17⇐⋒) ⅅ ⅄ ⅏ CTV TV available in bedrooms ⊗ 60P 3⌂ ⚓ Disco wkly Live music & dancing twice wkly Cabaret wkly ⌂ Ld9.30pm ♁ Ⅎ S% sB&B £6–£7.50 sB&B⇐⋒£6.50–£8.50 dB&B £11.50–£14 dB&B⇐⋒£12–£16 L £2.50–£3 Tea75p–£1.20 High Tea £3.25–£5.75 D £4–£6.50 Wine £3.20 ⊟ Credit card 1

Gunsborough, Earl Kitchener's birthplace, Listowel

LISTOWEL 3,021 Co Kerry Map6Q93 EcMon MdFri *Dublin170* Abbeyfeale11 Adare34 Ballybunion10 *Belfast248 Cork76* Glin15 *Limerick47* Newcastle West24 *Tralee17*
★★**Listowel Arms** ☎(068)21500
Lic; 34rm(22⇐⋒) Lift ⅅ ⅏ CTV ⊗ ₱ Disco wkly Ld8.30pm ♁ Ⅎ *sB&B IR£7.15–IR£7.70 sB&B⇐⋒IR£7.75–IR£8.30 dB&B IR£14.30–IR£15.40 dB&B⇐⋒IR£15.50–IR£16.60 L IR£3.52–IR£3.85 Tea IR£1–IR£1.20 High Tea IR£5alc Wine IR£3.20 ⊟
★**Stack's** Market St ☎(068)21094
Lic; 16rm(3⇐⋒) A4rm ⅅ ⅏ CTV ⊗ 30P ⥁ Ld7.30pm ♁ Ⅎ sB&B IR£5.50 sB&B⇐⋒IR£6.05 dB&B IR£11 dB&B⇐⋒IR£11.55 Lfr IR£3.50 Dfr IR£6
ↄ ***Moloney's*** Market St ☎(068)21033 **R** n⊕ Frd

LIXNAW 219 Co Kerry Map2Q92 EcThu *Dublin181 Cork88* Listowel18 *Tralee13*
ↄ20.00 ***Michael J O'Keeffe*** ☎(066)32157 **R**19.30 ⊕20.00

LONDONDERRY 51,850 Co Londonderry Map14C41
EcMon/Thu/Sat MdWed/Thu *Belfast72* Antrim55
Carrigart44 Coleraine31 Donegal43 Dublin147
Dungiven20 Greencastle22 Letterkenny21 Limavady17
Omagh34 Portrush37 Raphoe16 Rosapenna46
Strabane14 Stranorlar25
★★★★**Everglades** Prehan Rd ☎46722 Telex no 748005
Lic. 38⇄🛏 🌒 ⇒🍴 CTV CTV in bedrooms ⊘ 100P 4🏠 ⚓
🔲(heated) sauna bath Live music & dancing Sat
♀International Ld10pm ♦ ⌷ sB&B⇄🍴lfr£17.50
dB&B⇄🍴lfr£27.50 Llfr£4&alc High Teafr£3.50&alc
Dlfr£6&alc Wine£3.50 Credit cards ② ③ ⑤
◗*Desmond Motors Ltd* 173 Strand Rd ☎67613 **R** Frd
◗*Chas Hurst Mtrs Ltd* 78 Strand Rd ☎64181 ☎64184
R ⚙ BL RT
◗*G Nixon & Sons Ltd* Spencer Rd ☎42732 **R ⚙**
◗*John Street S/sta* 15 John St ☎63402 **R ⚙**

LOUGHBRICKLAND 349 Co Down Map15J14 EcThu
Belfast28 Armagh17 Downpatrick31 Dublin76
Londonderry93 Newry10 Portadown11
◗*Frank McGrath* Main St ☎Banbridge22396 **R ⚙**

LOUISBURGH 310 Co Mayo Map10L87 *Dublin175*
Cork189 Belfast205 Castlebar25 Leenane20 Westport14
◗21.00 *Harney's* Chapel St ☎5 **R ⚙** Frd

LURGAN 24,055 Co Armagh Map15J05 EcWed MdThu
Belfast25 Antrim27 Armagh16 Ballynahinch20
Banbridge9 Downpatrick29 Dublin80 Dundalk36
Dungannon26 Londonderry85 Newcastle30 Portadown6
◗*H Wilson & Sons* Portadown Rd ☎2278 ☎2874 **R ⚙**
Tal

MACROOM 2,256 Co Cork Map3W37 EcWed MdThu
Dublin186 Bandon19 Bantry34 Belfast289 Cork25
Dunmanway19 Glengarriff38

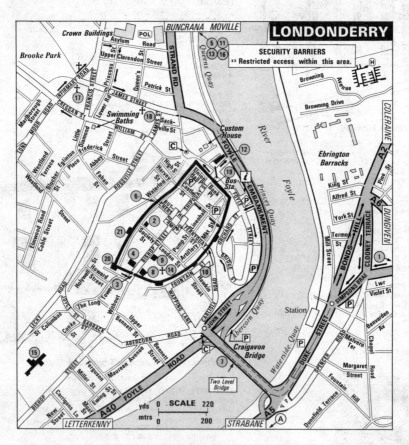

AA Road Service Centre ☎43467

A ★★★★ Everglades

places of interest
1 Altnagelvin Hospital and Princess
  Macha Statue
2 Apprentice Boys' Hall
3 Bishop Gate
4 Bishop's Palace
5 Boom Hall
6 Butcher Gate
7 Craigavon Bridge
8 Courthouse
9 Deanery
10 Ferryquay Gate
11 Foyle College
12 Guildhall
13 Magee University College
14 St Columb's Cathedral (CI)
15 St Columb's College
16 St Columba's Stone
17 St Eugene's Cathedral (RC)
18 Scot's Church
19 Shipquay Gate
20 Town Walls (Double Bastion)
21 Town Walls (Royal Bastion)

★★**Castle** ☎74
Closed 16 Dec–Jan. Lic. 23rm(3⇔🛁) A11rm(2⇔🛁) 🍴
CTV 6🚗 Ld8.30pm ⚭ ⬛ sB&BfrIR£6.50
sB&B⇔🛁fr IR£7.70 dB&Bfr IR£13 dB&B⇔🛁fr IR£14.20
L IR£3 D IR£5.50 Wine IR£3 Credit card ③

★**Victoria** ☎82
Lic. 20rm(4⇔🛁) 🗶 🍴 CTV ⚗ 20P 🚗 🛴 Ld8pm ⚭ ⬛ S%
sB&B IR£7–IR£7.50 sB&B⇔🛁 IR£8–IR£8.50
dB&B IR£14–IR£15 dB&B⇔🛁 IR£15–IR£16
L IR£3–IR£3.50 Tea IR£1.50 High Tea IR£3.50alc
D IR£5alc Wine IR£2
〰*Kelleher's* Main St ☎29 **R** n⬛ Frd

MAGHERA 2,108 Co Londonderry Map14C80 EcThu
MdTue/Fri *Belfast40 Dublin120 Londonderry33 Antrim23*
〰*Danny Otterson* Fair Hill ☎42651 ☎42305 **R**

Old watch tower, Malahide

MALAHIDE Co Dublin Map13O24 *Dublin10 Cork17*
Howth8 Galway145
★★**Grand** ☎(01)450633
Lic. 52rm(26⇔🛁) Lift 𝄪 🗶 🍴 CTV 200P 10🚗 🛴
Live music & dancing Sat 🎶 Ld10.30pm ⚭ ⬛
sB&B IR£11.25–IR£13.50 sB&B⇔🛁 IR£12.94–IR£15.19
dB&B IR£20.25–IR£24.75 dB&B⇔🛁 IR£23.63–IR£28.12
L IR£3.75 Tea IR£1.25 D IR£7 🍴 Credit cards ①②③⑤⑥

MALIN Co Donegal Map15C45 *Dublin176 Cork301*
Londonderry25 •
★★**Malin** ☎6
Lic. 15rm(2⇔) 🍴 CTV ⚗ 𝐏 Disco twice wkly
Live music & dancing wkly Ld9pm ⚭ ⬛ S%
sB&B IR£6.50–IR£8 dB&B IR£13–IR£16
dB&B⇔IR£15–IR£18 Lfr IR£3 Teafr IR£1
D IR£5.50alc Wine IR£2.70 Credit card ⑥

MANORHAMILTON 858 Co Leitrim Map11G83 EcWed
Dublin131 Belfast112 Bundoran16 Enniskillen26 Sligo16
〰*Thompson's Service Gar* ☎26 **R** 18.30 n⬛

MARKETHILL 954 Co Armagh Map13H93 EcWed
Belfast41 Armagh7 Dublin77 Dundalk24 Keady9
Londonderry77 Newry11 Portadown11
〰*RS Farson & Sons Mtr Engineers* ☎232 **R** ⬛

MILTOWN MALBAY 677 Co Clare Map6Q07
Dublin165 Belfast230 Cork106 Ennis19 Ennistymon10
Kilkee19 Lahinch8 Limerick42
〰19.00 *McCarthy's* ☎29 **R** 19.00 n⬛

MOHILL 868 Co Leitrim Map12N09 EcMon MdThu
Dublin93 Athlone45 Ballinamore11 Belturbet28
Belfast110 Carrick-on-Shannon11 Cavan31 Clones41
Cork182 Enniskillen35 Longford17
★**Sportsmans** ☎12
Hotel will not open until June 1980.
Lic. 11rm(4⇔🛁) 🍴 CTV 300P 2🚗 🛴 Disco wkly Live music
& dancing wkly Cabaret wkly 🎉Irish, English & Italian Ld9pm
⚭ ⬛ sB&B IR£7.50–IR£8.50 sB&B⇔🛁 IR£8.55–IR£9.55
dB&B IR£15–IR£17 dB&B⇔🛁 IR£16.35–IR£18.35 L IR£3
Tea IR£1.75&alc High Tea IR£3&alc D IR£6&alc
Wine IR£3.50 🍴 Credit cards ②④⑥

MOIRA 754 Co Down Map15J16 EcWed *Belfast18*
Dublin93 Lisburn10 Lurgan5
〰*Fernfield S/sta* (Brown Bros) 13 Lisburn Rd ☎611266
☎611389 **R** ⬛

MONAGHAN 5,256 Co Monaghan Map12H63 EcThu
MdMon *Armagh17 Athlone83* Aughnacloy12
Belfast57 Carrickmacross26 Castleblayney15
★★★**Hillgrove** ☎(047)81288
Lic. 45rm(38⇔🛁) 𝄪 🗶 🍴 CTV 600P 🛴 🚶 (hard) Disco
4 nights wkly Live music & dancing wkly Cabaret wkly
Ld9.30pm ⚭ ⬛ sB&B⇔🛁 IR£12 dB&B⇔🛁 IR£24 L IR£4
Tea IR£1.25 High Tea IR£8.50 D IR£6.50 🍴
〰*D & S Mtrs* North Rd ☎(047)81044 **R** n⬛ Aud Maz
MB VW
〰*Monaghan Mtr Wks* Old Cross Square ☎(047)82011
R n⬛ BL

MONASTEREVIN 1,619 Co Kildare Map8N61 EcThu
MdSat *Dublin40* Athy12 *Belfast140 Carlow24 Cork122*
Edenderry17 Kildare7 Naas19 Portarlington6
Port Laoise13 Rathangan7 *Tullamore24*
〰*Michael A Finlay & Sons Ltd* Automobile Engineers
☎(045)25331 **R** n⬛ Fia

MONEYMORE 1,177 Co Londonderry Map14H88 EcThu
Belfast42 Cookstown5 *Dublin110*
〰19.00 *Thomas John Boyce* 43 Lawford St ☎257
R 19.00 n⬛

MOUNTRATH 1,098 Co Laois Map8S39 EcMon
Dublin61 Cork108 Durrow14 *Port Laoise9*
〰23.59 *Dooley Mtrs* Dublin Rd ☎(0502)32221 **R**18.30
⬛

MOVILLE 1,089 Co Donegal Map14C63 EcWed
MdTue/Thu *Dublin167 Belfast92* Carndonagh12
Greencastle3 *Londonderry19* Malin Head24
★★**Inishowen Lodge** (formerly Keaveney's) ☎8
Closed Xmas. Lic. 20rm(6⇔🛁) 🍴 CTV ⚗ 𝐏
Live music & dancing 4 nights wkly Ld9.30pm ⚭ ⬛
sB&B IR£8–IR£12 sB&B⇔🛁 IR£8–IR£12
dB&B IR£14–IR£22 dB&B⇔🛁 IR£14–IR£22
L IR£3–IR£4 Tea75p High Tea IR£5 Dfr IR£6
Wine IR£3 🍴
★**Foyle** ☎25
Lic. 20rm(1⇔🛁) 🍴 CTV ⚗ 4P 1🚗 Disco wkly
Live music & dancing 3 nights wkly Ld9pm ⚭ ⬛ S%
sB&B IR£9–IR£9.50 dB&B IR£16.50–IR£17.50
dB&B⇔🛁 IR£18.50–IR£19.50 L IR£2.50–IR£3
Tea IR£1–IR£1.50 High Tea IR£2–IR£5&alc
D IR£3.75–IR£6&alc Wine IR£1.75 🍴 Credit cards ②③

MOY 926 Co Tyrone Map14H85 EcThu *Belfast43*
Armagh2 Dublin88 Dungannon6 *Londonderry70*
Portadown19
〰*McMullan Bros* 15/19 Dungannon St ☎252 **R**19.30

MULLINGAR 9,245 Co Westmeath Map12N45 EcWed
MdThu *Dublin51* Athboy22 *Athlone32 Belfast110*
Castlepollard13 *Cavan40* Ceanannus Mor26 *Cork148*
Drogheda50 *Dundalk58* Edenderry22 Enfield24
Longford26 Mostrim18 Oldcastle23 *Roscommon40*
Trim26 Tullamore2
○**Bloomfield House** ☎(044)80894
Lic. 33⇔🛁 𝄪 🍴 CTV CTV available in bedrooms 500P
🛴 𝄪 🚶 ⚗French Ld10.30pm ⚭ ⬛ S%
sB&B⇔🛁 IR£16–IR£18 dB&B⇔🛁 IR£28–IR£30
L IR£3.25–IR£4.25 Tea75p D IR£7.25&alc
Wine IR£3 🍴 Credit card ②

NAAS 5,078 Co Kildare Map9N81 EcThu *Dublin21*
Athy22 Baltinglass23 *Belfast125 Carlow31 Cork141*
Kilcock14 Kilcullen7 Kildare12 *Port Laoise32 Trim28*
〰*Hennessey's* Sallins Rd ☎(045)9598 ☎(045)97918 **R** ⬛
〰*Smith's (Naas) Ltd* ☎(045)97675 **R** n⬛ Ren

NEWCASTLE 4,621 Co Down Map13J33 EcThu

*Belfast*31 *Armagh*40 Ballynahinch16 Banbridge21
*Downpatrick*13 *Dublin*87 *Dundalk*34 Kilkeel13 Lisburn26
*Londonderry*99 Newry21 Newtownards33 Portadown32
Portaferry22
★★⚐♨ **Enniskeen** ☎22392
Closed Nov–Feb; Lic; 12rm(6⇋🚿) 🍴 CTV CTV available in
bedrooms ⊗ 45P ⚓ Live music & dancing wkly ⚘
Ld7.45pm ⚹ ⚗ S% sB&B£8.50–£10 sB&B⇋🚿£10–£12
dB&B£16.50–£19.50 dB&B⇋🚿£18.50–£21.50
L£3.50–£4&alc Tea£1.20–£1.50 High Teafr£3&alc
D£4.50–£5&alc Wine£3 🚩

NEWCASTLE WEST 2,680 Co Limerick Map7R23
EcWed MdThu *Dublin*150 Abbeyfeale13 Adare16
*Belfast*228 *Cork*54 Drumcollliher10 *Killarney*43
Limerick27 Listowel24 *Mallow*32 Tralee39
☆☆ **River Room Motel** ☎193
Lic; 15⇋🚿 🍴 CTV 200P Live music 4 nights wkly
Cabaret wkly ⚐ Irish, English & French Ld8.30pm ⚹ ⚗ S%
Credit cards 1 2
⏧ *Nash's* ☎3 **R** n⚙ Frd

NEW INN Co Laois Map8N50 *Dublin*48 *Cork*114
*Limerick*76 Naas27 *Port Laoise*5
★★ **Hotel Montague** ☎(0502)26154
Closed 25 Dec; Lic; 20⇋🚿 🍴 200P ⚓
Live music & dancing Sun ⚐ French Ld9.15pm ⚹ ⚗
*sB&B⇋🚿IR£9.35–IR£10.05 dB&B⇋🚿IR£16.50–
IR£19.80 LIR£3.10–IR£3.75&alc DIR£4.50–IR£5.75&alc
🚩 Credit cards 2 3

Urlanmore Castle, Newmarket-on-Fergus

NEWMARKET-ON-FERGUS 1,054 Co Clare Map7R36
*Dublin*138 *Cork*80 *Galway*50 Limerick15
★★★★ **Dromoland Castle** ☎(061)71144
Telex no 6854
Closed Nov–Mar; Lic; 67⇋🚿 🍷 🍴 CTV ⊗ 50P ⚓ ♪⚘
🏌(hard) ⏥ Live music nightly ⚘ ⚐ Continental Ld8.45pm
⚹ ⚗ *sB&B⇋🚿IR£43.45 dB&B⇋🚿IR£60.50
LIR£8.80 DIR£12.65 **(RS)**

NEWPORT 420 Co Mayo Map10L99 MdTue *Dublin*163
*Belfast*192 Castlebar12 *Cork*188 *Galway*59 Mulrany11
Westport8
★★★⚐♨ **Newport House** (Inter-Hotel) ☎12
Closed Oct–Mar; Lic; 12⇋🚿 A8⇋🚿 🏌 🍴 CTV ⊗ 40P ⚓
⏥ ○ billiards nc6 ⚐ Irish & French Ld9.30pm ⚹ S%
*sB&B⇋🚿IR£12–IR£15 dB&B⇋🚿IR£20–IR£28
LIR£4–IR£5.25&alc DIR£6.50–IR£8&alc Wine IR£2
Credit cards 2 3 5
⏧ *Kelly's* ☎3 **R** BL

NEW ROSS 5,153 Co Wexford Map5S72 EcWed
*Dublin*88 Arklow51 *Belfast*192 Borris17 Bunclody26
*Carlow*33 *Cork*94 Enniscorthy21 Graiguenamanagh12
*Kilkenny*27 Muine Bheag25 *Rosslare Harbour*36
Thomastown16 *Waterford*15 *Wexford*24 Wicklow68
★★★ **Five Counties** (Inter-Hotel) ☎(051)21703
Telex no 8771
Lic; 37rm(29⇋🚿) 🍷 🍴 CTV 200P ⚓ Disco wkly
Live music & dancing wkly Cabaret wkly ⚘ Ld9.15pm ⚹ ⚗
S% sB&B IR£14.05–IR£17.40 sB&B⇋🚿IR£16.05–
IR£19.30 dB&B IR£26.10–IR£29.95 dB&B⇋🚿IR£29.95–
IR£34.95 LIR£4.50&alc Tea IR£1.25–IR£2
High Tea IR£2.50–IR£4.50 DIR£7.50–IR£8&alc
Wine IR£2.85 🚩 Credit cards 1 2 3 5 6
⏧ *Central* South St ☎(051)21205 **R** n⚙ BL

NEWRY 11,393 Co Down Map13J02 EcWed
MdThu/Sat *Belfast*38 *Armagh*19 Banbridge13
*Downpatrick*30 Drogheda35 *Dublin*66 Dundalk13
Kilkeel18 Lisburn30 *Londonderry*89 Newcastle21
Portadown9 Rathfriland10 Warrenpoint7
⏧ *Cars Ltd* 19 Merchants Quay ☎3151 **R** Frd
⏧ 22.00 (18.00 Sat) *D J Cull Ltd* Kilmorey St ☎2801 **R** n⚙
⏧ *Hollywood Bros Ltd* Monaghan St ☎2208 **R** Vau VW
⏧ 21.00 *S H McCullough & Son* Downshire Rd ☎2144
R 21.00 n⚙
⏧ *McGraths S/sta* Patrick St ☎2857 **R** 19.00 n⚙
⏧ *Rowland & Harris Ltd* Railway Av ☎2201 **R** BL

NEWTOWNABBEY 57,936 Co Antrim Map15J38
*Belfast*6 *Dublin*110 Larne16
☆☆ **Chimney Corner** 630 Antrim Rd
☎Glengormley44925 Telex no.748158
Lic; 64rm(63⇋🚿) 🍷 🍴 CTV TV available in bedrooms ⊗
350P 🚐 sauna bath Disco 3 nights wkly Cabaret twice wkly
Ld9.15pm ⚹ ⚗ sB&B⇋🚿£16.50 dB&B⇋🚿£22
L£3 Tea£2 High Tea£3 D£5.50 Wine£2.25
Credit cards 1 2 3 4 5 6
★★⚐♨ **Abbeylands** Whiteabbey ☎Whiteabbey64552
Unlicensed; 10rm(1⇋🚿) 🍴 CTV ⊗ 60P 🚐 ⚓
Credit cards 1 2 3 4 5 6
★★ **Glenavna House** ☎Whiteabbey64461
Lic; 17rm7⇋🚿 🍷 🍴 CTV 60P 🚐 ⚓ Ld9pm
⏧ *Dick & Co Ltd* Mallusk, Glengormley ☎41515 **R** Fia
⏧ *Twinburn S/sta* 124 Monkstown Rd ☎Whiteabbey
63656 ☎Whiteabbey65969 **R**
⏧ *William James Walker* Glenville Trucks.
151 Glenville Rd ☎Whiteabbey64897 ☎Whiteabbey65950
R ⚙

NEWTOWNARDS 15,387 Co Down Map15J47 EcThu
MdSat *Belfast*10 Ballynahinch17 Ballywalter10 Bangor6
Donaghadee8 *Downpatrick*22 *Dublin*114 Greyabbey7
Newcastle33
⏧ *David R Jeffers* Brae S/sta, Church St ☎3541
☎3416 **R** n⚙

NEWTOWNHAMILTON 669 Co Armagh Map13H92
EcWed MdSat *Belfast*50 *Armagh*16 *Dublin*69 Dundalk16
*Londonderry*86 Newry12
⏧ *A Boyle & Co* 28–30 Newry St ☎207 **R** Toy

NEWTOWNSTEWART 1,458 Co Tyrone Map14H48
EcWed *Belfast*81 *Dublin*123 Enniskillen37
*Londonderry*24 Maghera33 Omagh10 Strabane10
⏧ *Wilson & Son* ☎239 **R** ⚙

OLDCASTLE 759 Co Meath Map12N58 EcMon
*Dublin*52 Cavan22 Ceanannus Mor15 *Cork*167
Mullingar23
★ **Naper Arms** ☎124
Closed Good Fri; Lic; 11rm(1⇋🚿) 🏌 🍴 CTV ⊗ 6P 3🚗
Ld9pm ⚹ ⚗ S% sB&B IR£7–IR£8 sB&B⇋🚿IR£8–IR£9
dB&B IR£14–IR£15 dB&B⇋🚿IR£15–IR£16
LIR£3–IR£4&alc Tea IR£1.50–IR£2&alc
High Tea IR£3–IR£4&alc Dfr IR£5 Wine IR£3.50
Credit cards 1 2 3 4 5 6

OMAGH 11,953 Co Tyrone Map14H47 EcWed MdThu/

Sat *Belfast71 Armagh36* Cookstown27 *Dublin113*
Dungannon29 *Enniskillen27 Londonderry34* Monaghan32
Strabane20
★★★ **Knock-na-Moe Castle** (Inter-Hotel) ☎3131
Closed Xmas Day; Lic; 11⇨🛏 D 🛏 CTV CTV available in
bedrooms 150P ⅃ Disco Tue Live music &dancing wknds
♀French Ld9.30pm ✿ ⚏ S% sB&B⇨🛏£15.50–£18.50
dB&B⇨🛏£25.50–£28.50 L£3–£3.50 D£5–£6 Wine£3 🅡
Credit cards ② ③
★★ **Royal Arms** 51 High St ☎3262
Lic; 22rm(15⇨🛏) D 🛏 CTV 200P ⅃ Live music & dancing
wkly ♀English & Continental Ld9.30pm ✿ ⚏ sB&B£6
sB&B⇨🛏£8 dB&B£12 dB&B⇨🛏£16 Lfr£3 Teafr£1
High Teafr£2 Dfr£3&alc Wine£3
⑊ *Sean Duncan* 52 Brookmount Rd ☎44161 **R** ⇨
⑊23.30 *Johnston King Mtrs Ltd* Derry Rd ☎2788
☎2147 **R** Frd

OMEATH 331 Co Louth Map13J11 *Dublin71*
Belfast45 Cork231 Dundalk18 Greenore9 Newry7
★ **Park** ☎(042)75115
RSOct–Apr; Lic; 16rm 🛏 CTV 200P ⅃ Ld8.30pm ✿ ⚏
sB&B£8.50 dB&B£17 L IRE5 Tea IRE1.40alc
High Tea IRE5.50alc D IRE6.50 Wine IRE4

OUGHTERARD 628 Co Galway Map10M14 EcWed
MdThu *Dublin153 Belfast216 Clifden32* Cong28 *Cork146*
Galway17 Leenane23 Westport43
✿✿✿ **Connemara Gateway** (Trusthouse Forte)
☎(091)82328 Telex no.5818
Closed 20 Oct–3 Apr; Lic; 48⇨🛏 D 🎨 🛏 TV 75P
⅃ (heated) Live music Wed Live music & dancing Fri
♀English & French Ld9pm ✿ ⚏ S%
Credit cards ① ② ③ ④ ⑤ ⑥
★★ **Corrib** ☎(091)82329
Lic; 18rm(17⇨🛏) A8⇨🛏 🛏 CTV 50P ⅃ ♀French
Ld9pm ✿ ⚏ sB&B⇨🛏IRE7.80–IRE14.40
dB&B⇨🛏IRE15.60–IRE28.80 D IRE7.80&alc
Wine IRE3.75 🅡 Credit cards ① ② ③ ⑤
★★ **Egan's Lake** ☎(091)82205
Lic; 24rm(17⇨🛏) D 🛏 TV 20P Ld9pm ✿
Credit cards ③ ⑥
★★ **Oughterard House** ☎(091)82207 Telex no.8370
Lic; 31rm(20⇨🛏) Lift CTV 30P 🚗 ⅃ Ld7.45pm ✿ ⚏
sB&B IRE22 dB&B⇨🛏IRE40 (Continental breakfast)
L IRE4alc Tea IRE2alc D IRE7alc Wine IRE4
Credit card ②

PARKNASILLA Co Kerry Map2V76 *Dublin227*
Belfast306 Cahirciveen34 *Cork74* Glengarriff32
Kenmare15 *Killarney35* Sneem2 Waterville24
★★★★ **Great Southern** ☎(064)45122 Telex no.6899
Closed 2 Jan–Mar; Lic; 60⇨🛏 D 🛏 CTV in bedrooms 60P
⅃ 🏊(heated) ♦9 🌊(hard) billiards sauna bath
Live music & dancing 3 nights wkly Cabaret 3 nights wkly
♦♦ ♀French Ld9pm ✿ ⚏ sB&B⇨🛏IRE18–IRE27
dB&B⇨🛏IRE27–IRE47 L IRE5&alc Tea IRE1
D IRE9&alc Wine IRE4 Credit cards ① ② ③ ④ ⑤ ⑥ **(RS)**

PORTADOWN 21,906 Co Armagh Map15J05 EcThu
MdSat *Belfast32 Antrim32 Armagh11* Banbridge11
Downpatrick39 Dublin85 Dundalk32 Dungannon17
Enniskillen61 Londonderry81 Lurgan6 *Maghera41*
Omagh46
⑊ *R Hewitt (Mtrs) Ltd* Church St☎33286 **R** ⇨ BL RT
⑊ *Edwin May Ltd* Bridge St ☎32238 **R** Vau

PORTAFERRY 1,592 Co Down Map15J55 EcThu
Belfast29 Bangor25 Donaghadee23
★★ **Portaferry** Shore Rd ☎231
Lic; 8rm(4⇨🛏) 🛏 CTV 🚗P Cabaret Fri & Sat
♀English & French Ld9.30pm ✿ ⚏ *L£3–£5&alc
Tea50p–£1.50&alc High Tea£2.50–£6&alc D£3–
£7.50&alc 🅡

PORTBALLINTRAE 496 Co Antrim Map14C94
EcThu *Belfast60* Bushmills1 *Portrush5*
★★ **Bayview** ☎Bushmills31453
Lic; 23rm(2⇨🛏) 🛏 CTV 🚗 23P ⅃ Ld8.30pm ✿ ⚏

---

*L£3.30–£5 Tea75p–£1 High Tea£2.75–£5
D£4.75–£5.50 Wine£3 🅡
★★ **Beach** ☎Bushmills31214
Lic; 28rm(14⇨🛏) D 🛏 CTV 🚗 100P 🚗 Ld8.15pm

PORTLAOISE 6,740 Co Laois *Dublin53 Cork109*
Limerick71 Rosslare Harbour84
⑊ *Cecil Lewis Mtrs Ltd* Mountrath Rd ☎(0502)21797
R n⇨ Opl

PORT-NA-BLAGH Co Donegal Map16C03 *Dublin170*
Belfast119 Carrigart12 Dunfanaghy2 *Dungloe30*
Letterkenny22
★★★ **Port-na-Blagh** ☎Dunfanaghy11
Closed 21 Sep–Mar; Lic; 58rm(28⇨🛏) D 🌊 🛏 TV 150P
🌊 (hard) Live music & dancing 4 nights wkly ♦♦
♀English & French Ld9pm ✿ ⚏ sB&B IRE7.50–IRE9
sB&B⇨🛏IRE9.50–IRE10.90 dB&B IRE15–IRE18
dB&B⇨🛏IRE18.50–IRE21.50 L IRE3.80–IRE5&alc
Tea70–85p High Tea IRE5alc D IRE6–IRE6.50 🅡
★★★ **Shandon** Marble Hill Strand ☎Dunfanaghy15 or
(021)292937 (winter)
Closed Oct–Apr; Lic; 55⇨🛏 Lift D 🛏 CTV 100P ⅃ 🌊
Ld8.30pm ✿ sB&B⇨🛏IRE10–IRE14 dB&B⇨🛏IRE18–
IRE22 L IRE5alc High Tea IRE5alc D IRE7.50alc 🅡

PORTRUSH 4,749 Co Antrim Map14C83 EcWed
Belfast61 Ballycastle18 Ballymena32 *Dublin159*
Giant's Causeway8 *Londonderry37* Portstewart4
★★ **Skerrybhan** Lansdowne Cres ☎822328
Closed Nov–Feb, RSOct, Mar & Apr; Lic; 42rm(10⇨🛏) Lift
🛏 CTV Disco wkly Ld8.30pm ✿ ⚏ S% *sB&B£6–£8
sB&B⇨🛏£6.50–£8 dB&B£12–£16 dB&B⇨🛏£13–£16
L£3 Tea£1 High Tea£3.30alc D£5&alc Wine£2.85 🅡
⑊ *Glenvale Garages (B Boyd)* 100 Coleraine Rd
☎823702 ☎822460 **R** ⇨ BL
⑊ *J S Mtrs* 119 Eglinton St ☎2760 **R** n⇨

PORTSTEWART 4,975 Co Londonderry Map14C83
EcThu *Belfast60* Coleraine5 *Portrush4*
★ **Windsor** 8 The Promenade ☎2523
Closed Jan & Feb; Unlicensed; 26rm(5⇨🛏) 🌊 🛏 CTV 9🚗
Ld7.15pm sB&B£9.25 sB&B⇨🛏£10.50 dB&B£18
dB&B⇨🛏£20 L£3–£3.50 High Tea£2.75–£4 🅡
Credit card ⑥

Government Forestry Centre demesne, Portumna

PORTUMNA 913 Co Galway Map7M80 EcMon
MdSat *Dublin97 Athlone37* Ballinasloe21 *Belfast178*
Birr16 *Cork108* Ennis46 *Galway42* Killaloe35
Limerick43 Loughrea19 Nenagh18 Roscrea26 Tulla35
Tullamore 38
★★★ **Westpark** ☎112
Lic; 29⇨🛏 D 🎨 🛏 CTV 🚗 500P ⅃ Live music & dancing wkly
Ld9.15pm ✿ ⚏ sB&B⇨🛏IRE12.10–IRE14.02
dB&B⇨🛏IRE22–IRE26.95 L IRE3.60–IRE3.90
D IRE5.95–IRE6.50&alc Wine IRE2.95 🅡 Credit card ②
⑊ *G A Claffey Ltd* ☎9 **R** n⇨ Frd

POYNTZPASS 320 Co Armagh Map13J03 EcTue MdSat
Belfast32 Armagh15 Dublin70 Dundalk22 Londonderry92

Ruined Bishop's Palace, Raphoe

Newry9 Portadown11
♪19.00 *Trainor Bros* Automobile Electrical Engineers
☎219 **R** 19.00 n♨

RANDALSTOWN 2,462 Co Antrim Map15J09 EcTue/Sat
MdWed *Belfast23 Antrim6* Ballymena9 Cookstown23
Dublin122 Londonderry50 Maghera17
♪*Robert Moore & Son* Main St ☎72286 ☎72287
R n♨ BL RT

RAPHOE 945 Co Donegal Map14C20 EcWed *Dublin139*
Belfast98 Donegal28 Letterkenny10 *Londonderry15*
Strabane7 Stranorlar10
★**Central** ☎8
Closed 23–31 Dec; Lic; 10rm(3⇔5🅵) ➡ CTV ⊗ 6P
Ld7.45pm ✿ 🗜 sB&B IR£6 sB&B⇔5🅵IR£7 dB&B IR£11
dB&B⇔5🅵IR£12.50 LIR£2.95 Tea60p High Tea IR£3.50
DIR£4.20

RATHCABBAN Co.Offaly Map8M90 *Dublin90*
Limerick44 Birr7 *Portumna10*
♪20.00 *Denis Duffy* The Garage ☎62 **R** 18.30 n♨

RATHDRUM 1,141 Co Wicklow Map9T18 EcWed MdThu
Dublin38 Arklow13 Aughrim8 Bray25 *Carlow43 Cork157*
Glendalough9 Rathnew9 *Wexford50 Wicklow11*
♪*Avonmore Service Gar* ☎(0404)6130 **R** n♨ Opl

RATHFRILAND 2,076 Co Down Map13J23 EcThu
MdWed *Belfast33* Ballynahinch18 Banbridge11
Downpatrick21 Dublin76 Dundalk24 Londonderry102
Newcastle12 Newry10
♪*T Lylrea & Sons Ltd* Downpatrick St ☎223 **R** 19.00 Frd

RATH LUIRC 2,232 Co Cork Map3R52 EcThu *Dublin138*
Cork40 Limerick25 Tipperary27
♪*Park* ☎(063)367 **R** ♨ Nov–Apr

RATHMULLAN 486 Co Donegal Map14C22 EcWed
Dublin165 Belfast113 Cork265 Letterkenny15
★★★🏖🍴 **Rathmullan House** ☎4
Closed 6 Oct–Mar; Lic; 21rm(16⇔5🅵) 🄳 CTV ⊗ 50P 🚗 🛒
🛶 (grass) ❀ Ld8.30pm ✿ S% sB&B IR£8.50–IR£11
sB&B⇔5🅵IR£12.50–IR£14.50 dB&B IR£17–IR£19
dB&B⇔5🅵IR£19–IR£25 (Continental breakfast)
DIR£6.75–IR£7.50 Wine IR£3 🍽 Credit cards ①②⑤ **(RS)**
★★🍴🛒 **Fort Royal** ☎11
Closed Oct–6 Apr; Lic; 17rm(7⇔5🅵) A10rm(2⇔5🅵) CTV
30P 🚗 🛒 &9 🛶 (hard) squash ⋒ Ld8.30pm ✿ 🗜
sB&B IR£10 sB&B⇔5🅵IR£12 dB&B IR£20

dB&B⇔5🅵IR£24 LIR£4 DIR£6.25 🍽 '**(RS)**
★**Pier** ☎3
Closed Oct–2 Apr; Lic; 16rm(1⇔5🅵) TV ⊗ 5P 🚗
Live music & dancing Wed 🔊 Ld8.30pm ✿ 🗜 S%
sB&B IR£5–IR£6 dB&B IR£10–IR£12 Tea75palc
High Tea IR£4alc Wine IR£3 🍽

RATHNEW 954 Co Wicklow Map9T29 *Dublin30*
Arklow17 Bray17 *Carlow52 Cork166* Dun Laoghaire25
Glendalough16 Rathdrum9 *Wexford58 Wicklow2*
★★**Hunter's** ☎(0404)4106
Lic; 17rm5⇔5🅵 CTV 40P 8🏠 🚗 🛒 🛶 (grass) ❀
🍴English & French Ld9.30pm ✿ 🗜 🍽 Credit card ④

RENVYLE Co Galway Map10L66 *Dublin189 Clifden14*
Cork184 Galway56 Leenane16 Westport36
★★★**Renvyle House** Tully Cross ☎3 Telex no 8338
Closed 2 Jan–26 Mar; Lic; 69rm(68⇔5🅵) ➡ CTV 60P 🛒
&9 🛶 (hard) ❀ ⋒ billiards sauna bath Live music & dancing
3 nights wkly 🔊 🍴Irish & French Ld9pm ✿ 🗜 sB&B IR£11–
IR£16 sB&B⇔5🅵IR£11–IR£16 dB&B IR£22–IR£32
dB&B⇔5🅵IR£22–IR£32 Teafr IR£2 Dfr IR£8.50
Wine IR£3.30 🍽

RICHHILL 658 Co Armagh Map14H94 EcWed/Sat
Belfast38 Armagh6 Dublin83 Dungannon15 Newry17
Portadown6
♪*J H Hutchison* Ballyleaney Garage, 171 Dobbin Rd
☎871633 ☎Portadown34864 **R** ♣

ROSCOMMON 2,821 Co Roscommon Map11M86
EcThu MdSat *Dublin91 Athlone20* Ballaghaderreen29
Ballina65 Ballinasloe28 Ballymahon22 *Belfast139* Boyle27
Carrick-on-Shannon26 Castlebar60 *Cork157 Galway51*
Longford19 *Mullingar40 Sligo53* Tuam37
★★**Abbey** ☎(090)6505
Lic; 10rm2⇔5🅵 ➡ TV 30P 🛒 Ld9pm ✿

ROSCREA 3,855 Co Tipperary Map8S18 EcWed MdThu
Dublin77 Athlone40 Belfast161 Birr12 Clonmel50 *Cork96*
Galway68 Kilkenny39 Limerick46 Nenagh21
Port Laoise25 *Portumna26* Thurles21 *Tipperary47*
Tullamore30
★★**Pathe** ☎241
Closed Xmas Day; Lic; 23rm(8⇔5🅵) ➡ CTV 10P 🚗 🛒
Ld9.30pm ✿ 🗜 S% sB&B IR£10 sB&B⇔5🅵IR£12
dB&B IR£18 dB&B⇔5🅵IR£20 LIR£2.50–IR£3.75
High Tea IR£2–IR£7 DIR£5–IR£7.50 Wine IR£2.50

Credit cards ① ② ③ ⑤
♨ *New Road Service Gar* ☎70 **R** n♠

ROSSCAHILL Co Galway Map10M13 *Dublin149
Belfast203 Galway13* Oughterard5
★★♨♨ **Ross Lake** ☎(091)80109
Closed Oct–Apr; Lic; 12rm3⇌🛏🖭 CTV 300P 🚗 ⅃
🌙(hard) sauna bath ♀Irish & Continental Ld9pm ♥ ☑ S%
🏳 Credit cards ③ ⑥

ROSSES POINT 464 Co Sligo Map11G63 EcWed
Dublin140 Belfast132 Cork215 Sligo5
★★ **Yeats Country Ryan** ☎(071)77211
Lic; 95⇌🛏 Lift TV 200P ⅃ 🌙(hard) Ld9pm ♥ ☑
sB&B⇌🛏IR£16–IR£20 dB&B⇌🛏IR£24–IR£30 🏳
Credit cards ① ② ③ ④ ⑤ ⑥

ROSSLARE 588 Co Wexford Map5T01 EcWed
Dublin140 Rosslare Harbour6 Wexford10
★★★ **Kelly's** ☎(053)32114
Closed mid Dec–mid Feb; Lic; 97rm(87⇌🛏) Lift 𝒟 🖭 CTV
TV available in bedrooms ⊛ 100P 🚗 ⅃ 🏊 &
squash billiards sauna bath Live music & dancing 5 nights
wkly ♨ Ld9pm ♥ ☑ sB&B IRE10.35–IRE12.60
sB&B⇌🛏IRE13.35–IRE15.60 dB&B IRE20.70–IRE25.20
dB&B⇌🛏IRE24.50–IRE26.90 LIRE5.25–IRE5.75
Tea75p–IRE1 DIRE7.55–IRE8.50 WineIRE3.50 🏳 **(RS)**
★★ **Golf** ☎(053)32179
Closed Xmas wk; Lic; 25rm(13⇌🛏) 🖭 CTV 25P 🚗 ⅃
🌙(grass) Ld9.15pm ♥ ☑ sB&B IRE9.62–IRE11
sB&B⇌🛏IRE11.55–IRE12.92 dB&B IRE19.25–IRE22
dB&B⇌🛏IRE22.55–IRE25.30 LIRE3.50 TeaIRE1.50
High Tea IRE3 DIRE7 WineIRE3.50 🏳 Credit card ②

ROSSLARE HARBOUR Co Wexford Map5T11 EcWed
Dublin101 Arklow50 *Belfast205 Carlow60 Cork129*
Kilkenny62 New Ross36 Rosslare5 *Waterford51
Wexford12*
★★★ **Great Southern** ☎(053)33233 Telex no 8788
Closed 4 Jan–9 Mar; Lic; 100⇌🛏 𝒟 🖭 CTV 200P ⅃
🏊(heated) 🌙(hard) ▷ billiards sauna bath Live music &
dancing nightly Jun–Sep ♀Irish & French ☑ S%
Credit cards ① ② ③ ④ ⑤ ⑥

ROSSNOWLAGH Co Donegal Map16G86 *Dublin135*
Ballyshannon5 *Belfast119* Bundoran10 *Donegal11
Galway117 Sligo32*
★★★ **Sand House** (Inter-Hotel) ☎(072)65343 Telex no
4858

Closed 2 Oct–Apr except Etr; Lic; 40rm27⇌🛏 🖭 CTV 60P
🚗 ⅃ 🌙 ◯ billiards Disco mthly Live music & dancing wkly
Cabaret wkly ♀English & French Ld9pm ♥ ☑
sB&B IRE9–IRE11 sB&B⇌🛏IRE10.50–IRE15.50
dB&B IRE18–IRE22 dB&B⇌🛏IRE21–IRE25
Credit cards ② ⑤

ROSTREVOR 2,064 Co Down Map13J11 EcWed
Belfast47 Dublin73 Kilkeel10 *Londonderry98*
Newcastle23 Newry9 Warrenpoint2
♨ *J C Campbell (NI) Ltd* 68 Shore Rd ☎391 **R** n♠
BL RT

ROUNDSTONE 204 Co Galway Map10L74 *Dublin184*
Ballyconneely8 *Cork177 Galway48* Oughterard31
Toombeola4
★ **Seal's Rock** ☎15
Closed Oct–Mar; Lic; 30rm CTV ⊛ 30P Ld8.30pm ♥ ☑
sB&B IRE5 LIRE1.50 DIRE4 WineIRE2.75

SALTHILL Co Galway see **GALWAY**

SCARIFF 619 Co Clare Map7R68 *Dublin121 Cork91
Galway47 Limerick26* Portumna24
★★ **Clare Lakelands** ☎18
Closed 23–31 Dec; Lic; 24rm(21⇌🛏) 𝒟 🇽 🖭 CTV
TV available in bedrooms 100P ▷ Ld9pm ♥ ☑
*sB&B IRE12–IRE14 sB&B⇌🛏IRE13–IRE16
dB&B IRE20–IRE24 dB&B⇌🛏IRE22–IRE26
LIRE2.75–IRE3.50 TeaIRE1–IRE1.50&alc
High TeaIRE3–IRE3.75&alc DIRE5–IRE7&alc
WineIRE2.50 🏳

SCHULL 457 Co Cork Map2V93 EcTue-*Dublin229
Belfast332 Cork68* Skibbereen15
♨18.30 *Schull Mtr Wks* ☎(028)28116 **R** 18.30 n♠

SHILLELAGH 246 Co Wicklow Map8M90 EcWed
Dublin58 Carlow20 New Ross37 *Rosslare Harbour50*
♨ *Shillelagh Mtrs* ☎(055)29127 **R** ♠ Fia

SKIBBEREEN 2,104 Co Cork Map3W13 EcThu MdSat
Dublin210 Bandon34 Bantry18 *Belfast314* Clonakilty20
Cork50 Dunmanway17 *Glengarriff29* Ross Carberry12
♨ *Hurley Bros* ☎(028)21555 **R** ♠ Fia

Dutch-gabled manor house, Richhill

ⅉ*Southern* ☎(028)21091 **R ♨** Ren

SLANE 483 Co Meath Map13N97 EcWed *Dublin29*
Navan8 Ardee13 *Belfast77* Carrickmacross25
Ceanannus Mor15 *Cork177* Drogheda9 *Dundalk26 Trim17*
★**Conyngham Arms** ☎(041)24155
Lic; 12rm(10⇌🛏) 📺 CTV ⊗ 10P Ld9pm ♿ ⌂
sB&B IR£7 50–IR£8 50 sB&B⇌🛏IR£8–IR£9
dB&B IR£15–IR£17 dB&B⇌🛏IR£16–IR£18
L IR£2 50–IR£4 Tea85palc High Tea IR£3 50alc
Wine IR£2.50 🍴 Credit cards ②③⑥

SLIGO 14.456 Co Sligo Map11G63 EcWed MdSat
Dublin134 Athlone73 Ballina37 Ballymote15.
★★★**Sligo Park** Cornageeha ☎(071)3291
Telex no 4397
Lic; 60⇌🛏① 📺 CTV 200P ♣ Live music & dancing Tue &
Sat Cabaret Sat ♿ ⌂English & French Ld9 15pm ♿ ⌂
sB&B⇌🛏IR£18 15–IR£23 92 dB&B⇌🛏IR£24 75–
IR£31 35 L IR£4 50 Tea IR£1 50 High Tea IR£4 50
D IR£7 50 Wine IR£2 50 🍴 Credit cards ①②③④⑤⑥
★★**Silver Swan** Hyde Bridge ☎(071)3231
Closed Xmas Day; Lic; 24rm12⇌🛏 Lift ① 📺 CTV 80P
Cabaret Fri Ld9 20pm ♿ ⌂ 🍴 Credit card ②
ⅉ*Henderson's Mtrs* Wine St ☎(071)2610 **R** n♨ Frd

SNEEM 285 Co Kerry Map2V76 EcWed *Dublin230
Belfast308 Cork76* Kenmare17 *Waterville22*
ⅉ*Sneem Mtr Wks* ☎(064)45101 **R ♨**

SPIDDAL (Spiddle) Co Galway Map6M12 *Dublin148
Galway12 Limerick77 Rosslare Harbour182*
★★**Bridge House** ☎(091)83118
Closed 20 Dec–6 Jan; Lic; 14rm(8⇌🛏) 📺 CTV ⊗ 20P
2🛏 ♨ ♣ ⌂Irish, English, French & Italian Ld10.30pm
♿ ⌂ S% *sB&B IR£7 50–IR£8 sB&B⇌🛏IR£9 50–IR£10
dB&B IR£15–IR£16 dB&B⇌🛏IR£19–IR£20 L IR£4
Tea IR£1&alc High Tea IR£2 50–IR£10&alc D IR£7
Wine IR£2 50

STEWARTSTOWN 720 Co Tyrone Map14H87 EcThu
MdWed *Belfast45 Armagh21* Cookstown6 *Dublin102*
Dungannon8 *Londonderry54 Maghera22* Portadown19
ⅉ*Megaw & McKeown* The Garage, 37 Hillhead ☎224
R ♨ BL

STRABANE 9,325 Co Tyrone Map14H39 EcThu
MdTue/Thu *Belfast80 Carrigart40 Donegal32 Dublin133
Dungloe45* Glenties41 Letterkenny17 *Londonderry14
Maghera40* Newtownstewart10 *Omagh20* Rosapenna42
ⅉ*Autoservices* Lower Main St ☎882650 ☎2524 **R** n♨

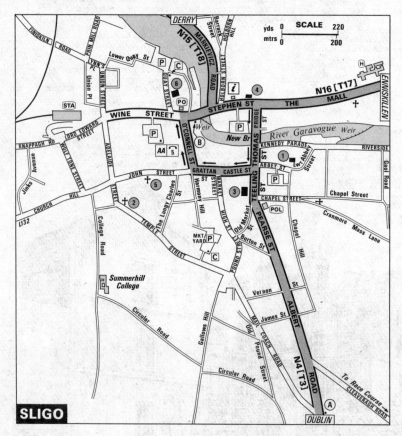

AA Road Service Centre ☎(071)5065

A ★★★ Sligo Park
B ★★ Silver Swan

places of interest
1 Abbey Remains
2 St John's Cathedral (RC)
3 Courthouse
4 Library and Museum
5 St John's Church (CI)
6 Town Hall

The Court House, Tralee

STRANORLAR 848 Co Donegal Map16H29 EcWed
MdFri *Dublin148 Belfast94 Cork268 Donegal18
Dungloe31* Glenties27 Letterkenny13 *Londonderry25*
Raphoe10 Strabane14
★★**Kee's** ☎Ballybofey18
Lic; 24rm4⇔卿卿 TV 4P 10爺 Ld11.40pm ◊ Credit card 5

STROKESTOWN 563 Co Roscommon Map11M98
*Dublin97 Athlone33 Ballina60 Belfast127 Cork169
Galway63* Longford14 *Roscommon12 Sligo45*
★★**Percy French** ☎46
Lic; 22rm11⇔卿卿 CTV 100P Music & dancing wkly
Ld9pm ◊ ✓ S%

SWINFORD 1,105 Co Mayo Map11M39 EcWed MdTue
Dublin132 Ballaghderreen17 *Ballina19 Belfast163*
Castlebar17 Claremorris20 *Cork181* Foxford9
Longford56 *Sligo36* Tobercurry14 Westport28
◗18 30 **St Patrick's S/sta** ☎111 **R** 18 30 n₷ Fia

TEMPLEMORE 2,174 Co Tipperary Map8S17 EcWed
MdWed/Thu/Fri *Dublin88* Abbeyleix25 *Athlone52
Belfast173* Birr24 Cashel23 Clonmel38 *Cork84*
Nenagh21 *Port Laoise37* Roscrea12 Thurles9
Tipperary35
◗18 50 **Hassetts Mtr Wks** ☎(0504)31051 **R** 18 50 n₷
BL

THOMASTOWN 1,270 Co Kilkenny Map5S54 EcThu
MdWed *Dublin77 Belfast181 Carlow25 Cork91*
Graiguenamanagh10 *Kilkenny11* Muine Bheag17
New Ross16 *Waterford21*
◗**Thomastown** ☎(056)24176 **R** n₷ Toy

THURLES 7,087 Co Tipperary Map8S15 EcWed MdSat
Dublin92 Athlone62 Belfast182 Cahir24 Cashel13
Clonmel28 *Cork75* Fermoy52 *Kilkenny30 Limerick40*
★★**Anner** ☎(0504)21799
Closed Xmas Day; Lic; 17rm(3⇔卿) ⅅ 卿卿 CTV 350P ✓
Disco Fri, Sat & Sun Ld9 30pm ◊ ✓ sB&B IR£8 80
sB&B⇔卿IR£9 90 dB&B IR£18 dB&B⇔卿IR£19 50

LIR£3 30 DIR£5alc Wine IR£3 Credit card 2
◗**Thurles Mtrs Ltd** The Mall ☎(0504)21355 **R** n₷ Frd

TIPPERARY 4,717 Co Tipperary Map4R83 EcWed
MdThu/Sat *Dublin112 Belfast208* Cahir14 Cashel13
Clonmel25 *Cork53* Fermoy30 *Kilkenny49* Kilmallock22
Limerick25 Mallow41 Mitchelstown20 *Waterford55*
★**Royal** Bridge St ☎(062)51204
RSXmas Day; Lic; 23rm(2⇔卿) ⅅ 卿卿 CTV 15P 10爺 ✓
Cabaret twice wkly Ld9pm ◊ ✓ sB&B IR£6–IR£6 80
sB&B⇔卿IR£8–IR£8 80 dB&B IR£12–IR£13.60
dB&B⇔卿IR£16–IR£17.60 LIR£3 50 Tea IR£1 50
High Tea IR£3.60alc DIR£6 50 Wine IR£6
◗20.00 **Hughes** ☎(062)51371 **R**20 00 ₷
◗22.00 **O'Doherty & O'Dwyer** ☎(062)51213 **R** ₷ Frd

TOBERMORE 570 Co Londonderry Map14H89 EcThu
Belfast42 Antrim25 Cookstown13 Draperstown4
Dublin118 Limavady26 *Londonderry36 Maghera3*
Magherafelt6
◗**Stockman & Sons** Maghera Rd ☎42320 **R** ₷ BL

TOOMEBRIDGE 386 Co Antrim Map15H99 EcWed
MdTue *Belfast29* Antrim12 Ballymena12 Cookstown17
Dublin100 Londonderry44 Maghera11 Magherafelt7
Randalstown7
◗**Robert Murray & Sons** The Garage ☎240 **R** n₷ Aud VW

TRALEE 13,263 Co Kerry Map2Q81 EcWed MdThu/Sat
Dublin188 Adare50 Ballybunion21 *Belfast267*
Cahirciveen43 Castleisland11 *Cork75* Dingle31
Killarney20 Killorglin16 *Limerick66* Listowel17
Newcastle West39
★★★**Ballyseede Castle** ☎(066)21585
Lic; 13rm10⇔卿 1 ⌣ 卿 CTV ⊗ 20P ✓ ♡ French Ld10pm
S%
★★★**Earl of Desmond** (Inter-Hotel) ☎(066)21299
Lic; 52⇔卿 ⅅ 卿卿 CTV ⊗ 300P ✓ ✤ (hard) ↳ Live music &
dancing twice wkly Cabaret nightly ◊ Ld9pm ◊ ✓ S%
sB&B⇔卿IRE13 50–IRE15.75 dB&B⇔卿IRE21 40–IRE27
LIRE3.50–IRE5 Tea80p–IRE1 High Tea IRE3–IRE5.50

D IR£8–IR£10 ♨ Credit cards ①②③④⑤⑥
★★★**Mount Brandon** ☎(066)21311 Telex no.8130
Closed 23–29 Dec; RSJan–Mar (1980); Lic; 162⇔🛏 Lift 𝄐
🍴 CTV TV available in bedrooms ⊛ 500P Live music &
dancing Sun ♀ International Ld8.45pm ✿ 🅿 S% sB&B⇔🛏
IR£13 50–IR£24 dB&B⇔🛏IR£23.05–IR£42
L IR£4 95–IR£5 50 D IR£7.30–IR£10.50&alc Wine IR£4 20
Credit cards ①②③⑤
⚓*Kelliher's* ☎(066)21688 **R** n⊛ Peu Toy
⚓*Rice* 100 Rock St ☎(066)21877 **R** n⊛ BL

TRAMORE 3,792 Co Waterford Map5S50 EcThu
Dublin107 Belfast211 Carrick-on-Suir20 Clonmel33

Cork75 Dungarvan26 *Waterford8*
★★★**Grand** ☎(051)81414
Lic; 50⇔🛏 Lift 𝄐 🍴 CTV TV available in bedrooms 100P
Live music & dancing 3 nights wkly Cabaret twice wkly
Ld9 30pm ✿ 🅿 S% sB&B⇔🛏IR£11 50–IR£13
dB&B⇔🛏IR£22–IR£25 L IR£3 50–IR£4 Tea75p
High Tea IR£3 50alc D IR£6–IR£7&alc Wine IR£2.65 ♨
Credit cards ①②③⑤⑥

TRILLICK 260 Co Tyrone Map14H35 EcWed *Belfast85
Dublin114 Enniskillen12*
⚓*G J Tunney* The Garage, Main St ☎249 **R** ⊛ Frd Hon
Ren Toy

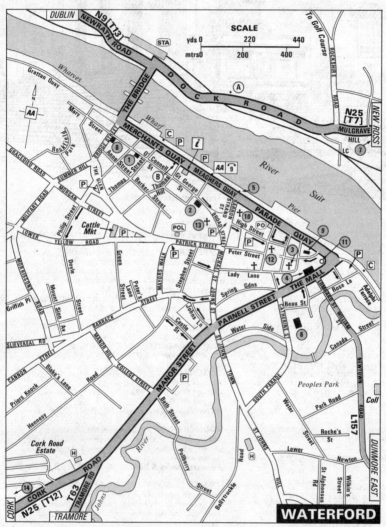

AA Road Service Centre ☎(051) 3765

A ★★★Ardree
B ★★Dooley's

places of interest
1 Art Gallery and Museum
2 Chamber of Commerce
3 Christchurch Cathedral
4 City Hall
5 Clock Tower
6 Court House
7 Cromwell's Rock
8 Dominican Friary
9 French Church
10 Holy Trinity Cathedral
11 Reginald's Tower
12 St Olaf's Church
13 St Patrick's Church (RC)
14 Waterford Glass Factory

TULLAMORE 7,474 Co Offaly Map8N32 EcMon MdTue *Dublin61 Athlone25* Ballinasloe35 *Belfast132* Birr23 *Cork126* Edenderry22 Kilbeggan7 *Mullingar22* Portarlington17 *Port Laoise22 Roscrea30*
♨***Offaly Mtrs Ltd*** Arden ☎(0506)21783 **R** n♨ Fia Lnc
♨***Tullamore Mtr Wks Ltd*** High St ☎(0506)21202 **R** n♨ BL

TULLOW 1,945 Co Carlow Map9S87 EcWed *Dublin50* Arklow30 Baltinglass11 *Belfast154 Carlow10 Cork120* Enniscorthy25 Bunclody13 Shillelagh10 *Wexford39 Wicklow44*
♨***Byrne's*** ☎(0503)51207 **R** n♨ Dat

VIRGINIA 583 Co Cavan Map12N68 EcTue MdThu *Dublin51* Navan22 Bailieborough8 *Belfast89 Cavan20* Ceanannus Mor12 *Cork178* Granard21 *Mullingar30* Oldcastle7
★★★**Park** ☎35 Telex no 31849
Closed mid Dec–mid Jan; Lic; 22rm(19⇌⋒) A4⇌⋒ CTV 100P ⚓ 9 (hard) English & French Ld10pm sB&B⇌⋒IR£12–IR£15.25 dB&B⇌⋒IR£24–IR£28 L IR£3.50–IR£5 Tea IR£1.20–IR£1.50 High Tea IR£2.20–IR£6 D IR£6–IR£7.20 Wine IR£2.75 Credit cards ①②③⑤⑥
♨19.00 ***Ramor Mtrs*** ☎69 **R**19.00 n♨
♨***Smiths*** Dublin Rd ☎25 **R** n♨

WARRENPOINT 4,278 Co Down Map13J11 EcWed *Belfast45 Dublin73* Kilkeel12 *Londonderry96* Newcastle25 Newry7 Rostrevor2
★**Crown** The Square ☎3665
15rm(7⇌⋒) CTV Irish & French Ld9.30pm sB&B £7.50–£10 sB&B⇌⋒£8.50–£11 dB&B £15–£20 dB&B⇌⋒£17–£22 L£3 High Tea £3&alc Wine £2.50 Credit card ③

WATERFORD 33,676 Co Waterford Map5S61 EcThu MdSat *Dublin99* Arklow66 *Belfast203* Cappoquin38 Carlow47 Carrick-on-Suir17 Clonmel30 *Cork78* Dungarvan29 Enniscorthy36 Fermoy59 *Kilkenny30 Limerick80* New Ross15 *Rosslare Harbour51* Thomastown21 Tramore8 *Wexford39*
★★★**Ardree** ☎(051)3491 Telex no 8684
Closed Xmas Day; Lic; 100⇌⋒ Lift ☽ CTV TV available in bedrooms 500P ⚓ (hard) Disco Tue & Sun International Ld9.15pm S% sB&B⇌⋒IR£20–IR£22.50 dB&B⇌⋒IR£30–IR£38.50 L IR£3.50–IR£4.50 Tea IR£1.30–IR£1.70 High Tea IR£3.50–IR£5 D IR£6–IR£8 Wine IR£3 Credit cards ①②③④⑤⑥
★★**Dooley's** 30 The Quay ☎(051)3531
Closed 25–27 Dec; Lic; 31rm(13⇌⋒) CTV International Ld9.30pm sB&B IR£12.10 sB&B⇌⋒IR£13.20 dB&B IR£20.90 dB&B⇌⋒IR£23.10 IR£4.50–IR£5.40 D IR£6.50–IR£8&alc Wine IR£4 Credit cards ①②③
♨***John Kelly*** St Catherine St ☎(051)74988 **R** ♨ Opl
♨***Sheridan's Motor*** ☎(051)72891 **R** n♨ Frd

WATERVILLE 547 Co Kerry Map2V56 EcWed MdTue *Dublin232 Belfast310* Cahirciveen11 *Cork99* Kenmare39 Killarney51 Killorglin36 Parknasilla24 Sneem22 *Tralee52*
★★**Bay View** ☎4
Closed mid Oct–Mar; Lic; 29rm(6⇌⋒) CTV 100P ⚓ Ld9pm *sB&B IR£6–IR£8.75 sB&B⇌⋒IR£7.70–IR£10.25 dB&B IR£12–IR£16.50 dB&B⇌⋒IR£15–IR£19.50 L IR£3 High Tea IR£3 D IR£6 Wine IR£3.75 Credit card ②
★★**Butler Arms** ☎5
Closed 12 Oct–Mar; Lic; 40rm(20⇌⋒) ☽ CTV 25P 6 ⚓ 18 (hard) billiards Irish & French Ld8.30pm sB&B IR£9–IR£10 sB&B⇌⋒IR£10.50–IR£11.50 dB&B IR£18–IR£20 dB&B⇌⋒IR£20–IR£23 D IR£7.50–IR£8 Wine IR£3 Credit cards ②⑤
♨19.00 ***Concannon's*** ☎10 **R**19.00 ♨

WESTPORT 3,023 Co Mayo Map10L98 EcWed MdThu *Dublin162* Ballinrobe21 *Ballina33 Belfast192 Belmullet51* Castlebar11 Claremorris28 *Clifden41 Cork181 Galway51* Leenane20 Mulrany18 *Roscommon71 Sligo64* Tuam41
★★★**Westport** ☎351 Telex no 6397
Closed Xmas wk; Lic; 49⇌⋒ ☽ CTV TV available in bedrooms 200P ⚓ Live music & dancing 6 nights wkly Ld9pm *sB&B⇌⋒IR£11–IR£16.50 dB&B⇌⋒IR£22–IR£30.80 L IR£3.85 Tea IR£1.25alc High Tea IR£3alc D IR£6.60 Wine IR£2.50 Credit cards ①②③④⑤⑥
★★**Clew Bay** ☎173 Telex no 6346
Lic; 33rm(24⇌⋒) ☽ CTV 4P Cabaret 3 nights wkly Irish & French Ld8.45pm sB&B IR£7.50–IR£9.50 sB&B⇌⋒IR£9.50–IR£10.50 dB&B IR£13–IR£16.50 dB&B⇌⋒IR£15–IR£19.50 L IR£3–IR£4 D IR£5–IR£6 Wine IR£3.50 Credit cards ②③

Tower of the west gate, Wexford

WEXFORD 13,293 Co Wexford Map5T02 EcThu MdSat *Dublin88* Arklow37 *Belfast192 Carlow48 Cork117* Enniscorthy15 Gorey26 *Kilkenny50* New Ross24 Rosslare10 *Rosslare Harbour12*
★★★★**Talbot** Trinity St ☎(053)22566 Telex no 8658
Lic; 100⇌⋒ Lift ☽ CTV 200P (heated) squash sauna bath Live music & dancing Sat Irish & Continental Ld8.45pm SB&B⇌⋒IR£19 dB&B⇌⋒IR£32 L IR£5–IR£6.50 D IR£7–IR£9 Wine IR£3 Credit cards ①②③④⑤⑥
★★★**Ferrycarrig** Ferrycarrig Bridge ☎(053)22999
Closed Nov–Mar; Lic; 40⇌⋒ Lift CTV TV available in bedrooms 100P ⚓ (hard) Ld8.30pm sB&B⇌⋒IR£12.10–IR£14.50 dB&B⇌⋒IR£20.90–IR£25.80 (Continental breakfast) D IR£5.25–IR£7.50&alc Wine IR£3 Credit cards ②③⑤
★★★**White's** ☎(053)22311 Telex no 8630
Lic; 100rm(59⇌⋒) Lift ☽ CTV P Disco Thu Live music & dancing Sat Ld10.45pm *sB&B IR£12.32–IR£14.57 sB&B⇌⋒IR£16.39–IR£18.42 dB&B IR£20.24–IR£24.75 dB&B⇌⋒IR£26.29–IR£30.80 L IR£4.95–IR£5.50 High Tea IR£3–IR£3.50 D IR£7.70–IR£8.25 Credit cards ①②③④⑤⑥
♨***Crescent*** Custom House Quay ☎(053)22223 **R** n♨

WHITEHEAD 2,618 Co Antrim Map15J49 EcThu *Belfast16 Antrim25 Dublin120 Larne9 Londonderry80*
♨18.30 ***Raw Brae S/sta*** ☎8532 **R**18.30 ♨

WOODENBRIDGE Co Wicklow Map9T17 *Dublin45*
Arklow5 Laragh15 *Rosslare Harbour54*
★**Woodenbridge** ☎(0402)5146
Closed Xmas Day & Good Fri; Lic; 12rm 🛏 ⊗ 40P ⟁
Live music & dancing Sat & Sun Cabaret Sat & Sun
Ld9pm ✿ ⚠ S% sB&B IR£6.50–IR£7.50
dB&B IR£13–IR£15 L IR£3.25–IR£3.75
High Tea IR£2.50–IR£4.95 D IR£6&alc Wine IR£3.60 🍴
Credit cards ① ② ⑤

YOUGHAL 5,626 Co Cork Map4X17 EcWed MdWed/Sat
Dublin144 Belfast249 Cappoquin19 Clonmel39 Cobh29
Cork30 Dungarvan19 Fermoy27 Lismor19 Midleton17
Waterford48
★★**Hilltop** ☎(024)2577
Closed 16 Oct–14 Apr; Lic; 50⇔🛏 🌙 🛏 CTV ⊗ 50P ⟁
⊇(heated) Disco twice wkly Live music & dancing twice
wkly Cabaret wkly ♨ ♨ Continental Ld9.30pm ✿ ⚠ S%
sB&B⇔🛏 IR£12.50–IR£15.50 dB&B⇔🛏 IR£16.50–IR£24
L IR£3.50–IR£3.80&alc Tea IR£1.50 D IR£6.50–
IR£7.50&alc Wine IR£3 🍴
★★⟁♨**Monatrea House & Country Club** ☎(024)4293
Closed mid Sep–mid May; Lic; 15rm(7⇔🛏) A6rm 🛏 CTV
50P 🚗 ⟁ ⊇(heated) ♨(hard) ∩ sauna bath ♨
♨ Continental Ld8.30pm ✿ ⚠ sB&B IR£10–IR£12
sB&B⇔🛏 IR£12–IR£14 dB&B IR£20–IR£24
dB&B⇔🛏 IR£22–IR£26 L IR£3 D IR£6.50 Wine IR£3.50
Credit card ②

Clock Gate, Youghal

FOG CODE

1 Slow down; keep a safe distance. You should always be able to pull up within your range of vision.

2 Don't hang on to someone else's tail lights; it gives you a false sense of security.

3 Watch your speed; you may be going much faster than you think.

4 Remember that if you are in a heavy vehicle you need a good deal longer to pull up.

5 Warning signals are there to help and protect; do observe them.

6 See and be seen – use headlights or fog lamps.

7 Check and clean windscreen, lights, reflectors and windows whenever you can.

8 If you must drive in fog, allow more time for your journey.

9 Headlights must be used during the daytime in conditions of bad visibility, *eg* fog.

Restaurants

Explanation of a gazetteer entry

The example is fictitious

Town name
Appears in bold type, followed by address in alphabetical order under county heading.

INCHIGEELA Map17W26
✕✕ **King Sitric** ☎(01)325235
Closed Sun, Xmas wk Lunch not served Sat. Lic; 70seats Ld11.15pm *Lunch £3.25–£6.50 Dinner £8.50alc Wine£2 Credit cards ① ② ③ ⑤ ⑥

Map reference
First figure is map page no. Then follows grid reference: read 1st figure across and 2nd figure upwards

Classification
See page 117.

Specific details
Closing times, facilities & restrictions. See page 114 for abbreviations and symbols.

Telephone number
The exchange is that of the town unless otherwise stated. In the Republic of Ireland, STD codes are shown where applicable.

✕	Modest but good restaurant
✕✕	Restaurant offering higher standard of comfort than ✕
✕✕✕	Well appointed restaurant
✕✕✕✕	Exceptionally well appointed restaurant
✕✕✕✕✕	A luxury restaurant

Co Antrim

TEMPLEPATRICK Map15J28 ·
✕ **Pig N'Chicken** 882 Antrim Rd ☎32310
Lic; 80seats 200P Disco Tue & Sat Cabaret wkly
Ld10.30pm

Belfast

BELFAST Map 15J37
✕✕ **Tavern Buttery** 82 Victoria St ☎22774
Closed Sat & Sun; Lic; 55seats ℙ ☐ International Ld6pm S% *L£3.50alc Wine£2.75
✕ **Carlton** Wellington Pl ☎26861
Closed Sun, Xmas, New Year, Etr & 12–13 Jul; Lic; 160seats ℙ Ld11pm S% *L£3alc D£3alc Wine£2.60
✕ **Errigle Inn** 320 Ormeau Rd ☎641410
Closed Sun & Xmas Day; Lic; 96seats Cabaret 6 nights wkly
Ld10.30pm
✕ **Thompsons Grill Bar** 47 Arthur St ☎23762
Closed Sun; Lic; 40seats ℙ Ld9pm S% *L£5alc D£5alc Wine£2.95 Credit cards ① ③ ⑤

Co Clare

SHANNON AIRPORT Map7R36
✕✕✕ **Shannon Airport** ☎(061)61444
Lic; 120seats ☐ English & French Ld10pm S%

Co Cork

CORK Map3W67
✕✕✕ **Lovett's** Churchyard Lane, Well Rd ☎(021)294909
Closed Sun, Public Hols & Holy week;
Lunch not served Sat; Lic; 30seats 15P ☐ French
Ld9.45pm *L IR£5–IR£6.50 D IR£8.50alc Wine IR£3
Credit cards ① ② ③ ⑤

KILBRITTAIN Map3W54
✕✕ **Pink Elephant** Harbour View ☎(023)49608
Lic; 54seats 60P Cabaret Thu ☐ Irish & Continental
Ld10pm S% High Tea IR£3.20alc D IR£7alc Wine IR£2.90
Credit card ③

KINSALE Map3W65
✕✕ **Bacchus** 13 Pearse St ☎(021)72659
Closed Sun, Mon, Sep, Etr & Xmas; Lic; 25seats
☐ Continental. Ld10pm S% Credit card ③
✕✕ **Bistro** Guardwell ☎(021)72470
Closed Sun, Mon & 20 Dec–20 Jan; Lunch not served; Lic; 50seats ℙ ☐ International. Ld11pm S% D IR£5–IR£14.50 &alc
✕✕ **Man Friday** Scilly ☎(021)72260
Closed Sun, Nov & Feb; Lunch not served; Lic; 45seats
☐ Irish & Continental. Ld10.15pm S%
✕ **Vintage** Main St ☎(021)72502
Closed Tue, Wed & Nov–Mar; Lunch not served; Lic;
40seats ℙ ☐ French. Ld10.30pm D IR£8alc Wine IR£2.75
MALLOW Map3W59
✕✕ **Longueville House** ☎(022)27156
Closed mid Oct–Etr except Sat; Lunch not served;
Dinner not served Sun & Mon; Lic; 50seats 50P
bedrooms available Ld9pm S% *D IR£9.40 Wine IR£3
SHANAGARRY Map4W96
✕✕ **Ballymaloe House (Yeats Room)** 2m S of Cloyne on
Ballycotton Rd ☎(021)62531
Lic; 80seats P bedrooms available ✗ Ld9.30pm L IR£3.75
D IR£9.50 Wine IR£4
YOUGHAL Map4X17
✕ **Aherne's Pub** 163 North Main St ☎(024)2424
Dinner not served Mon; Lic; 50seats 35P
☐ English & French. Ld10pm

Co Down

COMBER Map15J46
✕✕✕ **Old Crow** Glen Rd ☎872255
Lunch not served Sun. Lic; 65seats 18P Live music &
dancing Sat Cabaret Sat ☐ French. Ld9.30pm
L£2.50–£4 D£7.50alc Wine£3.80
HOLYWOOD Map15J37
✕✕ **Clanbrassil House** Seafront Rd, Cultra (1m E A2)
☎3147
Closed Sun & Public Hols; Lic; 180seats 50P
Live music & dancing Sat Ld9.30pm L£3.60&alc
High Tea£2.20–£5 D£5.20&alc Wine£4

PORTAFERRY Map15J55
✕✕ Scotsman Shore Rd ☎326
Closed Sun & 25 Dec; Lunch not served Good Fri; Lic;
75seats 7P Ld9.30pm L£5.10alc D£5.10alc Wine£3

Record Tower, Dublin Castle

Co Dublin

DALKEY Map9O22
✕ Guinea Pig Railway Rd ☎(01)859055
Lunch not served; Lic; 36seats ℗ ♀Irish & French.
Ld11.30pm D IR£15alc Wine IR£3 Credit cards ② ③ ⑤
DUBLIN Map9O13
✕✕✕ Amory Grant 39 Arran Quay, 7 ☎(01)711632
Closed Sun & Public Hols; Lunch not served; Lic;
48seats ♀Continental. Ld10.30pm *L IR£12alc
D IR£12alc Wine IR£4.05 Credit cards ① ② ③ ⑤
✕✕✕ Bailey Duke St, 2 ☎(01)770600
Closed Sun, Good Fri, 25 & 26 Dec; Lic; 100seats ℗
♀French Ld11.15pm L IR£5–IR£9.50&alc D IR£15alc
Wine IR£4.75 Credit cards ① ② ③ ④ ⑤ ⑥
✕✕✕ Le Bistro 5 Lord Edward St, 2 ☎(01)780663
Closed Good Fri, Xmas & Boxing Day; Lunch not served;
Lic; 60seats ℗ ♀French. Ld11pm *L IR£1.55–IR£5.60
D IR£8.50–IR£15 Credit cards ① ② ③ ⑤ ⑥
✕✕✕ Goat Grill Goatstown, 14 ☎(01)984145
Closed Sun, Xmas & Good Fri; Lic; 80seats 200P
♀Irish & French. Ld11.15pm L IR£4.60–IR£5.60
D IR£9.50alc Wine IR£3 Credit cards ① ② ③ ⑤
✕✕✕ Sachs 21-25 Morehampton Rd, Donnybrook, 4
☎(01)680995
Lic; 60seats 200P bedrooms available Disco 6 nights wkly
♀French. Ld10.45pm S% L IR£2.50–IR£7 Tea IR£1.50–
IR£2.50 D IR£15alc Wine IR£4 Credit cards ① ② ④ ⑤ ⑥
✕✕✕ Weigh Inn Phoenix Park Racecourse, Castleknock
☎(01)300042
Closed Sun; Lunch not served Sat; Dinner not served Mon;
Lic; 50seats P Disco Fri, Sat & Sun ♀International.
Ld10.30pm *L IR£10alc D IR£10alc Wine IR£3.25
Credit cards ① ② ③ ⑤
✕✕ Celtic Mews 109A Lower Baggot St ☎(01)760796
Closed Sun, Xmas wk & Two wks Jul; Lunch not served;
Lic; 65seats ℗ ♀International. Ld11.50pm S% D IR£10alc
Wine IR£3.75 Credit cards ② ③
✕✕ Coachman's Inn Cloghran ☎(01)401827
Closed Sun & Public Hols; Lic; 50seats 200P Ld11pm
Credit cards ① ② ③ ④ ⑤ ⑥
✕✕ Earl of Fingal Fingal House, Clontarf, 3 ☎(01)332680
Closed Sun & 23–26 Dec; Lunch not served; Lic;

70seats 30P bedrooms available ♀Irish & French
Ld10.30pm D IR£6.50&alc Wine IR£3 Credit cards ① ② ③
✕✕ Lord Edward Christchurch Pl, 8 ☎(01)752557
Closed Sun & Public Hols; Lunch not served Sat; Lic;
40seats ℗ ♀Irish & French. Ld10.45pm L IR£10alc
D IR£10alc Wine IR£4.35 Credit cards ② ③ ⑤
✕✕ Rafters 302 Lower Rathmines Rd ☎(01)960939
Lunch not served; Lic; 100seats ℗ ♀International.
Ld12.30am *D IR£7alc Wine IR£3.50 Credit cards ② ③
✕✕ Tandoori Rooms 27 Lower Leeson St, 2 ☎(01)762286
Closed Sun, Public Hols & 2 wks in Summer; Lunch not
served; Lic; 45seats ℗ ♀International. Ld12.30am
*D IR£8.70–IR£10.65&alc Wine IR£3.65 Credit cards ② ⑤
✕✕ Yellow House (Marley Room) Rathfarnham, 14
☎(01)905994
Closed Sun; Lic; 70seats ℗ ♀Irish & French. Ld11pm S%
L IR£3.25–IR£4&alc D IR£6.50–IR£7.50&alc
Wine IR£2.80 Credit cards ① ② ③ ⑤
✕ Kapriol Camden St, 2 ☎(01)751235
Closed Sun & Public Hols; Lunch not served; Lic; 28seats
℗ ♀Continental. Ld mdnt S% *D IR£8alc Wine IR£4.20
Credit cards ① ② ③ ⑤
✕ Old Dublin 91 Francis St, 8 ☎(01)751173
Closed Sun & Mon; Lunch not served; Lic; 30seats
Ld11pm S% Credit cards ① ② ③ ⑥
✕ Quo Vadis St Andrews Street ☎(01)773363
Closed Xmas & New Year; Lic; 94seats ♀Italian
Credit card ②
✕ Snaffles 47 Lower Leeson St, 2 ☎(01)762227
Closed Sun, Xmas & Public Hols; Lunch not served Sat;
Dinner not served Mon; Lic; 50seats Ld11pm S%
L IR£15alc D IR£15alc Wine IR£4 Credit cards ② ③ ⑤
✕ Unicorn 1 l Merrion Row, 2 ☎(01)762182
Closed Sun & Public Hols; Lunch not served; Lic; 50seats
℗ ♀International. Ld10.15pm *D IR£5.80&alc
Wine IR£3.20

DUN LAOGHAIRE Map9O22
✕✕✕ Mirabeau ☎(01)809873
Closed Sun & Public Hols; Lunch not served; Lic; 50seats
Ld11pm Credit cards ② ③ ⑤
✕✕✕ Restaurant Na Mara Crofton Rd ☎(01)806767
Closed Sun & Mon; Lic; 75seats 10P ✗ ♀International.
Ld10.30pm L IR£4–IR£5&alc D IR£7&alc
Credit cards ① ② ③ ⑤
✕ Creole 20A Adelaide St ☎(01)806706
Closed Xmas & Good Fri; Lunch not served; Lic; 48seats ℗
♀Irish & French. Ld12.30am *High Tea IR£8alc D IR£8alc
Wine IR£3.95 Credit cards ① ② ③ ④ ⑤ ⑥
✕ Trudi's 107 Lower Georges St ☎(01)805318
Closed Sun; Lunch not served; Lic; 55seats ℗ ♀French.
Ld11pm D IR£10.50alc Wine IR£3.40 Credit cards ② ③

HOWTH Map9O23
✕✕ King Sitric ☎(01)325235
Closed Sun, Public Hols & 10 days Xmas; Lunch not served;
80seats ♀Irish & French. Ld11.15pm D IR£12alc
Wine IR£4 Credit cards ① ② ③ ⑤ ⑥

KILLINEY Map9O22
✕✕ Rolland ☎(01)851329
Closed Sun, Mon & 3 wks Aug; Lunch not served;
No corkage charge; 55seats 15P ♀French. Ld10.30pm
D IR£12alc Credit cards ② ③ ⑥

MALAHIDE Map13O24
✕✕ Johnny's 9 St James Tce ☎(01)450314
Closed Sun, Mon, Etr, Xmas & mid Sep–mid Oct;
Lunch not served; Lic; 65seats ℗ ♀French. Ld10.30pm
D IR£13alc Wine IR£5 Credit cards ① ② ③ ⑤

STILLORGAN Map9O23
✕✕✕ Beaufield Mews Woodlands Av ☎(01)880375
Closed Sun, Mon, Public Hols, 1 wk Etr & 1 wk Xmas;
Lic; 125seats 100P ♀English & Continental. Ld10pm
*D IR£6.25–IR£6.85 Wine IR£3 Credit cards ② ③ ⑤

Co Galway

BALLYCONNEELY Map10L64
✕ Fishery ☎31

Closed Oct–May; Lic; 35seats 30P ♀Continental. Ld9 30pm
L IRE£3&alc D IRE£10alc Wine IRE£3 Credit card ②

BARNA Map10M22
✗**Ty-Ar-Mor** ☎(01)5031
Closed Sun; Dinner not served 15Jan–7Feb; Lunch not
served; Unlicensed; 40seats 15P ♀French. Ld11pm

CLARINBRIDGE Map7M41
✗✗**Paddy Burke's** ☎(091)86107
Closed Sun, Xmas Day & Good Fri; Lic; 40seats 30P
♀Irish & French. Ld10.30pm S% *L IRE£2.80alc
D IRE£7–IRE£7 50&alc Wine IRE£3 Credit card ②

CLIFDEN Map10L65
✗✗**Priory** Claddaghduff ☎234
Closed Mon & 15Sep–May; Lic; 38seats 10P ♀French.
Ld10pm *L IRE£4.90alc D IRE£7.75 Wine IRE£3.75
Credit card ③

MOYCULLEN Not on Map
✗✗**Silver Teal** ☎(091)85109
Lic; 40seats 60P ♀French. Ld10.30pm *L IRE£2–IRE£2.50
D IRE£5alc Wine IRE£3.20 Credit card ②

SPIDDAL Map 6M12
✗✗**Crooklog House** ☎(091)23091
Closed Oct–Apr; Lic; 45seats 25P bedrooms available
♀French. Ld10pm S% L IRE£3.50–IRE£5&alc
D IRE£6.50–IRE£7.50&alc Credit cards ①②③④⑤⑥

Co Kerry

DINGLE Map2Q40
✗**Doyle's Seafood Bar** John St ☎144
Closed Sun & mid Oct–mid Mar; Lic; 24seats ℙ Ld9pm S%
*L IRE£6.35alc D IRE£6.35alc Wine IRE£2.95 Credit cards ②③
SNEEM Map2V76
✗**Blue Bull** ☎(064)45231
Closed 16 Sep–Jun except Etr; Dinner not served Mon; Lic;
32seats P ♀Irish & Continental. Ld10pm S% *L IRE£2.50
D IRE£8alc Wine IRE£2.95 Credit cards ①②
SPA Map2Q71
✗**Lynch's Oyster Tavern** ☎(066)36102
Lunch not served Sun; Lic; 40seats Ld11pm
TEMPLENOE Map2V86
✗**Rockvilla** ☎(064)41331
Closed Nov–Feb; Lic; 30seats 30P bedrooms available
♀Irish & French. Ld8.30pm L IRE£5.50alc High Tea IRE£1–
IRE£3.50 D IRE£3.50–IRE£4.50&alc Wine IRE£3
TRALEE Map2Q81
✗✗**Cordon Bleu** The Square ☎(066)21596
Closed Sun & Feb; Lunch not served; Lic; 60seats
♀English & French. Ld11.30pm High Tea IRE£5alc
D IRE£8alc Wine IRE£3.90 Credit cards ①③

Co Kildare

CASTLEDERMOT Map9T78
✗✗**Doyle's Schoolhouse** ☎(0503)44282
Dinner not served Sun & Mon; Lic; 35seats 60P Ld10pm
D IRE£10alc Wine IRE£3.50
CURRAGH, THE Map11N71
✗✗**Jockey Hall** ☎(045)41416
Closed Sun; Lunch not served; Lic; 60seats 100P ♀French.
Ld9.45pm S% *D IRE£6.25&alc Wine IRE£4.25
Credit cards ①②③
DROICHEAD NUA Map9O81
✗✗**Red House Inn** ☎(045)31516
Closed Sun & Mon; Lic; 200seats 130P Ld10.30pm
D IRE£6.60–IRE£7.70 Wine IRE£3 Credit card ②
STRAFFAN Map9N93
✗✗**Barberstown Castle** ☎(01)288206
Lic; 60seats 80P bedrooms available ♀French. Ld9 30pm
*L IRE£5.95–IRE£7.85 D IRE£12alc Wine IRE£3.85
Credit cards ②③⑤⑥

Co Limerick

LIMERICK Map7R55

✗✗**Merryman** ☎(061)48738
Lunch not served Sun; Lic; 40seats Ld11pm

Co Londonderry

AGHADOWEY Map14C82
✗✗**Brown Trout** ☎209
Lic; 50seats 60P bedrooms available Disco Wed Ld10pm
L£3.50–£3.80 Tea85p–£1.40 High Tea£4alc D£6alc
Wine£3 Credit cards ②③⑤

Robert Burns statue, Dundalk

Co Louth

DUNDALK Map13J00
✗✗**Angela's** Rockmarshall ☎(042)76193
Closed Sun & 6–25 Oct; Lunch not served.; Lic;
52seats 60P ♀French. Ld10.30pm S% D IRE£8.50alc
Wine IRE£3 Credit cards ①②③⑤⑥
✗✗**Sportsman** Newry Rd ☎(042)71162
Lic; 75seats 200P ♀English & Continental. Ld10pm
Credit card ②
✗**Mounthamilton House** ☎(042)34417
Closed Xmas, Good Fri & Public Hols; Dinner not served
Mon; Lunch not served Sat & Sun; Lic; 50seats 50P
Ld10.30pm S% L IRE£2.50–IRE£4.50&alc D IRE£8alc
Wine IRE£3.50 Credit cards ②③

Co Meath

BETTYSTOWN Map13O17
✗✗**Coastguard Inn** ☎(041)27115
Closed Sun & Mon; Lunch not served; Lic; 35seats 60P
♀International. Ld10pm D IRE£8alc Wine IRE£2.60
Credit cards ②③
CLONEE Map13O04
✗**Grasshopper Inn** ☎(01)255265
Closed Xmas Day & Good Fri; Lic; 90seats 100P
♀French. Ld10.30pm *L IRE£2.85–IRE£2.95 D IRE£5–IRE£9
Wine IRE£3.30 Credit cards ②③
NAVAN (An Uaimh) Map13N86
✗✗**Beechmount House** Trim Rd ☎(046)21553
Closed Xmas Day; Lic; 75seats 100P Ld10.30pm S%
Credit cards ①②③

Co Monaghan

CARRICKMACROSS Map13H80
✗✗**Markey's** Main St ☎(042)61233
Lunch not served Sun; Lic; 55seats ℙ ♀Irish & French

Ld10.30pm S% L IR£2.95–IR£3.50&alc D IR£10alc
Wine IR£3.15 Credit cards ① ② ③ ⑤

Co Offaly

EDENDERRY Map8N63
✕ **Eden Inn** ☎146
Closed Xmas wk, Good Fri & Etr Sat; Lic; 45seats
♡ English & German. Ld9.30pm

12th to 15th century castle, Cahir

Co Tipperary

CAHIR Map4S02
✕✕ **Earl of Glengall** The Square ☎205

Closed Sun; Lic; 45seats ℗ ♡ Continental. Ld10pm
L IR£2.95–IR£6.50&alc D IR£8.95–IR£10.50&alc
Wine IR£2.95 Credit cards ① ② ③ ⑤

Co Wexford

CARNE HARBOUR Map5T10
✕ **Bakehouse** ☎(053)31234
Closed 3 Nov–Mar; Lic; 45seats 40P ♡ Irish, English &
French. Ld mdnt ✻L IR£5alc D IR£7alc Wine IR£2.90

NEWBAWN Map5S82
✕✕ **Cedar Lodge** Carrigbyrne ☎(051)24386
Lic; 36seats 70P bedrooms available Ld9.30pm
L IR£4.50alc Tea IR£1.25alc D IR£6.50alc Wine IR£3.
Credit card ①

Co Wicklow

ANNAMOE Map9T19
✕✕ **Armstrong's Barn** ☎(0404)5194
Closed Sun, Mon & Xmas–17 Mar; Lunch not served; Lic;
50seats 35P ✗ Ld10pm D IR£10–IR£13.50 Wine IR£3.50
Credit cards ② ⑤

DELGANY Map9O21
✕✕ **Delgany Inn** ☎(01)875701
Closed Sun; Lic; 45seats ℗ bedrooms available
Ld9.30pm ✻L IR£3.50–IR£5 D IR£10alc Wine IR£4.50
Credit cards ② ③ ⑥

ENNISKERRY Map9O21
✕✕ **Enniscree Lodge** Cloon ☎(01)863542
Lic; 45seats 25P Live music Fri ♡ Irish, French & Swiss
Ld10pm S%

Guesthouses

Additional abbreviations
(see also page 114)

Bdi inclusive dinner, bed & breakfast. Where
       B&B not shown rate always charged
       whether dinner taken or not
hc   no. of rooms with hot and cold water
Ł   no lunches included in weekly price

Ld   last time evening meal can be ORDERED
lake some rooms overlook lake
M   no main meals included in weekly price
river ⎱ some rooms overlook river and/or sea
sea ⎰

Explanation of a gazetteer entry
The example is fictitious

Town name
Appears in bold type
in alphabetical order
under county heading.

Map reference
First figure is map page
no. Then follows grid
reference: read
1st figure across
2nd figure vertically

Telephone number
The exchange is that of
the town name unless
otherwise stated.
In the Republic of
Ireland, STD codes
are shown where
applicable

Guesthouse name
followed by address

CORK Map3W67
▸ Quayside Western Rd ☎(021)531246 10hc 2⇔🅿 TV
6P 🕮 B&B IR£5.

Specific details
Opening times, facilities, prices and terms. See
'Abbreviations and Symbols' on page 114 and
gazetteer.

Co Antrim

BALLYCASTLE Map15D14
Atlantic The Promenade ☎62412 Closed Xmas 12rm
(A6rm) ⊗ TV P S% B&B£4–£6 Bdi£7–£9 W£56 ⅄
Ld7pm
Hillsea 28 Quay Hill ☎62311 22rm 20hc CTV 250P
🍴 S% B&B£4–£5 Bdi£6 –£7 Ld8pm

LARNE Map15D30
Derrin 2 Prince's Gdns ☎3269 7hc CTV 5P 2🏠 🍴 S%
B&B£4–£5 Bdi£6 50–£7 50 Ldnoon
Kaleedin 62 The Roddens ☎3439 3hc ⊗ nc4 CTV 3P 1🏠
🍴 S% B&B£4 Bdi£6 50 W£42 ⅄ Ld6pm
Linden 18 Curran Rd ☎2414 May–Sep 6hc ⊗ CTV S%
B&B£4–£4 50 Bdi£6 50–£7 50
Manor 23 Olderfleet Rd ☎3305 8hc ⊗ 8P 🍴 S%
B&B£4–£5 Bdi£6–£7 Ld6pm
Seaview 154–156 Curran Rd ☎2438
Further details for 1980/81 not confirmed.

PORTBALLINTRAE Map14C83
Ardvarna ☎Bushmills31371 May–Aug 5hc 4P *B&B£5

PORTRUSH Map14C83
Glencroft 95 Coleraine Rd ☎822902 4rm 3hc 1🛁🍴 ⋐
CTV 8P 2🏠 🍴 B&B£6–£8 Bdi£10–£12 W£70–£80 ⅄
Ld8pm
Mount Royal 2 Mount Royal ☎823342 13hc ⋐ CTV 🍴
S% B&B£4 50–£5 Bdi£7–£7 50 W£45 (W only Jul–Aug)
Ld6 30pm

WHITEHEAD Map15J49
Crestbank ☎2338 5hc
Further details for 1980/81 not confirmed.

Co Armagh

PORTADOWN Map15J05
Rockeden Watson St ☎34568 12hc CTV 6🏠 🍴 S%
B&B£6 Bdi£9 W£63 ⅄ Ld6 30pm

Belfast

BELFAST Map15J37
Camera 44 Wellington Park ☎660026 11hc 3🛁🍴 nc2
CTV P 🍴 B&B£8 Bdi£12 Ld7pm

Co Carlow

CARLOW Map9S77
Dolmen House Brownshill ☎(0503)42444 Apr–Sep Lic
6hc ⊗ TV 8P 🍴 S% B&B IR£6 Bdi IR£10 75 W IR£70 ⅄
Ld4pm

Co Clare

KILLALOE Map7R77
Canalside House ☎(061)76190 Etr–Sep 7hc CTV 10P
river S% B&B IR£5 50–IR£6

LISDOONVARNA Map6R19
Ballinalacken Castle ☎25 15 May–Sep Lic 6hc CTV P sea
S% B&B IR£5 50 Bdi IR£9 50 W IR£61 12 Ld6 30pm

Co Cork

BALLINHASSIG Map3W66
Laurel Wood House ☎(021)885103 7hc ⊗ CTV 12P S%
B&B IR£5 Bdi IR£9 Ldnoon

BALTIMORE Map3W02
Corner House ☎43 Etr–Oct rsNov–Mar 8hc (A2hc) ⊗ CTV
7P 🍴 B&B IR£5 50 Bdi IR£11 (Wonly Jun–Sep) Ld8 30pm
Customs House ☎44 May–Oct 7hc TV 🍴 sea Ld8 30pm

BLARNEY Map3W67
Elm Grove ☎(021)85136 5hc CTV 8P 🍴 S%
B&B IR£4 50

COBH Map4W86
Grand Union Hotel Pearse Sq ☎(021)811563 7hc ⊗ CTV
sea S% B&B IR£5 Bdi IR£10 50 W IR£70 ⅄ Ld3pm

The National Monument, Cork

CORK Map3W67
Gabriel House Summerhill, St Luke's ☎(021)500333
18🛁🍴 CTV 18P S% B&B IR£11

COURTMACSHERRY Map3W54
East Beach ☎(023)46119 Apr–Sep Lic 7hc ⊗ TV 🍴 sea
S% B&B IR£6 Bdi IR£11 W IR£60–IR£68 (W only Jun–Aug)
Ld6 30pm
Lislee House Lislee ☎(023)40126 Lic 7hc 1🛁🍴 nc12 TV
P 5🏠 S% B&B IR£12 50 Bdi IR£22 Ld7pm

CROSSHAVEN Not on Map
Whispering Pines ☎(021)831448 Lic 10hc 7🛁🍴 CTV
20P 🍴 *B&B IR£5 60–IR£8 20

INNISHANNON Map3W55
Celtic ☎(021)75218 Jun–Aug 6hc TV 6P

KANTURK Map3R50
Assolas ☎15 Etr–mid Oct Lic 7hc 4🛁🍴 ⊗ CTV 20P 6🏠
lake B&B IR£11 Bdi IR£19 25 W IR£104 50 ⅄

MALLOW Map3W59
Longueville House ☎(022)27156 Etr–mid Oct Lic 17rm
(A3rm) ⊗ nc10 CTV 50P 2🏠 🍴 S% B&B IR£12 50
Bid IR£22 50 Wfr IR£112 ⅄ Ld8 30pm

Co Donegal

CULDAFF Map14C4
McGrory's ☎4 Etr & Jun–Aug Lic 9hc TV 10P S%
B&B IR£5 Bdi IR£7 50 W IR£46 ⅄ Ld6pm

DONEGAL Map16G97
Four Master's Ballybofey Rd ☎205 Lic 12hc ⊗ TV 20P
🍴 S% B&B IR£5–IR£6 D7pm
White Gables Tirconnail St ☎106 Apr–Oct Lic 7hc TV P
S% B&B IR£4–IR£4 50 Ld8pm

KERRYKEEL Map16C23
Rockhill House ☎12 Etr–Aug 8hc 1⇨🛏 ⌀ CTV 100P 🍴
S% B&B IR£5 25–IR£5 75 W IR£56–IR£65 Ld8pm

KILMACRENAN Map16C12
Anglers' Haven ☎15 Lic 10hc CTV 6P 🍴 Ld8pm

Co Down

BANGOR Map15J58
Brentwood 2 Lorelei, Princetown Rd ☎60327 Apr–Sep
5hc ⌀ TV 4P sea S% B&B£5–£5 50 Bd£7 50–£8
W£50–£55 ₭ Ld6pm
Ennislare 9 Princetown Rd ☎2858 8hc ⌀ CTV sea S%
B&B£4–£4 50 Bd£7–£7 50
Malinmore 11 Princetown Rd ☎3303 Jan–16 Dec 6hc ⌀
CTV 🍴 B&B£5 Bd£7 W£49 ₭ Ld noon

NEWCASTLE Map13J33
Bayview 99 101 Central Promenade ☎23591
Etr & Jun–mid Sep Lic 10hc 2⇨🛏 ⌀ CTV sea B&B£6 50
W£45–£52 Ld6 45pm
Fountainville 103 Central Promenade ☎22317 Jun–Sep
10hc 1⇨🛏 ⌀ nc2 CTV sea S% B&B£4 Bd£5 50 W£42

Co Dublin

DUBLIN Map9O13
Abrae Court 9 Zion Rd Rathgar ☎(01)979944 10hc ⌀
TV 15P 🍴 Ld6 30pm
Ariel House 52 Lansdowne Rd, 4 ☎(01)685512
Jan–21 Dec 18⇨🛏 ⌀ nc5 CTV 15P 🍴 B&B IR£7 90–
IR£8 70
Iona House 5 Iona Park, 9 ☎(01)306217 16⇨🛏 ⚲ CTV
10P 2🏤 🍴 S% B&B IR£9 35–IR£11 55
Mount Herbert 7 Herbert Rd ☎(01)684321 88hc 77⇨🛏
CTV 36P 3🏤 🍴 Ld10 30pm
St Judes 17 Pembroke Pk, 4 ☎(01)680483 7hc ⌀ 🍴
B&B IR£6–IR£9

DUN LAOGHAIRE Map9O22
Ferry 15 Clarinda Park North ☎(01)808301 10hc ⌀ CTV
P 🍴 B&B IR£6 60–IR£7 70

Co Fermanagh

ENNISKILLEN Map12H24
Interlaken 54 Fort Hill St ☎22274 Closed Xmas 6hc ⌀
CTV 2P 2🏤 🍴 S% B&B£5–£7 Bd£7–£10 Ld6pm
Lack-a-Boy Farmhouse Tempo Rd ☎22488 6hc TV 10P
🍴 S% Ld6pm
Will-O-Brook 8 Willoughby Place ☎22420 7hc 1⇨🛏 ⌀
CTV 6P 4🏤 🍴 lake S% *B&B fr£4 50 Bd fr£7 W fr£45 ₭
Ld2pm
Willoughby 24 Willoughby Pl ☎22882 Closed Xmas wk
10hc CTV 8P 🏤 🍴 river S% Ld6pm

Co Galway

CLONBUR Map10M05
Fairhill ☎6 Etr–19 Oct Lic 12hc nc2½ CTV 20P B&B IR£5
Bd IR£10 Ld8 30pm

GALWAY Map7M22
Adare House Father Griffin Pl ☎(091) 62638 10hc 1⇨🛏
CTV 8P 🍴 B&B IR£6–IR£6 50
Knockrea House Lower Salthill ☎(091)62600 9hc CTV
12P 🍴 S% B&B IR£5–IR£6
Osterley Lodge Salthill ☎(091)64834 9rm 8hc CTV 10P
🍴 sea

KINVARRA Map7M30
Kinvarra House Main St ☎34 Etr–Sep 6hc nc12 TV P
Ld7 45pm

MOYARD Map10L65
Crocnaraw ☎9 May–Sep 10hc 6⇨🛏 30P 🍴 lake sea
B&B IR£10 50 Bd IR£18 W IR£120 Ld9 15pm

OUGHTERARD Map10M14
Currarevagh House ☎(091)82313 Etr–5 Oct Lic
12hc 3⇨🛏 (A 4hc 2⇨🛏) CTV 25P 3🏤 lake S%
B&B IR£12 55 Bd IR£19 80 W IR£135 85 Ld8pm

Co Kerry

ANASCAUL Map2Q60
Fitzgerald O'Donnell's ☎5 Tem 14hc 4⇨🛏 nc6 ⚲ CTV
16P 1🏤 🍴 B&B IR£5–IR£5 50 Bd IR£9 50–IR£10 50
W IR£60–IR£70 Ld9 30pm

BALLYBUNION Map6Q84
Eagle Lodge ☎(068)27224 Etr–Sep 11hc 2⇨🛏 CTV 11P
🍴 B&B IR£5 Ld7 30pm

BALLYLONGFORD Map6R04
Rusheen Park ☎21 May–Oct 7hc ⌀ ⚲ TV 7P S%
B&B IR£4–IR£5 Bd IR£8–IR£9 W IR£45–IR£49 Ld8pm

CARAGH LAKE Map2V79
Caragh Lodge ☎15 Apr–15 Sep 3⇨🛏 nc8 9P
🍴 lake S% B&B IR£10 45–IR£12 10 Ld7 30pm

CASTLEGREGORY Map2Q61
Aisling House ☎(066)39134 Jul & Aug rsMay, Jun & Sep
5hc ⌀ TV P *B&B IR£6 Bd IR£10 Wfr IR£55 ₭ Ldnoon

Aughnanure Castle, Oughterard

DINGLE Map2Q40
Alpine ☎15 Mar–Oct 15hc 4🛏 nc7 CTV 20P 🅿️
B&B IR£4–IR£4 50 Bdi IR£7 50–IR£7 75 Ld6pm
Milltown House Milltown ☎62 Etr–Sep 11hc 3⇋🛏 ⊗
nc10 TV 12P 🅿️ B&B IR£5–IR£5 50

INCH Map2Q60
Inch Heights ☎12 11hc ⊗ CTV 12P 🅿️ sea S%
B&B IR£6 Bdi IR£11 WIR£70 Ld5 30pm

KENMARE Map2V97
Commercial Arms 14 Henry St ☎(064)41453 Mar–Oct
Lic 10hc CTV 3P 5🏠 B&B IR£5 Bdi IR£9 WIR£60 Ld9pm

KILLARNEY Map2V99
Aisling House Countess Rd ☎(064)31112 Lic 10hc TV
25P 🅿️ Ld4pm
Cooldruma Muckross Rd ☎(064)31553 Lic 15hc TV 15P
Cum-a-Ciste Cork Rd ☎(064)31271 Etr–Aug Lic 8hc nc4
TV 8P B&B IR£5 40
Green Acres Fossa ☎(064)31454 Mar–Oct Lic 8hc
4⇋🛏 CTV 12P 🅿️ lake B&B IR£4 50–IR£5
Bdi IR£9 50–IR£10 Ldnoon
Loch Lein Fossa ☎(064)31260 Etr–Oct Lic 12rm
6hc 6⇋🛏 TV 14P 🅿️ lake B&B IR£4 75–IR£5 25
Bdi IR£10–IR£10 50 Ld5pm
Marian House Woodlawn Rd ☎(064)31275
10 Jan–20 Dec Lic 8hc TV 14P 🅿️ B&B IR£4 80–IR£5
Tuscar House Fossa ☎(064)31978 10hc 1⇋🛏 CTV 10P
🅿️ lake *B&B IR£4–IR£5 Bdi IR£9–IR£10 WIR£55–IR£60
ℓ Ld8pm

KILLORGLIN Map2V79
Bianconi Inn ☎46 Closed 24 Dec–1 Jan Lic 20hc
7⇋🛏 🅿️ B&B IR£5 50–IR£6 Ld9pm

TAHILLA Map2V76
Tahilla Cove ☎Sneem19 Etr–15 Oct Lic 4hc A5hc
CTV 30P sea Ld8 15pm

TRALEE Map2Q81
Kinard House Cloondara ☎(066)21658 Mar–Nov Lic
7hc 1⇋🛏 (A1⇋🛏) TV 8P 🅿️ S% B&B IR£5 Bdi IR£10
WIR£65 ℓ Ld11am

VALENTIA ISLAND Map2V37
Ring Lyne Chapeltown ☎3 Lic 10hc 2⇋🛏 ⚄ CTV
10P 🅿️ B&B IR£5 50–IR£6 Bdi IR£10 50–IR£11
WIR£72–IR£75 Ld8 30pm
Valentia Heights ☎38 Apr–Sep Lic 10hc 6⇋🛏 CTV 30P
🅿️ sea S% B&B IR£6–IR£8 80 Bdi IR£12–IR£15 40
WIR£75–IR£88 ℓ Ld8 30pm

Co Leitrim

CARRICK-ON-SHANNON Map12M99
Rutledge's ☎32 Lic 10hc CTV 10P 1🏠 🅿️ *B&B IR£5 50
Ld9pm

Co Londonderry

BALLYKELLY Map14C62
Bridge House 32 Clooney Rd ☎Limavady2193 12hc
4⇋🛏 CTV 14P 🅿️ S% *B&B £5–£5 50 Bdi £6 50–£7
Ld9pm

MAGHERA Map14C80
Glenburn House The Glen ☎Magherafelt42203
Closed Xmas rsNov–Mar 5hc ⚄ CTV 20P 6🏠 S%
B&B £4 50 Bdi £6.50 Ld9pm

PORTSTEWART Map14C83
Links 103 Strand Rd ☎2580 May–Oct 14hc ⊗ nc3
CTV 16P 🅿️ sea B&B £5 50 Bdi £8 50 W£59 Ld6pm

Co Louth

DUNDALK Map13J00
Failte Dublin Rd ☎(042)35152 Lic 15rm 17hc 5⇋🛏
(A3rm) CTV 15P 🅿️ S% B&B IR£6 Bdi IR£8 Ld6 30pm

Carved stones from the old town of Dingle

Co Mayo

ACHILL ISLAND Map10F80
Gray's Dugort ☎Dugort8 Mar–7 Oct Lic 8hc CTV 25P
sea *B&B IR£6 Bdi IR£11 WIR£55 ⚓ Ld6pm
CASTLEBAR Map10M19
Heneghan's Newtown St ☎(094)21883 21 Jan–21 Dec
13hc 1⇔🛏 ⊗ TV P 🍴 S% B&B IR£5.50
MULRANY Map10L89
Avondale House ☎5 Apr–15 Oct Lic 10hc ⊗ TV 10P 🍴
B&B IR£3.75–IR£4.75 Bdi IR£6.75–IR£8
WIR£42–IR£49 ⚓ Ld6.30pm
WESTPORT Map10L98
Riverbank House Louisburgh Rd ☎76 Apr–Oct 7hc ⊗ 10P
🍴 river S% B&B IR£5

Co Sligo

MULLAGHMORE Map16G75
Pier Head House ☎(071)76171 Etr–mid Sep 12hc ⊗
TV 50P Ld6.30pm

Co Tipperary

TIPPERARY Map4R83
Ach-na-Sheen ☎(062)51298 10hc 3⇔🛏 ⚗ CTV
10P 2🏠 🍴 S% B&B IR£5–IR£6 Bdi IR£10–IR£12 Ld4.30pm

Co Tyrone

COOKSTOWN Map14H87
Piper's Cave 38 Cady Rd ☎63615 Closed Xmas 6hc ⚗
CTV 12P 🍴 S% *B&B £6.50 Bdi £10 Ld7pm

Co Waterford

CAPPOQUIN Map4X19
Richmond House ☎(058)54278 Apr–Sep rsFeb & Mar
Lic 8hc 1⇔🛏 ⊗ ⚗ TV 12P 🍴 S% B&B IR£6–IR£7
Bdi IR£11–IR£12.50 WIR£60–IR£65 ⚓ Ld7.30pm
WATERFORD Map5S61
Diamond Hill Slieverue ☎(051)75543 Lic 10hc CTV P
🍴 S% B&B IR£5.75–IR£5.85 Bdi IR£10.75–IR£10.95
Ld7pm

Co Wexford

NEW ROSS Map5S72
Inishross House 96 Mary St ☎(051)21335 Tem 7rm
CTV 8P S% B&B IR£5–IR£5.50 Bdi IR£9–IR£11
WIR£84–IR£98 Ld7pm
ROSSLARE HARBOUR Map5T11
Fisherman's Lodge ☎(053)33137 May–Sep 6hc ⊗ TV
5P S% B&B IR£5 Bdi IR£9
WEXFORD Map5T02
Whitford House Clonard ☎(053)23405 Jan–20 Dec 22hc
12⇔🛏 CTV 30P 🍴 S% B&B IR£5.75–IR£6.25
WIR£57–IR£62 ⚓ Ld7.15pm

Co Wicklow

AVOCA Map9T27
Riverview House ☎(0402)5181 Jun–Sep 5hc CTV
10P 1🏠 river S% B&B IR£5.50
RATHDRUM Map9T18
Avonbrae House ☎(0404)6198 16 Mar–15 Nov Lic
6hc 5⇔🛏 CTV 10P 🍴 S% B&B IR£7.50 Bdi IR£13.50
WIR£87.50 ⚓

The 'Meeting of the Waters', Avoca

Farmhouses

For explanation of a gazetteer entry see page 160.

Additional abbreviations
(see also page 114)

ar	arable farming		Ld	last time evening meal can be ORDERED
Bdi	inclusive dinner, bed, breakfast. Where B&B not shown rate always charged whether dinner taken or not		lake	some rooms overlooking lake
			M	no main meals included in weekly price
			mx	mixed farming
dy	dairy farming		nw	non-working farm
hc	no. of rooms with hot & cold water		river	some rooms overlooking river
ʞ	no lunches included in weekly price		sea	some rooms overlooking sea

Co Antrim

BUSHMILLS Map14C94
Montalto Off Coleraine Rd ☎31257 Jun–Aug rsEtr, May & Sep 8hc TV 10P ⊶ 73acres mx S% B&Bfr£5 Bdifr£7.50 Ld3pm

CLOUGHMILLS Map15D01
Streamvale 77 Drumadoon Rd ☎213 3hc CTV 4P 2🏠 ⊶ 106acres mx S% B&B£4.50–£5 Bdi£6.50–£7.50 Ld8pm

CRUMLIN Map15J17
Ashmore Fourscore, 31 Garlandstown Rd ☎52377 2rm 1hc 4P 2🏠 ⊶ 56acres mx *B&B£4–£5 Bdi£6–£7

CUSHENDUN Map15D23
Villa Torr Rd, Ballycleagh ☎252 Etr–Sep 4hc TV 10P ⊶ 24acres mx *B&B£5 Bdi£8.50 W£48 ʞ Ld7.30pm

LISBURN Map15J26
Fruithill 45 Bresagh Rd, Boardmills ☎Bailie's Mills212 4rm 2hc CTV 12P 2🏠 65acres ar S% B&B£4.50 Bdi£8 Ld6pm
Trooperfield House Taghnabrick, Sprucefield ☎2860 3rm 2hc 1⇥🍴 ⊗ nc2 CTV 4P 3🏠 40acres nw S% B&B£4

PORTGLENONE Map15C90
Lowry's 268 Gortgole Rd ☎821262 3rm ⊗ CTV 4P 14acres mx S% B&B£4 Bdi£6 W£40 ʞ Ld7pm

PORTRUSH Map14C83
Ashlea 40 Magherabuoy Rd ☎822779 Apr–Sep 5hc ⊗ nc16 CTV 6P ⊶ 112acres nw S% B&B£4–£5 Bdi£8–£9.50 Ld6pm
Loguestown ☎822742 Closed Xmas 7rm 6hc TV 10P 🏠 ⊶ 28acres mx S% B&B£4.50–£5.50 Bdi£6–£7 W£40–£48 ʞ Ld6pm

Co Cavan

BELTURBET Map12H31
Mrs Wilson's Mullaghmeen ☎(0492)2184 Apr–Oct 3rm 2hc ⊗ CTV 52acres dy S% B&B IR£7 Bdifr IR£12 Wfr IR£63 ʞ Ld10am
Derryhoo House Milltown ☎(0492)2180 Apr–Oct 3hc ⊗CTV 6P ⊶ lake 72acres mx S% B&B IR£7 Bdi IR£12 WIR£63 Ld6pm

BUTLER'S BRIDGE Map12H41
Ford House 🏠 ☎(049)31427 Closed Dec 7rm 6hc ⌀ CTV 12P ⊶ lake river 54acres dy mx S% B&B IR£6 Bdi IR£8 WIR£56–IR£60 Ld6pm
Inishmore House ☎(049)31015 Apr–Aug rsSep–Mar 4hc ⊗ CTV 6P ⊶ river 54acres mx S% B&B IR£4.75–IR£5 Bdi IR£7.50–IR£8 WIR£48–IR£50 ʞ Ld3pm

Co Clare

COROFIN Map7R57
Caherbolane ☎(065)27638 May–Oct 4hc TV 5P 130acres dy S% B&Bfr IR£5.50 Bdifr IR£10 Wfr IR£58 ʞ Ld3pm
Fergus View Kilnaboy ☎(065)27606 May–Sep 5hc ⊗ TV 7P ⊶ lake river 16acres mx S% B&B IR£5.50 WIR£58 ʞ Ld2pm

CRUSHEEN Map7R38
Bakers House Galway Rd ☎(065)27115 May–Sep 3rm 2hc ⊗ CTV 10P ⊶ 37acres mx S% B&B IR£5.90 Bdi IR£9.75 Ldnoon
Lahardan House ☎(065)27128 8hc 5⇥🍴 ⊗ CTV 20P ⊶ 300acres beef S% B&B IR£5.75 Bdi IR£11.25 WIR£66.10 ʞ Ld3pm

ENNIS Map7R37
New Park House off Tulla Rd ☎(065)21233 rsEtr–Sep 6hc CTV 12P 85acres beef Ld3pm

KILKEE Map6Q86
Green Acres Doonaha ☎Querrin11 4hc TV 10P ⊶ 100acres beef dy sheep S% B&B IR£5 Bdi IR£8 Ld8pm

KILLIMER Map6R05
Ferryside ☎Knock9 5rm 4hc ⊗ TV 20P 4🏠 ⊶ 45acres mx S% B&B IR£6 WIR£50–IR£60 ʞ Ld6pm

KILRUSH Map6Q95
Bromehill House ☎97 5hc TV.P ⊶ river 35acres beef S% B&B IR£4.50 Bdi IR£8.50 Wfr IR£44 ʞ Ld4pm

LISDOONVARNA Map6R19
Fern Hill ☎40 Etr–Oct 4hc ⊗ TV 6P 60acres mx Ld2pm

NEWMARKET-ON-FERGUS Map7R36
Latoon ☎(061)71186 15 May–Sep 6hc ⊗ TV 20P ⊶ river 156acres mx S% *B&Bfr IR£4.85 Bdi IR£9.85–IR£10 Ld5pm

O'BRIEN'S BRIDGE Map7R66
Rye Hill Ardnatangle ☎(061)77188 4rm ⊗ CTV 20P 4🏠 ⊶ lake river 36acres mx S% B&B IR£4.50–IR£5 Bdi IR£6.50–IR£7 WIR£52.50–IR£56 ʞ Ld4pm

WHITEGATE Map7R36
Dromaan House ☎212 May–Sep 4hc 5P 100acres beef S% B&B IR£5 Bdifr IR£9 Wfr IR£50 ʞ Ld4pm

Co Cork

ARDFIELD Map3W43
Balteensbrack House ☎(023)40619 Etr–Nov 4hc ⌀ CTV P ⊶ 80acres dy S% B&B IR£4.75 Bdi IR£8.75 Ld3pm
Greenfield ☎(023)40613 Jun–Sep 4hc ⌀ TV P 78acres mx S% B&B IR£4.50 Bdi IR£8 WIR£53 ʞ Ld4pm

BALLINASCARTY Map3W44
Ard-na-Greine ☎(023)49104 15 May–14 Sep 5hc CTV 10P 150acres dy mx S% B&B IR£5.75 Bdi IR£11 WIR£63 Ld9.30pm
Lisnacunna ☎(023)49102 May–Sep 6rm 4hc ⊗ CTV P ⊶ 63acres mx B&B IR£5.75 Bdi IR£11 WIR£63 ʞ Ld5pm

BALLINEEN Map3W35
Gold Chest ☎(023)47168 7rm 1hc TV 100acres mx

BALLINGEARY Map3W16
Ard-an-Locha ☎12 May–Sep 5hc ⊗ P lake 60acres dy S% B&B IR£5.50 Bdi IR£10.50 Wfr IR£60 ʞ

BANDON Map3W45
Littlesilver House ☎(023)41262 May–Sep 5rm 3hc CTV P ⊶ 173acres mx Ld7pm

The Georgian mansion of Bantry House, Bantry

BANTRY Map3V94
Bay View Gories ☎241 Apr–Nov 8hc ⌘ CTV P sea
100acres dy mx S% B&Bfr IR£6 Bdifr IR£11 Wfr IR£60 ⱡ
Ld2pm
Island View ☎353 Apr–Oct 3hc P ▦ sea 30acres mx S%
B&B IR£4.70 Bdi IR£8 Ld6pm
Sand Bank Snave ☎245 10 Jan–10 Dec 6rm 5hc TV 5P
sea 10acres mx S% B&B IR£5 25 Bdi IR£10 Wfr IR£60 ⱡ
Ld4pm

CASTLEFREKE Map3W33
Kilkern House ☎(023)40643 Closed Xmas 5hc ♨ CTV
8P ▦ 75acres ar dy S% B&B IR£5.70 Bdi IR£10 70 Ld5pm

CASTLETOWNSHEND Map3W13
Fahoura East ☎(028)36113 4rm nc10 CTV 4P
🏠 45acres beef dy S% B&B IR£5 Bdi IR£8.50 Ld2pm

CLONAKILTY Map3W34
Desert House ☎(023)43331 Closed Xmas 7hc
(A3hc) ♨ TV P ▦ sea 100acres dy mx B&B IR£5 78
Bdi IR£11 28 WIR£66.15 ⱡ Ld7pm
Hillside ☎(023)43139 Apr–Sep rsOct, Nov & Mar 5rm
4hc (A2hc) TV 10P 114acres dy mx S% B&B IR£5 Bdi IR£9
WIR£52.50 ⱡ Ld4pm
Liscubba House Lyre ☎(023)48679 May–Sep 6hc ⌘ ♨
CTV P ▦ 130acres mx S% B&B IR£5 50 Bdi IR£10 50
WIR£60 ⱡ Ld6pm
Lyre View ☎(023)48624 4rm 3hc ⌘ CTV 6P 60acres mx
S% B&B IR£4.50 Bdi IR£8 WIR£49 ⋈ Ld6pm

DRIMOLEAGUE Map3W14
Hayes's Drominidy North ☎76 Jun–Sep 4rm 3hc TV
12P 20acres mx S% B&B IR£5.75 Bdi IR£11 WIR£59.85
ⱡ Ldnoon

DUNMANWAY Map3W25
Hillford House ☎(023)45240 Closed Dec–Feb 5rm 3hc
TV P ▦ 40acres ar dy S% B&B IR£5.35 WIR£55 65 ⱡ
Ld5pm

GRENAGH Map3W58
Birch Hill North of Cork off T11 ☎(021)886106
15 Mar–15 Oct 6hc ⌘ 6P 105acres ar mx B&B IR£5 75
Bdi IR£10.80 WIR£58.80 ⱡ Ld2pm

INNISHANNON Map3W55
Ballymountain House ☎(021)75366 Etr–mid Sep 6rm
5hc ⌘ TV P ▦ 120acres beef S% B&B IR£5 50
Bdi IR£8 50 WIR£59 50 ⱡ

KANTURK Map3R30
Inchwell ☎140 Apr–Nov 5rm 4hc ⌘ CTV P 15acres mx
S% *B&B IR£5

KILBRITTAIN Map3W54
Burren ☎(023)49622 Apr–Sep 3rm 2hc CTV P sea 40acres
mx S% *B&B IR£4.50 Wfr IR£49 ⱡ Ld4pm

KINSALE Map3W65
Murphy's ☎(021)72229 Mar–Oct 4hc CTV P 🏠 ▦ sea
80acres mx S% B&B IR£5 75 Bdi IR£10.75 WIR£73 ⱡ
D4pm

KNOCKRAHA Map4W77
Ashton Grove ☎(021)821537 Apr–14 Nov 4rm 6P
100acres mx S% B&B IR£5.50–IR£6 Bdi IR£10–IR£10.50
WIR£56–IR£58 ⱡ Ld3pm

SKIBBEREEN Map3W13
Abbeystrewery ☎(028)21713 Jun–Sep 5hc ⌘ TV P
90acres dy sheep S% B&B IR£6 Bdi IR£12 WIR£69 ⱡ
Ldnoon
Ahaerin Valley ☎119 May–Oct 4rm 3hc TV P 81acres dy
Ld6 30pm

YOUGHAL Map4X17
Cherrymount ☎(024)7110 6hc ♨ CTV 10P 2🏠
▦ 70acres dy S% B&B IR£4 Bdi IR£8 WIR£56 ⱡ Ld4pm

Co Donegal

BALLINTRA Map16G97
Carrig House ☎5 Jun–Sep rsMay 4hc P 20acres

BALLYSHANNON Map16G86
Carraig Donn Cavangarden ☎(072)65197 Jun–Sep 3rm
⌘ nc5 TV P ▦ 50acres mx S% B&B IR£4

CASTLEFINN Map14H29
Gortfad ☎16 Etr–Sep 6hc CTV P 180acres mx S%
*B&B IR£5 50 Bdi IR£9.50 WIR£56 ⱡ Ld4pm

PORT-NA-BLAGH Map16C03
Mweelfin Marble Hill ☎Dunfanaghy34 Etr–Sep 5hc TV
8P 80acres mx sheep S% *B&B IR£4–IR£4 50 Bdi IR£8
WIR£45 Ld6pm

RAPHOE Map14C20
The Tops ☎19 Jul–30 Oct 5rm 4hc ⌘ nc10 TV 10P ▦
24acres nw B&B IR£5 50 Bdi IR£9.50 WIR£56 Ld1pm

RATHMULLAN Map16C22
Carrig Lough The Saltpans ☎45 Apr–Oct 8rm 6hc ♨ TV
10P 4🏠 ▦ lake 40acres mx S% B&B IR£5 Bdi IR£9–
IR£9 50 Wfr IR£90 Ld4pm
Creevery House (Longhill Farm) ☎29 Apr–Sep 5hc ⌘ CTV
15P lake 7acres beef S% B&B IR£5 50 Bdi IR£10

TAMNEY Map16C13
Sweeney's ☎11 Apr–Sep 5rm 2hc ⌘ nc8 CTV P 100acres
mx S% B&B IR£5 50 Bdi IR£9 50 Ld3pm

Co Down

BALLYMARTIN Map13J31
Slieve Mor ☎Annalong210 5hc ♨ TV P 17¾acres mx S%
B&B £3 50–£4 Bdi £4 50–£5 W£38–£40 Ld6pm

BALLYNAHINCH Map15J35
Corner House 182 Dunmore Rd ☎2670 4rm 1hc ♨ TV
8P ▦ 30acres mx S% B&B IR£5–IR£5 50 Bdi IR£8–IR£8.50
WIR£56–IR£58 Ld8pm

BALLYWALTER Map15J67
Abbey Ballywalter Rd, Greyabbey ☎Greyabbey207 3hc ♨

TV 6P 卌 50acres ar beef S% B&B£5 Bdi£7.50 Ld6pm

BOARDMILLS Map15J36
Bressa 55 Bresagh Rd ☎Baillie's Mills316 2hc ⊘ nc13 TV 4P 3🏠 卌 60acres mx S% B&B£4–£4.50 Bdi£6–£6.50 Ld6pm

DROMARA Map15J25
Hill House 10 Mullaghdrin Rd ☎221 3rm TV 10P 40acres beef S% B&B£4 Bdi£5.50 Ld6pm

KILKEEL Map13J31
Eastwood 8 Cranfield Rd ☎62387 4rm ⊘ P sea 1acre nw S% B&B£3 Bdi£4.50 W£25

MAGHERA Map14C80
Ivybank ☎Newcastle22450 4hc CTV 6P 卌 50acres mx S% B&B£5–£5.50 Bdi£8–£8.50 W£50 ⱡ Ldnoon

Co Dublin

RATHCOOLE Map9O02
Calliaghstown House ☎(01)589745 May–Sep 3rm 2hc 8P 60acres dy Ld6.30pm

SHANKHILL Map9O22
Brides Glen House reach from Loughlinstown ☎(01)853731 Apr–Oct 6rm 5hc ⊘ TV 9P 60acres mx Ld3pm

Co Fermanagh

ENNISKILLEN Map12H20
Dragon Killadeas ☎Irvinestown554 Apr–Sep 3rm ⊘ TV 6P lake 130acres mx S% B&B£4–£4.50
Gortadrehid Culkey P.O. ☎22725 4rm ♧ TV 15P river 75acres beef
Further details for 1980/81 not confirmed.
Lake View Drumcrow, Blaney P.O. ☎Derrygonnelly263 Etr & Summer mths 5hc ⊘ CTV 8P 卌 lake 40acres mx S% *B&B£4–£4.50 Bdi£6.50–£7 Ldprevious day

KESH Map16H16
Clonelly ☎225 4hc ⊘ TV 10P 100acres mx

TULLY Map16H15
Bayview ☎Derrygonnelly250 Etr–Oct 3hc TV 12P 卌 sea 60acres dy S% B&B£3.50–£4.50 Bdi£6.50–£7.50 W£45.50–£50 Ld5.30pm

Co Galway

ANNAGHDOWN Map11M23
Corrib View ☎(091)89114 Apr–Oct 4rm 3hc ⊘ 5P 卌 mx B&B IR£5.50 Bdi IR£10

ARDRAHAN Map7M41
Woodlands ☎32 Jun–mid Sep 3hc TV 50acres mx

CORNAMONA Map10M05
Mrs Carney's Ballydoon Lough 4hc TV 5P 卌 river 30acres mx S% *B&B IR£4 Bdi IR£7 W IR£50
Joyce's Carrick West Apr–Sep 4hc TV 10P lake 10acres mx Ldnoon

CORRANDULLA Map7M23
Corrib House ☎(091)89117 Apr–Sep 10hc CTV P 卌 4½acres ar beef S% B&B IR£7 Bdi IR£12.50 W IR£65 ⱡ Ld7pm

CRAUGHWELL Map7M51
Bungalow ☎22 3hc nc10 TV P 50acres mx S% B&B IR£5.50 W IR£60 ⱡ Ld3pm

HEADFORD Map11M24
Balrickard ☎(093)21421 May–Sep 4hc ♧ CTV 25P 10🏠 卌 60acres mx S% B&B IR£6.50 Bdi IR£13 Ld6pm
Hill View Cloughanover ☎(093)21458 Etr–Sep 3hc TV P 2🏠 卌 60acres mx S% B&B IR£6.50–IR£7 Bdi IR£10.50–IR£11.50 W IR£70 Ld4.30pm
Lisdonagh Manor Caherlistrane ☎(093)21428 Closed Dec 5hc nc6 CTV 15P 2🏠 卌 lake 230acres beef mx S% *B&B IR£8 Bdi IR£17 W IR£119 ⱡ Ld5pm

KINVARA Map7M30
Burren View Doorus ☎(091-602)13 Etr–Oct 4hc 1⇌⁋ ⊘ TV 15P 卌 60acres mx S% B&B IR£5.60 Bdi IR£11.10 W IR£63 ⱡ Ld3pm

KNOCKFERRY Map10M24
Knockferry Lodge (Lough Corrib) ☎(091)80122 3 Apr–Oct 10hc 2⇌⁋ 15P 卌 35acres nw *B&B IR£6 Bdi IR£11 W IR£65 Ld9pm

MAAM BRIDGE Map10L95
Brooklawn ☎(091)71125 Apr–Sep 4rm 3hc CTV 4P 卌 river 1,000acres sheep S% B&B IR£5.50 Bdi IR£11 W IR£63 ⱡ Ldnoon

MOYARD Map10L65
Rose Cottage Rockfield ☎17 May–Oct 6hc P 卌 36acres mx S% B&B IR£5 Bdi IR£9 Ld5pm

STREAMSTOWN Map10L65
Taobh-a-Locha ☎Clifden136 May–Sep 4hc 4P 卌 sea 19acres mx Ld5pm

WOODFORD Map7M20
Shannon Vale Douras ☎30 3rm 2hc ⊘ TV 20P 卌 lake 70acres mx

Co Kerry

ARDFERT Map2Q72
Kilgulbin House off Abbeydorney Rd ☎(066)34116 Jun–14 Oct 5hc CTV P 150acres dy S% B&B IR£6 Bdi IR£11 W IR£56 ⱡ Ld5pm

BALLYBUNION Map6Q84
Lighthouse View Doon ☎107 6hc TV 10P 卌 56acres dy Ld7pm
Trippol ☎43 5hc TV 30P 1🏠 卌 river 60acres dy Ld7pm

BALLYMACELLIGOTT Map2Q91
Hillview ☎(066)37120 Jun–Aug 3hc TV P 85acres dy S% B&B IR£5.60 Bdi IR£10.60 W IR£58 ⱡ D3pm

A view of Gearhane, Camp

CAMP Map2Q70
Cova Meenascarty ☎(066)30124 Jul & Aug rsJun & Sep 4⇌⁋ nc5 5P sea 37acres mx *B&B IR£5–IR£5.50 Bdi IR£9.50–IR£10.50 W IR£50–IR£55 ⱡ Ld4pm

CAHIRCIVEEN Map2V47
Valentia View ☎130 Mar–Oct 6hc ♧ TV 10P 卌 sea 43acres dy S% B&B IR£5.50 Bdifr IR£11 Wfr IR£60 ⱡ Ld3pm

CASTLEGREGORY Map2Q61
Griffin's Country Goulane ☎(066)39147 Apr–Oct 7rm 3hc 3⇌⁋ ♧ CTV 10P 卌 lake 100acres dy S% B&B IR£6 Bdi IR£12.50 Wfr IR£63 ⱡ Ld4pm
Lakeside ☎(066)39121 Etr–Oct 3hc CTV P 卌 lake 35acres mx S% *B&B IR£5
Lake View House ☎(066)39110 end Jun–Aug 6hc TV P lake 100acres dy mx S% B&B IR£6 Wfr IR£60 ⱡ Ld3pm

FARRANFORE Map2Q90
Hill Top Knockaderry ☎35 Apr–Sep 6hc ⊘ ♧ CTV 10P 卌 70acres dy S% B&B IR£5.75 Bdi £10.75 W IR£60 ⱡ D5pm

Dunkerron Castle, Kenmare

KENMARE Map2V95
Bay View Greenane ☎(064)41383 Apr–Sep 6hc ⌘ ✿ CTV
P 🐾 sea 90acres mx S% B&B IR£5 Bdi IR£15 WIR£65 ⅄
Ld5pm
River Park Killarney Rd ☎(064)41161 Jun–Aug 5hc ⌘
CTV 7P river S% B&B IR£5.50 Bdi IR£10.50 WIR£63 ⅄ Ld am
Shelbourne House Cork Rd ☎(064)41013 Apr–27 Sep
7hc ⌘ nc7 CTV 12P 21acres mx S% B&B IR£5
Bdi IR£9 WIR£60 Ld3pm
Templenoe House Greenane ☎(064)41538 May–Sep 5hc
⌘ TV 6P sea 45acres dy B&B IR£5.75 Bdi IR£10.50 WIR£60
⅄ Ld3pm

KILGARVAN Map2W06
Glanlea ☎14 Etr–Sep 4hc 2🕅 CTV 6P 4🏠 🐾 river
750acres mx S% B&B IR£5.75 Bdi IR£10 Ld4pm
Hawthorn ☎26 Closed 15 Oct–Mar 10hc CTV 15P 🐾
87acres mx S% B&B IR£5.75 Bdi IR£11.25 WIR£66.15
Ld3pm

KILLARNEY Map2V97
Inchagree Tralee Rd ☎(064)31095 Apr–Sep 5hc TV 🐾
40acres dy Ld3pm
Ross Villa Ross Rd ☎(064)31510 Etr–Sep 4hc TV 6P
22acres mx

KILLURLEY Map2V65
Waterville View Emlaghmore PO ☎Ballinskelligs34
Jun–Aug 6rm 4hc TV 20P lake sea 100acres mx Ld7pm

LISTOWEL Map6Q93
Mount Rivers outskirts of Listowel ☎(068)21494
May–Sep 4hc (A1hc) 10P river 39acres dy S% B&B IR£5.60

STRADBALLY Map2Q51
Farrantoolen ☎(066)39150 May–Sep 5hc 3⇔🕅 nc2 TV P
70acres mx dy *B&B IR£5.50 Bdi IR£10.50
Kilcummin House Castlegregory ☎(066)39152 Mar–Oct
5hc TV 10P 60acres dy S% *B&B IR£4.50–IR£5
Bdi IR£8.50–IR£9 Ld7pm
Sea View Castlegregory ☎(066)39171 Jun–Sep 4hc TV
4P sea 37acres mx S% B&B IR£5 Bdi IR£9 Ld4.30pm

TRALEE Map2Q81
El Ranco Ballyard ☎(066)21840 Apr–Oct 4hc ⌘ TV 10P
🐾 sea 35acres horses S% B&B IR£5.75–IR£6.50
Bdi IR£9.75–IR£10.50 WIR£60–IR£65 ⅄ Ld3pm

WATERVILLE Map2V56
Benmore Oughtive Mar–Oct 5hc ⌘ CTV 10P 250acres mx
S%B&B IR£5.75 Bdi IR£11.25 WIR£60 ⅄ Ld7pm

Co Kildare

KILCULLEN Map9N80
Mrs B O'Sullivan's Gormanstown ☎(045)81325
Closed Dec & Jan 6hc ⌘ CTV 10P 🐾 22acres beef
S% B&B IR£6–IR£6.50 Bdi IR£11 WIR£63 ⅄ Ld6pm

NAAS Map9N81
Westown Johnstown ☎(045)97006 Mar–Oct 5hc ⌘ CTV
12P 🐾 98acres mx S% *B&B IR£6 Bdi IR£10 Ld2pm

Co Kilkenny

BALLYFOYLE Map8S56

Drumherin House ☎(056)27626 Etr–Oct 5rm TV 10P
77acres mx Ld7pm

BALLYHALE Map5S54
Kiltorcan House ☎(056)28617 12rm 10hc 4⇔🕅 CTV 40P
6🏠 🐾 27acres dy S% B&B IR£5–IR£5.50 Bdi IR£10–
IR£10.50 WIR£70–IR£73.50 ⅄ Ld9pm

THE ROWER Map5S73
Cullintra House ☎(051)23614 5hc P 🐾 230acres mx S%
B&B IR£6 Bdi IR£11.50 WIR£63 ⅄ Ld3pm
Garranavabby House ☎(051)23613 Mar–Oct 3hc CTV
10P 92acres mx S% B&B IR£6 Bdi IR£11.50 WIR£66
Ld5pm

Co Laois

BALLYBRITTAS Map8N50
Jamestown House ☎(0502)26163 Apr–Sep 6rm TV P
lake 80acres mx

Co Leitrim

BORNACOOLA Map12NO8
Tooman House ☎(043)24119 Apr–Oct 4hc ⌘ CTV 8P
4🏠 🐾 river 40acres beef S% B&B IR£5.80 Bdi IR£10.80
WIR£57.50 ⅄ Ld noon
GARVAGH Map12HOO
Drumcollip House Carrick-on-Shannon ☎Keshcarrigan22
Apr–Sep 4hc ⌘ TV P 60acres mx S% B&B IR£5.50
Bdi IR£9.95 Ld3.30pm

ROOSKY Map12O8
Killianiker House ☎16 Mar–Nov 5hc 2⇔🕅 TV 6P 🐾
river 45acres beef S% B&B IR£5.50 Bdi IR£9.50
WIR£54–IR£55 ⅄ Ld3pm

Co Limerick

ADARE Map7R44
Woodlands Knockanes ☎(061)94118 7hc ⌘ CTV 10P 🐾
60acres beef S% B&B IR£5.50 Bdi IR£10.50 WIR£60 ⅄
Ld6pm

BALLYSIMON Map7R65
High Park ☎(061)95209 Apr–Sep 4hc 1⇔🕅 ⌘ ✿ CTV
8P 2🏠 🐾 200acres mx *B&B IR£6 Bdi IR£10 Ld8pm

BRUREE Map3R52
Ballyteigue House ☎75 Apr–Sep 4hc 1⇔🕅 (A4rm) CTV
20P 30acres mx S% B&B IR£5 Bdi IR£10 Ld3pm

CROAGH Map7R44
Clonshire ☎Rathkeale55 May–Aug 5hc ⌘ 6P 1🏠
15acres mx S% B&B IR£5.50 Bdi IR£10.50 WIR£63 ⅄
Ld noon

CROOM Not on Map
Old Rectory ☎(061)88245 May–Sep 5hc 2⇔🕅 CTV 10P
30acres mx S% B&B IR£5.50 Bdi IR£10 WIR£60 Ld4pm

GRANGE Map7R64
Bridge House ☎(061)89195 Apr–Aug 4hc ⌘ nc5 CTV
6P 2🏠 🐾 200acres mx S% B&B IR£6 Bdi IR£10
WIR£60 ⅄ Ld4pm

KILMALLOCK Map3R62
Roseville Kilbreedy East (3m E of Kilmallock)
☎Martinstown9 Jun–Aug 4hc ⌘ nc2½ CTV 10P 50acres
mx S% B&B fr IR£5.50 Bdi fr IR£10.50 WIR£65 ⅄ Ld3pm

Co Londonderry

BALLARENA Map14C63
Ballycarton 239 Seacoast Rd ☎216 5rm 3hc ⌘ CTV 10P
2🏠 🐾 45acres nw B&B£4–£4.50 Bdi£7–£7.50
W£49–£52.50 ⅄

CASTLEDAWSON Map14H99
Moyola Lodge ☎224 4hc ⌘ ✿ CTV 50P 4🏠 🐾 10acres
nw S% B&B£7.50 Bdi£10 Ld9pm

COLERAINE Map14C83
Riverside Drumslade ☎Portstewart2668 Mar–Oct 3rm

⊗ CTV 6P 2🐾 📞 river 80acres dy B&B£4 50 Bdi£7
W£45 ⚹ Ld3 30pm
Rockmount 241 Windyhill Rd ☎2914 May–Sep 2rm CTV
4P 📞 10acres nw S% B&B£3 50 Bdi£5

DUNGIVEN Map15C60
Mount Prospect Magheramore ☎262 Etr–Sep 2rm 1hc
⊗ nc10 CTV 5P 1🐾 📞 1,760acres mx S% Ld8pm

KILLALOO Map14C51
Bondsglen House ☎Dunamanagh253 3rm 350acres ar
Further details for 1980/81 not confirmed.

Co Louth

DUNLEER Map13O08
Primrose House ☎(041)51137 May–Sep 3hc CTV 4P
3acres nw S% B&B IR£5 25 WIR£55 ⚹ Ld5pm

GREENORE Map13J21
Mrs J Toal W of Greenore ☎(042)73235 3hc CTV 6P lake
22acres mx S% B&B IR£4 50 Bdi IR£8 WIR£45 ⚹ Ld3pm

Co Mayo

AYLE Map10M08
Ayle Crest ☎Westport240 Apr–Oct 3hc TV 4P 60acres mx

TURLOUGH Map10M19
Turlough Park House ☎(094)22843 Jun–Sep 8hc 2🐾 📞
30acres mx Ld am

Co Meath

CEANANNUS MOR (Kells) Map12N77
Latimor House ☎133 Closed 2wks Xmas rs wknds
5hc ⊗ CTV 10P 📞 40acres beef S% B&B IR£6 Bdi IR£11
Ld3pm

CROSSAKEEL Map12N76
Deerpark (½m from Crossakeel) ☎9 May–Aug 3hc 1🍽
⊗ CTV P 📞 30acres mx S% B&B fr IR£5 Bdi fr IR£10
Ld4 30pm

NAVAN Map13N86
Balreask House ☎(046)21155 Apr–Oct 3rm 2hc CTV 4P
20acres mx S% B&B IR£6 05 Ld3pm

Co Offaly

BIRR Map8N00
Woodville Shinrone ☎Shinrone42 Mar–Nov 4rm ⊗ CTV
P river 238acres ar beef dy S% B&B IR£5 50 Bdi IR£10 50
WIR£63 ⚹ Ld5 30pm

CLONEYGOWAN Map8N41
Ashmount House ☎(0506)23533 May–Sep 3rm 2hc
⊗ nc CTV 4P 175acres mx

Co Roscommon

ATHLEAGUE Map11M85
Clooneyourish N of Athleague ☎(0903)7334 3hc CTV
5P 2🐾 📞 40acres mx S% B&B IR£5 Bdi IR£8 WIR£65
Ld8pm

BOYLE Map11G80
Rushfield Croghan ☎276 Etr–Oct 5rm 4hc TV 7P 80acres
mx S% B&B IR£5 Bdi fr IR£9 WIR£50 ⚹ Ld4 30pm

CASTLECOOTE Map11M86
Lisheen ☎(0903)7413 9rm 6hc ⊗ nc10 CTV 8P ⊗ river
80acres beef & dy S% B&B IR£5 Bdi IR£10 Ld6pm

KILGLASS Map11M98
Church View House Strokestown ☎Strokestown47
Apr–Sep 5hc CTV P 245acres beef S% B&B IR£6
Bdi IR£10 WIR£60 ⚹ Ld7pm

KILTOOM Map12M94
Ballycreggan House Athlone ☎(0902)38101 Apr–Oct
3rm 2hc CTV P 🐾 📞 175acres mx S% B&B IR£5
Bdi fr IR£9 50 Ld5 30pm

Co Sligo

BALLYSADARE Map11G62
Sacré Coeur Drumiskabole ☎(071)2811 Jun–Aug 3hc
🐕 TV 3P 📞 13acres mx S% B&B IR£4 50 Bdi IR£7 50
Ld4pm

DRUMCLIFF Map11G64
Urlar House N of Drumcliff ☎(071)73110 Etr–Sep 5hc
6P 📞 sea 50acres dy Ld3pm

GLENCAR Map11G74
Langley Cottage ☎(071)2833 Apr–Sep rsOct–Mar 3hc
⊗ nc8 TV 10P 📞 5acres nw S% B&B IR£4 Bdi IR£8
WIR£56 ⚹ Ld10am

GLENEASK Map11G31
Lough Talt Inn Lough Talt, Aclare ☎Bonniconlon7
Feb–Oct 4rm 3hc nc8 TV 4P lake 128acres mx Ld7pm

KNOCKNAREA Map11G63
Primrose Grange ☎(071)2005 Mar–Oct 6hc 1🍽 ⊗ TV
10P 40acres mx S% B&B IR£5 50 Bdi IR£10 50 WIR£58
⚹ Ld3pm

MONEYGOLD Map16G65
Island View ☎(071)70156 4hc 1🍽 TV
10P 📞 sea 150acres mx S% B&B IR£4–IR£4 50
Bdi IR£7–IR£7 50 WIR£48–IR£50 Ld5pm

RIVERSTOWN Map11G72
Coopershill ☎(071)75108 Etr–Sep 5rm 4hc 🐕 TV P
500acres mx B&B IR£6 Bdi IR£11 WIR£70 ⚹ Ld2pm

ROSSES POINT Map11G64
The Farmhouse Cregg ☎(071)77189 Mar–Sep 3hc TV
6P sea 134acres beef dy S% B&B IR£5 Bdi IR£9 WIR£50
⚹ Ld6pm

SLIGO Map11G63
Hillside Glencar Rd ☎(071)2808 Apr–Oct 3hc CTV 10P
2🐾 60acres mx S% B&B IR£5 Bdi IR£9 Ld2pm

TEMPLEBOY Map11G43
Ave Maria Corkamore ☎(071)72174 5rm 1hc 🐕 TV 2🐾 📞
dy S% B&B IR£4 50 Bdi IR£8 50 WIR£50 Ld9pm

TOBERCURRY Map10G51
Bawn House Ballymote Rd ☎90 Closed Xmas 6hc CTV
6P 📞 35acres beef S% B&B IR£4 50 Bdi IR£8.50 Ld3pm

Co Tipperary

ARDFINNAN Map4S01
Clonacody House ☎(052)38150 Apr–Sep 3hc nc5 TV
P 📞 130acres mx S% B&B IR£4 50 Bdi IR£9 WIR£70
Ld7pm

BANSHA Map4R93
Bansha House ☎(062)54194 7hc ⊗ CTV P 📞 100acres
mx S% B&B IR£5 Bdi IR£10 Wfr IR£55 ⚹ Ld4pm

CAHIR Map4S02
Lissava House ☎277 Etr–Sep 4hc TV P 📞 120acres mx
S% B&B IR£5 Bdi IR£8–IR£10 Ld4pm

CASHEL Map4S04
Knock-Saint-Lour House ☎(062)61172 Closed Dec & Jan
6hc 2🍽 ⊗ CTV 20P 📞 30acres mx S% B&B IR£5 75
Bdi IR£11 75 WIR£70 Ld1pm

CLONMEL Map4S22
Abbeyview ☎(052)22307 5hc CTV 7P 90acres beef
B&B IR£5 50 WIR£58 ⚹ Ld3 30pm
Inislounaght Marlfield (2m W) ☎(052)22847
15 Mar–15 Oct 7rm 6🍽 🐕 CTV 10P 📞 15acres mx
S% B&B IR£10 50 Bdi IR£18 75 WIR£115 ⚹ Ld3pm
Mullinarinka NE of Clonmel ☎(052)21374 May–Aug 5hc
P 📞 100acres mx S% B&B IR£6 Bdi IR£12 WIR£63 ⚹
Ld3pm

DUNDRUM Map4R94
Cappamurra House E of Dundrum ☎(062)71127
Closed Xmas 8hc CTV P 2♨ 105acres dy S% *B&B IR£6
Bdi IR£12 WIR£70 ⅄ Ld7.30pm

HORSE & JOCKEY Map8S15
Parkstown House ☎Littleton 15 May–Sep 5hc ⊗ CTV
10P 2♨ 撈 200acres mx

KNOCK Map8S28
Sacré Coeur ☎Borris-in-Ossory37 Jun–Sep 3rm TV P
77acres mx S% B&B IR£3.85 Bdi IR£6.85 Wfr IR£48 ⅄
Ld7pm

MONARD Map7R83
Ballyryan House ☎(062)51321 Etr–Sep 6hc ♨ CTV 10P
撈 104acres beef S% B&B IR£6.50 Bdi IR£11.50 WIR£70

PRIORSTOWN Map4S22
Kilheffernan House ☎(052)22549 Apr–Sep 4hc ⊗ CTV
P 60acres mx S% B&B IR£5.70 Bdi IR£10.70 WIR£60
Ld3pm

PUCKANE Map7R88
Ashling ☎96 4rm 3hc ♨ CTV 10P lake 50acres mx S%
B&B IR£4.50 Bdi IR£9 Wfr IR£55 ⅄ Ld6pm
Lodge House ☎8 Apr–Sep 3rm TV 10P 撈 160acres dy
S% B&B IR£6 WIR£65 ⅄ Ld noon

ROSCREA Map8S18
Streamstown House W of Roscrea ☎172 Apr–Sep
4rm 3hc (A2hc) ⊗ CTV P 撈 74acres dy S% B&B IR£5
Bdi IR£8.50 Ld4pm

TIPPERARY Map4R83
Barronstown House Emly Rd ☎(062)55130 May–Aug
4hc ⊗ CTV P 撈 100acres dy S% B&B IR£6 Bdi IR£12
WIR£62 ⅄ Ld3.30pm

Co Tyrone

BALLYGAWLEY Map14H65
Grange 15 Grange Rd ☎266 May–Sep 3hc 1⇨🚿 CTV 6P
撈 3acres nw B&B £4.50 Bdi £7.50 Ld5pm

BREADY Map14C52

Glebe House ☎3ß5 4hc TV 12P 撈 2acres S% B&B £4
Bdi £7 Ld7.30pm

LISLAP Map14H48
Hillcrest ☎Gortin284 Closed Dec 4rm 2hc TV 12P
101acres beef & dy S% B&B £4.50 Bdi £6.50 Ld6pm

OMAGH Map14H47
Copperbeech Strathrey Rd ☎2368 4rm
Further details for 1980/81 not confirmed
Green Mount Lodge 58 Greenmount Rd, Gortaclare
☎Fintona325 6hc 1⇨🚿 CTV 12P 撈 150acres beef sheep
S% B&B£4–£4.50 Bdi£7–£7.50 W£40–£45 ⅄ Ld9pm

Co Waterford

BALLIGUIRY EAST Map4X29
Mrs Kiely's ☎(058)41194 Etr–Oct 4hc CTV 10P 撈
165acres mx S% B&B IR£5.65 Bdi IR£10.60 WIR£58 ⅄
Ld3pm

DUNMORE EAST Map5S60
Creaden Cottage ☎(051)83191 Apr–Sep 3hc nc10 TV P
4♨ 撈 sea 177acres ar beef S% B&B fr IR£5.50
Bdi fr IR£10.50 Wfr IR£58 ⅄ Ld4pm

ROSSDUFF Map5X60
Elton Lodge Dunmore East ☎(051)82117 Jun–Sep
5⇨🚿 TV 6P 撈 130acres dy S% B&B IR£6 Bdi IR£10.50
Ld4.30pm

WATERFORD Map5S61
Ashbourne House Slieverue ☎(051)3003 Apr–Oct 6hc
TV 6P 撈 20acres mx S% B&B IR£5.50 Bdi IR£10
Wfr IR£64 ⅄ Ld3pm
Blenheim House Ballymaclode ☎(051)74115 Closed Xmas
5hc 4⇨🚿 ⊗ CTV 10P 撈 river 10acres ar S% B&B IR£6.50
Bdi IR£12 WIR£72 ⅄ Ld previous day
Foxmount Halfway House ☎(051)74308 May–Aug 3hc
⊗ ♨ CTV 5P 220acres mx S% B&B fr IR£6 Bdi fr IR£11
Wfr IR£64 ⅄ Ld6.30pm
River View House Golfclub Rd, Ferrybank ☎(051)75206
Mar–Nov 4hc ⊗ CTV 4P 撈 16acres nw S% B&B IR£6
Bdi IR£10.50 WIR£60 ⅄ Ld2pm

Bell's Bridge on the River Strule, Omagh

Co Westmeath

DYSART Map12N34
Grasslands ☎(044)26146 Closed Nov & Dec 5rm 4hc ✿ CTV 12P ₩ 100acres mx S% B&B IR£5 50 Bdi IR£9 50 Ld5 50pm

KILLUCAN Map12N55
Annascanan House ☎(044)74130 May–Sep 4hc CTV P 350acres S% B&B IR£5 75 Bdi IR£9 75 WIR£60

RAHARNEY Map12N65
Craddenstown House ☎(044)74165 Apr–Sep 4rm ⊘ TV P 2⌂ ₩ river 18acres ar beef S% B&B IR£5 Bdi IR£7 50 Ld8pm

STREAMSTOWN Map12N24
Woodlands off Mullingar/Moate Rd ☎(0902)36114 Mar–Oct 6rm 3hc ✿ CTV 15P ₩ 120acres mx S% B&B IR£4 60 Bdi IR£8 50 WIR£48 Ł Ld3pm

Co Wexford

BOOLAVOGUE Map5T04
Ballyorley House ☎(054)6287 3hc ⊘ CTV P ₩ 200acres mx S% B&B IR£4 80 Bdi IR£9 30

FERNS Map9T05
Clone House S of Ferns ☎(054)6113 Apr–Sep 4rm 3hc 2⇌ CTV P 4⌂ ₩ 236acres ar beef sheep S% B&B IR£6 Bdi IR£11 50 WIR£67 Ł Ld4pm

FOULKESMILL Map5S81
Crosbie's E of Foulkesmill ☎(051)63616 Mar–Oct 12hc TV P 150acres mx Ld7pm
Horetown House S of Foulkesmill ☎(051)63633 Closed mid Jan–Feb 12rm 10hc CTV P ₩ 214acres dy mx S% B&Bfr IR£5 75 Bdifr IR£8 75 Ld3pm

GOREY Map9T15
'Kia-Ora' Courteencurragh ☎(055)21166 Mar–Sep 3hc ⊘ CTV P beef S% B&B IR£6 Bdi IR£12 WIR£65 Ł
Woodlands Ballynestragh (3m N unclass rd) ☎(0402)7125 Apr–Sep 3hc CTV 4P ₩ 8acres nw S% B&B IR£6 Bdi IR£12 WIR£65 Ł Ld4 30pm

KILRANE Map5T11
Killilane St Helen's Bay ☎(053)33134 14hc TV 20P ₩ sea 75acres mx S% B&B IR£4 50 Bdi IR£7 50 WIR£52 50 Ł Ld10am

TAGOAT Map5T01
Orchard Park Churchtown ☎(053)32182 rsSep–May (B&B only) 10hc CTV 15P 23acres ar S% B&B IR£5–IR£7 Bdi IR£9 50–IR£11 50 WIR£52 50–IR£59 50 Ł Ld3pm

Co Wicklow

ARKLOW Map9T27
Killinskyduff House ☎(0402)2185 Jun–Oct 3hc CTV P ⌂ ₩ 200acres ar beef S% *B&B IR£7 Bdi IR£12 Ld6pm

AUGHRIM Map9T17
Cronemore House (on unclass rd joining L32 & T7) ☎(0402)5185 May–Sep 3rm 2hc TV 4P 78acres ar S% B&B IR£5.75 Bdi IR£10 75 WIR£63 Ł Ld3pm

AVOCA Map9T18
Rose Linn Kilmacoo ☎(0402)5247 May–Sep 4hc TV 6P 51acres ar S% *B&B IR£5 75 Bdi IR£10 75 WIR£63 Ł Ld1pm

CARRACOLE Map9T27
Bay View ☎(0402)2245 Jun–Sep 3hc ⊘ TV 4P sea 200acres mx
Beeches ☎(0402)2245 4hc ⊘ CTV P 200acres mx Ld6pm

DUNLAVIN Map9N80
Rahoon Colbinstown ☎(045)53138 Apr–Sep 4rm 2hc TV 80acres dy Ld5pm

GLENEALY Map9T29
Ballyknocken House ☎(0404)5627 Apr–Oct 6hc TV 8P ₩ 100acres dy S% B&B IR£5 75 Bdi IR£11 WIR£63 Ł Ld5pm

NEWTOWN MOUNTKENNEDY Map9O20
Ballyronan House ☎(01)819131 Etr–mid Sep 4rm ⊘ ✿ TV 5P sea 60acres dy S% *B&B IR£4 50

WICKLOW Map9T39
Knockrobin House (between Rathnew & Wicklow) ☎(0404)2344 Mar–Oct 4rm 1hc 3⇌ (A2⇌) ⊘ TV 30P ₩ sea 100acres mx S% B&B IR£9 Bdi IR£17 50 WIR£112 Ł Ld6pm

IT'S UP TO YOU!

Think ahead! Never take a chance. Always wear your seat belt, even on short journeys. Be sure your vehicle is in good condition, with sound tyres at the correct pressures. Check that all lights are working and correctly set to avoid dazzling other road users. Maintain clear vision all round. The police say that 70% of thefts of and from motor vehicles can be avoided by motorists locking all doors, securing all windows, fitting a security device, and getting into the habit of removing all valuables. It's up to you!

Camping and caravanning sites

Abbreviations and symbols

acres	total area available for *touring* pitches	wc	water closet
all year	site open all year	wash	washing machine
C	century	① ❷ △	AA qualitative assessment symbols:
CC	Countryside Commission	① ② ③	environment – (1) adequate (2) good (3) excellent
cdp	chemical closet disposal point	❶ ❷ ❸	sanitary installations – as above
central hc	hot water from a central source	△ △ △	equipment and facilities – as above
	(*eg* geyser installation)	►	AA pennant classification
CTV	colour television	*	1979 prices
dry	facilities for drying clothes	☎	public telephone available
E	east	☏	site telephone number
Etr	Easter	⊕	touring caravans
fr	from	⛟	motor caravans
hc	hot and cold water	▲	tents
hrs	hours	Ⓐ	separate tent enclosure
iron	iron(s) and ironing board(s)	⇆	bath(s)
ltr	long term rates	⋔	shower(s)
Map	atlas page and National Grid reference	⊙	electric razor points
m	mile	⛫	shop (on or within 200yd of site)
mdnt	midnight	mobile⛫	mobile shop calls at site at least
N	north		5 days a week
nc	no children (with age limit)	▭	swimming pool (indoor)
OSref	Ordnance Survey map reference	⊃	swimming pool (outdoor)
pub	public house with facilities for children	⚲	tennis court
rs	restricted service	⊘	no dogs
S	south	⚲	drinking water stand-pipes
signposted	signed by officially prescribed sign	⊞	first aid facilities
spin	spin dryer	⊖	amenities within three miles of site
stables	horse riding stables	⅁	golf
static	static/residential pitches	⌌	fishing
TV	black and white television	⛵	boats for hire
W	west	( )	chargeable facilities
warden	warden in attendance on site		

Explanation of a gazetteer entry
The example is fictitious

Town name
Appears in bold type in alphabetical order, under county heading.

Map reference
First figure is atlas page no. Then follows grid reference: read 1st figure across, 2nd figure upwards

BALLYREAGH 16 C83
► ► ► **Clonea Caravan Park** Clonea ☏42150
② ❸ △ signposted
Level, grass site set in meadowland, adjacent to sea and beach looking across to Helvick Head. On coast road Waterford to Dungarvan.
3acres 20pitches 12static
May27–Aug rsSep last arrival 20.00hrs last departure 20.00hrs ⊘ 5⇆ 7wc lit all night 1cdp central hot water (2⋔hc) 3⊙ CTV camping gaz ⛫
20⊕fr£2 or 20⛟fr£2 or 20▲fr£2 (awnings)

Pennant rating, camp site name and telephone number. In Republic of Ireland, STD codes are shown

Qualitative assessment and whether signposted from nearest main road by officially prescribed sign

Description
Description of site, size and number of pitches

Specific details
Opening dates, arrival and departure information and facilities

Touring units accepted & terms
Number of caravans, motor caravans and/or tents including price per unit where possible. Prices quoted are those applicable at the time of going to press. See page 117 for price details.

► Site with six or more pitches for the touring caravanner or camper and full range of basic facilities
► ► Site with extended range of facilities including hot water
► ► ► Site with improved facilities and limited range of services
► ► ► ► Well equipped site with wider range of services
► ► ► ► ► Very well equipped and well laid out site with full range of services

Co Antrim

BALLYCASTLE Map 15D04
►►**Moyle View Caravan Park** ☎62550
2 ❷ △
*Part level site with trees and bushes, adjacent to River
Glenshesk and beach. ¼m W of town.* 3acres 48pitches
365static
Etr–Oct Last arrival 22.00hrs Last departure 10.00hrs
10☝ individual pitches late arrivals enclosure 32wc
lit all night 2cdp 48washbasins hc 2central hot water
8🖪hc 12⊖ warden (spin dry) iron games room TV
calor gas ☎ ⊞ ♨ ⊖ ♂ ↩ cinema ↪ launderette
36🖵 or 36🚐 12▲ ltr

CUSHENDALL Map 15D22
►**Cushendall Caravan Camp** Apply to : Moyle District
Council, 61 Castle St, Ballycastle, Co Antrim ☎333
2 ❷ △ Signposted
Level, grass site, adjacent to sea, beach and main road.
3½acres 8pitches 46static
Etr–Oct Must book 5☝ individual pitches ❹~9wc
lit all night 1cdp 7washbasins hc central hot water
2🖪hc 9⊖ warden (wash spin) dry ☎ ⊞ ♨ ⊖ ♂
cinema ↪ pub
4🖵£2.13 4🚐£2.13

CUSHENDUN Map 15D23
►►►**Cushendun Caravan Park** ☎254
3 ❷ △ Signposted
*Level grass site with trees and bushes; adjacent to sea,
beach, river and hills.* 15pitches 40static
Etr–Sep Last arrival 21.00hrs ☝ individual pitches wc
lit all night washbasins hc central hot water 🖪hc ⊖
(wash spin) dry iron TV ☎ ♨ ⊖ ♂ ↩ cinema ↪
launderette pub
9🖵fr£1.62 6🚐fr£1.62 or 15▲fr£1.30

LARNE Map 15D30
►►►**Curran Caravan Park** 131 Curran Rd ☎3797
2 ❷ △
3acres 44pitches
Mar–Oct Last arrival 21.30hrs 6☝ 8wc lit all night cdp
4washbasins hc 3🖪hc 2⊖ wash spin dry ☎ ⊞ ⊖ ↩
cinema ↪
20🖵 9🚐 15▲

PORTBALLINTRAE Map 14C94
►►**Ballintrae Holiday Caravan Camp**
☎Bush Mills 31478
1 ❶ △ Signposted
A level grassy site near to sea and beach. 2acres
30pitches 100static
🖵 🚐 ▲
Further details for 1980/81 not confirmed.

PORTRUSH Map 14C84
►**Golf Links Caravan Park** Bushmills Rd ☎823539
2 ❶ △
*Level, grass site in urban area adjacent to sea and beach.
½m from town centre on Bushmills road.* 10acres 150pitches
🖵 🚐 ▲
Further details for 1980/81 not confirmed.

Co Cavan

SHERCOCK Map 12H70
►►►**Lakelands Caravan Park** ☎(042)69206
3 ❷ △
*Mainly level grass and gravel site amidst young trees and
bushes. Set in hilly country, close to lake and main road.*
½acre 12pitches 10static
Etr–Sep Must book Jul & Aug Last arrival 23.00hrs
Last departure 12.00hrs 9☝ individual pitches ❹ 11wc
lit all night 2cdp 🖵 washbasins hc central hot water
(↩hc) (🖪hc) ⊖ warden (wash spin dry iron) cold storage
calor gas camping gaz toilet fluid cafe restaurant & bar ☎ ⊞
children's playground & private beach ♨ ⊖ stables ↩ ↪
launderette pub
12🖵IRE2.90 or 12🚐IRE2.90 20▲IRE2.90 (awnings) ltr

Co Clare

KILRUSH Map 6Q95
►►►**Aylevarroo Caravan Park** ☎102
3 ❷ △
*Level grass site, set in meadowland, adjacent to beach,
river and Shannon estuary. 2m from Kilrush.* ❀ 6½acres
38pitches 10static
16 May–18 Sep Last arrival 21.00hrs Last departure
12.00hrs 7☝ individual pitches 15wc lit all night 1cdp
washbasins hc central hot water (🖪hc) ⊖ warden
(spin dry iron) ❧ games room TV color gas camping gaz
☎ ⊞ children's playground ♨ ⊖ stables ↩ cinema ↪
launderette
28🖵IRE2.80 or 28🚐IRE2.80 or 28▲IRE2.80 awnings

LAHINCH Map 6R18
►►►►**Lahinch Camping & Caravan Park**
☎(065)214
2 ❸ △
*Situated south of village near sandy beach. If approaching
from Ennistymon pass through village turn left, then right
opposite church.* 4½acres 92pitches
26 May–11 Sep Last arrival 20.00hrs Last departure
12.00hrs 10☝ individual pitches for caravans only ❹
19wc lit all night 2cdp 🖵 washbasins hc (🖪hc) ⊖
(wash spin dry iron) games room CTV (cold storage)
camping gaz toilet fluid cafe restaurant ☎ ⊞
children's playground ♨ ⊖ stables ♂ ↩ cinema ↪
launderette pub
62🖵IRE3 or 62🚐IRE3 30▲IRE3 (awnings)

Co Cork

BANDON Map 3W45
►►**Murray's Caravan & Camping Park** Kilbrogan Rd
☎(023) 41232
1 ❶ △
*Part level, part sloping, grass and gravel site with various
trees and bushes, set in meadowland within the urban
area and close to river and main road.* 4acres 19pitches
Apr–Sep rsOct–Mar Last arrival 22.00hrs Last departure
13.00hrs 10☝ individual pitches ❹ late arrivals enclosure
8wc lit all night 1cdp 🖵 washbasins hc central hot water
🖪hc ⊖ warden wash spin iron cold storage calor gas
camping gaz ☎ ⊞ children's playground ♨ ⊖ stables
♂ cinema ↪ launderette pub
19🖵IRE1.80 or 19🚐IRE1.80 or 19▲IRE1.80 awnings

CORK Map 3W67
►►**Cork Caravan Co & Camping Park** ☎(021) 961611
2 ❷ △ Signposted
*Sheltered by trees near to soccer pitch and close to the
Cork–Kinsale road.* 6acres 80pitches
Must book Last arrival 24.00hrs Last departure 12.00hrs
36☝ individual pitches ❹ late arrivals enclosure 14wc
lit all night cdp 🖵 6washbasins hc 1central hot water
(8🖪hc) 2⊖ warden (2wash) 1spin (1dry 1iron)
games room CTV (cold storage) calor gas camping gaz
licensed bar ☎ ⊞ Licensed club horse riding & soccer
pitch ♨ ⊖ stables ♂ cinema ↪ launderette pub
30🖵IRE2.85 30🚐IRE2.85 20▲IRE2.85 awnings ltr
►►**Cork City Caravan & Camping Park** Togher Rd
☎(021) 42111
2 ❷ △
*Level, grass and gravel site with mature trees. 2½m from
city centre.* 2acres 40pitches
Apr–Oct Last arrival mdnt Last departure 12.00hrs 4☝
6wc lit all night 1cdp washbasins hc central hot water
🖪hc ⊖ warden (wash spin) dry (iron) TV cold storage
calor gas camping gaz paraffin toilet fluid ⊞
children's playground ♨ ⊖ stables ♂ ↩ cinema ↪
launderette pub
20🖵IRE1.60–IRE2.25 or 20🚐IRE1.60–IRE2.25
20▲IRE1.60–IRE2.25 awnings ltr

CROOKHAVEN Map 2V82
►►► **Barley Cove Caravan Park** ☎(028) 35302
🔟 ❸⚠
*Level, grass and gravel site with trees and bushes set in
mountains, hills and meadowland. Adjacent to sea and
beach.* ✿ 4½acres 70pitches 65static
20 May–15 Sep rs Etr & 16–30 Sep Must book Jul & Aug
Last arrival 21.00hrs Last departure 12.00hrs 14🛁
individual pitches (caravans only) ⊛ 24wc lit all night
1cdp 🚰 washbasins hc central hot water (⇱hc ⇲hc) ☉
warden (wash spin dry iron) games room calor gas
camping gaz toilet fluid ☎ ⊞ children's playground ♨
⊖ ♿ ➳ ☍ launderette pub
20🏕IRE3 40 5🚎IRE2 40 50▲IRE3 40 (awnings) ltr

GARRYVOE Map 4X06
►►► **O'Brien's Holidaycenter** ☎(021) 62749
🔢 ❸⚠
A level, grassy site near sea and beach. ✿ 4acres
10pitches 30static
Jun–14 Sep rs Etr–May & 15–30 Sep Last arrival mdnt
Last departure mdnt 6🛁 lit all night 1cdp washbasins hc
central hot water (1⇱hc 2⇲hc) ☉ warden (1wash)
(2iron) (games room) CTV cold storage calor gas
camping gaz toilet fluid ☎ ⊞ children's playground &
private beach ♨ ⊖ stables ➳ cinema ☍ launderette
pub
10🏕IRE3 or 10🚎IRE3 awnings ltr

GLENGARRIF Map 2V95
►►► **Dowling's Caravan Park** ☎(021) 154
🔟❷⚠
*Mainly level, grass site with various trees and bushes, set in
mountainous woodland and meadowland country. Close
to sea, river and main road. On L61. 1½m W of Glengarriff
village.* 18acres 160pitches 20static
Etr–10 Oct Must book Jul & Aug Last arrival 23.00hrs
Last departure 13.00hrs 16🛁 individual pitches 22wc
lit all night 🚰 washbasins hc central hot water (⇲hc) ☉
warden (wash spin dry iron) cold storage camping gaz
paraffin toilet fluid ☎ ⊞ children's playground ♨ ⊖
stables ♿ ➳ ☍ launderette pub
40🏕IRE3 50 20🚎IRE3 50 100▲IRE3 50 awnings ltr

Co Donegal

KERRYKEEL Map 16C23
►►► **Rockhill Caravan Park** ☎12
🔢 ❷ ⚠ Signposted
Level grass site, set in meadowland, adjacent to Mulroy Bay.
20acres
Jul & Aug rsMar–Jun & Sep 20🛁 individual pitches ⊛
21wc lit all night 3cdp 🚰 washbasins hc central hot water
(⇱hc⇲hc) ☉ (wash spin dry iron) (🐕) games room TV
(cold storage) calor gas camping gaz toilet fluid ☎
⊞ children's playground, horse riding ♨ ⊖ stables ♿
cinema ☍ launderette ♨
20🏕IRE2 80 30🚎IRE2 80 or 30▲IRE2 80 awnings

NARIN Map 16G79
►►► **Campbell Caravan Park** ☎Clooney 11
🔢❷⚠
*Partly level site set in mountains and moorland
adjacent to sea, beach and lake.*
Etr–Oct individual pitches 4wc lit all night 1cdp
4washbasins hc central hot water ⇲hc ☉ (spin) (iron)
calor gas toilet fluid ♨ ⊖ ♿ ➳ ☍
🚰 🚎 ▲

PORTSALON Map 16C24
►►► **Knockalla Holiday Centre**
Ballynashannagh P.O. ☎8
🔟 ❸⚠
13acres 46pitches 59static
Mar–Sep Last arrival 20.00hrs Last departure 12.00hrs
3🛁 individual pitches 14wc lit all night 1cdp
22washbasins hc 1⇱hc 11⇲hc 4☉ warden (2wash)
(2spin) iron games room TV cold storage calor gas
camping gaz cafe restaurant ☎ ⊞ children's
playground & pony trekking ♨ ⊖ stables ➳ ☍ ♨
23🏕IRE2 50 or 23🚎IRE2 50 23▲IRE2 50 awnings

ROSBEG Map 16G69
►►► **Tramore Beach Caravan Park** ☎Glenties 6
🔢❷⚠
*Part level, part sloping, grass and sand site set in hilly
country with access to sea, beach and main road.*
10acres 52pitches 30static
Apr–Oct Must book Jul & Aug Last arrival 20.30hrs
Last departure 12.00hrs 5🛁 individual pitches 12wc
lit all night 2cdp washbasins hc ⇲hc ☉ spin iron
calor gas toilet fluid cafe restaurant ☎ ⊞ ♨ ⊖ ♿ ➳ ☍
launderette pub
🚰 🚎 ▲

Co Down

CASTLEWHELLAN Map 13J33
►►► **Castlewhellan Forest Park** Apply to Ministry of
Agriculture, Forestry Division, Castlewhellan ☎664
🔟 ❷ ⚠ Signposted
*A level, grass site with bushes, set amid lakes, hills,
moorland and woodland. 24m S of Belfast on A24*
3acres 60pitches
🚰 🚎 ▲
Further details for 1980/81 not confirmed.

CLOUGHEY Map 15J64
►►► **Silver Bay Caravan Park** Ballyspurge
☎Portavogie 321
🔢❷⚠
*A level, sandy and grassy site with mature trees and
bushes, set in mountainous moorland and woodland country
near to sea and beach.* 14pitches 150static
1 wk before Etr–15 Nov Last arrival 20.00hrs
Last departure 12.00hrs 8🛁 wc lit all night 2cdp
washbasins hc (⇲hc) ☉ calor gas toilet fluid ☎
private beach ♨ ⊖ ♿ ➳ cinema ☍ pub
14🏕£1 50 or 14🚎£1 50 or 14▲£1 50 awnings

CRANFIELD Map 13J21
►►► **Chestnut Caravan Park** ☎Kilkeel 653
🔟 ❶⚠ Signposted
Level, grass site near sea. Off B27 Kilkeel/Greencastle road.
10½acres 40pitches 12static
🚰 🚎 ▲
Further details for 1980/81 not confirmed.
►► **Cranfield Caravan Site** ☎Kilkeel 572
🔟 ❶⚠ Signposted
*Mainly level, grass site with direct access to main road and
beach.* 15acres 9pitches 200static
🚰 🚎
Further details for 1980/81 not confirmed.

KILKEEL Map 13J31
►► **Leestone Caravan Park** Leestone Rd ☎62567
🔟 ❶⚠
*Part level, part sloping grass site set in hilly country,
with access to sea, river, beach and main road. 1m
from town on A2 Newcastle road.* 10pitches 110static
Mar–Oct Last arrival 21.00hrs Last departure 12.00hrs
16🛁 individual pitches 20wc lit all night 2cdp
washbasins hc central hot water ⇲hc ☉ warden (iron)
games room CTV (cold storage) calor gas camping gaz
toilet fluid cafe ☎ ⊞ children's playground ♨
⊖ ♿ ☍ launderette pub
10🏕£1 65 or 10🚎£1 65 awnings ltr

MILLISLE Map 15J57
►► **Rathlin Caravan Park** Moss Rd ☎861386
🔟 ❶⚠
*Mainly level, grass site set in meadowland, adjacent to main
road. On B172.* 6acres 12pitches 70static
Etr–Oct Must book Jul Last arrival 22.30hrs
Last departure 12.00hrs 4🛁 14wc lit all night 1cdp
9washbasins hc (1⇲hc) 1☉ warden iron games room
TV calor gas ⊞ ♨ ⊖ ♿ ➳ ☍ launderette pub
6🏕 6🚎

►►**Sea View Caravan Park** Ballycopeland ☎861248
🛱 ➊ ⚠
Part level, part sloping, grass site, set in downland,
close to sea, beach and main road. 8m S of Bangor on A2
from Belfast. 1acre 276static
Apr–Oct Last arrival 22.00hrs Last departure 12.00hrs
15☛ individual pitches 30wc lit all night 2cdp
18washbasins hc central hot water (4⬛hc) ☉ warden
iron calor gas games area ⚨ ⊖ stables 𝔰 ↩ cinema
↳ launderette pub
20🔲 20🚐 ltr

NEWCASTLE Map 13J33
►►**Newcastle Caravan Trailer Park** ☎22351
🛱 ➊ ⚠
Part level, part sloping, grass site with mature trees and
bushes, near sea, beach and river. Set amid hills,
mountains, moorland and woodlands. 2m W of
Newcastle on A2. 2acres 30pitches 500static
🔲 🚐
Further details for 1980/81 not confirmed.
►**Tollymore Forest Park** ☎22428
🛱 ➌ ⚠ Signposted
Part level, part sloping, grass site with various trees and
bushes. Set in woodland countryside, adjacent to River
Shimna and Tollymore Forest. 2m W of Newcastle on B180.
7½acres 70pitches
Must book Last arrival dusk Last departure 17.00hrs
8☛ ⊛ 20wc 2cdp 24washbasins hc central hot water
4⬛hc ☉ (1wash 1iron) cafe restaurant 🍴 ⊞ ⚨ ⊖
stables 𝔰 ↩ ↳ launderette pub
35🔲£1.60 or 35🚐£1.60 35▲£1.60 awnings

Co Dublin

KILLINEY Map 9O22
►►►**Cromlech Caravan Park** Killiney Hill Rd
☎(01) 852415
🛱 ➌ ⚠
Level, grass site amidst various trees and bushes, near
sea, beach and mountains. ⊛ 5½acres 65pitches 9static
Etr–mid Sep Last arrival 22.00hrs Last departure 12.00hrs
10☛ individual pitches (caravans only) ⊛ 16wc
lit all night 1cdp 🔲 17washbasins hc (2central hot water)
(8⬛hc) 4☉ (wash spin) (iron) (cold storage)
camping gaz 🍴 ⊞ ⚨ ⊖ stables 𝔰 ↩ cinema ↳
launderette pub
29🔲IR£3 or 29🚐IR£3 36▲IR£3 awnings

SHANKHILL Map 9O22
►►**Sherrington Park** ☎(01) 820011
🛱 ➋ ⚠
A grassy site with mature trees and bushes. 7acres
55pitches 50static
Etr–Sep no bookings Last departure 12.00hrs 10☛
lit all night 2cdp 12washbasins hc central hot water
(⬛hc) ☉ iron (cold storage) calor gas 🍴 ⊞
children's playground & table tennis ⚨ ⊖ stables
𝔰 ↩ cinema ↳ launderette pub
40🔲IR£2.40 or 20🚐IR£2.40 or 55▲IR£2.40 (awnings)
ltr

Co Fermanagh

CASTLE ARCHDALE Map 16H15
►►►**Castle Archdale Caravan Park** ☎Irvinestown 333
🛱 ➋ ⚠ Signposted
Level, grass site with trees and bushes, set in woodland,
close to a lake. 20pitches 100static
🔲 🚐 ▲
Further details for 1980/81 not confirmed.

Co Kerry

CASTLEGREGORY Map 2Q61
►►►**Anchor Caravan Park** ☎(066) 39157
🛱 ➋ ⚠
Mainly level, grass site with mature trees and bushes, set
in mountainous, meadowland country close to sea and
beach. 5acres 30pitches 9static
Etr–Sep Last arrival 23.00hrs Last departure 12.00hrs
10☛ 6wc lit all night 1cdp 🔲 8washbasins hc
2central hot water 4⬛hc 4☉ warden iron games room
TV cold storage ⊞ children's playground, private beach &
hot snacks ⚨ ⊖ stables ↩ ↳ pub
30🔲IR£3 or 30🚐IR£3 (awnings)

KILLARNEY Map 2V98
►►►**Fossa Caravan Park** ☎(064) 31497
🛱 ➋ ⚠
A level and grassy site with mature bushes and trees, near
lake and woodland. 2½m from town on N70. 8acres
100pitches 20static
Etr–Oct Must book Jul & Aug Last arrival 23.00hrs
8☛ individual pitches ⊛ 16wc lit all night 1cdp 🔲
16washbasins hc (6⬛hc) 2☉ warden (2wash 2spin 2dry
1iron) games room CTV cold storage camping gaz cafe
restaurant 🍴 ⊞ children's playground & private beach ⚨
⊖ stables 𝔰 ↩ cinema ↳ launderette pub
42🔲IR£2.40 or 42🚐IR£2.40 58▲IR£2.40
(awnings) ltr
►►►**White Bridge Caravan Park** Ballycasheen
☎(064) 31590
🛱 ➋ ⚠
A grass site set in woodlands and mountains, and near
river. 1m E of Killarney, 300yds off Killarney–Cork road.
46pitches
Etr–Sep Must book Jul & Aug Last arrival 22.00hrs
Last departure 12.00hrs 8☛ individual pitches ⊛ 11wc
lit all night 1cdp 🔲 washbasins hc (⊖hc ⬛hc) ☉ (iron)
calor gas camping gaz 🍴 ⊞ children's playground ⚨ ⊖
stables 𝔰 ↩ cinema ↳ launderette pub
25🔲IR£2.05–IR£3.10 or 25🚐IR£2.05–IR£3.10
21▲IR£2.05–IR£3.10 (awnings) ltr

Co Londonderry

BALLYREAGH Map 14C84
►►►**Carrick-Dhu Caravan Park** 12 Ballyreagh Rd
☎Portrush 3712
🛱 ➌ ⚠
Part level, part sloping, grass site, set in downland within
the urban area, close to sea, beach and main road.
8acres 28pitches
Apr–10 Oct Last arrival 20.00hrs Last departure 12.00hrs
20☛ individual pitches ⊛ 60wc lit all night 4cdp
washbasins hc central hot water ⬛hc ☉ warden spin
dry iron games room TV calor gas camping gaz
paraffin toilet fluid 🍴 ⊞ children's play area ⚨ ⊖ 𝔰 ↩
cinema ↳ launderette
28🔲 or 28🚐 or 26▲

CASTLEROCK Map 14C73
►►►**Castlerock Caravan Park** ☎Portstewart 3092
🛱 ➋ ⚠
Level grass site with bushes, set in meadowland, adjacent
to sea, beach and River Bann estuary. 20 pitches
Apr–Oct Must book Last arrival 21.00hrs ☛ wc
lit all night calor gas camping gaz toilet fluid 🍴 ⊞
children's playground ⚨ ⊖ 𝔰 ↳ pub
20🔲£2 12▲£2 awnings

PORTSTEWART Map 14C83
►►►**Juniper Hill Caravan Park** ☎2023
🛱 ➋ ⚠
Part level, part sloping site, set in downland within the
urban area, close to sea and beach. 2m from
Portstewart. 2acres 17pitches 🔲
Further details for 1980/81 not confirmed.

Co Louth

CLOGHERHEAD Map 13O18
►►► **Ashling Caravan Park** ☎(041) 22271
2❷⚠
*A level and grassy site near sea and beach. 7m N of
Drogheda.* 6acres
Apr–Sep 8⚑ 31wc lit all night 2cdp washbasins hc
8⬛hc 6⊝ warden dry ⚒ games room TV calor gas cafe
☎ ⊞ ⚌ ⊖ stables ♪ ← ↰
20⚐ or 20⇶ or 20▲

Co Meath

BETTYSTOWN Map 13O17
►►► **Bettystown Caravan Park** ☎(041) 27173
2❶⚠
*Slightly sloping grass site, set in meadowland, close to river
and main road.* ❀ 2acres 20pitches 120static
May–13 Sep Must book Jul & Aug Last arrival 22.00hrs
Last departure 13.00hrs 10⚑ individual pitches 16wc
lit all night 2cdp washbasins hc central hot water ⬛hc ⊙
iron (games room) calor gas ☎ ⊞ children's playground
⊖ ♪ ← ↰ ⚌ pub
20⚐IR£3.50 or 20⇶IR£3.50 or 5▲IR£3.50 awnings

Co Roscommon

BOYLE Map 11G80
►►►► **Lough Key Forest Caravan Park** ☎212
3❸⚠
A level and grassy site in woodland 2½m E of town on N4.
13acres 5static
Apr–Sep Last arrival 23.00hrs 13⚑ 11wc lit all night
cdp washbasins hc 4⬛hc 3⊝ warden wash dry ⚒
games room cafe ☎ ⊞ ⚌ ⊖ stables ♪ ← cinema ↰
⚐ ⇶ ▲ ltr

Co Tipperary

ROSCREA Map 8S18
►► **Streamstown House** ☎172
2❶⚠
Level and grass site in meadowland. 1½m from town on L34
2½acres 30pitches
Jun–Sep rs Etr Must book Last arrival mdnt 4⚑ individual
pitches 5wc lit all night 1cdp ⚐ 6washbasins hc
central hot water 1⬛hc 5⊝ (iron) calor gas camping gaz
paraffin toilet fluid ⊞ children's playground ⚌ ⊖ ♪
cinema ↰ launderette pub
15⚐IR£2 or 15⇶IR£2 15▲IR£2 (awnings) ltr

Co Waterford

ARDMORE Map 4X17
►► **Ardmore Caravan Site** ☎(024) 4129
2❷⚠
Level, grass site near sea and beach. ❀ 5acres
10pitches 10static
May–Sep Must book Last arrival 20.00hrs
Last departure 16.00hrs 2⚑ ④ 20wc lit all night
washbasins hc 4⬛hc 4⊝ warden calor gas ☎ ⊞ ⊖
stables ← ↰
10⚐ or 10⇶ or 10▲
►► **Curragh Caravan Park** ☎(024) 2218
2❶⚠
*Mainly level, grass site with bushes, close to sea, beach and
main road.* 3acres 40pitches
15 May–15 Sep Last arrival 18.00hrs Last departure
12.00hrs 8⚑ ④ 14wc 1cdp 10washbasins hc
(4⬛hc) 2⊝ (1spin) ⚌ ⊖ ← ↰ pub
40⚐ or 40⇶ 40▲ (awnings) ltr

DUNGARVAN Map 4X29
►►► **Clonea Caravan Park** Clonea ☎(058) 42150
2❷⚠
*Level grass site set in meadowland, adjacent to sea and
beach looking across to Helvick Head. On coast road
Waterford to Dungarvan.* ❀ 3acres 36pitches 12static
15 May–14 Sep Last arrival 21.00hrs Last departure
15.00hrs 5⚑ ④ 7wc lit all night 1cdp ⚐ washbasins hc
central hot water (⬛hc) ⊙ warden (iron) CTV
⊞ private beach ⊖ stables ♪ ← cinema ⚌
10⚐IR£2.50–IR£3 5⇶IR£2.50–IR£3 20▲IR£2.50–
IR£3 (awnings)

TRAMORE Map 5X50
►►► **Atlantic View Caravan Park** Riverstown
☎(051) 81330
2❸⚠
*A sloping and grassy site near sea and beach. ½m from town
on the Waterford road N25.* ❀ 9acres 114pitches
80static
mid May–mid Sep Last arrival 22.00hrs Last departure
15.00hrs 16⚑ individual pitches ④ 15wc lit all night
1cdp 16washbasins hc 3central hot water 8⬛hc 8⬛hc
5⊝ warden (3wash 2spin 1dry 4iron) TV camping gaz
cafe restaurant ☎ ⊞ ⚌ ⊖ stables ♪ ← ↰ launderette
pub
54⚐IR£2.70 or 54⇶IR£2.70 60▲IR£2.70 (awnings) ltr

Co Westmeath

MULLINGAR Map 12N45
►►► **Lough Ennel Caravan Park** ☎(044) 8101
2❷⚠
*Level, grass and gravel site set in woodland and
meadowland. Access to Lough Ennel.* 15acres 10static
Apr–Sep Last arrival 22.30hrs Last departure 12.00hrs
14⚑ individual pitches ④ 9wc lit all night 1cdp
16washbasins hc central hot water (4⬛hc) 6⊝ warden
(1wash) (iron) cold storage calor gas camping gaz cafe
☎ ⊞ ⚌ ⊖ ♪ ← ↰ launderette
50⚐ or 50⇶ 30▲ ltr

Co Wexford

BROADWAY Map 5T00
►►► **Carne Beach Caravan Park** ☎(053) 31131
3❷⚠
*Mainly level and grass site with sand, gravel and bushes.
Near to sea, beach and main road.* 3acres 35pitches
80static
20 May–12 Sep Last arrival 22.00hrs Last departure
22.00hrs 4⚑ ④ 24wc lit all night 2cdp washbasins hc
central hot water ⬛hc ⊙ warden (spin) iron TV
calor gas camping gaz paraffin toilet fluid cafe
restaurant ☎ ⊞ ⚌ ⊖ stables ← ↰ launderette
10⚐ 10⇶ 15▲ ltr

COURTOWN HARBOUR Map 9T15
►►► **Parklands Caravan Park** ☎(055) 25202
2❷⚠
*Mainly level, grass site with mature trees and bushes set in
the urban area; access to sea and beach.* 8acres
25pitches 50static
26 May–5 Sep Last arrival 20.30hrs Last departure
14.00hrs 14⚑ ④ 21wc lit all night 2cdp 21washbasins hc
(6⬛hc) 8⊝ (2wash spin dry) games room TV
camping gaz ☎ ⊞ ⚌ ⊖ ♪ ← launderette
25⚐ or 25⇶ or 25▲ (awnings)

KILMUCKRIDGE Map 5T14
►►► **Morriscastle Strand Caravan Park**
☎(053) 30124 (summer), (01) 972027 (winter)
🅿 ❷ ⚠
*Part level, part sloping, grass site, set in meadowland with
direct access to sea and beach.* ✤ 6acres 90pitches
140static
Jun–Aug rs May & Sep Must book 15 Jul–15 Aug 6⚲
individual pitches for caravans only ④ 30wc lit all night
2cdp washbasins hc (�+ hc) ☉ warden (wash spin) (iron)
(cold storage) calor gas camping gaz 🏕 ⊞
children's playground & private beach 🛒 ⊖ ↪
launderette pub
40🚐IR£2.70 10🚍IR£2.70 50▲IR£2.70 (awnings)

WEXFORD Map 5T02
►►► **Ferrybank Caravan Park** ☎(053) 22611
🅿 ❸ ⚠
*A level and grassy site with bushes near sea, beach and
river. N side of bridge.* 10acres 44pitches
26 May–mid Sep Must book peak periods
Last departure 12.00hrs 14⚲ individual pitches. 12wc
lit all night 12washbasins hc 8�+ hc 4☉ warden wash
dry iron 🔲 cafe 🏕 ⊞ ⊖ stables ⚡ ↩ cinema ↪
launderette
22🚐 or 22🚍 22▲ ltr

Co Wicklow

ARKLOW Map 9T27
►►► **Arklow Holiday Ltd** North Beach ☎(0402) 2156
🅿 ❷ ⚠
*A level and grassy site with trees and bushes set in
mountainous country near sea and beach.*

50acres 100pitches
Jun–Sep rs Apr–May Last arrival 22.00hrs
Last departure 14.00hrs 20⚲ ④ 35wc lit all night 3cdp
30washbasins hc central hot water (6�+ hc) 8☉ warden
↪ games room TV calor gas camping gaz toilet fluid
🏕 ⊞ 🛒 ⊖ stables ⚡ ↩ cinema ↪ launderette
60🚐 or 60🚍 40▲

RED CROSS Map 9T28
►►► **River Valley Caravan Park** ☎(0404) 8647
🅿 ❸ ⚠
✤ 5½acres 32pitches 10static
Etr–Sep Must book Public Hols Last arrival 22.00hrs
Last departure 12.00hrs 5⚲ individual pitches for
caravans only ④ late arrivals enclosure 7wc lit all night
1cdp 🚿 12washbasins hc (2central hot water) (�+ hc)
2☉ (3wash) (iron) (games room) CTV (cold storage)
calor gas camping gaz paraffin toilet fluid 🏕 ⊞
children's playground 🛒 ⊖ launderette pub
18🚐IR£2.30 or 18🚍IR£2.30 14▲IR£2.30 (awnings) ltr

ROUNDWOOD Map 9O10
►► **Roundwood Caravan Park** ☎(01) 818163
🅿 ❷ ⚠
*Part level, part sloping grass site with trees and bushes,
set in mountains and woodland, adjacent to Vartry river.
12m from Bray.* 6acres 77pitches
Mar–Sep Last arrival 23.00hrs Last departure 12.00hrs
6⚲ individual pitches ④ 10wc lit all night 1cdp
13washbasins hc central hot water (�+ hc) ☉ warden
(wash) (iron) (cold storage) camping gaz 🏕 ⊞
children's playground 🛒 ⊖ stables ⚡ ↩ ↪ launderette
pub
42🚐IR£1.80 or 42🚍IR£1.80 35▲IR£1.80 (awnings) ltr

FOLLOW THE
COUNTRY CODE

Guard against all risk of fire

Fasten all gates

Keep dogs under proper control

Keep to the paths across farmland

Avoid damaging fences, hedges and
walls

Leave no litter

Safeguard water supplies

Protect wild life, wild plants and trees

Go carefully on country roads

Respect the life of the countryside

Picnic sites

P = parking spaces

Northern Ireland

Co Antrim

A2 Ballygalley Map **15** D30 5m N of Larne. P70.
A2 Ballypatrick Forest Map **15** D13 6½m SE of Ballycastle. Toilets. P50.
A2 Carnlough Harbour Map **15** D21 On A2 near harbour. P70.
A2 Carrick-a-Rede Map **15** D04 5m W of Ballycastle. P30.
A2 Cushendall Map **15** D22 On A2 at Cushendall adjacent to caravan site. P30.
A2 Drains Bay Map **15** D30 2½m N of Larne. On Seafront. P60.
A2 Garron Point Map **15** D22 4½m N of Carnlough. On Seafront. P40.
A2 Glenarm Map **15** D31 In Glenarm.
A2 Magheracross Map **14** C83 3m E of Portrush. P55.
A2 Whiterocks Map **14** C84 2m E of Portrush. Signposted at entrance. 1 acre. Furniture. Toilets. P80.
A2 Red Bay Map **15** D22 1½m SE of Glenariffe. P10.
A2/unclass Slieveanorra Forest Map **15** D12 Off A2 5m W of Cushendall.
A6 Brackfield Map **14** C41 7m SE of Londonderry. Signposted at entrance. ½ acre elevated site with pleasant views. Furniture. P10.
A6 Carrieknakieft Map **14** H89 On Maghera Bypass NW of Castledawson. Signposted at entrance. 15 acre pleasantly situated site with good views of surrounding countryside and Sperrin Mountains. Furniture. P4.
A6 Craigadick Map **14** H89 1m S of Maghera on Maghera Bypass at junction with A29. Signposted at entrance. ½ acre. Furniture. P4.
A6 Curran Bridge Map **14** H89 On Maghera Bypass 4m NW of Castledawson. Signposted at entrance. ¾ acre site on the banks of Moxala River. Furniture. P8.
Off A6 Ness Wood Map **14** C51 9m SE of Londonderry signposted off A6 at a point 7m SE of Londonderry. Signposted in advance and at entrance. Pleasant site. Furniture. P40.
A6 Kanaghan Map **14** C70 4m NW of Maghera. Signposted at entrance. 1½ acre pleasantly situated at SE end of Glenshane Pass with superb view towards Lough Neagh. Furniture P25.
A42 Knockstacken Map **15** D21 2m SW of Carnlough. P15.
A42 Portglenone Forest Map **15** C90 1m S of Portglenone. Signposted. P70.
A43 Glenariffe Glen Map **15** D22 ¾m SW of Waterfoot.
A43 Parkmore Map **15** D22 4¾m SW of Waterfoot. P50.
A54 Castleroe Wood Map **14** C83 3m S of Coleraine. Signposted at entrance. ½ acre, forest walks, furniture. P20.
A55 Belvoir Park Map **15** J37 Off A55 Belfast road. Signposted. P.
B15/unclass Ballycastle Forest Map **15** D04 Off Ballycastle–Armoy via Glenshesk road. Toilets. P.
B55 Cairn Wood Map **15** J47 ½m ENE of Belfast. P.
B59 Tardree Forest Map **15** J19 ½m E of Kells. Signposted. P8.
B94 Tildarg Map **15** J29 5m N of Ballyclare. P30.
B90 Brown's Bay Map **15** J49 On Island Magee on B90 from Ballycarry.
Off B145 Portballintrae Map **14** C94 Off B145 which is off A2: adjacent to Beach Hotel. P127.
B201 Largantea Map **14** C72 5½m E of Limvady. Signposted at entrance. ½ acre site by small river and waterfall. Furniture. P15.

Co Armagh

A29/B31 Fews Forest Map **13** H92 3m NW of Newtownhamilton. P60.
Off A29/B31 Gosford Forest Park Map **13** H93 Adjacent to Market Hill entrance of forest. Toilets. P200.
B31/B78 The Fews Forest, Carrickatuke, Deadmans Hill Map **13** H92 Off B31/B78 4m N of Newtownhamilton. P12.
B79 Fathom Wood Map **13** J02 4m S of Newry. P20.
B134 Slieve Gullion Map **13** J02 2m from Forkhill. P200.
B32 The Fews Forest, Carnagh Map **13** J02 On B32 Keady/Castleblayney road, 3m S Keady. P30.

Co Down

A1 Large Park Map **15** J25 In Hillsborough on A1. P50.
A2 Ballywalter Map **15** J66 At S end of village. P41.
A2 Bloodybridge Map **13** J32 2¾m S of Newcastle. P50.
A2 Cloughey Car Park Map **15** J65 In Cloughey. P190.
Off A2 Harbour Car Park Map **15** J65 At Portavogie Harbour ¼m E of Portavogie on unclassified road. P34.
A2 Harbour Car Park Map **15** J66 In Ballyhalbert. P39.
A2 Killard Road Map **15** J54 On Ballyhornan/Strangford road. P100.
A2 Millisle Car Park Map **15** J57 In Millisle. P390.
A2 Sliddery Ford Bridge Map **13** J33 2¼m N of Newcastle on A2. P200.
A20 Ballyfrench Car Park Map **15** J66 Near junction on Ballyhalbert road. P40.
Off A22 Quoile Low Road Map **15** J44 1m N of Downpatrick near Quoile Bridge. P50.
On A24 Clough Village Map **15** J44 On A24. P12.
A24 Seaforde Demesne Map **15** J44 ¾m N of Seaforde Village on A24. P18.
A25 Castlewhellan Forest Map **13** J33 In Castlewhellan Forest. P800.
A25 Creegduff Map **15** J44 1m NE of Clough. No toilets. P40.
B7/unclass Drumkeeragh Forest Map **15** D24 On unclass road 4½m SE of Dromara.
B25 Rostrevor Forest Map **13** J11 Adjacent to Rostrevor Village. Toilets. P220.
B27 Crockafeola Forest Map **13** J21 5½m N of Kilkeel. P.
B170 Ballysallagh Map **15** J47 2m NE of Craigantlet. P50.
B180 Tollymore Park Map **13** J33 2m NW of Newcastle. P500.
B511 Groomsport Harbour Map **15** J38 In Groomsport. P38.

Co Fermanagh

Off A4 Brook Park Map **14** H24 In Enniskillen. P30.
Off A4 Fardross Forest Map **14** H44 Signposted from Clogher–Fivemiletown road. 3m SE of Fivemiletown. P.
Off A35 Muckrise Map **16** H16 1¼m W of Kesh. P16.
A46 Elylodge Forest Map **16** H15 On Enniskillen–Belleek road 6m NW of Enniskillen. P.
A46 Loughside Map **16** H15 Between Enniskillen and Belleek. P20.
A47 Castle Caldwell Map **16** G95 5m E of Belleek. P40.
A47 Stonefort Map **16** H16 On A47 at W end of Boa Island. P10.
B81/unclass Lough Navar Forest Map **16** H05 5m NW of Derrygonnelly. Toilets. P.
B82 Castle Archdale Map **15** H15 1m W of Lisnarrick. No toilets. P40.
B127 Corradiller Map **12** H33 On B127 between Lisnakea and Derrylin. P30.
Unclassified road Carry Bridge Map **12** H34 2¼m S of Lisbellaw on unclassified road. P15.

Co Londonderry

A2 Bishop's Gate Map **14** C73 1m E of Downhill. Signposted in advance and at entrance. ½ acre. Close to forest walk and walk through gardens to Musseden Temple. Furniture. P25.
A2/unclass Binevenagh Forest Map **14** C73 On Bishop's road 4¾m SW of Downhill. Parking.
A2 Carrakeel Map **14** C41 5m NE of Londonderry. No toilets. P25.
A2 Castleroe Map **14** C82 3m S of Coleraine on A54. P15.
A2 Downhill Map **14** C63 On A2 Coleraine/Downhill road 1½m from road. P50.

Off A2 Gortmore Map **14** C73 4m SW of Downhill on unclassified road. Signposted in advance and at entrance. 7 acres. On high ground with views of Donegal Hills and coast of Scotland. Furniture. P50.
A2 Quilly Map **14** C82 3m W of Coleraine. No toilets. P15.
Off B40 Moydam Laght Map **14** H79 1½m NW of Moneyneaney. P20.
A29/unclass Carndaisy Forest Map **14** H88 4m NW Moneymore. P.
A29/unclass Iniscarn Forest Map **14** H88 6m NW Moneymore. P.
B44 Banagher–Learmount Wood Map **14** C50 1m W of Park Village on B44. P20.
B69 Loughermore Map **14** C51 At Loughermore Bridge 8m SW of Limavady. P30.

Co Tyrone
A28 Favour Royal Forest Map **14** H65 Between Aughnacloy and Augher. P10.
Off A29 Drum Cairne Map **14** H86 In Drum Cairne Forest 2m ESE of Stewartstown on unclassified road. P20.
B48 Gortin Forest Park Map **14** H48 7½m N of Omagh and 2½m S of Gortin off B48. Signposted. Toilets. P250.
B48 Gortin Lakes Road Map **14** H48 9m N of Omagh and 1m S of Gortin on unclassified road off B48 and B46. Signposted. P100.
B50/unclass Lough Bradan Forest Tully Hill Map **14** C37 5m W of Drumquin. P.
B72 Lough Bradan Forest Scraghey Map **16** H26 4m W of Ederney. P.

Republic of Ireland
Approved by the Forest and Wildlife Service of the Republic of Ireland. Sites in *italics* have been inspected by the AA.

Co Cavan
N3 (T35) Corronagh Map **12** N68 On S shore of Lough Ramor. Turn W off N3 3m S of Virginia or E off L49. 3m SW of Virginia. Lakeside picnic site.
L5 *Dun a Ri* Map **13** N89 In Forest Park 1m N of Kingscourt towards Carrickmacross. 1 acre. Nature trails, forest walks, drinking water, furniture. P50.
L15 Killykeen Map **12** H30 8m W of Cavan Town turn NW off L15.

Co Clare
N18 (T11) Dromore Map **7** R38 Off N18 (Ennis–Gort) near Crusheen Village. Wooded lakeland area.
L11 Cullaun Map **7** R47 1½m from Kilkishen off L11.
L34 Doon Map **7** R57 3m from Broadford on Tulla road. Lakeside site.

Co Cork
Off N8 (T6) Corrin Hill Map **4** W89 1m S of Fermoy town. Entrance on second road leading to golf course.
Off N25 (T12) *Glenbower* Map **4** W97 Entrance at eastern end of Killeagh village. Signposted in advance and at entrance. Open mature forest. Trout fishing, nature trail, forest walks, furniture. P40.
N22 (T29) Ummera Map **3** W37 3m E of Macroom on N22.
L34 Ballynoe Map **4** W98 8m S of Tallow on L34.
N71 (L42) Barnegeehy Map **2** W04 3m from Bantry on L42.
N71 (L42) Dromilihy Map **3** W23 4m from Rosscarbery on L42 to Skibbereen.
N71 (L42) Castlefreke Map **3** W33 Off L42 6m from Clonakilty. On sea coast.
T64 Gortnacarriga Map **3** W26 2½m SW of Inchigeelagh.
N71 (T65) Glengarriff Map **2** V95 Adjacent to Town on N71 to Kenmare. Nature trail.
T65 Clashnacrona Map **3** W24 3m from Dunmanway 5m from Drimoleague on T65.
N71 (T65/L41) Innishannon Map **3** W55 Junction of T65/L41.
L41 Shippool Map **3** W55 2m from Innishannon on L41 to Kinsale.
Off L42 or L60 Rinneen Map **3** W13 On unclassified Leap/Castletownsend road.

L59 Lough Hyne Map **3** W02 On unclassified road near Baltimore off L59.
L65 Kilbrittain Map **3** W54 On L65 from Bandon. 1m from Kilbrittain.

Co Donegal
N15 (T18) Drumboe Wood Map **16** H19 200 yds from Stranorlar Riverside Walk.
N56 (T72) *Ards* Map **16** C03 Entrance 2m N of Creeslough, plus 2m drive through forest. (C 208434). Signposted in advance and at entrance. Grassy area at forest edge overlooking beach and sea. Forest walks, swimming, drinking water, furniture. Toilets. P200.
T72 *Woodquarter* Map **16** C12 2m NW of Milford towards Carrigart. Signposted in advance and at entrance. Pleasant site in narrow strip of forest along coast. Forest walks, furniture. P40.
L77 *Rathmullan Wood* Map **14** C22 1m SW of Rathmullan on Letterkenny Road. Signposted in advance and at entrance. Open forest. Forest walks, furniture. P30.
L82 Churchill Map **16** C01 Overlooking Gartan Lough near Glendowan RC Church. 2m from Churchill, 11m from Letterkenny.

Co Dublin
L201 *Tibradden* Map **9** O12 5m S of Rathfarnham. Signposted in advance and at entrance. Natural site in rocky area. Forest walks, nature trail, furniture.

Co Kerry
N21 (T28) Dooneen Map **2** RO1 2m N of Castleisland.
N70 (T66) Ballygamboon Map **2** Q80 On Tralee/Castlemaine road N70 2m from Castlemaine.
N70 (T66) Gleensk Map **2** V68 On ring of Kerry 8m W of Glenbeigh.
N70 (T66) *Parknasilla* Map **2** V78 2m E of Sneem on Waterville/Kenmare road. Viewpoint from low mountain ridge in mature forest, furniture. P30.
L62 Rossacrue Map **2** W07 2m from Morley's Bridge on L62 linking Kilgarvan.
Unclassified road Ballaghisheen/Derreenageeha Map **2** V67 W of Ballaghisheen pass on road between Waterville and Caragh Lake 13m from Waterville.
Unclassified road Lickeen Map **2** V79 At southern end of Caragh Lake on lakeside road from Killorglin to Ballaghisheen Pass, quiet attractive site with access to forest walks. 1½ acres. Furniture. P20.
Unclassified road Mastergeehy Map **2** V57 Lay-by Glencar/Waterville road 5m from Waterville.

Co Kildare
L25 Dunstown Wood Map **9** N81 4½m from Naas (N 870135), forest clearing. Forest walks, furniture. No toilets. P30.

Co Kilkenny
N78 (T6) Jenkinstown Map **8** S56 6m N of Kilkenny. Signposted in advance and at entrance. 15 yds up side road in forest clearing. 10 acres. Furniture. P35.
T20 Woodstock Park Map **5** S63 1m S of Inistioge Village off T20 at Inistioge travelling from Kilkenny.
L18/L32 Graiguenamanagh Map **9** S74 Adjacent to Graiguenamanagh Village.

Co Laois
N8 (T36) Bishops Wood Map **8** S37 1m S of Durrow (S 385765). Signposted in advance and at entrance. Large circular gravelled area surrounded by pine forest. Drinking water, furniture. P30.

Co Leitrim
Off N16 (T17) Glenfarne Map **12** H03 Eastern side of Glenfarne/Kiltyclogher road at Lough Macnean.

Co Limerick
N69 (T68) Foynes Map **6** R25 Near Foynes Village.

Co Louth

N51 (T26) Townley Hall Map **13** O07 3m W of Drogheda (O 035650), at entrance to a forest park. Forest walks, nature trail, furniture. No toilets. P40

T62 Carlingford Map **13** J11 2m from Carlingford on T62 towards Omeath.

Unclassified road *Bellurgan* Map **13** J11 5m NE of Dundalk off Carlingford/Ravensdale road on mountain slope above Ballymakellett (J 111113). Signposted in advance and at entrance. Wide view over Dundalk Bay and surrounding area, furniture.

Co Mayo

L22 Drummin/Lough Cullin Map **11** G20 2m from Foxford on Pontoon road.

Off N59 (T40) Ballina Map **10** G21 ½m N of Ballina on West Bank of Moy Estuary.

L134 Clydagh Map **10** M19 3m from Castlebar on Pontoon road.

L140 Coryosla/Coryosla Bridge Map **10** G10 1m from Pontoon towards Crossmolina.

T40 Morehall Map **10** M17 E of T40 via Ballintober Abbey, S of Carnacon.

N59 (T71) Sheefrey Map **10** L96 14m SW of Westport between L100 and T71.

Unclassified road *Tourmakeady Demesne* Map **10** M16 Access from Tourmakeady Village. Signposted in advance and at entrance. ½ acre facilities laid out in small forest clearing. Forest walks, furniture. P25

Co Meath

L17 Tardree Forest Map **13** N77 3½m E of Ceanannus Mor. Signposted. P8

L24 Lough Bracken Map **13** N88 1m SW of Drumcondra off L24.

Co Monaghan

L45 Annaghmakerig Map **12** H51 On side road 5m NW of Cootehill.

L45 Ballamont and Dartry Wood Map **12** H51 1m N Cootehill on L45 to Monaghan. Furniture. P30

Co Offaly

Unclassified road Glenletter Map **8** N20 5m SE of Kinnitty on Kinnity/Mountrath road between T9 and L147

Co Roscommon

N4 (L107A) Picnic site within Lough Key Forest Park Map **11** G80 2m E of Boyle, signposted in advance and at entrance. 13 acres. Drinking water, furniture. Toilets. P200

Co Sligo

L3 Union Wood/Ballygawley Lough Map **11** G72 5m S of Sligo.

L16 Hazelwood Map **11** G73 ½m off L16, 3m from Sligo.

L117 Dooney Rock Map **11** G73 4m from Sligo.

Co Tipperary

N8 (T6) *Glengarra Wood* Map **4** R92 8m SW of Cahir on road to Cork. Signposted. 2 acres. Furniture, riverside walks, parking in small clearings.

N62 (T32) Golden Grove Wood Map **8** S19 1m from Roscrea (S 212192). Signposted in advance and at entrance. 2 acres. Forest clearing. Furniture. P30

N24 (T13) *Bansha Wood* Map **7** R93 Tipperary/Cahir 1½m NW of Bansha (R 935332). Signposted in advance and at entrance. Forest clearing. 2 acres. Furniture. P25

Co Waterford

N25 (T12) Drum Hills/Monameen Map **4** X28 7m W of Dungarvan.

N25 (T12) Glendalligan Map **4** X39 7m from Dungarvan on Dungarvan/Waterford road.

T27 Nier Valley Map **4** S11 On scenic route from Clonmel 4m from Ballymacarbry.

Off N72 (T30) Glenshellane Map **4** X19 2m N of Cappoquin.

T36 Knockaun Map **4** X09 4m S of Tallow on Tallow/Youghal road.

L27 Gurteen Map **4** S22 3m from Kilsheelan.

Off L27 Lyreanearla Map **4** S22 5m from Clonmel on Nier Valley road.

L36 Cooleydoody Map **4** W99 N side of Tallow/Fermoy road. 2m W of Tallowbridge.

Unclassified road Bohadoon/Maw Maw Road Map **4** S30 Comeragh drive near Kilrossanty village.

Unclassified road Carnglass Map **4** X08 8m S of Cappoquin on hill route.

Unclassified road Killahaley Map **4** X09 On Blackwater opposite Dromana Cappoquin/Youghal road.

Co Wicklow

T7 *Avoca* Map **9** T18 Off T7 1m S Avoca. Signposted in advance and at entrance. Small elevated area backed by trees. Nature walks. Furniture. P30

T61 *Trooperstown* Map **9** T19 2m S of Annamoe, to Laragh. Signposted at entrance. Forest and riverside walks, furniture.

Off T61 Avondale Map **9** T18 1m S of Rathdrum. Toilets.

Off T61 Deer Park Map **9** O21 An old long hill road from Enniskerry to Roundwood.

L107A *Glendalough* Map **9** T19 By lakeside. Scenically and historically famous. Signposted at entrance. Nature trail, forest walks, lakes and mountain scenery, furniture. Toilets P400

Off L161 *Devil's Glen* Map **9** T39 2m W of Ashford on road to Glendalough (T 323189). Signposted in advance and at entrance. Furniture. P45

Golf Courses

Due to the large number of golf and race courses listed in this guide, the map location references can be found on the larger scale Ordnance Survey Maps of Ireland (½ inch series), and not in the atlas starting after page 192.

Co Antrim

Ballycastle Golf Club	18 hole
Map D1241	
Ballyclare Golf Club	9 hole
Map J2632	
Ballymena Golf Club	18 hole
Map D1305	
Bushfoot Golf Club	18 hole
Map D9241	
Cairndhu Golf Club	18 hole
Map J3707	
Carrickfergus Golf Club	18 hole
Map J4187	
Cushendall Golf Club	9 hole
Map D2328	
Dunmurry Golf Club	18 hole
Map J2969	
Greenisland Golf Club	9 hole
Map J3685	
Larne Golf Club,	9 hole
Island Magee	
Map D4202	
Lisburn Golf Club	9 hole
Map J2461	
Massereene Golf Club	18 hole
Map J1486	
Rathmore Golf Club	18 hole
Map J8740	
Royal Portrush Golf Club,	2×18 hole
Portrush	
Map J8740	
Whitehead Golf Club	18 hole
Map J4692	

Co Armagh

Armagh Golf Club	18 hole
Map H8844	
Lurgan Golf Club	18 hole
Map J0958	
Portadown Golf Club	18 hole
Map J0351	
Tandragee Golf Club	18 hole
Map J0245	

Belfast

Balmoral Golf Club	18 hole
Map J3170	
Belvoir Park Golf Club	18 hole
Map J3570	
Cliftonville Golf Club	9 hole
Map J3277	
Fortwilliam Golf Club	18 hole
Map J3378	
Malone Golf Club	18 & 9 hole
Map J3167	
Ormeau Golf Club	9 hole
Map J3472	
Shandon Park Golf Club	18 hole
Map J3772	

Co Carlow

Borris Golf Club	9 hole
Map S7351	
Carlow Golf Club	18 hole
Map S7276	

Co Cavan

Belturbet Golf Club,	9 hole
Erne Hill	
Map H3617	
Blacklion Golf Club	9 hole
Map H0838	
County Cavan Golf Club,	18 hole
Drumelis, Cavan	
Map H4204	
Virginia Golf Club,	9 hole
Park Hotel	
Map N6187	

Co Clare

Ennis Golf Club,	18 hole
Drumbiggle	
Map R3377	
Kilkee Golf Club	9 hole
Map Q8860	
Kilrush Golf Club	9 hole
Map Q9955	
Lahinch Golf Club	2×18 hole
Map R0988	
Shannon Golf Club,	18 hole
Shannon Airport	
Map R3862	
Spanish Point Golf Club,	9 hole
Miltown Malbay	
Map R0387	

Co Cork

Bandon Golf Club,	18 hole
Castlebernard	
Map W4954	
Bantry Golf Club	9 hole
Map V9948	
Charleville Golf Club,	18 hole
Ráth Luirc	
Map R523	
Cork Golf Club,	18 hole
Little Island	
Map W7572	
Doneraile Golf Club	9 hole
Map R5907	
Dunmore Golf Club	9 hole
Map W3838	
East Cork Golf Club,	9 hole
Goracrue	
Map W8873	
Fermoy Golf Club	18 hole
Map W8198	
Glengarriff Golf Club	9 hole
Map V9256	
Kanturk Golf Club	9 hole
Map R3803	
Kinsale Golf Club,	9 hole
Ringerare, Belgooly	
Map W6351	
Macroom Golf Club,	9 hole
Luckaduve	
Map W3472	
Mallow Golf Club	18 hole
Map W5698	
Mitchelstown Golf Club	9 hole
Map R8112	

Monkstown Golf Club	18 hole	Kirkistown Castle Golf Club	18 hole
Map W7666		*Map J6357*	
Muskerry Golf Club	18 hole	Knock Golf Club	18 hole
Map W6572		*Map J4074*	
Skibbereen Golf Club	9 hole	Mahee Island Golf Club	9 hole
Map W1233		*Map J5263*	
Youghal Golf Club	18 hole	Mourne Golf Club	18 hole
Map X1077		*Map J3832*	

Co Donegal

Ballybofey & Stranorlar Golf		Royal Belfast Golf Club,	18 hole
Club,	18 hole	*Graigavad*	
Ballybofey		*Map J4382*	
Map H1494		Royal Co Down Golf Club,	18 hole
Ballyliffin Golf Club	18 hole	*Newcastle*	
Map C3848		*Map J3832*	
Buncrana Municipal Golf Club	9 hole	Scrabo Golf Club	9 hole
Map C3532		*Map J4672*	
Bundoran Golf Club	18 hole	Spa Golf Club	9 hole
Map G8158		*Map J3549*	
Donegal Town Golf Club,	18 hole	Warrenpoint Golf Club	18 hole
Murvagh		*Map J1319*	
Map G9278			
Dunfanaghy Golf Club	18 hole	## Co Dublin	
Map C0237		Balbriggan Golf Club	9 hole
Greencastle Golf Club	9 hole	*Map O2064*	
Map C6640		Ballinascorney Golf Club	9 hole
Gweedore Golf Club,	9 hole	*Map O0823*	
Derrybeg		Carrickmines Golf Club	9 hole
Map B8126		*Map O2224*	
Letterkenny Golf Club,	18 hole	Castle Golf Club,	18 hole
Barnhill		*Rathfarnham*	
Map C1912		*Map O1428*	
Narin & Portnoo Golf Club,	18 hole	Clontarf Golf Club,	18 hole
Narin		*Malahide Road*	
Map G7198		*Map O1836*	
North West Golf Club,	18 hole	Deerpark Golf Club,	18 hole
Fahan, Lifford		*Howth*	
Map C3329		*Map O2739*	
Otway Golf Club,	9 hole	Donabate Golf Club	18 hole
Rathmullan		*Map O2548*	
Map C2927		Dublin & County Golf Club,	18 hole
Portsalon Golf Club	18 hole	*Corballis*	
Map C2439		*Map O2447*	
Rosapenna Golf Club,	18 hole	Dublin Sport Golf Club,	9 hole
Downings		*Kilternan*	
Map C1238		*Map O2121*	
		Dun Laoghaire Golf Club,	18 hole
## Co Down		*Eglinton Park*	
Ardglass Golf Club	9 hole	*Map O2327*	
Map J5635		Edmondstown Golf Club,	18 hole
Banbridge Golf Club	9 hole	*Rathfarnham*	
Map J1147		*Map O1326*	
Bangor Golf Club	18 hole	Elm Park Golf & Sports Club,	18 hole
Map J5181		*Nutley Lane, Donnybrook*	
Carnalea Golf Club	18 hole	*Map O1931*	
Map J4882		Forest Little Golf Club,	18 hole
Clandeboye Golf Club	2×18 hole	*Cloghran*	
Map J4978		*Map O1644*	
Donaghadee Golf Club	18 hole	Foxrock Golf Club	9 hole
Map J5881		*Map O2325*	
Downpatrick Golf Club	9 hole	Grange Golf Club,	18 hole
Map J5045		*Rathfarnham*	
Helens Bay Golf Club	9 hole	*Map O1625*	
Map J4582		Hermitage Golf Club,	18 hole
Holywood Golf Club	18 hole	*Lucan*	
Map J4078		*Map O0535*	
Kilkeel Golf Club	9 hole	Howth Golf Club,	18 hole
Map J2715		*Carrickbrack Road, Sutton*	
		Map O2739	

Island Golf Club,   18 hole
Corballis
Map O2447
Killiney Golf Club   9 hole
Map O2625
Lucan Golf Club   9 hole
Map O0234
Malahide Golf Club   9 hole
Map O2446
Milltown Golf Club,   18 hole
Lower Churchtown Road
Map O1830
Newlands Golf Club,   18 hole
Clondalkin
Map O0729
Portmarnock Golf Club   9 & 18 hole
Map O1227
Rathfarnham Golf Club   9 hole
Map O1227
Royal Dublin Golf Club,   18 hole
Dollymount
Map O2137
Rush Golf Club   9 hole
Map O2531
Skerries Golf Club   18 hole
Map O2561
Slade Valley Golf Club,   18 hole
Saggart
Map O0426
Stackstown Golf Club,   9 hole
Rathfarnham
Map O1324
St Anne's Golf Club,   9 hole
Dollymount, North Bull Island
Map O2237

Co Fermanagh
Enniskillen Golf Club   18 hole
Map H2543

Co Galway
Athenry Golf Club   9 hole
Map M5028
Ballinasloe Golf Club   9 hole
Map M8428
Connemara Golf Club,   18 hole
Clifden
Map L6650
Galway Golf Club,   18 hole
Salthill
Map M2823
Gort Golf Club   9 hole
Map M4502
Loughrea Golf Club   9 hole
Map M6216
Mountbellow Golf Club   9 hole
Map M6248
Oughterard Golf Club   9 hole
Map M1243
Portumna Golf Club   9 hole
Map M8304

Co Kerry
Ballybunion Golf Club   18 hole
Map Q8642
Ceann Sibeal Golf Club,   9 hole
Ballyferriter
Map Q3504

Dooks Golf Club,   18 hole
Glenbeigh
Map V5888
Kenmare Golf Club   9 hole
Map V9171
Killarney Golf & Fishing Club   18 hole
Map V9391
Parknasilla Golf Club   9 hole
Map V7164
Tralee Golf Club   9 hole
Map Q8315
Waterville Golf Club   18 hole
Map V4867

Co Kildare
Athy Golf Club,   9 hole
Geraldine
Map S6995
Bodenstown Golf Club,   18 hole
Sallins
Map N8925
Cill Dara Golf Club,   9 hole
Newbridge
Map N8015
Curragh Golf Club   18 hole
Map N8010
Naas Golf Club,   9 hole
Kerdiffstown
Map N9123

Co Kilkenny
Callan Golf Club   9 hole
Map S4143
Castlecomer Golf Club   9 hole
Map S5373
Kilkenny Golf Club,   18 hole
Glendine
Map S5056

Co Laois
Abbeyleix Golf Club   9 hole
Map S4482
Heath Golf Club,   18 hole
The Heath, Portlaoise
Map N5201
Mountrath Golf Club,   9 hole
Knockinina
Map S3592
Portarlington Golf Club   9 hole
Map N5412
Rathdowney Golf Club   9 hole
Map S2878

Co Leitrim
Ballinamore Golf Club   9 hole
Map H1311
Carrick-on-Shannon Golf Club,   9 hole
Woodbrook
Map M8901

Co Limerick
Adare Manor Golf Club,   9 hole
Adare
Map R4646
Castletroy Golf Club   18 hole
Map R6258
Limerick Golf Club,   18 hole
Map R6257
Newcastle West Golf Club   9 hole
Map R2833

Co Londonderry
Castlerock Golf Club   18 hole
Map C7735
City of Derry Golf Club   18 hole
Map C4114
Kilrea Golf Club   9 hole
Map C9211
Portstewart Golf Club   2×18 hole
Map C8136

Co Longford
County Longford Golf Club   18 hole
Map N1375

Co Louth
Ardee Golf Club   9 hole
Map N9690
County Louth Golf Club,   18 hole
Baltray
Map O1578
Dundalk Golf Club,   18 hole
Blackrock
Map O0603
Greenore Golf Club   18 hole
Map O2211

Co Mayo
Achill Golf Club,   9 hole
Keel, Achill Island
Map F6405
Ballina Golf Club   9 hole
Map G2618
Ballinrobe Golf Club   9 hole
Map M1765
Ballyhaunis Golf Club   9 hole
Map M5079
Belmullet Golf Club   9 hole
Map F7032
Castlebar Golf Club   9 hole
Map M1786
Claremorris Golf Club   9 hole
Map M3572
Mulrany Golf Club   9 hole
Map L8496
Swinford Golf Club   9 hole
Map G3300
Westport Golf Club   18 hole
Map L9985

Co Meath
Bettystown Golf Club   18 hole
Map O1673
Headfort Golf Club,   18 hole
Kells
Map N7675
Royal Tara Golf Club   18 hole
Map N9061
Trim Golf Club   9 hole
Map N8056

Co Monaghan
Clones Golf Club,   2×9 hole
Map H4919
Nuremore Golf Club,   9 hole
Map H8502
Rossmore Golf Club   9 hole
Map H6632

Co Offaly
Birr Golf Club   18 hole

Map N0606
Edenderry Golf Club   9 hole
Map N6433
Tullamore Golf Club   18 hole
Map N3121

Co Roscommon
Ballaghaderreen Golf Club   9 hole
Map M6195
Boyle Golf Club   9 hole
Map M8002
Castlerea Golf Club   9 hole
Map M6780
Roscommon Golf Club,   9 hole
Moate Park
Map M8961

Co Sligo
Ballymote Golf Club   9 hole
Map M6615
County Sligo Golf Club,   18 hole
Map G6341
Enniscrone Golf Club   18 hole
Map G2731
Strandhill Golf Club   18 hole
Map G6035

Co Tipperary
Cahir Park Golf Club   9 hole
Map S0423
Carrick-on-Suir Golf Club   9 hole
Map S2040
Clonmel Golf Club   18 hole
Map S2420
Nenagh Golf Club   18 hole
Map R8679
Roscrea Golf Club   9 hole
Map S1188
Templemore Golf Club   9 hole
Map S1171
Thurles Golf Club   18 hole
Map S1455

Co Tyrone
Dungannon Golf Club   18 hole
Map H7863
Fintona Golf Club   9 hole
Map H4360
Killymoon Golf Club   9 hole
Map H8276
Newtownstewart Golf Club   18 hole
Map H3784
Omagh Golf Club   9 hole
Map H4571
Strabane Golf Club   9 hole
Map H3496

Co Waterford
Dungarvan Golf Club   9 hole
Map X3092
Lismore Golf Club   9 hole
Map X0598
Tramore Golf Club   18 hole
Map S5801
Waterford Golf Club   18 hole
Map S6112

Co Westmeath
Athlone Golf Club,   18 hole
Hodson Bay

Map N0146
Moate Golf Club — 9 hole
Map N1839
Mullingar Golf Club — 18 hole
Map M4248

Co Wexford
Courtown Golf Club, — 18 hole
Map T2058
Enniscorthy Golf Club — 9 hole
Map S9438
New Ross Golf Club — 9 hole
Map S7028
Rosslare Golf Club — 18 hole
Map T0916
Wexford Golf Club — 9 hole
Map T0621

Co Wicklow
Arklow Golf Club — 18 hole

Map T2473
Baltinglass Golf Club — 9 hole
Map S8785
Blainroe Golf Club — 18 hole
Map T3291
Bray Golf Club — 9 hole
Map O2717
Delgany Golf Club — 18 hole
Map O2717
Greystones Golf Club — 18 hole
Map O3011
Coollattin Golf Club, — 9 hole
Shillelagh
Map T0068
Wicklow Golf Club — 9 hole
Map T3193
Woodenbridge Golf Club — 9 hole
Map T1977

Hotels with sporting facilities

Co Antrim
Ballygally — *** — Ballygally Castle
⚑ Hard ⬡

Dunadry — **** — Dunadry Inn ⬡
Dunmurry — **** — Conway ⌓(Heated)

Co Cavan
Virginia — *** — Park ♒⚑ Hard

Co Clare
Bunratty — *** — Fitzpatrick's Shannon
Shamrock
⌓ (Heated)

Ennis — *** — West County Inn ⬡
Lisdoonvarna — ** — Spa View
Newmarket-on- — (RS) **** — Dromoland Castle ⚑ (Hard)
Fergus — ⬡
Scariff — ** — Clare Lakelands ⚑ ⬡

Co Cork
Ballinascarty — *** — Ardnavaha House
⌓(Heated) ⚑Hard ⌒
Ballylickey — (RS) *** — Ballylickey House
⌓(Heated)
Bantry — *** — Westlodge ⌓(Heated)
⚑ (Hard) squash
Garryvoe — ** — Garryvoe ⬡
Glenbeigh — ** — Towers ⌒
Glouthaune — ** — Ashbourne House
⌓(Heated)
Gougane Barra — ** — Gougane Barra ⬡
Inchgeela — * — Creedons ⌒
Innishannon — ** — Innishannon ⬡
Kinsale — *** — Acton's ⌓ (Heated)
Youghal — ** — Hilltop ⌓(Heated)
— ** — Monatrea House &
Country Club
⌓(Heated)
⚑Hard ⌒

Co Donegal
Dunfanaghy — ** — Arnold's ⚑Hard ⬡ ⌒
Dungloe — ** — Ostan Na Rosann
⌓(Heated)
Killybegs — *** — Killybegs ⚑ Hard
Port-Na-Blagh — *** — Port-Na-Blagh
⚑ Hard ⬡
— *** — Shandon ⚑Grass
Rathmullan — (RS) *** — Rathmullan
House ⚑ (Grass) ⬡
— (RS) ** — Fort Royal ⚑ (Hard) Squash
♒ ⌒

Co Down
Holywood — **** — Culloden ⚑ Hard

Co Dublin
Dublin — **** — Burlington
⌓(Heated)
— **** — Jury's ⌓ & ⌓ (Heated)
— **** — International Airport
⌓(Heated)
— *** — Marine ⌓ (Heated)
Killiney — **** — Fitzpatrick's Castle
⌓(Heated) ⚑Hard Squash
— *** — Court Squash

Co Galway
Carraroe — ** — Ostan Cheathru Rua
Cashel — (RS) *** — Cashel House ⚑ (Hard)
Clifden — *** — Abbeyglen House
⚑ Hard ⌓ (Heated)
Galway — **** — Great Southern
⌓ (Heated)
— *** — Corrib Great Southern
⌓ (Heated)
Oughterard — *** — Connemara Gateway
⌓ (Heated)
Renvyle — *** — Renvyle House ♒
⚑ Hard Squash ⬡ ⌒
Billiards
Rosscahill — ** — Ross Lake ⚑ Hard

Co Kerry
Caherdaniel — *** — Derrynane
⌓ (Heated) ⚑ Hard
Dingle — *** — Sceilig ⌓ (Heated)
⚑ Hard
Glenbeigh — ** — Falcon Inn ⬡
— ** — Glenbeigh ⚑
— ** — Towers ⚑
Killarney — **** — Dunloe Castle (Heated)
(Hard) ⬡ ⌒ Billiards
— **** — Europe ⌓(Heated) ⌒
— **** — Great Southern
⌓(Heated) ⚑Hard
— *** — Aghadoe Heights ⚑ (Hard)
— *** — Castlerosse ⌓⚑ Hard
— *** — Lake ⚑Hard
— *** — Torc Great Southern
⌓ (Heated) ⚑Hard
— ** — Glen Eagle ⚑Hard)
Squash ♒
Listowel — * — Stack's ⬡

185

Parknasilla (RS) **** Great Southern ⌧(Heated) [symbols]
Tralee *** Earl of Desmond [symbol] Hard
Waterville ** Butler Arms [symbol] Hard Billiards

Co Kilkenny
Kilkenny *** Newpark [symbol] Grass

Co Laois
Durrow ** Castle Arms [symbol]

Co Limerick
Adare *** Dunraven Arms [symbol]

Co Londonderry
Londonderry **** Everglades ⌧ & ⌧ (Heated)

Co Louth
Drogheda ** Boyne Valley [symbol]
Dundalk *** Ballymascanlon House [symbol] ⌧ (Heated)
** Fairways Squash

Co Mayo
Achill Island * Achill Head [symbol] Hard
Ballina *** Downhill ⌧ (Heated)
Foxford *** Pontoon Bridge [symbols]
Newport *** Newport House [symbols]

Co Meath
Drumconrath ** Aclare House [symbols]

Co Sligo
Rosses Point ** Yeats Country Ryan [symbol] Hard

Co Tipperary
Cahir *** Kilcoran Lodge [symbol]
Dromineer ** Sail Inn [symbol]

Co Waterford
Ballyduff ** Blackwater Lodge
Lismore ** Ballyrafter House [symbol]
Waterford *** Ardree [symbol] (Hard)

Co Westmeath
Mullingar * Bloomfield House [symbols]

Co Wexford
Courtown Harbour ** Bay View Squash
** Courtown ⌧ (Heated)
Rosslare (RS) *** Kelly's ⌧ & ⌧ (Heated)
[symbol] Squash
** Golf [symbol] Grass
Rosslare Harbour *** Great Southern ⌧ (Heated) [symbol] Hard [symbol] Billiards
**** Talbot ⌧ (Heated) Squash
Wexford *** Ferrycarrig [symbol] (Hard)

Co Wicklow
Ballymore Eustace ** Ardenode [symbol] Hard
Blessington *** Downshire House [symbol] Hard
Greystones *** La Touche [symbol] Hard/Grass
Rathnew ** Hunter's [symbol] (Grass)

Hotels with facilities for children

Co Cavan
Virginia ★★★⚑ Park

Co Clare
Bunratty ★★★ Fitzpatrick's Shannon Shamrock
Killaloe ★★ Lakeside
Newmarket-on-Fergus ★★★★ Dromoland Castle

Co Cork
Bantry ★★★ Westlodge
Cork ★★★ Silver Springs
Garryvoe ★★ Garryvoe
Youghal ★★ Hilltop

Co Donegal
Dunfanaghy ★★ Arnold's
Dungloe ★★ Ostan Na Rosann
Killybegs ★★★ Killybegs
Port-na-Blagh ★★★ Port-na-Blagh
Rathmullan ★ Pier

Co Down
Newcastle ★★★⚑ Enniskeen

Co Dublin
Dun Laoghaire ★★ Hotel Victor
Malahide ★★ Grand

Co Fermanagn
Irvinestown ★★ Mahons
Kesh ★★ Lough Erne
Lisnaskea ★★ Ortine

Co Galway
Carraroe ★★ Ostan Cheathru Rua
Cashel ★★★ Zetland
Galway ★★★ Ardilaun House
★★ Anno Santo
Renvyle ★★★ Renvyle House

Co Kerry
Caherdaniel ★★★ Derrynane
Dingle ★★★ Sceilig
Kenmare ★★★ Kenmare Bay
Killarney ★★★ Aghadoe Heights
Parknasilla ★★★★ Great Southern
Tralee ★★★ Earl of Desmond

Co Kilkenny
Kilkenny ★★★ Newpark

Co Mayo
Ballina ★★★ Downhill
Ballinrobe ★ Lakelands
Castlebar ★★★ Breaffy House
Westport ★★★ Westport

Co Meath
Drumconrath ★★★⚑ Aclare House

Co Sligo
Sligo ★★★ Sligo Park

Co Tipperary
Cahir ★★★ Kilcoran Lodge
Dromineer ★★ Sail Inn

Co Waterford
Dunmore East ★★ Haven

Co Wexford
New Ross ★★★ Five Counties
Rosslare ★★★ Kellys

Co Wicklow
Arklow ★★ Arklow Bay
Blessington ★★★ Downshire House
Greystones ★★★ La Touche

BREAKDOWNS: prevention and cure

Avoiding breakdowns

The AA exists to help members in case of breakdowns, but very often motorists can help themselves. Apart from mechanical and electrical component failures, the causes of breakdown are often simple and easy to resolve. A large percentage are due to minor faults which would not occur if preventive maintenance was carried out. It is best to follow the instructions in the manufacturer's handbook, but if this is not available the following checks should be made.

Daily check
(or before each journey)
Check visually for damaged tyres, clean windscreen, lights and mirrors; check oil and coolant levels; ensure that all lights are working; look where the car has been standing for signs of leaks dripping on the ground, and ensure that there is sufficient petrol for the journey.

Remember the code word POWER – Petrol, Oil, Water, Electrics and Rubber. This will remind you to check the essentials.

Weekly check
In addition to the daily routine, once a week check the level of the brake and clutch fluid, top up the battery with distilled water; top up the windscreen washer bottle, check the tyres carefully and remove any flints or stones from the treads, check tyre pressures and ensure that there is at least 2mm of tread depth; check the free pedal movement of both brake and clutch pedals (this should usually be about 1 inch), and check the fanbelt for tension and damage (replace as soon as any wear, fraying or cracks can be seen).

Driving checks
When driving take note of any unusual behaviour by the car and of any excessive noises or smells. If there are any, investigate them before continuing your journey.

Self-help hints

Trouble	Fault	Remedy
Starter will not turn engine (headlights dim)	Flat battery	Push or tow start (except automatics) or use jump leads to another car
	Loose or corroded battery terminals	Clean terminals and battery posts. Tighten locking screws or clamps
	Jammed starter	Free by using a spanner on the square end of the starter shaft
(headlights bright)	Defective starter solenoid or switch	Press solenoid manual button or start as for flat battery
Engine turns but will not start (if there is no spark at the plugs)	Damp ignition system	Dry with clean cloth or spray with a moisture repellent.
	Loose or disconnected leads	Check security of all leads
	Contact breaker points out of adjustment or dirty	Clean and adjust or replace
(if there is a good spark)	Fuel shortage	Check contents of tank and refill if necessary
	Clogged vent in fuel filler cap	Clear vent with a pin or wire
	Clogged fuel filter	Remove – clean and replace
	Air leak in petrol pipe joints	Tighten
	Vapour lock	Allow engine to cool
	Excess fuel – over rich mixture	Turn engine on starter with accelerator fully depressed. If this does not clear excess – remove sparking plugs, dry and replace
	Carburettor flooding	Tap carburettor float chamber lightly with the handle of a screwdriver or hammer

Warning signs of other troubles

Symptom	Cause	Remedy
Oil warning light stays on when engine is running	Very low oil pressure	Stop and check oil level. Find cause before topping up and driving on
Oil warning light flashes on cornering	Low oil level	Top up
Ignition warning light stays on above idle speed	a Broken or slipping fanbelt	a Tighten or renew
	b No generator output	b Check security of leads to generator. If secure – seek help
Temperature gauge climbs, then drops to cold	Overheating and loss of coolant	Stop and let engine cool before checking hoses and radiator for leaks
Brakes pull to one side	a Soft tyre on one side	a Check pressure and rectify
	b Worn or contaminated linings	b Overhaul
Burning smells	a Wires shorting	a Disconnect battery immediately
	b Oil or rag on exhaust	b Locate and remove
	c Brakes binding	c Allow to cool and adjust
	d Clutch slipping	d Allow to cool and adjust
Electric fuel pump clicking fast	a Shortage of fuel in tank	a Fill tank
	b Air lock on suction side	b Tighten petrol pipe joints
Engine speed increases when climbing hills at steady speed	Clutch slip	Allow to cool and adjust
Loss of braking after long descent	Brake fade	a Check brake linings
		b Renew brake fluid
Petrol smells	a Carburettor flooding	a Check needle valve for dirt and float for damage
	b Overfilled tank	b Siphon off if serious
	c Venting into boot	c Clear vent pipes
	d Leaks	d Locate and rectify immediately
Grinding noise from wheels	a Brakes binding	a Adjust brakes
	b Dry wheel bearings	b Remove – grease and replace. Essential to check correct loading
Steering vibration	a Wheels out of balance	a Have wheels balanced by a garage
	b Loose wheels	b Check and tighten wheel nuts

Rosette awards

The following establishments in Ireland were awarded one or two rosettes by the Automobile Association for their cuisine. These awards are reconsidered annually.

One rosette ❀   Hotel or restaurant where the cuisine can be especially recommended.
Two rosettes ❀❀   Hotel or restaurant offering very much above average food irrespective of the classification, together with a high standard of service within the classification.

Two rosettes

Co Cork	Cork	★★★	Arbutus Lodge

One rosette

Co Cork	Ballylickey	(RS) ★★★✕♀	Ballylickey House
	Cork	★★★	Jury's (Vintage Room)
	Cork	XXX	Lovett's
	Kinsale	X	Vintage
	Mallow	XX	Longueville House
	Shanagarry	XX	Ballymaloe House (Yeats Room)
Co Dublin	Dublin	XXX	Bailey
	Dublin	XXX	Le Bistro
	Dublin	XX	Celtic Mews
	Dublin	XX	Tandoori Rooms
	Dublin	X	Snaffles
	Dun Laoghaire	XXX	Mirabeau
	Dun Laoghaire	XXX	Restaurant Na Mara
	Dun Laoghaire	X	Creole
	Howth	XX	King Sitric
	Killiney	XX	Rolland
	Malahide	XX	Johnny's
Co Galway	Ballyconneely	X	Fishery
Co Kerry	Dingle	X	Doyle's Seafood Bar
	Glenbeigh	★★	Towers
Co Kildare	Curragh (The)	XX	Jockey Hall
Co Limerick	Limerick	★★★	Jury's (Copper Room)
Co Meath	Bettystown	XX	Coastguard Inn
Co Wicklow	Enniskerry	XX	Enniscree Lodge

Country-house hotels

Co Antrim			
Newtownabbey	★★	Abbeylands	
Co Cavan			
Virginia	★★★	Park	
Co Cork			
Ballylickey	(RS) ★★★	Ballylickey House	
	(RS) ★★	Sea View	
Youghal	★★	Monatrea House & Country Club	
Co Donegal			
Rathmullan	(RS) ★★★	Rathmullan House	
	(RS) ★★	Fort Royal	
Co Down			
Newcastle	★★	Enniskeen	
Co Galway			
Cashel	(RS) ★★★	Cashel House	
Rosscahill	★★	Ross Lake	
Co Kerry			
Tralee	★★★	Ballyseede Castle	
Co Mayo			
Newport	★★★	Newport House	
Co Meath			
Drumconrath	★★	Aclare House	
Co Waterford			
Lismore	★★	Ballyrafter House	
Co Wexford			
Gorey	★★★	Marlfield	

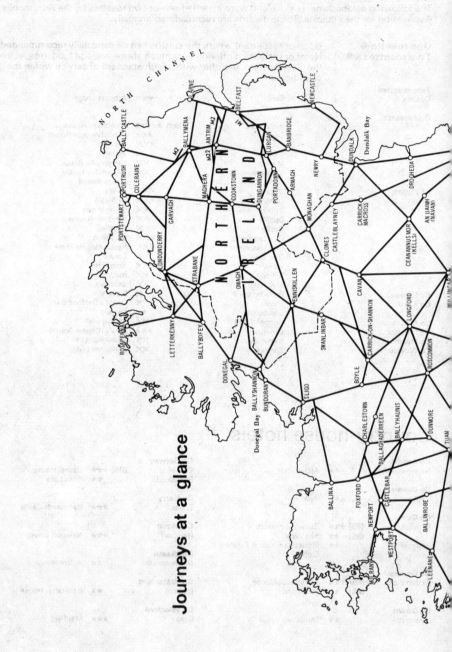

Journeys at a glance

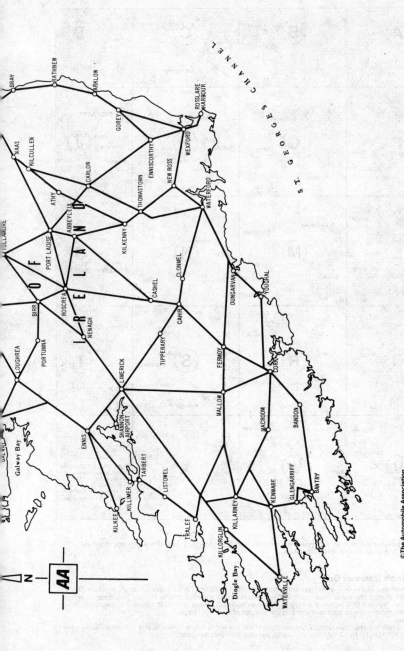

ST. GEORGE'S CHANNEL

BRAY
RATHNEW
ARKLOW
GOREY
ROSSLARE HARBOUR
NAAS
KILCULLEN
WEXFORD
CARLOW
ENNISCORTHY
ATHY
THOMASTOWN
NEW ROSS
ABBEYLEIX
KILKENNY
WATERFORD
TULLAMORE
PORT LAOISE
CASHEL
CLONMEL
DUNGARVAN
YOUGHAL
BIRR
ROSCREA
CAHIR
NENAGH
TIPPERARY
FERMOY
CORK
LOUGHREA
PORTUMNA
LIMERICK
MALLOW
MACROOM
BANDON
ENNIS
SHANNON AIRPORT
Galway Bay
KILLIMER
TARBERT
LISTOWEL
KENMARE
GLENGARRIFF
BANTRY
KILKEE
TRALEE
KILLARNEY
KILLORGLIN
Dingle Bay
WATERVILLE

I R E L A N D   O F

N
AA

© The Automobile Association

191

The Irish National Grid

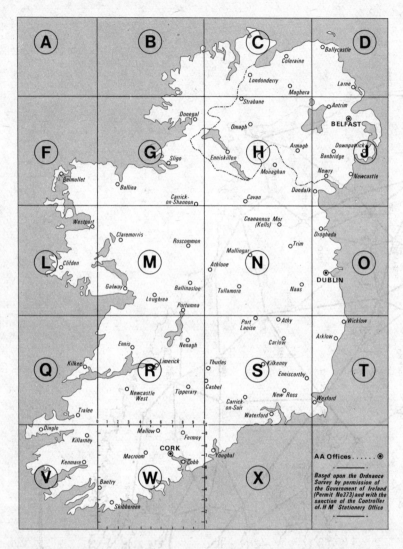

The Irish National Grid is superimposed by permission of the Ordnance Survey of the Republic of Ireland and the Ordnance Survey of Northern Ireland.

The Irish National Grid

The advantage of this Grid is that it provides one system of reference for the whole country correct for any scale of map. The major squares are 100 kilometres across and each smaller division 10 kilometres across. In the Irish National Grid system the letter of the major square is always given first, followed by the numbers into which the major squares are sub-divided (in the margins of each map page).

Example

The Grid reference for Cork is **W67** indicating that Cork lies within major square **W** and is **6** sub-divisions **east** (or from left to right) and **7** sub-divisions **north** (reading from zero upwards).

Key to page numbers

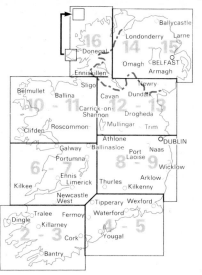

ATLAS
Northern Ireland and the Republic of Ireland

Contours	610			2000
	457	Metres	Feet	1500
	305			1000
	152			500
	61			200

Legend

ROADS IN THE REPUBLIC OF IRELAND:

National primary routes

National secondary routes

Trunk roads

Link roads

Other roads

Road numbering in the Republic is currently undergoing a changeover to a National system. The National network is numbered accordingly and, until the changeover is completed, the existing Trunk and Link road numbers are shown in smaller type.

ROADS IN NORTHERN IRELAND:

Motorways with access points

Motorways under construction and projected

Dual carriageways

Primary routes

Class A roads

Class B roads

Other roads

Border Crossing Prohibited

Places with AA hotels or guesthouses   ●

Places with AA garages   ○

Places with AA hotels or guesthouses and garages   ◉

Places with AA restaurants   ※

Places with AA farmhouses

Places with AA camping and caravanning sites   ▲

AA Viewpoints

Spot heights

AA service centres (Emergency services)

AA road service centres (Emergency service normally 09.00 - 17.00 hrs)

AA and RAC telephones   ☎·

Rivers and loughs

Vehicle ferries

Airports

Distances in miles between motorway access points

Distances in miles between places and road junctions

Frontier Customs   Republic of Ireland   ℗
Post   Northern Ireland   ▶

County boundaries

Country border

Tidal Constants (Belfast) see tide table

Tidal Constants (Dublin) see tide table

Towns shown in black lettering have a detailed entry of an AA approved establishment in the gazetteer

Towns shown in red lettering are for location purposes only

Overlaps and numbers of continuing pages

Based upon the Ordnance Survey by permission of the Government of Ireland (Permit No.373) and with the sanction of the Controller of H M Stationery Office

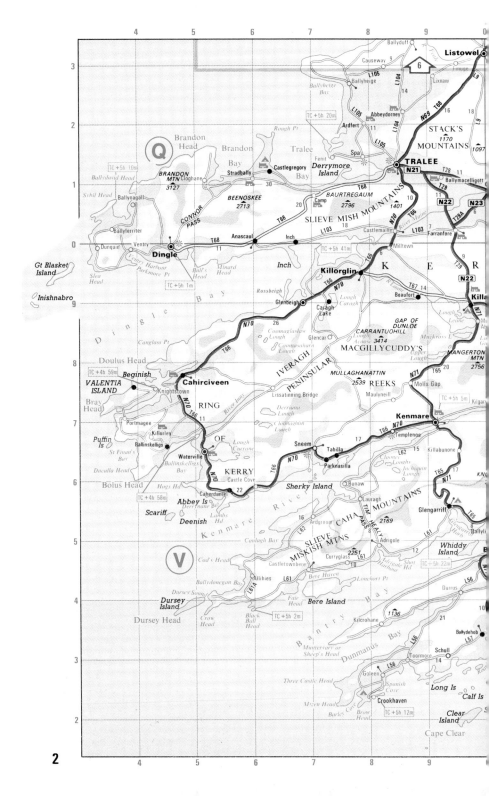

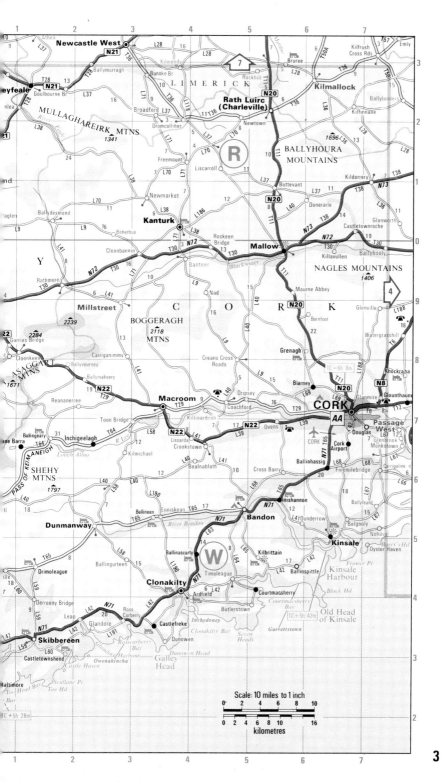

Scale: 10 miles to 1 inch

0   2   4   6   8   10

0 2 4 6 8 10   16

kilometres

3

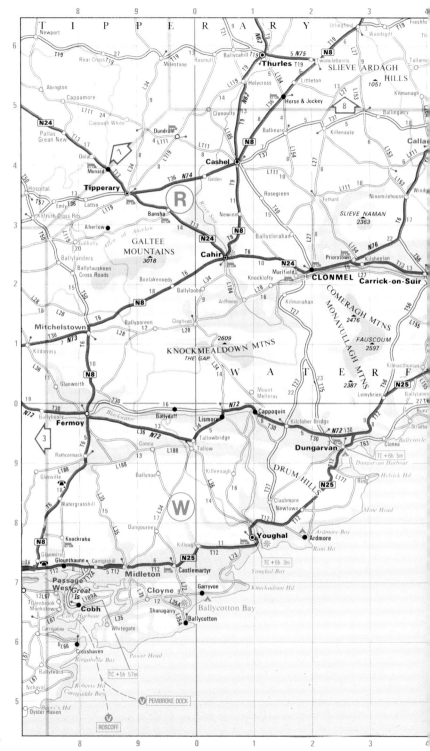

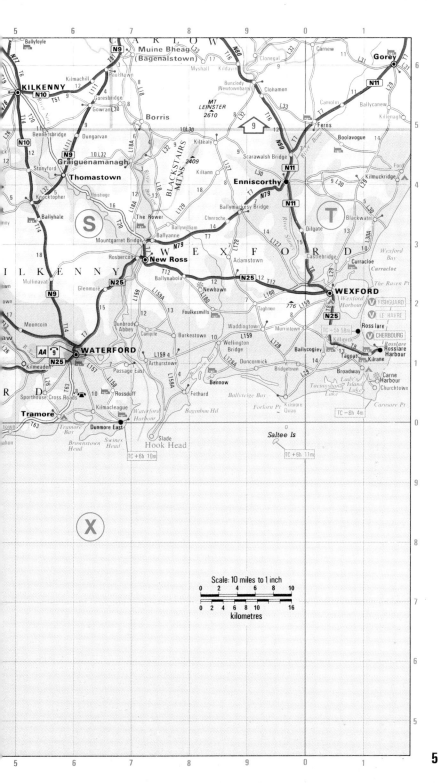

Scale: 10 miles to 1 inch

0 2 4 6 8 10

0 2 4 6 8 10   16
kilometres

5

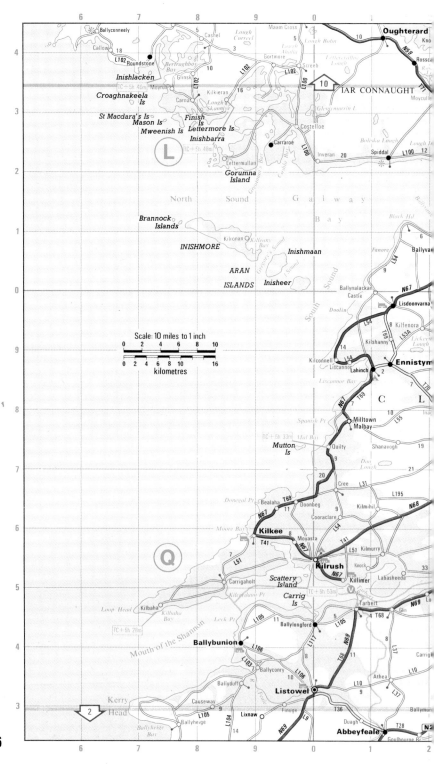

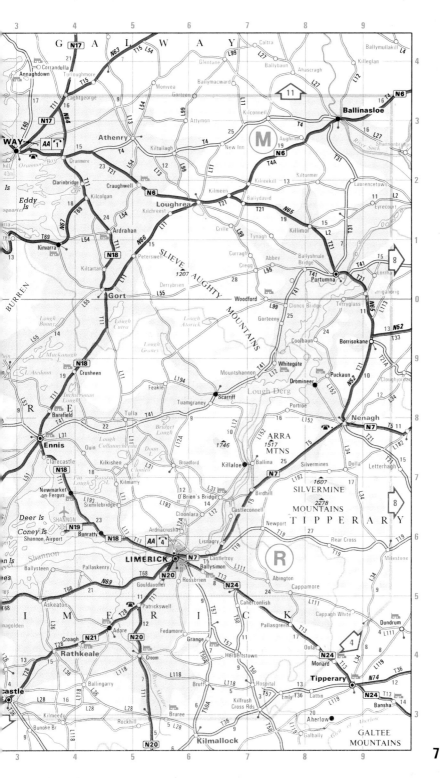

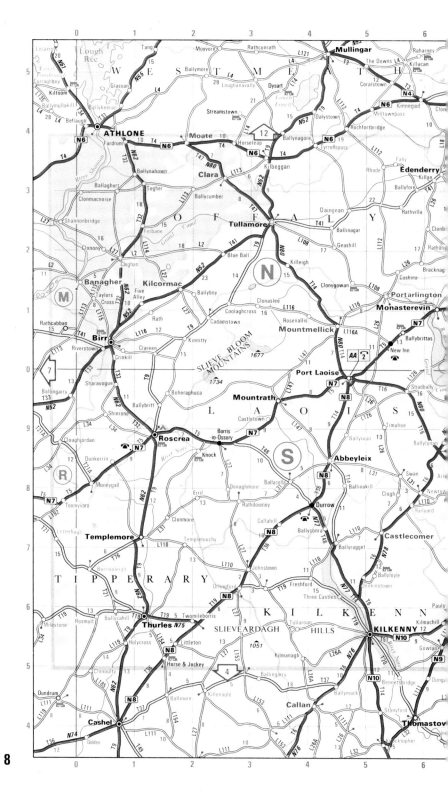

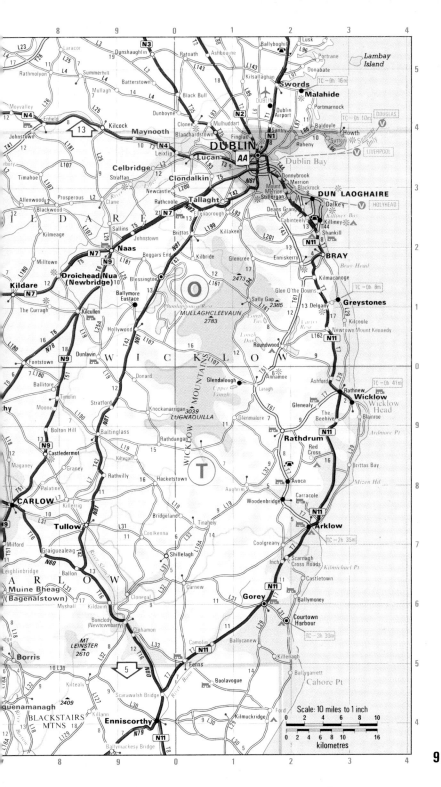

Scale: 10 miles to 1 inch

| 0 | 2 | 4 | 6 | 8 | 10 |

miles

| 0 | 2 | 4 | 6 | 8 | 10 | | 16 |

kilometres

9

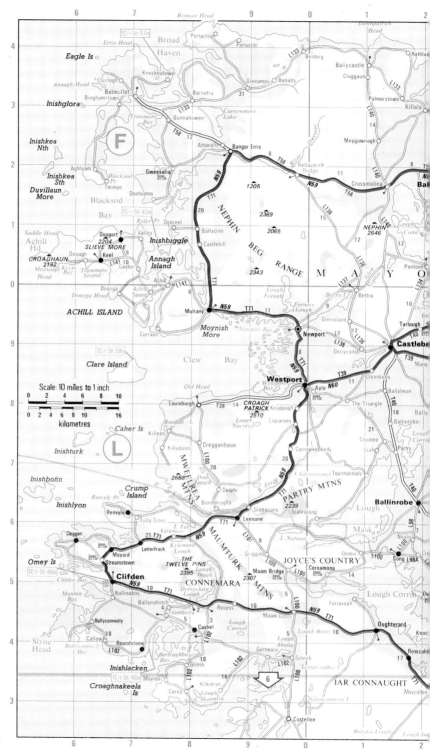

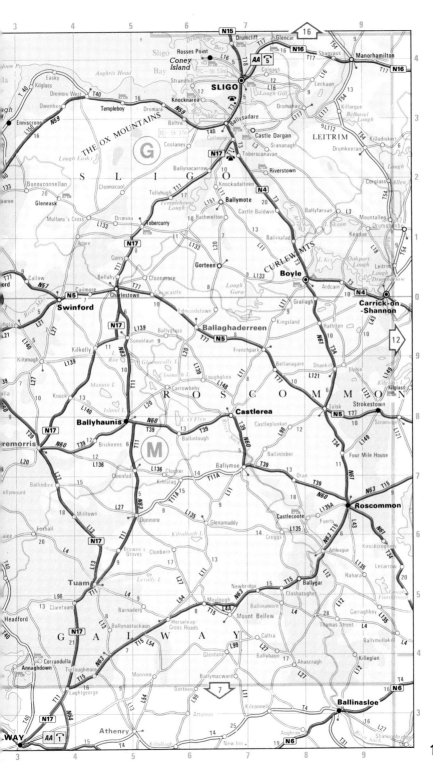

11

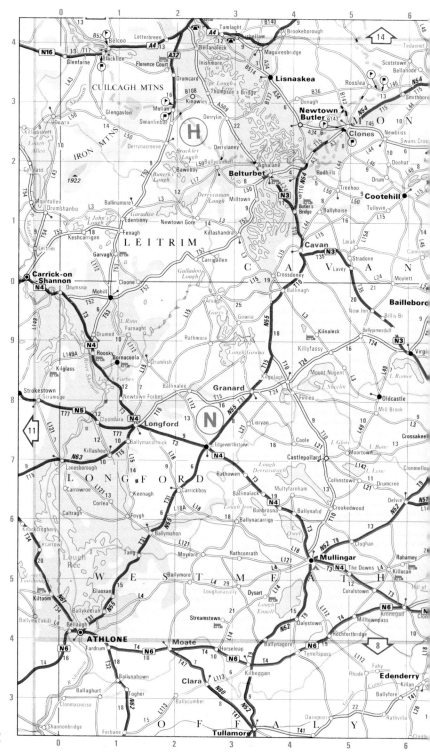
12

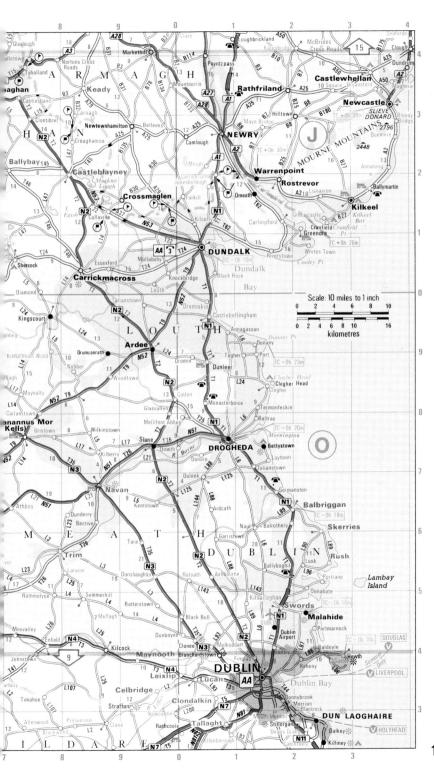

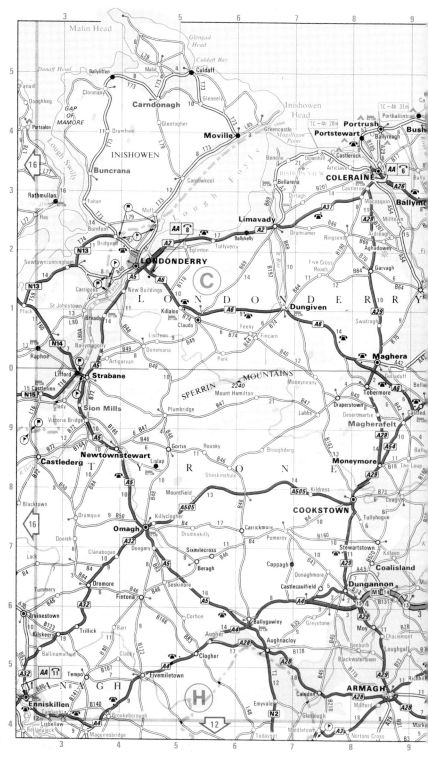

14

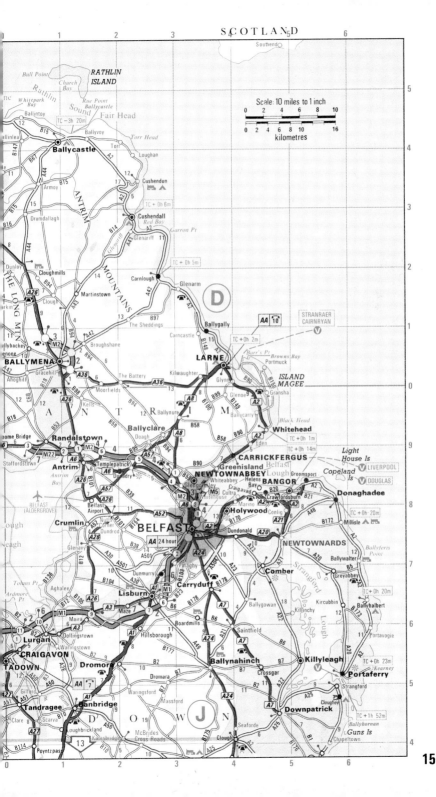

15

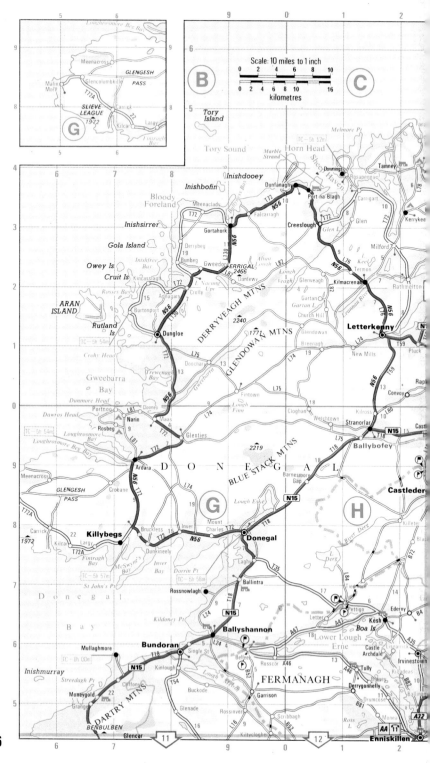

Inset B (Scale)

Scale: 10 miles to 1 inch

0 2 4 6 8 10

0 2 4 6 8 10 16
kilometres

Inset G (top left)

Loughrosmore Beg Bay
Meenacross
GLENGESH PASS
Glencolumbkille
Malin More
T72A
SLIEVE LEAGUE 1972
Carrick
Kilcar
Largy
Fintragh Bay

Main map

Tory Island

Tory Sound

Horn Head
Melmore Pt
Marble Strand
Sheep Haven
Downings
Rosapenna
Tamney

Inishdooey
Inishbofin
Dunfanaghy
Port-na-Blagh
Carrigart
Glen
Kerrykee

Bloody Foreland
Meenaclady
Falcarragh
N56
Creeslough
Glen L
Milford

Inishsirrer
Gortahork
N56
T72

Gola Island
Derrybeg
L130
Keel
Termon
N56

Owey Is
Inishfree Bay
Bunbeg
Gweedore
ERRIGAL 2466
L82
Dunlewy
Lough Veagh
Glenveagh
Kilmacrenan
Rathmelton

Cruit Is
Kincasslagh
T72
L Nacung Upr
Crolly
DERRYVEAGH MTNS
Gartan
Gartan L
Church Hill

ARAN ISLAND
Rosses Bay
Burtonport
Annagar
N56
L130
2240
1771
GLENDOWAN MTNS
Glendowan
Breenagh
Letterkenny
N56

Rutland Is
Dungloe
Glenties
New Mills
Pluck
T59

Crohy Head
Doochary
L75
L74
Convoy
Raph
N56

Gweebarra Bay
Trewenagh Bay
13
Gweebarra
Fintown
Lough Finn
L75
Clogham
Welchtown
Kilross
Stranorlar
Castl
N15

Dunmore Head
Portnoo
L81
Clooney
Maas
Narin
L74
18
T18
Ballybofey
N15

Dawros Head
Rosbeg
T72
Glenties
L75

Loughrosmore Bay
Loughrosmore Beg Bay
Meenacross
L81
Ardara
2219
BLUE STACK MTNS
Barnesmore Gap
T18
Castleder

GLENGESH PASS
Crobane
N56 T72
L74
Lough Eske
N15

T72A
Carrick 1972
Kilcar
Largy
Killybegs
Bruckless
Inver
Mount Charles
T72
Donegal
River Derg
Killeter

T72A
Fintragh Bay
McSwyne's Bay
Dunkineely
Inver Bay
Laghy
L Derg
T35

St John's Pt
Dorrin Pt
Ballintra
Tievmore
B4

Donegal Bay
Rossnowlagh
T18
Letter
Pettigo
Ederny

Kildoney Pt
N15
L24
Ballyshannon
A47
Kesh
Boa Is
A35

Mullaghmore
Bundoran
Single St
Lower Lough Erne
Castle Archdale
Irvinestown

Inishmurray
T19
Kinlough
Bellek
Rosscor A46
B52
Tully
Killadeas
B82

Streedagh Pt
N15
L24
FERMANAGH
Derrygonnelly

Moneygold
Cliffony
T54
Buckode
Garrison
Drumcose
B81

Grange
DARTRY MTNS
Glenade
Rossinver
Scribbagh
Ross L
Money

BENBULBEN
Glencar
11
Kittyclogher
B52
12
A32
Enniskillen
AA

16